HEALTH
PROMOTION
IN CANADA

DATE DUE

HEALTH

PROMOTION

IN CANADA

PROVINCIAL,

NATIONAL &

INTERNATIONAL

PERSPECTIVES

Ann Pederson   Michel O'Neill   Irving Rootman

W.B. Saunders Canada
a division of
Harcourt Brace & Company, Canada
Toronto, Philadelphia, London, Sydney, Tokyo

W.B. Saunders Canada
a division of
Harcourt Brace & Company Canada, Ltd.
55 Horner Avenue
Toronto, Ontario M8Z 4X6

Health Promotion in Canada

ISBN 0-920513-09-3

Canadian Cataloguing in Publication Data

Pederson, Ann P.
   Health promotion in Canada

Includes bibliographical references and index.
ISBN 0-920513-09-3

1. Health promotion — Canada. I. O'Neill, Michel, 1951- . II. Rootman, I.
III. Title.

RA427.8.P43 1994   613'.0971   C93-094780-0

DESIGN/DESKTOP PUBLISHING: Jack Steiner Graphic Design
EDITING/PRODUCTION: Francine Geraci

Printed in Canada at Webcom Limited
Last digit is print number: 9 8 7 6 5 4 3 2 1

Dedication

We dedicate this book to two people who have been enormously important to health promotion in Canada, Ron Draper and Wendy Farrant. Ron has probably had the greatest influence on Canada's role in contemporary health promotion. A former Director-General of the federal Health Promotion Directorate, Ron has exceptional bureaucratic skills and a very special sense of humour. He provides daily testimony to the fact that one can be magnificently healthy despite living with a profound medical condition.

We also dedicate this book to the late Wendy Farrant, an uncompromising champion of health promotion in Africa and her native Britain. Wendy, like so many others, was an immigrant to Canada. She came here in part because of her faith in health promotion in this country. Now she lies in peace in one of the most supportive environments on the planet — overlooking Active Pass in the tiny cemetary on Galiano Island, British Columbia. The field is lessened by her passing.

Acknowledgements

While the span of this book is almost twenty years, the history of the project itself is barely three. This is a comparatively short time frame for preparing a book, and each of the contributors deserves special thanks: without them, this book would have been a lot shorter and much less valuable. We were impressed with their good-natured tolerance for the constant niggling to meet our deadlines and the overall enthusiasm with which they participated in the project. We think this reflects the co-operative culture of health promotion as well as the temperaments of the individual contributors.

Thanks are also owed to Victor W. Marshall, Ph.D., and the Centre for Studies of Aging at the University of Toronto for providing a very supportive environment to Ann Pederson in which to do the difficult work required to change this book from a dream to a reality.

We would also like to thank the Ontario Ministry of Colleges and Universities, as well as the University of Toronto (specifically, the Bertha Rosenstadt Endowment Fund) and Laval University for providing some financial support for this project. We hope that the final product justifies their investment.

In addition, we would like to thank Gerry Mungham and W.B. Saunders, who had the faith to support this book, and Francine Geraci, who had the patience and skill to edit the copy.

We also would like to express our appreciation to our respective spouses and families for standing by us through this sometimes difficult endeavour and having confidence in us.

Finally, we would like to acknowledge the many individuals who have contributed significantly to the development of the field in Canada who are not formal contributors to this book but who daily toil to improve the health of Canadians. We hope these pages are something of a testimony to their efforts, enthusiasm, and vision, without which what is documented here would have been impossible.

Ann Pederson
Michel O'Neill
Irving Rootman
April 1994

Contents

Preface

This book describes and analyzes the development of health promotion in Canada since the release in 1974 of *A New Perspective on the Health of Canadians* by then federal Minister of Health and Welfare, Marc Lalonde (Lalonde, 1974; hereafter referred to as the Lalonde Report). We believe that Canada's contribution to the field has been both significant and misunderstood; this book aims both to celebrate and clarify it.

Canada is generally believed to be a world leader in health promotion policy and practice, in part because the Lalonde Report was the first statement by a national government that health resulted from the interplay of biology, environment, lifestyle, and the system of health care. By introducing lifestyle and the environment into the equation, the Lalonde Report contributed to a re-examination of the role of health care delivery in fostering health. Mounting evidence on the social (not medical) determinants of health continues to support the claims of the Lalonde Report and to encourage the resurrection of a tradition of public health which argues that health is intimately tied to overall conditions of living. The "new public health" is the expression of this renewed understanding that interventions outside of the traditional domain of the health field (in income and education, for example) are key to improving population levels of health.

Since the 1970s, many nations have prepared their own versions of the Lalonde Report and considered the potential contributions of social, economic, and environmental conditions to fostering health and well-being for their populations. Much — but not all — of the enthusiasm for health promotion has arisen from concern over spiralling health care expenditures, costs borne in most advanced industrialized countries by the state through various systems of publicly funded health care. Support for health promotion has also come from individuals and agencies committed to fostering health in addition to focussing on the elimination or prevention of disease.

The approach taken in this book is historical and sociological. We adopted this approach because we are convinced that in order to understand the emergence of health promotion in Canada, we must look at events contextually, and consider how social, political, and economic forces have contributed to current interest in health and health promotion. We are influenced in thinking about health promotion by those who encourage critical reflection on health promotion itself (e.g., Thorogood, 1992). As Eakin and Maclean argued in a special edition of the *Canadian Journal of Public Health*, much research is currently undertaken to inform the practice of health promotion but little is done "to analyze health promotion as a social institution" (Eakin & Maclean, 1992, p. S75). By stimulating such analysis, we hoped to provide some insights to the activists and practitioners around the world who support health promotion. Moreover, we hoped that social scientists, typically concerned more with understanding than intervention, would find this book a useful case study of a significant social phenomenon that has arisen in developed countries in the late twentieth century.

This book does not offer prescriptions for how to change health-related behaviour or focus on exemplary programs for particular populations of interest. Instead, it offers various accounts of the way in which health promotion has developed in different jurisdictions in the country, from which we hope readers will be able to discern patterns that strengthen or inhibit the development of this domain.

Despite our historical approach, in order to generate the greatest possible theoretical diversity in the book, we did not articulate a particular analytic framework for all the contributors to use. Rather, we chose to encourage each author or team of authors to develop their own perspective. We trust that the resultant diversity is both thought-provoking and illuminating.

A Brief Overview

Canada is an extremely large country with a small population concentrated in the southern third of the land mass. The nation is currently organized into a federal political system with ten provinces and two territories, each with its own government, in addition to the national government. While this structure has largely been in place since Confederation, the political structure of the country has not been static and continues to be in flux. For example, a third territory in the north, Nunavut, has recently been proclaimed and is slated to come into being in 1999. Further, sovereignty for Québec remains a possibility, although not a certainty, at this time. Changes such as these will undoubtedly alter the structure of Canada and possibly the distribution of powers between the various levels of government.

In Canada, formal jurisdiction over health is split between the various levels of government. The largest responsibility for health has been constitutionally defined as residing with the provinces and territories, but the federal government has always played a significant role. (The shifting understanding of the nature of the health field is also forcing a rethinking of the traditional division of responsibility for health in Canada.) The federal role has been traditionally tied to its greater revenue-generating capacity; consequently, federal involvement in the health field has been virtually inevitable — if largely indirect — from the earliest days of the nation (Renaud, 1981). Since the advent of universal hospital and medical insurance in the 1950s and 1960s, all levels of government have been concerned with the cost of health care services, particularly the rate of increase in costs (Mhatre & Deber, 1992). This jurisdictional and fiscal context is important in situating the development of health promotion in Canada in the 1970s and '80s.

Even as this book goes to print, however, events are unfolding that could alter the details of what is documented here. Health care system reform in every jurisdiction in the country is changing organizational, institutional, and fiscal arrangements. Subsequent study of health promotion in Canada will undoubtedly add much to the initial portrait we offer here. Yet, we believe that the general pattern of development of health promotion offered in the following chapters is accurate, notwithstanding the limits to our understanding imposed by writing about current events.

The international community may be most familiar with the health promotion initiatives of the federal government such as the Lalonde Report and *Achieving Health for All: A Framework for Health Promotion* (Epp, 1986) or with the *Ottawa Charter for Health Promotion* (in which Health and Welfare Canada collaborated with the World Health Organization and the Canadian Public Health Association). But most people are likely to be less familiar with the role of the provinces and territories in health promotion, a role which, given their responsibility for health care, is at least as important as that of the federal government.

In this book, we offer accounts of health promotion at the federal, provincial, and territorial levels. In addition, several chapters explore Canadian developments in health promotion from an international perspective, examining the impact of Canadian activities elsewhere and the link between external initiatives and developments here.

We are pleased to have Ilona Kickbusch, Director of the Lifestyles and Health Program for the World Health Organization's Regional Office for Europe, introduce the book as a whole. Ilona has been a leading figure in health promotion worldwide and has been familiar with developments in Canada from the early days post-Lalonde. Her chapter is useful for providing a context for the case studies that follow.

To situate the case studies within the developing discourse of health promotion, the first section of the book offers a conceptual perspective. The first chapter, by medical sociologist Robin Badgley, is actually an "old" paper, republished here because we believe it makes an important contribution to understanding health education and health promotion prior to and in the 1970s and because his observations, first offered in 1978, seem prescient in their continuing applicability. In the second chapter in this section, O'Neill and Pederson discuss how the sociology of knowledge and the study of social movements have been useful to them in analyzing health promotion sociologically, and invite readers to see how these intellectual strands apply to the material in this book. Then we turn to an examination of the concepts of health and health promotion. First, Irv Rootman and John Raeburn review several definitions of health and offer a Canadian view, building on previous work they conducted to reconceptualize the "health field concept" first articulated in the Lalonde Report (Raeburn & Rootman, 1989). This discussion is followed by one by Ron Labonté, who co-authored an important critical analysis of Canadian health promotion some years ago (Labonté & Penfold, 1981). Ron offers a personalized account of the reformulation of the concept of health promotion since the late 1970s, linking an account of the shifting territory of health promotion to his personal experiences as a health promotion practitioner.

The second section of the book deals with health promotion at the national level. Lavada Pinder, a former Director-General of the Health Promotion Directorate of Health and Welfare Canada, outlines the Directorate's leadership role in health promotion; she notes important contributions made by the Directorate but also notes missed opportunities and clarifies the limited impact of health promotion on formal policy.

The other chapters in this section discuss health promotion endeavours noteworthy for their visibility and nationwide scope. The first chapter is by Sharon Manson-Singer, who was a member of the national Steering Committee of the Canadian Healthy Communities Project from 1986 to 1991. Sharon describes the genesis and achievements of the Healthy Communities project from the vantage point of one of the project organizers. The next chapter analyzes a project also undertaken in the late 1980s to support local community initiatives in health, the Strengthening Community Health Program. Written by Ken Hoffman, former Associate Director of the Strengthening Community Health Program, the chapter offers insights into the evolution and contribution of the program. Together, the Healthy Communities Project and the Strengthening Community Health Program reflect the growth of interest in fostering health at the local level in Canada.

The last chapter in this section describes a different sort of program: the federal government's Knowledge Development in Health Promotion Project. Co-authored by Irving Rootman and Michel O'Neill, the chapter explores federal efforts to encourage health promotion research through supporting conferences, commissioning literature reviews, funding research projects, and establishing health promotion research centres across Canada.

From a consideration of developments at the national level, the next section shifts the focus to provincial developments. Nine case studies describe the variation in health promotion activities in every region of the country. The contributors were asked to examine who has been advocating health promotion, how the concept has been used over time, what form health promotion activities have taken, what the consequences of these developments have been, how current circumstances have been conducive to the growth of health promotion, and what has shaped the development of health promotion in the area they studied.

There are notable similarities and differences in the accounts from across the country. In British Columbia, Jack Altman and Sharon Martin, both active within the City of Vancouver Department of Public Health and the British Columbia Public Health Association, note the high degree of interest by the province in supporting the Healthy Communities Project and research. In contrast, Healthy Communities is much less visible in Saskatchewan, where, however, Joan Feather, a researcher at the University of Saskatchewan in Saskatoon, observes that formal health promotion activity predates the Lalonde Report. In Alberta, Nancy Kotani and Ann Goldblatt, of the Health Promotion Division of the Edmonton

Board of Health, find that health promotion has been a relative newcomer to a well-developed system of locally based community development structures. John English, from the Department of Nursing and Health Studies at the University of Brandon in Brandon, Manitoba, observes that Manitoba has committed itself to an intersectoral approach to policy-making in the context of major health care system reform. In the Yukon and the Northwest Territories, Sharon Matthias and Susan Yazdanmehr, respectively — both former employees in the Territorial Departments of Health — describe the innovative arrangements that both territories had to develop in order to accommodate their unique jurisdictional and Aboriginal contexts. In Ontario, Ann Pederson and Louise Signal, both from the University of Toronto, argue that the major achievement of health promotion to date has been in establishing the legitimacy of a broad, social view of health, a process given significant support by the establishment of a Premier's Council on Health Strategy in 1987. Meanwhile, Michel O'Neill from Laval University and Lise Cardinal from the regional health department in Québec City question whether health promotion ever really caught on in Québec and why or why not. Finally, in a chapter that grapples with all four Atlantic provinces, Dale Poel from the Department of Public Administration at Dalhousie University in Halifax and Frances Pym from the University of New Brunswick in Fredericton catalogue the diverse experiences of each province and their different approaches to similar geographic, economic, and political conditions. Together, these case studies provide a previously unavailable survey of health promotion across Canada.

The fourth section of the book offers international perspectives on health promotion in Canada. The first chapter in this section is by Larry Green, a well-known author and educator in the health promotion field from the United States. Larry has recently become a Canadian and is currently the Director of the Institute for Health Promotion Research at the University of British Columbia. He provides a thoughtful discussion of the supposed distinctions between American and Canadian health promotion, challenging the view that American efforts have been individualistic rather than structural.

In the second chapter, John Raeburn, from the University of Auckland, offers a commentary on how Canadian health promotion developments have affected the field in New Zealand. In the last chapter in this section, David McQueen, now with the Centers for Disease Control in Atlanta, but formerly the Director of the Research Unit in Health and Behavioural Change in Edinburgh, Scotland, considers the development of health promotion in Canada, with a focus on research.

The last section of the book contains two reflection pieces. The first is by Trevor Hancock, a public health physician and consultant of international reputation in health promotion and sustainable development, as well as the man who coined the phrase "healthy public policy" and who co-parented the international Healthy Cities movement. Following a presentation by Nancy Milio for the Centre for Health Promotion at the University of Toronto in the fall of 1991, Trevor remarked that he wondered to what extent we "had won the battle but lost the war" with respect to significant changes in the direction of health policy and priorities; he explores this idea here. In the final chapter, the editors offer their own conclusions on the pattern of development of health promotion in Canada, taking into account the range of experiences described throughout the book. We conclude with our views of where we think health promotion is headed in the future.

Collaboration Across Boundaries

This book is a collaborative project of the University of Toronto's Centre for Health Promotion in Toronto and the Groupe de recherche et d'intervention en promotion de la santé (GRIPSUL) at Laval University in Québec City. It is the continuation of a productive association between the two centres, and we hope it will spark such collaborations between other centres across the country.

As this book goes to press, we would like to say a word or two about the title because, while clear now, it posed a significant challenge in the early phases of the project — to the editors, many of the contributors, and potential publishers. Questions about the title arose because in the intial stages of the project, no one was sure that Canada would still be a single country by the time the book was published. Various political forces were at play that appeared poised to transform the structure of the nation.

These forces included the wish by a significant proportion of Québec's population to separate from Canada and create a country of its own, and the desire by Aboriginal peoples to use the constitutional debate finally to achieve significant political recognition. As well, western and maritime Canadians were striving for greater say in the evolution of a country that had been run in the interests of what they call Central Canada, that is, Ontario and Québec, since Confederation in 1867. These struggles were occurring, moreover, in an increasingly multicultural society — one in which the proportion of the population from ethnic backgrounds other than those of the two "founding peoples" — the French and the English — already constitute the majority in many areas of the country. For these new and not-so-new Canadians, the old struggle between the French and the English is not necessarily a meaningful one.

To reflect this complex political situation, the working title of the book was initially *The Development of Health Promotion in Canada and Québec*. We agreed to make a final decision on the title following the October 26, 1992 referendum on a proposed constitutional structure for the country. As is obvious, we agreed on a title recognizing that, at the time of writing, Canada remains one country, fragile though it may be. The federal election of October 1993 — with the election of new, regionally based parties and the demise of two traditional parties — reminds us, however, that the structure of Canadian politics and policy will continue to reflect the concerns that prompted our original debate over the appropriate title for this book. Yet, whatever the political decision made by the

Québécois(es) and Canadians in the years to come, the fact that this book is in your hands testifies once again that beyond geographic and linguistic boundaries, it is possible for people of good will who share similar lines of thought to unite around common, meaningful projects.

Ann Pederson, Michel O'Neill, Irving Rootman
November 1993
Toronto and Québec City

References

Badgley, R.F. (1978). *Health promotion and social change in the health of Canadians.* Ottawa: Health & Welfare Canada.

Eakin, J.M., & Maclean, H. (1992). A critical perspective on research and knowledge development in health promotion. *Canadian Journal of Public Health, 83*(Supp. 1), S72-76.

Epp, J. (1986). *Achieving health for all: A framework for health promotion.* Ottawa: Minister of Supply & Services.

Labonté, R., & Penfold, S. (1981). *Health promotion philosophy: From victim-blaming to social responsibility.* Vancouver: Health Promotion Directorate, Western Regional Office.

Lalonde, M. (1974). *A new perspective on the health of Canadians.* Ottawa: Minister of Supply & Services.

Macdonald, G., & Bunton, R. (1992). Health promotion: Discipline or disciplines? In R. Bunton & G. Macdonald (eds.), *Health promotion: Disciplines and diversity* (pp. 6-19). London and New York: Routledge.

Mhatre, S.L., & Deber, R. B. (1992). From equal access to health care to equitable access to health: A review of Canadian provincial health commissions and reports. *International Journal of Health Services, 22,* 645-668.

Renaud, M. (1981). Les reformes québécoises de la santé ou les aventures d'un état narcissique. In Bozzini et al. (eds.), *Médecine et société, les années '80* (pp. 513-579). Montréal: Éditions cooperatives Albert Saint- Martin.

Raeburn, J.M. & Rootman, I. (1989). Towards an expanded health field concept: Conceptual and research issues in a new age of health promotion. *Health Promotion International, 3,* 383-392.

Thorogood, N. (1992). What is the relevance of sociology for health promotion? In R. Bunton & G. Macdonald (eds.), *Health promotion: Disciplines and diversity* (pp. 42-65). London and New York: Routledge.

Introduction: Tell Me a Story

Ilona Kickbusch

"Institutions learn from data; people learn from stories." The first time I heard that statement was in Canada — in Toronto in 1984, to be exact, at the Beyond Health Care Conference. Telling stories, according to Gregory Bateson, is a characteristic of human beings. He tells a beautiful story about a researcher asking his computer if it would ever be able to think like a human being. The computer replies: *"Let me tell you a story...."*

Paradigm Shift

The main story in health promotion is about a conscious bid to support a paradigm shift — to change the way decision makers think about health and to introduce new principles and priorities into health policy. Health promotion offered — and still offers — a legitimate social and professional space to challenge a health agenda focussed on the consumption of services and care rather than on the production of health. Health promotion is not, and in my view never was, a social movement. But it cannot be understood without the experiences, knowledge, and wisdom of social movements, most of all the women's health movement and, later, the environmental/ecological movement. Many of the professionals involved in health promotion had participated in or supported social movements, and had been influenced by the means of social activism as well as its goals. Health promotion was and remains profoundly committed to democracy and participation. In particular, it aimed to change professional, institutional, organizational, and political approaches to health. Under the banner of a "new" public health, it insisted that each and every health professional had a responsibility for public health, and redefined the image and role of professionals to include advocating, enabling, and mediating.

This book, then, is not only an academic exercise; it is also a book of stories. And some authors have rightly chosen to write a story rather than an academic analysis. Let me add a few of my own.

The Child

Health promotion is coming of age, and people are starting to tell its life history. More and more books, articles, dissertations, and requests for information are crossing my desk. Health promotion is being analyzed and scrutinized — in these fast-paced times, you need to prove yourself rapidly. "But the child is so young!" I am tempted to exclaim. It is only eight years ago — in 1986 — that the Ottawa Charter for Health Promotion was accepted. And already we expect so much of it. In view of all our expectations, will it be forced to grow up too soon and lose out on some crucial developmental steps?

Of course, we are proud of the child. And — as with all successful children — there are many claims to parentage, or at least to major influences on the child's upbringing and development. Since the child moved mainly among people with a social rather than a biological view of the world, there are many views as to who taught the child the most crucial skills, gave it the most attention, proved to be the best role model. This child — so the common view was of those involved in the process — was going to be different.

The Face in the Mirror

Having been one of the key actors in the development of health promotion, I would have loved to add my personal version of some of the stories told in this book. ("*No*, it was *not* like that!", I was tempted to exclaim now and then. "I was *there*.") But as a German baby boomer, I have read and heard (and told) too many stories about those wonderful times in 1968 when we were out to change the world. Too easily, the present will seem boring compared to the past, and the future even more so. And then — as someone recently wrote in *The New York Times* — you look at yourself in the mirror one morning and you realize: "A guy my age is now President of the United States," and you will be able to watch him (you) age day by day on the television screen. This brings home the issue of responsibility and accountability, and this is also true in health promotion. The vantage point has changed from "us against them" to us *being* them. The authors (we!) are now, without exception, professors, directors, even deputy ministers and — very typical for the development in health promotion — private consultants. There is no getting away from it: *we* shaped health promotion; do we like what we did when we look in the mirror? Are we still doing enough? Have we been good parents?

Parentage: Made in Canada

What cannot be denied is that the child is the fruit of a close relationship between Canada and Europe. The sweet scent of change was in the air. Supporting a paradigm shift can be romantic and exciting — a point Kuhn (1962) misses in his analysis. As the late 1970s were still permissive, there were some other flirtations and influences: experiences with new types of health projects in the United States and in Finland, social movements, democratic approaches to how people learn, feminist research, critiques of Newtonian science, doubts about the medical model, and many more. It seemed possible to effect change, to create a synergy.

Explorations

In the early 1980s I was given the task to develop a social model of health education for the European Office of the World Health Organization (WHO). The decision had been taken in our governing bodies that by 1984 we would have a health promotion program in place, the first in WHO. To prepare for this, we commissioned a thorough review of the literature and a collection of whatever examples of health promotion programs we could identify. The explorer who was sent out to map this territory was an English medical sociologist, Robert Anderson, and part of his brief was a visit to the United States and Canada. I joined him for part of these explorations.

> *Inquisitive question regarding parentage:*
> *"Mummy, why did you fall in love with Daddy and not Uncle Sam?"*
> *"Well, I will tell you a story...."*

Discoveries

The result of our visit was perhaps typical of what many Europeans interested in health promotion experienced: While the United States was full of exciting programs and initiatives, particularly at the grass-roots level, the barriers facing health promotion at the structural and political level were mounting. The Reagan years had begun and the *Healthy People's Objectives for the Nation* was struggling to survive. In order to do so, it had to put some of its key social concerns — for example, the difference in health status between White and Black Americans — on hold. But the enormous amount of research and data available from the many intervention programs, as well as the innovations coming from the wellness and the self-care movements, illustrated clearly that health promotion had to build on a positive image of health rather than on a risk-factor model; it needed to contain a strong element of community action and self-care; it needed to highlight exactly what many of our U.S. colleagues found lacking — a political commitment and a government-based infrastructure. At that time, a policy approach in which the state was virtually absent was difficult to integrate with European thinking on health reform, and seemed hard to transfer.

The Canadian welfare state, on the other hand, was easily recognizable to Europeans. Of course, we Europeans saw some things through rose-coloured glasses, and many of the critical Canadians never quite understood what we got so excited about. Following Anderson's report, which was widely disseminated in Europe, health promotion tourism to Canada began to expand. Looking back, one can see that many of the most admired things were not implemented or could not be sustained. But the mystique of "made in Canada" was a key ingredient of the process to get health promotion on the agenda worldwide.

Canada in the late 1970s symbolized a special mix of vision and pragmatism, of public and private action, a willingness to try to do things in a different way, that was felt to be lacking in many European societies. At the time, we could not put a name to it. In the mid-1980s it would be called "the new welfare mix." It seemed to combine the best of North American pioneer and community spirit with a base in European-style commitment to the welfare of populations. Some of these elements were to lead us to look more closely at a new public health.

In the mid-1980s Canada could capitalize on a range of factors that helped strengthen health promotion, and that served as a signal for other countries:

- A concept and framework for what it was doing, *A New Perspective on the Health of Canadians*, otherwise known as the Lalonde Report (1974);
- A much-envied infrastructure: the Canadian Health Promotion Directorate, a large governmental body to deal with health promotion;
- A wide social approach recognized through the appointment of a non-medical Director of the Directorate;
- A strong non-governmental organization, the Canadian Public Health Association, willing to advocate for change;
- A Minister willing to give political clout to the new direction;
- A range of campaigns and projects that built on a positive concept of health; and
- A range of extraordinary professionals committed to developing health promotion and thinking ahead with a very strong commitment to policy-focussed approaches.

To this day, these remain the key elements for a successful health promotion strategy.

Synergy

Many Canadian colleagues were very clear in their wish to move toward a more social/environmental approach in health promotion, and they were keen to hear that WHO Europe was set to move in this direction. That is when the Canadian-European alliance for health promotion was born. It was this synergy that led to constant exchange and joint commitments, the highlight of which was the First International Conference on Health Promotion which produced the Ottawa Charter in 1986. The Ottawa conference has become a landmark, seen by many authors as a watershed in public health and health promotion (we speak of the times before, the times after Ottawa), and through it Canada will be talked of for many years to come.

Mentors

Many of the key individuals writing or mentioned in this book acted as mentors and supporters of the European health promotion development — and unabashedly, we in Europe took what we could get. Two key examples are Healthy Public Policy and Healthy Cities/Communities.

"Healthy public policy" became the heading of Target 13 of the Health for All policy targets of the WHO Regional Office for Europe, which were accepted in 1984 (World Health Organization, 1985). It was also included as one of the five key elements of health promotion in 1986 in the Ottawa Charter. The Beyond Health Care Conference in 1984 in Toronto brought together many of the future key actors in the development of health promotion and Healthy Cities: Trevor Hancock, Nancy Milio, Len Duhl, Ron Draper, Ron Labonté, and many more. They continue to exert a major influence in the international debate.

Healthy Cities took its lead from the Healthy Toronto 2000 initiative and several workshops at the Beyond Health Care Conference, and has since become one of the most widely known public health initiatives worldwide.

Grandparents, Aunts, and Uncles: Canadians Everywhere...

WHO's work on health promotion cannot be understood without the Health for All strategy adopted in 1977 and the Alma Ata Declaration on Primary Health Care of 1978. Both documents were influenced by the Lalonde Report in many direct and indirect ways. The WHO regions were requested to develop regional strategies, and the European region adopted such a strategy in 1980. It contained the four key action areas that were to shape European health policy for the next twenty years: health status, health care, lifestyles, and environment. With great foresight, a decision was taken to merge Canadian health field thinking with the U.S. approach of setting concrete health objectives. The outcome was the 38 European targets of Health for All. It will not surprise anyone to hear that the person hired to write and co-ordinate the final version of the target book was a Canadian, who went on to become the Planning Officer at the Regional Office and was supplanted by another Canadian, then yet another! (The person now responsible for health promotion at the global level, Jean Rochon, is well known to Canadians.)

This influence continues. We have followed with great interest the development of a new type of health policy in Ontario and are using these materials and experiences to stimulate the European debate. This seems to be the kind of outcome envisaged by the Beyond Health Care Conference: how can we get closer to a health policy that deals with health, rather than with provision of sickness care and technology? This remains a key question worldwide, and is getting additional attention in view of the fact that most societies are not willing to spend more than the present average of eight to ten percent of their GNP on sickness care.

We have meanwhile sharpened the approaches laid down in the Ottawa Charter to look more consistently at investment in health. While doing so, we were again assisted by work done in Canada on population health — Evans and Stoddart's (1990) seminal article on producing health vis-à-vis consuming health care has become standard reading for health promotion advocates in Europe.

Combining Process and Outcome

I think we relate to stories because they are about process and we can *enter* the story, whereas we are *confronted* with data. Data, says René Dubos, often hide what is most important. If people learn from stories, successful health promotion must be able to tell stories that relate to their experience; stories that give a possibility for ownership and identification, that give courage for change; stories about where people live, love, work, and play — in short, about everyday life.

It was critical to state that health promotion is a process: a process for initiating, managing, and implementing change. This process definition was heavily criticized in an environment that was focussed on cause-and-effect, risk-factor outcome studies. The early 1980s saw behavioural epidemiology in its heyday. But the process definition opened a vista to expand health promotion thinking and move into realms beyond health care through the settings approach. The many criticisms of defining health promotion as a process led us to sharpen our thinking and be challenged to explain it with more clarity. In particular, the understanding of health promotion as a process of personal, organizational, and policy development has helped us move away from simplistic cause-and-effect intervention models. The key question has always been how to transform the complex knowledge of social epidemiology into practice and at the same time be able to document an effect. It is only natural, therefore, that health promoters become consultants for the process of change. The health promotion questions are not simply, "How do I get X to change her behaviour?" but "How do we make the school/workplace/city a healthier place, in order to support X in practising healthier behaviour?" Setting better health as a goal (possibly translating it into quantifiable targets) and managing the process of change toward that goal are crucial elements of health promotion.

A Parent's Pride

This is where a certain pride enters the picture. Health promotion did not just sit back after the Ottawa Charter. It has been constantly refined, challenged, adjusted, and continues to move ahead — not only through conferences such as those held in Adelaide and Sundsvall, but through a wide range of initiatives throughout the world involving policy makers, practitioners, academics, community groups, and activists. The ecological elements have been strengthened, the economic issues have come into sharper focus, and organizational thinking has moved to centre stage. Most important of all, in many cases the health promotion debate has moved from the margins of the health policy debate to its centre.

Health promotion is not the social work of medicine, for which a few extra dollars should be made available. It is truly about a new public health, a new type of health policy based on the determinants of health. It implies a basic shift. At the WHO Regional Office for Europe, this shift has been taken quite seriously: the Lifestyles and Health Department is presently the largest in the house, the settings projects are the key to the implementation of Health for All (cities, schools, workplaces, hospitals, prisons), the major action plans on tobacco and alcohol are structured according to the principles of the Ottawa Charter, and two key initiatives focus on investment in health: HIV/AIDS prevention for central and eastern Europe, and Women's Health Counts, an initiative on women's health for central and eastern Europe.

How Radical?

In terms of the medical paradigm and existing policies and structures, health promotion was a radical agenda. To many social activists, it was a reform agenda that reeked of co-option, not to be trusted. As such, it was seen as a highly delicate balancing act, full of contradictions. The key to making it work was to be open about such contradictions — the Concepts and Principles paper (WHO, 1984) consciously draws attention to dilemmas — and to draw energy from the tension. The aim was to get away from the either/or thinking of personal versus societal responsibility for health and to propose an approach that integrated the best thinking of the time, forward-looking and open to continuous challenge. The document on Concepts and Principles states:

> At a general level, health promotion has come to represent a unifying con-
> cept for those who recognize the need for change in the ways and conditions
> of living, in order to promote health. Health promotion represents a mediat-
> ing strategy between people and their environments, synthesizing personal
> choice and social responsibility in health to create a healthier future (WHO,
> 1984).

Made in Europe

The Concepts and Principles strategy paper marked the birth of health promotion in Europe. The Lalonde Report had given us a word that needed clarification: lifestyle. In the six years between the two documents, a malaise had set in with regard to the narrow behavioural focus of the word. Since we could not get rid of it, we reclaimed it in its original European sense as used by Max Weber. In 1981, the Member States accepted a social concept of health education and in 1983, we presented the Regional Committee with the following definition:

> Lifestyles are patterns of choices made from the alternatives that are available to people according to their socio-economic circumstances and the ease with which they are able to choose certain ones over others.

The specifically European flavour we brought to health promotion was the foundation in European social philosophy, the insistence that a new approach needed a clear conceptual foundation. To create this, we made use of a wide range of disciplines and scientific research. The decision to express this concept in a tangible and understandable form in order to make it relevant for policy and practice has led some people to underestimate the amount of academic research that went into its production. For example, in order to produce the lifestyle and health targets of the Regional Office for Europe, several hundred experts and academics were brought together for discussion: social philosophers, economists, ecologists, political scientists, medical and health experts.

But just as important was the input of community activists. What a step it was when, as part of the health promotion debate, the feminists, self-help advocates, and gay activists advised WHO on its strategies. This inclusiveness was heavily criticized at the time; now, it is the norm in the work of the WHO Global Program on AIDS.

The Gender of the Child

Health promotion balances between the soft and the hard. It is crucial not to let it become the social work of medicine (now that nursing has gotten organized) but still to take seriously the personal aspects of health, the dreams of quality of life, the need to understand and like our bodies. Health promotion needs to keep and strengthen its tough political dimension: the slogan to "Make the healthier choice the easier choice" is not just about types of milk offered at the supermarket; it opens the debate towards those who have no choice at all. We have found three questions useful when examining priorities for action:

- Where is health created?
- Which investment creates the largest health gain?
- Does this investment reduce inequities in health and respect human rights?

Tougher Than the Rest

The analogy is quite appropriate: once children enter school, the relatively unstructured time of their lives ends and they enter the mainstream. This is very much the case with health promotion right now. It is popular. People use the term and its approaches for a multitude of reasons. It is successful. It has shown in its short life that it can make a difference. It has stimulated debate. It is a key factor in the policy debate in the health care reforms of central and eastern Europe. It has to continue to prove itself, be sharp in its arguments, be a little bit smarter than the rest. It has a lot waiting for it.

Health promotion has been a major agent for change. It was crucial to understand it as a part of a new public health and to link it to the ecological movement. Its current challenge is to create a synergy with the classic public health issues that are demanding our attention again: tuberculosis, cholera, polio are returning to parts of the world where we thought we would never see them again.

The child now has to prove itself in building successful alliances and bringing the benefit of its new ideals to the old problems that have returned.

The Parents Today

Some assessments in this book are, to my mind, too impatient and pessimistic. Children do not grow up that quickly. Sometimes a parent despairs of them. But a good parent helps them through, mistakes and all.

Of course, public health is about politics and power. It took fifty years for John Snow's message of the Broad Street pump to be heeded by policy makers and to be translated into action. And in many countries of the world and in many projects in the developing world, this lesson has still not been learned. The power struggle over public health will continue, but it will be different from those of the 1970s and 1980s. And it should be — since, as we see from the authors in this book, many of the parents, aunts, and uncles now hold positions of influence.

If anything, the going will get tougher. Increasingly, it will be at the local level where we will see change occur. The success of the Healthy Cities Project is an indication of this trend.

I am confident that the child will be one of the brightest in class. It will also need to be one of the toughest.

Afterthought:
Daughter: "I still don't understand. What does it all mean?"
Father: "If you were in love, you would not ask."

References

The Adelaide recommendations: Healthy public policy (1988). *Health Promotion* (International), 3(2), 183-186.

Anderson, R. (1984). Health promotion: An overview. *European Monographs in Health Education Research, 6,* 1-126.

Bateson, G. (1975). *Steps to an ecology of mind.* New York: Ballantine Books.

Evans, R.G., & Stoddart, G.L. (1990). Producing health, consuming health care. *Social Science & Medicine, 31,* 1347-1363.

Green, L.W., & Raeburn, J.M. (1988). Health promotion — What is it? What will it become? *Health Promotion* (International), 3, 151-159.

Kickbusch, I. (1986). Lifestyles and health. *Social Science & Medicine, 22,* 117-124.

Kickbusch, I. (1989). Healthy Cities: A working project and a growing movement. *Health Promotion* (International), 4, 77-82.

Kuhn, T. (1962). *The structure of scientific revolutions.* Chicago: University of Chicago Press.

Lalonde, M. (1974). *A new perspective on the health of Canadians.* Ottawa: Information Canada.

World Health Organization (1984). *Health promotion: A discussion document on the concept and principles.* Copenhagen: WHO Regional Office for Europe (Document ICP/HSR 602[m01]).

World Health Organization (1985). *Targets for Health for All.* Copenhagen: WHO Regional Office for Europe.

World Health Organization (1992). *The Sundsvall statement on supportive environments for health.* Geneva: Author (Document WHO/HED/92.1).

CONCEPTUAL

PERSPECTIVES

Health Promotion and Social Change in the Health of Canadians[1]

Robin F. Badgley

"Ne pereat populos Scientia absente" [2]

In terms of reduced infant mortality, greater longevity, and a broader accessibility to health services under national health insurance, there can be no doubt that considerable gains have been achieved in recent decades in the health of Canadians. But it is less certain why these changes have occurred than the fact that they have come about. Historically, each period in the expansion of Canadian health services has relied upon a somewhat different strategy of intervention, initially regulatory, then an extension of public services, and in more recent times, an emphasis upon health promotion. At the social roots of these contrasting ways of seeking deliberately to alter the health of Canadians have been basic changes in the national economy and the structure of Canadian society, which are usually considered to have been too diffuse and indirect to have had measurable consequences.

For the field of health promotion a central issue is whether and how it may have contributed to the improved life chances of the population, or if it has evolved as an institutional by-product accompanying broader shifts in the nation's health conditions. The principal premises of the field are positive and prescriptive, assuming that the health status of individuals and groups can be altered. This perspective is congruent with the increasing rationalization of health services by government. As the demand for health care has mounted and led to larger public expenditures, nations, including Canada, have imposed budgetary ceilings resulting in a direct or implicit rationing of health care resources. In turn, these economic pressures have fostered a more critical appraisal of how such services are used, have led to a search for ways to make existing programs more efficient and effective, and have highlighted the nature of personal choice in the use of publicly paid-for resources.

[1] Originally published in the Proceedings of *Seminar on Health Education and Behaviour Modification Programs,* September 15-16, 1978, Health & Welfare Canada, 1978. Reproduced, with minor modifications, with the permission of the author and Minister of Supply & Services Canada, 1993.
[2] Motto of Ontario Provincial Board of Health, 1882: "Let not the people perish for lack of knowledge."

The altruistic objectives set for health promotion in 1952 by the appointment of the first Expert Committee by the World Health Organization have gradually been recast as a pragmatic cost efficiency strategy in health programs. Accompanying this perceptible shift in perspective has been a greater emphasis turned to the documentation of these programs and a search for more precise information and research methods. This intent was the basis for the 1978 national symposium on Evaluation of Health Education and Behaviour Modification Programs. It is within the context of these broader changes affecting health promotion that this review, prepared for the 1978 Symposium, traces the historical development of the field in Canada, outlines in broad terms its major concepts and research methods, and assesses its current status.

Development of the Field

For a period covering some 250 years, a regulatory philosophy was the main means by which government sought to protect and modify the health of Canadians. The role of government in health affairs in colonial times was through direct subsidies to hospitals and charitable organizations, the setting of professional standards for practice, and the enactment of sanitation and quarantine regulations. Under the French regimen, medical standards were set by *médecin du roi*, the work of hospitals was heavily subsidized, and salaried midwives were elected to care for mothers and the newborn. This regulatory philosophy, coupled with modest government grants, was continued under British rule. In 1786, Québec magistrates in an appeal to the Governing Council wrote that "the most necessary and effectual means, both of preserving the lives of His Majesty's Subjects and advancing the population is that of regulating systematically the practice of Physic, Surgery and Midwifery" (Canada, 1918). Stiff penalties were then set for breaches of health regulations, as in the case of ship captains who faced the double jeopardy of "death without benefit of clergy" for the failure to report passengers who suffered from infectious diseases.

Friendly societies and benevolent associations, which were found in most villages and towns, were concerned with providing relief through direct aid for indigent women with children, the sick, and the aged. The predominant concern was to control the scourge of killer epidemics, the regulation of sanitary conditions, and the provision for the needs of destitute immigrants. An early recognition of the need for health promotion came from H.J. Boulton, Solicitor-General of Upper Canada, who testified in 1827 before a British Parliamentary Select Committee on Emigration. Boulton's concerns, some still valid today, were then largely unheeded:

> The town of York. . . [is] a healthy part of the country. . . . I impute most of the disease in York, and all over the country, to a want of proper attention to diet and to not having proper nutrition, drinking too much water, perhaps, and sometimes too much whisky (Great Britain, 1827).

Until towards the end of the nineteenth century, the major emphasis was still on the building and maintaining of public general hospitals and the enactment of sanitary regulations. According to surgeon William Kelly, who undertook a detailed review of mortality statistics in 1834, improvements in the health of the population were to be gained by "an enlightened police. . . and the drainage that must accompany an improved system of cultivation" (Kelly, 1834). In the 1870s and 1880s, several physician Members of Parliament sought to have a national bureau of health statistics established. These efforts were turned aside on the constitutional grounds that such an agency would infringe upon the provincial jurisdiction in health matters. The federal government then started a program, which is still continued, of selectively providing grants to voluntary and professional associations, some of which undertook health promotion activities.

The importance of direct health promotion was first formally recognized in 1882 when the Ontario Provincial Board of Health was established. One of the Board's listed objectives was the dissemination of sanitary information and under the leadership of its indefatigable secretary, Dr. Peter Bryce, an active program was started which included the preparation of pamphlets, the scheduling of public lectures, the issuing of weekly bulletins published in newspapers, and the distribution of annual reports of the Board (7000 in 1883). Repeatedly in its Annual Reports, the Board stressed that "the dissemination of sanitary information is one of the first and most important steps in the progress of sanitary reform", one which "is so apparent to everyone as not to need proof" (Ontario, 1883). Based on this philosophy, an evaluation of the efficacy of these public information efforts was unnecessary and irrelevant. This health promotion program was continued for four decades with its purposes unaltered when a Division of Public Health Education was formed in 1921. The Division continued the publication of pamphlets and the preparation of a weekly newspaper column. Without documentation which might have been useful for subsequent ventures, the Division's Director then concluded that "it has been found to be comparatively easy to gain public support of sanitary measures when the public understand their value" (Ontario, 1921).

At the national level, the federal government continued its policy of providing grants to voluntary and professional associations, but it took no direct action in health promotion work. In the parliamentary debate of 1904 over whether direct assistance and regulation should be implemented to control smoking, a basic issue was raised which as yet has not been clearly resolved. The debate turned on the nature of state intervention in health affairs, what types of issues were appropriate to be dealt with, and who should be involved in these efforts. In commenting upon the anti-smoking resolution, Sir Wilfrid Laurier, then the Prime Minister, observed:

> . . . the resolution. . . goes too far. I think we should be careful not to enact legislation which would not be observed by the community. . . . More can be done by the beneficial influence of women in teaching and educating our youth than in seeking legislation in this respect (Canada, 1904).

A year later, the Report of a Joint Senate–House Committee on Tuberculosis, which called for strong federal intervention, was allowed to die on the order paper on the grounds that the federal government did not have constitutional jurisdiction in these matters. In rejecting the Report on Tuberculosis, the Prime Minister stated: ". . . if we commit ourselves to contributing a further amount than that stipulated in the British North America Act, where do we stop" (Canada, 1905). Instead of direct involvement, the government provided modest annual grants to the Canadian Association for the Prevention of Consumption.

One of the first ventures by the federal government in a direct program of health promotion came at the end of World War I through the establishment of $200 000 annual grants for the control of venereal disease. This came about as a result of widespread apprehension that returning soldiers would create an epidemic of sexually transmitted diseases across the land. Remarkably comprehensive in scope and anticipating the blending of contemporary approaches that were only to become prominent again half a century later, the strategy then adopted included: enabling legislation, designated public administrative channels, changes in health services by means of clinical facilities providing free care for veterans, a strong partnership between government and voluntary agencies, and mobilization at the local level, often led by well-known community leaders. In addition, mass media campaigns were launched by the newly formed National Council for Combatting Venereal Disease. This organization, a precursor of the Health League of Canada, was given support until this federal–provincial cost-sharing program was discontinued in 1931. Singularly, the dimensions and implications of this comprehensive health promotion activity have been largely forgotten in this field.

About the time of World War II, several provinces had established health promotion programs (Ontario, 1921; Manitoba, 1929; Québec, 1943; Newfoundland, 1949). In 1938, following a reorganization of the Health Section of the Department of Pensions and National Health, a section on Publicity and Health Education was formed with F.W. Rowse as its first director (May, 1938). Over half of the unit's budget was for salaries, with most of the remainder set aside for advertising purposes (Canada, 1939). At both the federal and provincial levels health promotion was then seen to involve the work of all public health personnel, and its methods relied on lectures and the preparation of news releases. When the Department of National Health and Welfare was formed in 1944, the section on Publicity and Health Education was reassigned to the Administration Branch, retitled the Information Services Division, and given a substantially larger budget with five permanent staff positions. During its first year, the Division's work involved the preparation of 29 film strips, 28 pamphlets, and 19 posters.

Anticipating the argument that reappeared thirty years later in the 1974 federal green paper on lifestyles, the sharply increased budget for this Division was defended by the Minister of Health in terms of its economic utility. ". . . We believe these expenditures pay dividends just as industrialists believe their expenditures pay. We believe that these expenditures have paid dividends in the past" (Canada, 1946). For these reasons the benefits accruing from health promotion were still considered to be self-evident, and either no evaluation was undertaken or selective measures were used. In discussing the impact of the widely circulated pamphlet *Mother and Child*, Health Minister Brooke Claxton stated in 1946 that "since that book has been distributed infant mortality rates in Canada have improved. We do not claim credit for the improvement, but we do say that you cannot have information unless people know what should be done" (Canada, 1946).

As part of the federal government's 1948 grants-in-aid program which was intended to develop services, provide capital for the construction of facilities, and expand professional training programs, direct support was offered to the provinces for the support of health education programs. These general public health grants, which were in operation during the 1950s, were picked up by the western provinces, notably Saskatchewan and Manitoba, and were used to pay for positions for health educators, graduate training at American schools of public health, the purchase of equipment, and as a way to expand rural health education services. During this period the listing of what had been done, or the extent of the circulation of items, continued to be the main means of evaluating health promotion programs. Even this social marketing approach was opposed by some health officials as being conceptually irrelevant or a way to reduce the prestige of traditional public health workers. Expressing these concerns, one provincial director of health education wrote in the mid-1950s that:

> We see no point in trying to evaluate the results of educational efforts integrated in preventive services offered to the public. . . . We shall not attempt to measure the results of health education in terms of mortality or morbidity statistics or even of changed behaviour. . . . We have no intention of crediting health educators alone with improvements that may be due to education from other sources. . . . Even though we cannot yet measure accurately the results of health education, we are firmly convinced of its importance and its true usefulness (Gilbert, 1953, 1954, 1966, 1967).

This outlook gave way to a growing reliance upon external, accessible measures, and then later, to the use of descriptive social survey techniques. Commenting on the impact of a 1957 series of eight, half-hour health promotion programs on local television, the health educator who was involved commented, "while there has not been a formal evaluation of our series, we know of several concrete results." The appraisal of this program included strong endorsement by the local medical profession and good viewer ratings (Geekie, 1957).

The objectives of the first national symposium on health education held in Saskatoon in 1961 were "to assess current concepts and techniques in the diffusion of health information and to develop a fresh approach to understanding and educating the public" (Badgley, 1961). While these aims were too ambitious to be realized then, the 1961 workshop set the stage for the inception of the Canadian Health Education Society, fostered the development of the federal Health Education Unit in 1963, and gave momentum to an expansion of work carried out in the field. Under the leadership of M.E. Palko, the new Unit's responsibilities were "the coordination of educational activities and resources within the Branch and to facilitate their implementation in the provinces." Subsequently, a national health education bulletin (which is still published) was issued and health educators were involved in the federal Smoking and Health Program (1964) (Wake, Andrews & Laughlin, 1967). About this time (1960), the Medical Services Branch started its community health representatives' program which by the mid-1970s had placed over 500 workers in Indian and Inuit centres. National reviews of the state of health education in the curriculum of public schools and some hospitals were also undertaken (Marshall, 1966; Palko, 1965).

Despite these sizeable developments for a small field, the centre stage of public concern with health affairs was preoccupied during this period by issues related to the introduction of national health insurance. Health education, despite its substantial growth, was then little more then a supporting player that was relegated to the wings. *The Royal Commission on Health Services* (1964), for instance, the most comprehensive review undertaken up to that point of health care in the nation, tabled 200 recommendations calling for an expansion and strengthening of health services (Canada, 1964). None of these recommendations dealt directly with health promotion. Likewise, five years later scant attention was given to the field among the 337 recommendations of the federal *Task Force on the Cost of Health Services in Canada* (Canada, 1969). The five recommendations on this theme put forward by the Task Force relegated health education to a consultancy role, advocated attention be given to dietary and family life education, and stressed the need for education involving medically underreported conditions. Almost as an afterthought given with casual justification, the Task Force recommended "that health education activities should be expanded and intensified, but subjected to more critical evaluation with respect both to their effectiveness in informing the public, and especially in influencing behaviour in the desired direction" (Canada, 1969). The rationale given was that health education was a means of "fostering a sense of responsibility" by individuals in their use of health services.

During the 1970s two distinctive approaches to health education crystallized in Canadian programs, one focussing attention on the intimate world of the values and attitudes of individuals, while the second led to the development of large-scale national campaigns. The psychological approach resulted in a number of small-scale, often clinical, studies about how individuals perceive their health and in turn how their perceptions may influence their subsequent health behaviour. In contrast, the work of ParticipAction Canada focussing on physical fitness, the Hole-in-the-Fence program (1973) seeking to curtail drug use, and the Dialogue on Drinking campaign (1976) (Canada, 1978b) aimed at reducing alcohol consumption, relied heavily on channelling information through the mass media. The priority given to this strategy was underscored by the 1974 federal green paper, *A New Perspective on the Health of Canadians*, which called for an expansion of social marketing techniques in health education (Canada, 1974). The document outlined a health promotion strategy "aimed at informing, influencing and assisting both individuals and organizations so that they will accept more responsibility and be more active in matters affecting mental and physical health" (Canada, 1976, p. 66). Twenty-three steps were listed as possible courses of action.

Much has been accomplished for the field of health promotion since the publication of the 1974 green paper. Thousands of Canadians have taken part in a self-administered inventory of their health status, a national health survey was started (and discontinued in 1978), and the country hosted an international symposium on health promotion. During this period, momentum accelerated for the mounting of academic training programs, a federal–provincial health promotion committee sought to develop the research side of the field, and a series of federal–provincial conferences on health education were convened to develop guidelines and identify evaluation methods (Canada, 1973). At its 1973 meeting this latter body endorsed a definition of the field, advocated that a detailed review of research be undertaken to identify "the most effective methods of health promotion", and recommended that a national depository of health promotion materials be established. The 1978 reorganization of the federal Department of National Health and Welfare designated a Promotion and Prevention Directorate whose objectives included "the fostering of intra- and extramural research required to establish the scientific basis for the programs as well as the appropriate strategies and techniques to be employed."

The rapid, recent growth of the field is reflected by the existence of health promotion programs in all provincial health ministries and the large number of voluntary health associations which now employ these specialists. In some instances the traditional role of disseminating information is being coupled with the enactment of health ordinances, such as in the AWARE and FEELIN' GOOD projects in Saskatchewan, seat-belt legislation, or the Ontario Occupational Health Hazards Act. Recommendations for the reorganization of the Toronto health department have called for legal controls as the major way of limiting the use of tobacco, alcohol, and harmful drugs and as a means to reduce chemical hazards and automobile accidents (Toronto, 1978). Health education was assigned an advocacy role in achieving these objectives, but where regulation was deemed to be inadvisable or was seen to have a limited impact (e.g., mental illness, family planning, physical fitness), the responsibilities for the field were expanded.

The experience with a Toronto anti-smoking bylaw illustrates well the dilemma between the enactment and the enforcement of statutes as well as the impact that established vested interests can have in this regard. Fines for breaching this ordinance were levied in 1978 against the Toronto General Hospital, a major university teaching centre, and the Toronto Western Medical Building. Similar charges were dismissed against the Canadian Cancer Society on the grounds that the terms of the law were unclear (Strauss, 1978). Somewhat reminiscent of Sir Wilfrid Laurier's observation in 1904 about enacting legislation that would not be observed, the president of the local academy of medicine concluded:

any suggestion that smoking be totally prohibited in this health care setting [hospitals] results in cynical, supercilious or derisive comments. How can the public be given the message when the educators need educating (Mahood, 1978, p. A8).

Some of the larger voluntary health associations that are dependent upon public subscription for their revenues may assume a low public profile on controversial issues involving legal enforcement. A charge of a conflict of interests in this regard has been made against the cancer, lung, and heart associations in Ontario, which while raising some $15 million in 1977 contributed less than $500 to an umbrella organization to combat smoking of which they were council members. A former president of one voluntary society concluded that "there is no doubt that there is a consideration with respect to [our] campaign. We do not want to alienate smokers who might support the society" (Mahood, 1978, p. A8).

The growing public endorsement of health promotion has not always been matched by a corresponding allocation of resources for these purposes. The Red Queen hypothesis from *Alice in Wonderland* about running twice as fast to keep up with other developments is partly borne out. At the level of the federal government, for instance, while funds designated for the dissemination of information, publicity and health education rose substantially between 1920–70, these allocations declined over time as a proportion of general departmental expenditures (Canada, n.d.). In 1940–41, 1.40% of health expenditures were set aside for health promotion and publicity. This proportion was 0.53% in 1955–56, 0.30% in 1960–61, 0.52% in 1965–66, and 0.80% in 1970–71. If the total expenditures of the federal ministry are included, then the amount of funds spent on designated health promotion activities decreased from 0.04% in 1970–71 to 0.02% in 1975–76.[3]

The recent changes in health promotion programs and related research activities are measures of a field that is in transition. An anomaly emerges in the gradual retitling of the field from health education to health promotion, for while much of the emphasis in the 1970s was with education, the term promotion connotes a wider range of means including regulation, community action, and basic changes in social structure. Looked at from a historical perspective, the recent developments in the field represent substantial accomplishments. Paradoxically, these gains may be constrained by financial restraints, which while accelerating its initial growth may come in time to contract its scope on a basis of cost efficiency.

Conceptual Frameworks

There is a broad debate and much uncertainty about the first principles upon which health promotion is based. Seldom clearly specified as they

---

[3] Excluded from the rates cited here are the amounts spent on federal-provincial cost-sharing programs.

apply to this field, how these premises are interpreted determines its perceived utility, how its priorities are set, what programs are undertaken, and
how these in turn are evaluated. Health education, as it is commonly
thought of in most definitions of the field, is a narrowly gauged form of
radical utopianism that seeks a reordering of individual behaviour toward
the attainment of an optimal level of well-being. The premises of this
approach assume that a man's actions are rationally based and can be modified by the provision of information or result from unilateral intervention
schemes.

Implicit here is the idea that the individual makes critical and responsible choices that are little influenced by his or her social circumstances, or the
prevailing structure of a society. The emphasis in a majority of the health
promotion literature to date is with how individual attitudes and behaviours
can be modified. What is often ignored is that this interpretation constitutes
only one of several approaches that have in fact been adopted, as exemplified by the national venereal disease program of the 1920s.

A vast theoretical and research literature drawn from several fields dealing with human behaviour and social organization relates directly to the
work done in health promotion. Sketched in broad terms, these schools of
thought can be called: (i) nihilist; (ii) incremental adaptation; (iii) structural; (iv) regulatory; and (v) activist intervention. Each approach assumes
different premises about why and how change occurs in society and, in
particular, how health services and individual health behaviour may be
modified.

As represented differently in the work of Cochrane and Illich, the
nihilist approach either questions the utility of intervention until there is
evidence to the contrary (Cochrane, 1972), or rejects much of such effort
as having negative social consequences. For Illich the positive potential of
health promotion is limited by its actual use as an ideologically fuelled
means of hygienic behavioural control. He sees the field as a form of
human engineering that instills a greater dependence upon medicine. Illich
concludes that health promotion, as it is practised, has little utility, multi-
plies risks, and generates fear (Illich, 1974, 1977). While most health
workers would reject Illich's thesis, few health promoters would deny the
pervasive impact of an entrenched scepticism that surrounds their work. In
part, such scepticism is partially responsible for the search for evaluation
procedures that may demonstrate the utility of the field.

The incremental adoption or diffusion approach assumes that the major
changes which have occurred in health status have resulted from broader
social forces which gradually transform society. From this perspective,
health promotion is seen as being little more than an irrelevant social frill
accomplishing little of real benefit for society. McKeown, for instance, has
argued that historically the major improvements in mortality and morbidity
were gained by advances made in agriculture, the development of more
effective means of providing water and sewage disposal, and in recent
times, the introduction of effective preventive therapeutic measures. At the
individual level of the modification of health behaviour, McKeown asserts
that convincing evidence is lacking "whether public intervention in per-

sonal habits is justified or likely to be effective" (McKeown & Lowe, 1974). In the absence of effective ways of controlling human behaviour, this epidemiologist reaches the morose conclusion that "the death of the susceptible at an early age is the price that must be paid". Putting aside McKeown's pessimism, his analysis pinpoints the limited relevance of applying a classical epidemiological analysis to the complex matter of how social and economic forces may affect health behaviour, a dilemma still encountered in the substance of most health promotion research.

From the perspective of the structural and conflict theories of health promotion, the current predominant emphasis on the modification of individual behaviour precludes a consideration of the impact that the structure and power relations of society may have in determining the distribution of health resources and affecting individual circumstances. In his critique of western systems of medical care, Navarro attacks this individualistic ideology which he believes "absolves the present pattern of class power relations — a pattern that determines the current economic, political and social environments — from responsibility for creating and conditioning the individual's behaviour and for causing much of the mortality, morbidity, disease and unease to which our populations are subject" (Navarro, 1978). This analysis of health promotion highlights issues that are seldom considered in the field, namely, the competing social forces and vested interests that may affect individual choice in the use of alcohol, drugs, or tobacco, or the extent to which a society's social class system affects the life chances of individuals. How health promotion studies in Canada have dealt with these issues is considered more fully later in the consideration of the research methods that have been used to date in this field.

The regulation by the state of factors affecting health grew out of an evolving public concern to control the spread of infectious disease and was gradually extended to the provision of water and the disposal of sewage. In most western countries there has been a reluctance by legislators to deal directly with certain areas affecting the health risks faced by individuals, unless it can be shown that the public good is jeopardized. It is implicitly recognized in such instances that preserving the freedom of choice relative to health hazards may accelerate death or impose the need for expensive therapy paid for from the public purse. This anomaly is accounted for by the widespread prevalence of certain health-injurious customs, often assuming epidemic proportions, coupled with a finely tuned sense of political pragmatism. The experience with prohibition, fluoridation, and marijuana attests to the difficulty of implementing legislation about which there is little sense of apparent urgency in terms of safe-guarding health or that runs counter to the values of a sizeable number of the population. Such legislation may even be ignored by those groups which might be expected to uphold these principles.

Despite the fact that there are a large number of health statutes in force across Canada, and a sizeable body of legislation that has a bearing on health, there has been no review of their collective and accumulative effects in influencing health behaviour, or of their comparative utility relative to other means that are used in health promotion work.

In contrast to the four conceptual positions which question the relevance and the utility of health promotion, the activist intervention and community mobilization approaches assume that changing individual and collective behaviour is a positive and feasible objective. While numerous redefinitions have been developed since 1954, when the WHO Expert Committee put forward its objective for the field as helping "people to achieve health by their own actions and efforts" (World Health Organization, 1954), this concern remains predominant. As currently conceived, it assumes a large measure of personal and local community culpability in the discretionary use of health care or the occurrence of disease. This perspective is consonant with the idea that the onus for change in health status lies more with recipients than with the providers of services.

For the most part, government agencies have followed the high road of undertaking large-scale campaigns, thereby avoiding the procedural and ethical dilemmas involved in more detailed inquiries relying on smaller and more direct local community and behaviour modification ventures. Such campaigns have become an established feature of recent health promotion work in Canada. Apparently, while it has been feasible to obtain resources for these purposes, rather less effort has focussed upon an evaluation of what in fact may have been achieved. The hallmarks of these mass media programs initiated by government have been an omission of clear-cut statements of expected outcomes, their short duration, a lack of co-ordination along these lines between government agencies, and an absence of rigorous evaluation. The conceptual underpinnings of this social marketing approach are seldom, if ever, enunciated, the assumption often being that the benefits are self-evident.

Two other approaches, mostly at the level of clinical trials or university-based research, have been followed within the context of the interventionist school of thought. Focussing alternatively either on the psychological or the situational circumstances of individuals, the concern with these inquiries has dominated the field, often to the exclusion of a consideration of other approaches and also standing in sharp contrast with the major work being done involving mass media campaigns. This anomaly has resulted in an imbalance in the allocation of resources for research evaluation between these strategies as well as in the relative rigour of the methods used.

The Health Belief Model developed over the past twenty years adopts a psychological–phenomenological approach, namely, it is the intimate world of the individual that shapes what he/she will or will not do (Becker, 1974). This model assumes that each person: (i) is affected by positive and negative values; (ii) holds different ideas about his/her expected susceptibility to illness; (iii) makes different assumptions about the seriousness of actual or potential illness; and (iv) reacts differently to the perceived relative effectiveness of treatment solutions. For two proponents of this approach, I.M. Rosenstock and J.P. Kirsht, a central dilemma is that key premises of the model such as "group dynamics", "the teachable moment", or "fear arousal" are not readily operationalized for research purposes (Rosenstock, 1966; Rosenstock & Kirscht, 1974). Based on a review of several hundred studies of the Health Belief Model, these authors concluded that it had "sadly failed the challenge of external validity" and that a broader view of how health beliefs and behaviours changed should include an assessment of the impact of modifying health care systems, a conclusion reached by Navarro. At the time of this major review, little research had been done to test the relative weighting of the variables used, their durability of impact, or how they might be applied to larger population groups.

Another approach that can be labelled a Health Behaviour Model assumes that it is the attributes of individuals and the nature of their affiliations with groups and organizations which account for different patterns of health behaviour. While this approach has been a popular one in Canada, such studies do not account for why change itself occurs, but rather document the existence of different outcomes involving a limited number of associated variables. This approach has essentially been adapted in the evaluation of the federal Dialogue on Drinking program. Another study following this research strategy found that higher income groups and persons with strong religious beliefs, in contrast to those who did not have these attributes, were more positive about the need for physical exercise and more negative about smoking (MacKie, 1975). Left unstated in this inquiry was how the standard of living of the poor or the religious beliefs of the unconverted individuals might be modified to alter their health behaviour.

An initial review and listing of some of the work done in health promotion in Canada was completed by Susan McCoy in 1974 for the Health Promotion Branch of the Department of National Health and Welfare (McCoy, 1974). Constituting a useful starting point, the review did not examine the conceptual premises of the work that had been done nor undertake a comparative assessment of techniques and programs. In this regard, the recommendations of a number of commissions and advisory groups remain yet to be implemented.

Research Methods

Reflecting the historical development of the field, the research methods used in some fifty studies completed during the past decade have varied substantially. Because small numbers of individuals have usually been involved, often in special settings, and different research methods have been used, few generalizations can be made about the general course or success of these health promotion programs. A majority were primarily descriptive assessments involving neither a random selection of participants nor the use of matched control groups in two out of three studies. While the use of study control groups may pose difficult ethical and methodological questions, there is the possibility that without them, spurious conclusions may be drawn about the effectiveness of particular intervention strategies. As has often been shown in medical research, unless control groups are used, the effects of a particular treatment may remove from consideration the potential impact of alternative procedures.

The immediate and short-term effects of particular programs were considered in four out of five recent intervention studies. What the long-term effects of these programs might have been or the extent to which change has preceded the intervention was usually unknown or undocumented. In considering the impact of belief or behaviour modification, a longer time perspective than is usually used is indicated, a point illustrated by changes in Canadian infant and maternal mortality rates. Some observers have concluded that these rates were substantially reduced following the introduction of national hospital insurance (Armstrong, 1975; Leclair, 1975). The evidence here is unconvincing. While significant improvements were made in the fourteen years following the program's inception, the gains were greater during a similar period before it started.

A usual "shopping list" of psychological and social variables has been developed that includes such items as age, sex, residence, occupation, education, income, and family size, among others. The typical questions asked of respondents may inquire about the occurrence of illness, the use of health services, and attitudes toward health matters. Many of these items have come to be so widely used that sometimes their social meanings have been uncritically accepted. The importance of work as it relates to health risks is well known, but relatively little care has been taken in the use of occupational or income scales in these investigations. Without further specification, it is usually not self-evident what qualitative attributes of a person's work may affect different health attitudes or behaviours, result in stress, or induce risks.

Analytically more powerful statistical tools in health promotion research are starting to be used, but this is a recent development, with earlier work often being based on the separate analysis of variables. As the use of both multivariate and qualitative analysis develops, it should be possible to gauge in greater detail the factors associated with modified behaviour as well as how extensive the changes are.

Considerable work remains to be done to determine how much effort is required to achieve significant changes, and at what cost. Nathan Keyfitz of Harvard University has concluded that if the effects of cancer were eliminated in the United States, the average life expectancy would be extended by about one-thirtieth of the average life span (Keyfitz, 1978). But as cancer occurs more extensively among older age groups and in conjunction with other fatal conditions such as heart disease, this gain would be sharply reduced. Keyfitz calls for a reordering of research effort to focus on where the greatest gains to longevity might be made within available resources, a strategy that might serve as the basis for assigning priorities for health promotion programs and research. If this approach were to be followed in Canada, it would result in greater attention being paid to certain conditions and high-risk groups in the population.

Because the constitutional jurisdiction for health services in Canada is divided between the federal and provincial governments, there is a blurring of where responsibility lies for the field of health promotion. In practice, both levels of government have initiated programs, with support given by the provinces varying considerably across the nation. The federal role has primarily dealt with the support of programs deemed to be in the interests of national well-being and the financing of selected research ventures. With the exception of the 1974 *New Perspective* document, there has been an absence in the past of clearly enunciated, national priorities for health services generally, and in particular, for health promotion. This fact is evident in the focus of research that has been done. Accidents, for instance, accounted for 14.5% of deaths and 30.8% of potential years of lost life in 1974 (Canada, 1976). That year, the federal green paper on lifestyles called for greater effort to control smoking and to limit injuries resulting from car accidents. Between 1974–77 less than 2% of federally supported research studies have tackled these problems (Canada, 1978a). The role that industries supplying commodities potentially injurious to health (tobacco, alcohol, etc.) may have had in influencing health behaviour has not been investigated, nor the extent to which they may constitute a strong counterforce of vested interests in health promotion efforts.

A small number of federally supported investigations have dealt with the health problems of known high-risk groups, such as the poor, Indians, and Inuit. Between 1974–77 less than 3% of federally funded research dealt with these groups; half of these studies resulted from crisis intervention, reflecting public concern with the effects of mercury pollution or parasitic infection. These groups are known to have higher infant and maternal mortality rates, experience significantly more physical disabilities, and in the case of the poor, to have more ill health and disability (Beck, 1973).[1]

The body of health promotion research undertaken in Canada has dealt predominantly with ways to alter the health status of individuals such as modifying levels of physical activity, reducing weight, improving dietary habits, reducing primary depression or increasing effective communication, and raising levels of health knowledge. The broad thrust of these studies suggests that operational lines may exist within which intervention studies are generally undertaken, resulting in minimal attention being turned to those issues having potentially divisive social policy implications.

The aegis under which health promotion research is done, which issues are studied, and which outcome measures are used raise questions requiring critical consideration. The extent to which public agencies are capable of undertaking independent and impartial assessments of the utility of their own programs, particularly when much is at stake in terms of institutional resources or professional interests, has not been considered in health promotion research. It is apparent from other studies of organizations or groups that unintended influences may limit the scope of an inquiry or determine the types of measures that are used. This is done most commonly by focussing an inquiry on the role of recipients, with negligible attention being given to the potential impact of how services are organized or provided.

---

[1] Between 1963–71 in Saskatchewan, for instance, the average dollar value of health services for each person rose from $67.04 to $109.25. This amount increased by $36.10 for the lowest income group and by $61.24 for the highest income earners. During this period the difference between these income groups more than doubled so that while all had gained, it was the highest income groups that had gained the most in terms of using health services.

Incisive health promotion research implies an invidious comparison of programs in terms of how well they may or may not achieve their intended objectives. To demonstrate, for instance, that established programs may not be achieving their goals requires a steeled fortitude and an institutional independence that may be hard to come by. Faced with such a dilemma, either peripheral issues may be chosen for investigation or evaluation measures used that have limited long-term validity. Much of the work in the field is still permeated with a staunch conviction about its utility, a belief that may not always accord well with measurable outcomes relating to durable changes in health status. Reflecting the different approaches followed in intervention programs, there is considerable ambiguity about what is meant by evaluation itself.

Trends and Implications

This review suggests the need for a full and detailed reappraisal of the health promotion field, one that takes into account its conceptual premises, the nature of its intervention strategies, and its evaluation methods. Some basic questions may be asked such as the types of problems with which it deals, how its programs are directed, what types of strategies are involved, how change is measured, how extensive and durable are these changes, and what are their cost and social policy implications.

Commenting on these issues in 1954, the WHO Expert Committee called for:

> . . . attention [to be] given to implementing carefully planned field studies, research, and experimental programmes in this field.
>
> It is recommended that a technical conference or study-group be convened to delineate the areas. . . where the need for stimulating studies and experimental programmes seems to be particularly urgent.
>
> This study could. . . foster closer collaboration between the health disciplines.
>
> The Committee recommends. . . [exploration] of fostering training programmes in health education. . . (World Health Organization, 1954).

The 1969 WHO Scientific Group on Research in Health Education reiterated these concerns and called for a codification of pertinent available research.

> The most general and yet the most significant problem is the lack of adequate research concerned with health education in various circumstances. . . codification could serve several useful purposes simultaneously: it would reveal gaps in knowledge and research needs and assist in the refinement of theory: it would relate research findings to concepts. . . ; and it would guide practitioners in coping with field problems. . . (World Health Organization, 1969).

At the level of an ongoing evaluation of research in health promotion, these steps remain to be taken in Canada. Their implementation could serve as a valuable baseline upon which programs could be developed in the future. Acting upon these recommendations would entail:

(1) a comprehensive evaluation of completed health promotion research in Canada;

(2) the designation of health promotion priorities in terms of the potential effectiveness of various intervention strategies, the resources required and the costs involved;

(3) the convening of interdisciplinary planning workshops to develop the design and evaluation methods for specific programs;

(4) the support of carefully mounted and evaluated health promotion demonstration projects; and

(5) the development of academic health promotion research training programs at the master's and doctoral levels.

In some respects, the situation of health promotion in the 1970s is analogous to an assessment of the needs of the field given by the Provincial Board of Health in Ontario almost a century ago. In its Second Annual Report for 1883, the Board concluded:

> However much progress has been made in general knowledge, it is only here and there that organization, comprehensive and effective in its nature, is seen actively and boldly devising schemes for the attainment of definite improvement. . . (Ontario, 1884).

Health promotion in Canada is now at a critical turning point in terms of how its research is conducted and the extent to which resources may be available for intervention programs during a continuing period of financial retrenchment. The field has reached a stage where more rigorous research is indicated and is feasible. But having said this, it is equally relevant to remember the nature of the constraints that limit the scope of the field. The concepts and intervention strategies that have been adopted bear the overriding imprint of the values of Canadian society and its medically dominated health system. It may be that only when there is a fuller understanding of these usually ignored dimensions of health promotion that the reoccurring dilemmas that circumscribe the work of the field can be accounted for. These broader social values and the structure of Canadian society epitomize a sharp division of legislative authority in health affairs, give emphasis to curative services and the clinical model of therapy, and stress consensus and accommodation while seeking to avoid conflict. The impact of these broader Canadian values on health promotion is reflected in the tacit acceptance of existing political and economic interests which are not to be disturbed. As a result, what emerges is a field accorded a high place in the public rhetoric of numerous government reports, yet one that is constrained to a limited role in public service.

In *Knowledge for What?*, written in 1939, Robert S. Lynd reminds us of the need to re-examine critically the central premises of a discipline, what it seeks to accomplish, how it goes about achieving its purposes, and the nature of its impact for the people who are involved (Lynd, 1939). In particular, Lynd called for a consideration of the concepts and issues that were guarded by posted "No Trespassing" signs. Included among these issues is a critical examination of the usual ways used to educate the public and the curtailing effects of key institutions in this process. Lynd concluded that "while all possible improvements in education and personnel must be pushed for all they are worth. . .", it may be "impossible to rely primarily upon popular education to effect such changes." In this effort (which includes health promotion), it is "only when an intricate culture like ours is better structured to support rather than to obstruct, or merely to tolerate, humanly important lines of behaviour, can we justifiably expect secondary agencies like education to carry on effectively."

With respect to Lynd's observations, health promotion as it is presently constituted has had a negligible role to play in effecting changes in the internal organization of health services, the reordering of health priorities, the redistribution of services, or in the reducing of inequitable mortality and morbidity along class lines and by high-risk groups. Such changes are well beyond the mandate of the field and the powers actually assigned to it. But until these limitations inherent in the field are clearly recognized and resolved, it will continue to face the dilemma of experiencing constantly thwarted purposes and will flounder in an absence of demonstrable major achievements in ameliorating the health status and social well-being of the population. While this conclusion may be unpalatable, it is well within the discretion of those working in health promotion, by removing the "No Trespassing" signs, to document more fully the nature and the scope of those social forces limiting its fuller development, and thereby enabling a better informed public to resolve them. Based on the past experience of the field, such fundamental changes are unlikely to come about soon or easily, leaving health promotion in its traditional role of a discipline continuing to promise great, but as yet unfulfilled, expectations.

References

Armstrong, R.A. (1975, February). *Notes for an address at Washington journalism seminar.*

Badgley, R.F. (1961). An interdisciplinary assessment of health education. *Food for Thought, 21,* 26-31.

Beck, R.G. (1973). Economic class and access to physician services under public medical care assistance. *International Journal of Health Services, 3,* 341-355.

Becker, M.H. (1974). The health belief model and personal health behaviour. *Health Education Monographs, 2*(4).

Canada (n.d.). *Public Accounts,* 1919-77. Ottawa.

Canada (1904, March 3). *House of Commons debates.* Ninth Parliament, Fourth Session.

Canada (1905, July 10). *House of Commons debates.* Tenth Parliament, First Session.

Canada (1918). Archives. *Documents relating to the constitutional history of Canada, 1759-1791.* Part II, pp. 926-28. Ottawa: King's Printer.

Canada (1939). Department of Pensions and National Health. *Report of the Auditor General.* Ottawa: Author.

Canada (1946, March 31) *House of Commons debates.* Twentieth Parliament, Second Session.

Canada (1964). *Royal Commission on health services.* Ottawa: Queen's Printer, Volume I.

Canada (1969). *Task force on the cost of health services in Canada* (3 volumes). Ottawa: Department of National Health & Welfare.

Canada (1973). *Proceedings of the meeting of provincial directors and consultants in health education,* Winnipeg, October, 1973. Ottawa: Department of National Health & Welfare.

Canada (1974). Department of National Health & Welfare. *A new perspective on the health of Canadians: A working document.* Ottawa: Information Canada.

Canada (1976). *Health field indicators: Canada and provinces.* Ottawa: Department of National Health & Welfare, 1976.

Canada (1978a). Department of National Health & Welfare. *Summary of projects approved January 1974 to March 1977.* Ottawa: National Health Research & Development Program.

Canada (1978b). *Dialogue on drinking: Briefing paper.* Ottawa: Department of National Health & Welfare.

Cochrane, A.L. (1972). *Effectiveness and efficiency: Random reflections on health services.* Abington, Berkshire: The Nuffield Provincial Hospitals Trust.

Geekie, D.A. (1957). Television and health education. *Canadian Journal of Public Health, 48,* 254-255.

Gilbert, J. (1953). Health education in the province of Quebec. *Canadian Journal of Public Health, 44,* 452-455.

Gilbert, J. (1954). Evaluation in health education. *Canadian Journal Of Public Health, 45,* 51-54.

Gilbert, J. (1966). The technique of health education and its evaluation in a health unit. *Canadian Journal of Public Health, 57,* 25-28.

Gilbert, J. (1967). The grandeur and decadence of health education. *Canadian Journal of Public Health, 58,* 355-358.

Great Britain (1827). Parliament. *Report from the Select Committee on Emigration from the United Kingdom.* London, pp. 13-22.

Illich, I. (1974). *Hygienic nemesis.* Cuernavaca, Mexico: CICOC Cuaderno No. 86.

Illich, I. (1977). *Limits to medicine: Medical nemesis.* Harmondsworth, England: Penguin Books.

Kelly, W. (1834). On the medical statistics of Lower Canada. *Transactions of the Literary & Historical Society of Quebec, 3,* 193-221.

Keyfitz, N. (1978). How much would a cure for cancer affect life expectancy? *Surgical Rounds, 1,* 24-29.

Leclair, M. (1975). The Canadian health care system. In S. Andreopoulos (ed.), *National health insurance* (pp. 11-96). New York: Wiley & Sons.

Lynd, R.S. (1939). *Knowledge for what? The place of social science in American culture.* Princeton: Princeton University Press.

MacKie, M. (1975). Perception of beneficial health behaviour: Smoking and exercise. *Canadian Journal of Public Health, 66,* 481-487.

Mahood, G. (1978, November 2). Time to get tough on smoking. *Toronto Star,* p. A8.

Marshall, J.M. (1966). Teacher preparation in health and health education. *Canadian Journal of Public Health,* 458-462.

McCoy, S. (1974). *Annotated bibliography on health education in Canada 1969-1974.* Ottawa: Department of National Health & Welfare (mimeo).

McKeown, T., & Lowe, C.R. (1974). *An introduction to social medicine.* Oxford: Blackwell.

Navarro, V. (1978). The crisis of the western system of medicine in contemporary capitalism. *International Journal of Health Services, 8,* 179-211.

Ontario (1883). Provincial Board of Health. *First annual report, 1882.* Toronto: C. Blackett Robinson.

Ontario (1884). Provincial Board of Health. *Second annual report, 1883.* Toronto: C. Blackett Robinson.

Ontario (1921). Provincial Board of Health. *Thirty-ninth annual report, 1920.* Toronto: King's Printer.

Palko, M.E. (1965). Highlights of a report on the preparation of elementary school teachers in Canada in health and health education. *Canadian Journal of Public Health, 56*, 207-209.

Rosenstock, I.M. (1966). Why people use health services. *Milbank Memorial Fund Quarterly, 44*, 94-127.

Rosenstock, I.M., & Kirscht, J.P. (1974). Practice implications. In M.H. Becker (ed.), The Health Belief Model and personal health behaviour. *Health Education Monographs, 2*(4), 472-473.

Strauss, M. (1978, November 3). Law considered ambiguous: Anti-smoking charge against cancer groups is dismissed by court. *The Globe & Mail*, p. 5.

Toronto (1978). *Public health in the 1980s.* Report of the Health Planning Steering Committee. Toronto: Board of Health.

Wake, F.R., Andrews, D.A., & Laughlin, T.J. (1967). *Methods involved in successful and unsuccessful attempts to stop smoking.* Ottawa: Carleton University (mimeo).

World Health Organization (1954). *Expert Committee on health education of the public.* Geneva: WHO Technical Report Series No. 89.

World Health Organization (1969). *Research in health education: Report of a scientific group.* Geneva: WHO Technical Report Series No. 432.

Two Analytic Paths for Understanding Canadian Developments in Health Promotion

Michel O'Neill and Ann Pederson

This book is about the development of health promotion in Canada and throughout there are descriptions of programs, policies, and strategies aimed at improving health. But underlying all that activity is a different form of action — and this book is about that as well. This other form of action is the evolution of thinking about what determines health and disease and about societal choices for reducing inequities in the distribution of health problems. Through its challenge to traditional views of health and its determinants, health promotion offers a knowledge challenge to health practitioners and planners. In this chapter, we suggest how two theoretical strands, the sociology of knowledge and the study of social movements, can be useful in understanding the contribution of health promotion beyond the level of new programs and policies.

The Context: A Brief Historical Review

From Health Education to Health Promotion

Our focus is on the contemporary health promotion enterprise as it has taken shape since the early 1970s. This time frame was chosen because the birth of the term "health promotion" is typically traced to a 1974 Canadian federal discussion paper, the so-called Lalonde Report (referring to then federal Minister of Health and Welfare, Marc Lalonde) (see, for instance, Green & Kreuter, 1991; Illich, 1974; Kickbusch, 1986; MacDonald, 1991). *A New Perspective on the Health of Canadians,* as the report was officially entitled, discussed the determinants of health, the nature of the health field, and strategies for improving health and reducing illness. More specifically, the Lalonde Report argued that medical care was not the most significant determinant of health and has been subsequently referred to as the first such statement by a national government (Hancock, 1986; Kickbusch, 1986). The report also suggested that the greatest improvements in health in the future were likely to come through changes in individual lifestyles and improving the quality of the environment. "Health promotion" was the term used to refer to a strategy of education and mass communication intended to explain to individuals how their personal lifestyles were putting them at risk for major health problems. While the term "health promotion" had been in circulation prior to 1974, the Lalonde Report was among the earliest public documents to use it (Pederson, 1989).

Although Canada was prominent in articulating a role for health promotion, throughout the 1970s and early 1980s the field was still dominated by the United States and, intellectually, by the discipline of social psychology as it had been since the early 1950s. Both health education and mass communication were based on a model of individual behaviour emphasizing personal volition and control. Health education, practised as it had been since the Second World War (O'Neill, 1977), consequently focussed on changing individual behaviour. In the latter half of the 1970s, however, parallel with an emerging critique of medicine (see Bozzini et al., 1980; Illich, 1976; Krauze, 1977; McKeown, 1976; Powels, 1973), these approaches came to be criticized as being overly individualistic and as "blaming the victim" for his or her health problems, borrowing the phrase from the well-known book by William Ryan (1971). Self-reflectively, both American and Canadian practitioners criticized the practice of health education (Brown & Margo, 1978; Crawford, 1977; Freudenberg, 1978, 1981; Labonté & Penfold, 1981; Watts & Breindel, 1981) and argued for a more social view of health and health education, an evolution that was to pave the way for a broader concept of health promotion.

An Expanded Definition

In the early 1980s, a second major trend was under way with which Canada was more centrally involved. Through skilled political manoeuvring, the World Health Organization (WHO) and Canada's federal department of Health and Welfare reformulated the concept of health promotion and, in our opinion, accelerated and legitimized the burgeoning critique of health education, as has been described by Green and Raeburn (1988). The new health promotion was based on the perspective that health is determined in important ways by social and environmental factors (Kickbusch, 1986; World Health Organization, 1984).

This vision of health promotion was reinforced in 1986 when Canada hosted the First International Conference on Health Promotion which was marked by the release of the *Ottawa Charter for Health Promotion* (Charter, 1986). Concurrently, Jake Epp, then Minister of Health and Welfare, used the conference to suggest a new policy direction regarding health promotion with the release of *Achieving Health for All: A Framework for Health Promotion* (Epp, 1986). Both documents adopted the view of health promotion as "the process of enabling individuals and communities to increase control over and to improve their health", first used in a 1984 WHO discussion paper on the concept and principles of health promotion (World Health Organization, 1984, p. 3), but with earlier roots (Labonté & Penfold, 1981b, p. 45).

The WHO-based view of health promotion is that of a strategy for improving health which recognizes the interaction between individual health-related behaviour and the social, political, physical, and economic environment in which that behaviour occurs (see, for instance, Green & Kreuter, 1991). Both collective and individual behaviour-changing strategies are embraced by the term, including health education, social marketing, mass communication, community development, organizational change, and public policy.

The Lalonde Report did little to shift health policy or practices immediately in Canada (Evans, 1982; Hancock, 1986; McEwen, 1979), but it was part of a larger trend of thought throughout the Western world. Similar reports were issued in the United States (DHEW, 1979) and Great Britain (DHSS, 1976) in short order. However, it took more than a decade before health promotion was highly visible in Canada. It is as if important elements of what would become health promotion were triggered in Canada but had also to be articulated elsewhere (especially in Europe and the United States) before finally being accepted here. This book fills in some of the story of health promotion thinking and practice in the years between the Lalonde Report and the early 1990s, following the shift in health promotion from an individualistic to a more ecological approach.

One reason that two of us collaborated on this book was because we shared a view on how we think about the development of health promotion. Our approach reflects our training as sociologists of health and illness, our experiences as practitioners and activists within the health promotion field, and our subsequent integration into academia. Two influences on our thinking are the sociology of knowledge and the study of social movements. The sociology of knowledge poses questions about the content of health promotion thought as well as who its proponents were at different times. The sociology of social movements suggests mechanisms by which the ideas and practices of health promotion emerged and developed over time. Together, these two theoretical strands provide a provocative way of considering the development of health promotion in Canada.

The Sociology of Knowledge

While there are various definitions of the nature and scope of the sociology of knowledge, ". . . there has been a general agreement to the effect that [it] is concerned with the relationship between human thought and the social context in which it arises" (Berger & Luckmann, 1967, p. 4). The sociology of knowledge stems from the work of Max Scheler in the 1920s and from Karl Mannheim's writings in the 1940s (Scheler actually having coined the term). The field was significantly revitalized in the 1960s with Thomas Kuhn's *The Structure of Scientific Revolutions* (1962) and Berger and Luckmann's *The Social Construction of Reality* (1967).

While the sociology of knowledge is not a unified field, in general, sociologists of knowledge argue that knowledge is socially distributed and that it is a social product. What counts as knowledge and the actual content of knowledge on particular subjects, including health, varies across time and social cleavages (e.g., class, culture, gender, age). In keeping with this awareness, sociologists of knowledge also argue that knowledge is produced and shaped by social, particularly historical, context.

Scientific knowledge has long been regarded as a special form of knowledge, derived through uniquely logical and rational procedures and hence less (if at all) susceptible to social influences. In the past two decades, however, the sociology of knowledge has expanded its gaze from its early concerns with "irrational" knowledge (ideology and religion) to include scientific and technical knowledge. Sociologists of scientific knowledge have argued that it too is a social phenomenon, with what counts as truth or facts depending upon the particular frame of reference of the observer/scientist. This more relativist approach to scientific knowledge challenges positivist traditions about how knowledge is produced and how it changes. Facts are not simply discovered by objective scientists who are observing a natural world, but rather are perceived and championed by members of competing schools of thought. Similarly, new ideas emerge and either flourish or diminish, in part, because of their exponents' ability to persuade influential social actors of their usefulness.

This approach to the production of knowledge has important implications for the understanding of social problems. As Best (1989) argues, objectivist accounts of social problems typically define them in words such as: "A social problem is a social condition that has been found to be harmful to individual and/or societal well-being" (Bassis, Gelles, & Levine, 1982, p. 2). Social problems are consequently seen as existing "out there" in the world, apart from observers. Constructivist approaches, in contrast, argue that what becomes defined as a social problem is not solely dependent upon objective conditions but rather a function of claims-making activities by various actors. Thus, social problems are to some extent social constructions (Best, 1989).

The usefulness of this approach to thinking about knowledge and social problems is that it directs analysts' attention to questions of how it is that certain ideas take hold and others do not, why certain conditions are identified as social problems and others are not — to the processes by which social phenomena occur. This approach is not especially useful for understanding how to "solve" social problems, however they are identified, but that is not its purpose. Reflecting on the developments of knowledge in a field can expand our capacity to think creatively about our collective problems, thus perhaps contributing to improvements through helping to challenge the political agenda.

Recently, it has been suggested that social movements are one of the mechanisms by which new ideas and knowledge are introduced into societies (Eyerman & Jamison, 1991). In contrast to more classical approaches to examining social movements, Eyerman and Jamison suggest that through their knowledge projects, social movements are important avenues of change.

Social Movements

There are numerous definitions of social movements, depending on the particular theoretical lens through which one is looking. One reason for the various views of social movements is that they appear differently in different societies and during different historical periods, varying with socio-historical conditions and traditions. At risk of oversimplification, therefore, we say that a social movement occurs when a large enough group of people with a particular vision of the world challenges the dominant social order.

Classical approaches, influenced by the rise of fascism and communism, tended to view social movements as representing deviant collective behaviour and to examine either the structural forces that could account for the rise of revolutionary or reform movements or the social psychological mechanisms by which individuals could be recruited into engaging in such activities. Since the student and civil rights movements of the 1960s and 1970s, and the rise of feminism, environmentalism, and the peace movement, renewed interest in social movements has led to the development of additional theories directed at explaining these quite distinct social movements. Rather than seeing social movements as unusual and therefore requiring explanation (a view based on a homeostatic view of society), theorists, among them Touraine (1978), who built a general theory of society around the idea of social movements, began to argue that they are ubiquitous and normal parts of society. They are of interest not so much because they threaten to destroy the existing social order but because they constitute the very core of social change processes, they involve the expression of countervailing ideas and lifestyles, and they are involved in reforming the social order.

Two dominant schools of thought in recent years in looking at the "new" social movements (as opposed to the "old" ones like the labour movement) are new social movement theory and resource mobilization theory. Each offers distinct views of what constitutes a social movement, what the project of a movement is, how they exist in relation to the state and civil society, and the appropriate level at which to analyze the phenomenon. Some authors believe that the two schools of thought are fundamentally incommensurate, while others argue for various attempts at synthesis (e.g., Canel, 1991).

New social movement theory, which developed largely in Europe, situates social movements in civil society and sees them principally as carriers of expressions of new forms of social identity (e.g., the gay and lesbian rights movement, the women's movement, various artistic movements). Resource mobilization theory, in contrast, is concerned more with how social movements manage the challenges of being a movement, that is, of recruiting members, linking people together, promoting its agenda, and surviving. A focus in resource mobilization theory has been to examine the role of organizations in social movements (Zald & McCarthy, 1987). Furthermore, resource mobilization theorists do not necessarily assume that social movements exist strictly within civil society, suggesting that it is possible for a movement to occur within the institutions of the state.

Another dimension on which social movement theories differ is the question of who participates in a movement. New social movement theory, emphasizing the importance of movements in supporting alternative social identities, argues that the members of a movement are those people who stand to benefit from whatever gains the movement manages to create on behalf of its members. Thus, the participants in the homosexual rights movement are gay and lesbian people themselves (and possibly, but not primarily, sympathizers). But resource mobilization theory treats the question of who participates more broadly, encompassing various types of movement supporters who are not necessarily the beneficiaries of the social movement, as predicted by earlier relative deprivation theories of social movement participation.

Recently, a third approach to social movements that is very compatible with the general approach of the sociology of knowledge has been articulated. As noted earlier, Eyerman and Jamison (1991) describe a view of social movements as "cognitive praxis" which argues that social movements are fundamentally knowledge developers and transmitters. "Movement intellectuals" play a significant role in this approach because the social movement creates social space for them to articulate new ideas.

Social movements are transient processes of defining or redefining political projects; they open up new conceptual spaces and frame issues in new ways, thus enabling changes in how "problems" are defined and solutions conceived.

Eyerman and Jamison take an interactional view of social movements. Movements must articulate an "Other" (Touraine, 1981) (or an "Enemy", as Turner and Killian [1972] refer to it in an earlier view) against whom they act. Thus, a movement is, fundamentally, the interaction between actors and this opposition over some historically situated problem.

In this view, the location of a social movement, its membership, and its capacity to mobilize resources are of less interest than the question of the new ideas or knowledge that the movement introduces. For Eyerman and Jamison, knowledge production is a form of social action.

"Knowledge," as used here, is defined very broadly and includes "both [the] formal and informal, objective and subjective, moral and immoral, and most importantly, professional and popular" (Eyerman & Jamison, 1991, p. 49). Further, "knowledge" includes categories of human activity not always thought of as knowledge per se, such as new practices, organizational forms, and social arrangements. For example, the student movements introduced, among other things, new ways of being political (participatory democracy) and learning (teach-ins) (Eyerman & Jamison, 1991).

Another contribution to the study of social movements which is enlarged by Eyerman and Jamison's framing of movements as knowledge producers is the function and role of "movement intellectuals." While intellectuals have been identified as important in earlier theorizing about movements (e.g., Gramsci, 1971), Eyerman and Jamison have expanded the number of roles that can rightfully be considered to contribute to the knowledge production of a movement. Thus, movement intellectuals are not restricted to those individuals with formal credentials. In addition, movement intellectuals not only shape a movement but they are in turn shaped by it; this is a dialectical, interactional process by which participation in a movement changes the people who participate. From case studies, Eyerman and Jamison (1991) have noted the following types of movement intellectual: teacher, publicist, journalist, facilitator, diplomat, lecturer, technocrat, counterexpert, public educator, administrator, and elite pressure group.

Through Eyerman and Jamison's formulation, we can link the sociology of knowledge with the study of social movements. With regard to health promotion, both approaches encourage us to examine its knowledge project and to consider how it has contributed to changes in thinking about health, illness, and medical care. In the next section, we apply these two approaches to health promotion, first through a description of the theory and practice of health education that occurred in the 1970s and early 1980s and then through a brief examination of the development of health promotion in Ontario.

The Sociology of Knowledge and Social Movements Applied to Health Promotion

To illustrate the usefulness of Eyerman and Jamison's (1991) cognitive praxis approach to examining social movements, we can reconstruct from the writings of a handful of key authors the major characteristics of a critical approach to health education as it emerged in North America during the second half of the 1970s and which has been at the core of the knowledge challenge offered by health promotion. By examining the ideological and theoretical assumptions and the intervention strategies proposed by these challengers of health education, we shall see that much of what health promotion was to promote in the mid-1980s was already well formulated in the mid-1970s. We think that, among other things, what contributed to the growth of health promotion in the 1980s was the spreading of the health education critique through a loose network of critical health educators and public health activists.

Critical Health Education[1]

A major characteristic of the critical approach to health education is a "society-blaming" ideology. Almost without exception, authors writing

[1] This subsection comes from the preliminary work done by Michel O'Neill for his PhD dissertation at the Boston University Department of Sociology (O'Neill, 1986), work funded by grants from the National Health Research and Development Program of Health and Welfare Canada and from the Conseil de la recherche en santé du Québec. Although some of it was presented at the Third Pan-American Health Education Conference in Mexico in 1985 and at the New Delhi meeting of the International Sociological Association in 1986, this material has never been published previously. Michel wishes to thank Ron Labonté, William Shannon, Ilona Kickbusch, and Ron Draper for their useful comments on this material.

within the critical perspective openly criticize the ideology that had inspired most health education programs since the Second World War: Allison (1982), Brown and Margo (1978), Crawford (1977), Freudenberg (1978, 1981), Labonté and Penfold (1981), and McKinlay (1974) — all these authors share an "anti-victim blaming" conviction that could be labelled a "society-blaming" stance.

Some critical authors deny almost any individual responsibility in health matters; Freudenberg (1978) is especially blunt in this regard. Other writers are less clear about how the individual should contribute to his or her own health, such as Brown and Margo (1978) or O'Neill (1980), for instance. However, even Allison, who suggests ways to maintain personal responsibilities over health matters, ultimately argues ". . . that the problem of health education does not lie in the individual approach itself but in the fact that focusing only on individual behaviour tends to neglect the environmental and social factors which are also influencing health" (Allison, 1982, p. 12). All the authors of the critical approach thus agree in ascribing to society the major responsibility for the production of illness, a perspective leading, according to Labonté and Penfold (1981), to a philosophy emphasizing social rather than individual responsibility.

The "society-blaming" ideology of the critical approach stems from a theory of the determinants of health and illness that emphasizes various social, economic, cultural, and political factors (as opposed to more individualistic factors such as personal behaviour, lifestyle, or genetics). For example, in a famous paper, McKinlay (1974) was among the first to argue that health education should consider such societal factors to understand illness better. He argued that the dominant culture of Western capitalist societies rewarded all the "bad" habits health educators sought to alter. He further suggested that these habits are supported by the profit motives of large corporations, the "manufacturers of illness."

Similarly, Brown and Margo (1978, p. 12) suggested an "ecological" perspective on health and illness, contending that ". . . undoubtedly, individual behaviour works hand in glove with the physical environment and social conditions in the etiology of many important diseases". More concretely, Labonté and Penfold (1981, pp. 7-9) single out four factors having a major impact on the health status of populations: economic inequalities, gender inequalities, occupational risks, and environmental risks.

Using the same type of epidemiological evidence as the other critical commentators, Freudenberg (1978, p. 373) made the following argument: "I would argue that one's position in the class structure determines the range of potential behaviours and life styles. Furthermore, an environment itself may be either health promoting or health damaging." Allison, referring to authors like Minkler and Cox (1980), Brown and Margo (1978), as well as Watts and Breindel (1981), argues for a "structural" approach to health education to take into account environmental and social factors related to health and illness and correct that "disequilibrium in favour of the behavioural approach that currently exists" (Allison, 1982, p. 13).

Clearly, all the authors writing with a critical perspective in health education share the same theoretical assumptions, despite minor differences of terminology and minor disagreements about the importance that should be given to individual factors as compared to social ones in identifying the determinants of health and illness.

Based on their more structural approach to the causes of ill health, critical health educators recommended changes in the practice of health education. As opposed to traditional health education which aimed to change individuals, the critical perspective suggested intervention strategies that can be characterized as environmental, political, and "Freireian."

By "environmental," the critics meant that health educators ought to try to alter the physical and social environment that makes so difficult the adoption of individual health habits. As Brown and Margo (1978, p. 5) put it, "health educators should not only explain to people what behaviours or conditions would be beneficial to their health; they should also help them to remove health-damaging conditions and substitute health-promoting ones".

In the same line of thought, McKinlay (1974, p. 13) argued for the necessity of intervening on broader political–economic forces shaping so-called at-risk behaviours, a vision that was pushed much further at the beginning of the 1980s by the work of Milio (1981). Freudenberg (1978, p. 376), in the same spirit, suggested an approach he labelled "health education for social change." Quotes could be added from Labonté and Penfold, Allison, and others, but the point is always the same: if society is causing health problems, changing society, and not individuals, should be the major, if not the only, goal for health education. But how should health educators change society?

Most critical authors suggest similar methods for bringing about the social changes they advocate. First, they contend that health should be "politicized." This means ". . . the raising of awareness and capacity in groups and communities to build political pressure on decisions in a way which fits their needs" (O'Neill, 1980, p. 5). Second, as McKinlay, Allison, Watts and Breindel, and especially Freudenberg propose, a shift in the power structure of society is required in order to improve the health of the population.

There are many ways in which health educators could act in a political fashion to alter the social environment, some of which are seen as potentially more fruitful than others. Freudenberg's strategy of "health education for social change," although not directly linked to Freire, includes the basic characteristics of Paulo Freire's "dialogical" method to raise the consciousness of people. Although it was originally devised for the teaching of literacy to the rural Brazilian population, Freire's method has been used in various fields, including the health sector, as Minkler and Cox (1980) and Allison (1982) have convincingly shown.

As Minkler and Cox (1980, p. 312) summarize it, "in sharp contrast to movements for change which place the burden of responsibility for action on a relatively small group of 'leaders', the Freire method stresses the imperative nature of the total participation of the people themselves in a process based upon dialoguing between equals." This is probably the key feature of Freire's approach: both the change agent and the people are in a process of learning and changing, although their relationship at the outset is not equal; the change agent, as a professional, is given a certain status by the population based upon his or her knowledge. However, this difference is not negated, and "dialoguing" about it is part of the approach itself, assisting in equalizing the relationship.

Thus, the approach to health education advocated by proponents of the critical vision demanded starting from the viewpoint of people to construct, with them, a collective understanding of daily life. This understanding would be used subsequently to deal, through political means, with the dominant power structure in order for the oppressed to gain more freedom (or better health). This was — and arguably still is — a dramatic departure from traditional health education practice!

The term "critical" was chosen to describe this proposed vision of health education for three reasons. First, all the authors quoted are "critical" of the traditional fashion of health education practice. Secondly, they are also "critical" of the type of society that permitted the traditional approach to health education to develop. Finally, they all suggest intervention strategies in which raising the "critical consciousness" of individuals and collectivities, using Freire's approach, is identified as one of the major tools.

This critique of health education formed the foundation of the vision of health promotion subsequently articulated by the World Health Organization. More locally, this same vision penetrated the policy and planning mechanisms of the federal, provincial, and municipal governments, challenging the way in which health promotion was conducted. While the process was undoubtedly distinct in all locales, the case of Ontario, described below, raises some interesting questions on the processes of the development of health promotion generally.

The Professional Health Promotion Movement in Ontario[2]

Some people speak of the rise of health promotion since the mid-1980s, both internationally and in Canada, in terms of its being a movement, and many people refer to one of the most visible offsprings of health promotion as "the Healthy Cities movement" (Tsouros, 1990). Yet, several observers question whether health promotion or Healthy Cities are social movements at all and suggest considering who promotes and profits from these activities (e.g., Grace, 1991; Stevenson & Burke, 1992). These same questions have been applied to the development of health promotion in Ontario (Pederson, 1989) and to the practice of health education in Québec (O'Neill, 1986). As suggested earlier, the question of whether such activities constitute social movements depends in part upon how one defines a movement and where one considers social movements to be located in the social structure.

[2] This subsection is based upon work conducted by Ann Pederson for her MSc in the Department of Community Health at the University of Toronto and was supported by the National Health Research and Development Program.

In a qualitative study of the emergence of health promotion thinking and practice in Ontario during the 1970s and '80s, it was observed that the key actors in the field were what Moynihan (1965) called "professional social reformers" (Pederson, 1989). That is, the people advocating health promotion did so principally within the mandates of their jobs. These people were public health workers, educators, social workers, civil servants, community developers, social scientists, and health administrators. They combined careers with social activism and used their professional knowledge, skills, and prestige to argue for an alternative vision of health and health interventions.

When asked to identify the major contributors to health promotion in Ontario, these activists identified one another. Missing, however, were individuals who represented the "community." The major participants in the Ontarian movement were not community residents concerned about health issues but professionals acting on behalf of community members. This should not be construed as evidence that there is no popular support for health promotion in Ontario, but rather that the people most involved in health promotion in the 1980s had some specialized training, worked in organizations, and "did" health promotion for pay.

Supporting this argument is an observation made by the Minister's Advisory Group on Health Promotion. During a community consultation, the group found that Ontarians did not know what the term "health promotion" meant, but they could certainly describe the things in their community that fostered or damaged their health (Podborski, 1987, p. 51). Community members did not cling to a view that it was the medical care system that fostered health but rather identified such things as "environmental pollution, the amount of money they have, what they learn, their lifestyles, and the kinds of family and community resources available to them" (p. 6). In sum, Ontario residents were aware of a broad set of factors capable of influencing their health, but they did not always associate this view with something called "health promotion." (If asked what health promotion was, they would likely have described it in social marketing terms or as analogous to disease prevention.)

Thus in Ontario, at least, health promotion has been a professional rather than a popular social movement. More recent activities under the Healthy Communities banner are altering the pattern of support for health promotion somewhat, but such activity is still confined to relatively few communities.

The aim of the Ontario health promotion movement has been to challenge the equating of medical care with health. Movement intellectuals have used their writing, public speaking, and organizing skills to generate opportunities for arguing for a broad view of health and its determinants. Conferences, such as the 1984 Beyond Health Care conference in Toronto and the Seeking Consensus series, have provided forums for exposing large numbers of people interested in health reform to the view that health arises from conditions of living and not from medical care. While relatively marginal ideas in the early 1970s, they were sufficiently mainstream by the 1990s to have become part of the rhetoric of Ontario's Premier's Council on Health Strategy.

Implications of the Sociology of Knowledge and the Study of Social Movements for Studying Health Promotion in Canada

As the example on critical health education illustrated, the significance of a sociology of knowledge perspective for the study of the development of health promotion in Canada is that it suggests, as do Eakin and Maclean (1992), that we pause to look at the knowledge project of health promotion. What case does health promotion make? What claims about the world does health promotion suggest? What ideas does it challenge or champion? One question that we hope this book illuminates is why health promotion became prominent in the mid-1980s, despite the articulation of critical health education a decade earlier.

While the sociology of knowledge analytic approach says little about whether health promotion is "correct" in its view of the world, it can be an interesting tool for thinking about how, despite the persistence of previously identified problematic conditions (e.g., the cost of health services delivery, the rise of chronic diseases, the inadequacy of health education for behavioural change), these "problems" became more significant at one time rather than another. One mechanism for this transformation may have been an informal movement of public health activists, sympathetic bureaucrats, and community health academics — what we have called a professional health promotion movement.

The usefulness of considering the development of health promotion in terms of a social movement is also among the questions that we are encouraged to ask as observers and/or participants in the phenomenon.

Taken collectively, social movement theories suggest numerous lines of inquiry. For instance, who are the members of a particular social movement? Are the people involved in the movement its beneficiaries or are they unlikely to stand to gain directly from the movement's goals, if accomplished? What are the aims of the movement? What is the relationship between the movement and the state and/or civil society? How are people recruited into the movement? Is the movement aimed at revolution or reform?

The case study of Ontario offers a sense of the link between the two analytic strands we have outlined. The professional health promotion movement in Ontario sought to articulate a new set of ideas about health. To date, the movement has had as one of its goals the aim of convincing societal decision makers that health is about more than health care. New phrases have been coined ("healthy public policy"), new jobs developed (health promotion specialists in public health), new training programs established (the University of Toronto's Masters of Health Science program in health promotion), and new policy-making processes and institutions have emerged — in part as a result of the efforts of a reform-minded group of professional (public) health workers.

Implications for This Book

The contributors to this volume were not explicitly asked to examine health promotion from the two perspectives described above. We hope that the remainder of the book could serve as an opportunity to assess the usefulness of these approaches to understanding developments throughout the country. In the concluding chapter, we discuss our own view of many of the questions we have just raised; the extent to which contributors and readers agree with our assessment should stimulate interesting and, we hope, productive debate. It is our belief that such dialogue will foster continuing reflection among practitioners, analysts, and students of health promotion, in keeping with the tradition that self-reflective praxis is a vital means of contributing to our individual and collective health and well-being.

References

Allison, K. (1982). Health education: Self-responsibility vs. blaming the victim. *Health Education, 20*(3-4), 11-13.

Bassis, M.S., Gelles, R.J., & Levine, A. (1982). *Social problems.* New York: Harcourt Brace Jovanovich.

Berger, P.L., & Luckmann, T. (1967). *The social construction of reality: A treatise in the sociology of knowledge.* Garden City, NY: Anchor Books.

Best, J. (ed.) (1989). *Images of issues: Typifying contemporary social problems.* New York: Aldine de Gruyter.

Bozzini, L. (1981). "L'expertise et la hiérarchie sanitaires en question." In Bozzini et al. (ed.), *Médecine et société, les années 1980* (pp. 389-425). Montréal: Éditions Saint-Martin.

Bozzini et al. (eds.) *Médecine et société, les années 1980.* Montréal: Éditions Saint-Martin.

Brown, E.R., & Margo, G.E. (1978). Health education: Can the reformers be reformed? *International Journal of Health Services, 8,* 3-25.

Canel, E. (1991, June). *New social movement theory and resource mobilization: The need for integration.* Paper presented at the Learned Societies Conference, Queen's University, Kingston, Ontario.

Charter (1986). The Ottawa Charter for Health Promotion. *Health Promotion, An International Journal, 1,* iii-v.

Crawford, R. (1977). You are dangerous to your health: The ideology and politics of victim blaming. *International Journal of Health Services, 7,* 663-680.

Department of Health and Social Services (1976). *Prevention and health: Everybody's business.* London: Author.

Department of Health, Education & Welfare (1979). *Healthy people: The Surgeon-General's report on health promotion and disease prevention.* Department of Health, Education & Welfare Publication No. 79-55071. Washington, DC: U.S. Government Printing Office.

Eakin, J.M., & Maclean, H.M. (1992). A critical perspective on research and knowledge development in health promotion. *Canadian Journal of Public Health, 83* (Supp.1), S72-76.

Epp, J. (1986). *Achieving health for all: A framework for health promotion.* Ottawa: Minister of Supply & Services.

Evans, R. (1982). A retrospective on the "new perspective." *Journal of Health Politics, Policy and Law, 7,* 325-344.

Eyerman, R., & Jamison, A. (1991). *Social movements: A cognitive approach.* University Park, PA: The Pennsylvania State University Press.

Freire, P. (1968). *Pedagogy of the oppressed.* New York: Seaburg Press.

Freudenberg, N. (1978). Shaping the future of health education: From behavior change to social change. *Health Education Monographs, 6,* 372-377.

Freudenberg, N. (1981). Health education for social change: A strategy for public health in the U.S. *International Journal of Health Education, 24(3),* 1-8.

Grace, V.M. (1991). The marketing of empowerment and the construction of the health promotion consumer: A critique of health promotion. *International Journal of Health Services, 21,* 329-343.

Gramsci, A. (1971). *Selections from the prison notebooks.* New York: International Publishers.

Green, L.W., & Raeburn, J.M. (1988). Health promotion. What is it? What will it become? *Health Promotion, An International Journal, 3,* 151-159.

Green, L.W., & Kreuter, M. (1991). *Health promotion planning: An educational and environmental approach.* Mountain View, CA: Mayfield Publishers.

Hancock, T. (1986). Lalonde and beyond: Looking back at "A new perspective on the health of Canadians." *Health Promotion, An International Journal, 1,* 93-100.

Illich, I. (1974). *Medical nemesis.* London: Calder & Boyars.

Kickbusch, I. (1986). Health promotion, a global perspective. *Canadian Journal of Public Health, 77,* 321-326.

Krauze, E. (1977). *Power and illness.* New York: Elsevier.

Kuhn, T. (1962). *The structure of scientific revolutions.* Chicago: University of Chicago Press.

Labonté, R., & Penfold, S. (1981a). Canadian perspectives in health promotion: A critique. *Health Education, 19*(3-4), 4-9.

Labonté, R., & Penfold, S. (1981b). *Health promotion philosophy: From victim-blaming to social responsibility.* Vancouver: Health Promotion Directorate, Western Regional Office.

Lalonde, M. (1974). *A new perspective on the health of Canadians.* Ottawa: Health & Welfare Canada.

Macdonald, G. (1991). Has health promotion matured as a discipline? *Health Promotion International, 6,* 85-87.

McEwen, E. (1979). Whatever happened to the Lalonde report? *Canadian Journal of Public Health, 70,* 13-16.

McKeown, T. (1976). *The role of medicine: Dream, mirage, or nemesis?* London: Nuffield Provincial Hospitals Trust.

McKinlay, J.B. (1974). A case for refocusing upstream: The political economy of illness. In *Applying behavioral science to cardiovascular risk.* Proceedings of the American Heart Association Conference, Seattle, pp. 7-17.

Milio, N. (1986). *Promoting health through public policy.* Ottawa: Canadian Public Health Association.

Minkler, M., & Cox, K. (1980). Creating critical consciousness in health: Applications of Freire's philosophy and methods to the health care setting. *International Journal of Health Services, 10,* 311-323.

Moynihan, D.P. (1965). The professionalization of reform. *The Public Interest, 1*(Fall), 6-16.

Ogden, H. (1978). Recent developments in health education policy. *Health Education Monographs, 6*(Supp.), 67-73.

O'Neill, M. (1977). *Vers une problématique de l'éducation sanitaire au Québec.* Unpublished master's thesis, Laval University, Québec City.

O'Neill, M. (1980). A perspective on politics and health education policies. *Health Education, 18*(4), 4-7.

O'Neill, M. (1986). *Innovative practices in governmentally funded community health agencies: The case of Quebec's DSCs.* Québec: Centre de Recherche sur les services communautaires, Université Laval (No.1 de la collection Édition Speciale).

Pederson, A.P. (1989). *The development of health promotion in Ontario.* Unpublished master's thesis, University of Toronto.

Podborski, S. (1987). *Health promotion matters in Ontario.* Toronto: Government of Ontario.

Powels, J. (1973). On the limitations of modern medicine. *Science, Medicine and Man, 1*(1), 1-30.

Ryan, W. (1971). *Blaming the victim.* New York: Pantheon Books.

Stevenson, H.M. & Burke, M. (1992). Bureaucratic logic in social movement clothing: The limits of health promotion research. *Canadian Journal of Public Health, 83*(Supp. 1), S47-S53.

Touraine, A. (1978). *La voix et le regard.* Paris: Seuil.

Tsouros, A. (ed.) (1990). *World Health Organization Healthy City project: A project becomes a movement.* Copenhagen: FADL Publishers.

Turner, R.H., & Killian, L.M. (1972). *Collective behavior* (2nd ed.). Englewood Cliffs, NJ: Prentice-Hall.

Watts, A., & Breindel, C. (1981). Health education: Structural vs. behavioral perspectives. *Health Policy and Education, 2,* 7-57.

World Health Organization (1984). *Health promotion, a discussion document on the concept and principles.* Copenhagen: World Health Organization, Regional Office for Europe.

Zald, M.N., & McCarthy, J.D. (1987). *Social movements in an organizational society.* New Brunswick, NJ: Transaction Books.

The Concept of Health

Irving Rootman and John Raeburn

E ven a cursory look at the literature on the concept of health shows that it is a minefield. One reason for this is that health is both personal and social, and therefore an emotional issue that touches all our lives in an important way. Another, and probably more important, reason is that it is an area that consumes enormous amounts of public and private money. As a consequence, the way in which health is defined will have a major impact on how a country allocates its resources for this area. Thus, we believe that the topic has considerable practical relevance to health promotion in Canada and elsewhere.

Although we do not attempt an exhaustive review of the concept of health in this chapter, we do present a range of views about health including lay, medical, nursing, political, academic, holistic, and Canadian concepts. We then draw some implications from this material, and conclude with an attempt to define health from the point of view of health promotion in Canada.

Range of Concepts

Historical, Dictionary, and Lay Concepts

Most discussions of the concept of health begin with its etymology. In English, the word has Germanic roots, from a word meaning "whole" (that is, not dismembered). The Old English version was *haelth,* meaning safe, sound, or whole. (In medieval times, *haelthing* meant to share a few drinks with one's friends!)

The idea of "soundness" has continued over the centuries, and is reflected in modern dictionary definitions. For example, the *Concise Oxford Dictionary* (Sykes, 1984) defines health as "soundness of body or mind" (p. 460), and sound is defined as "not diseased or injured or rotten" (p. 1013).

Although readers of this chapter will mainly be professionals and academics, those who most often use the term health are, of course, lay people. A relatively recent British book (Calnan, 1987) looks at the whole area of lay views of health, based mainly on surveys in the U.K. and other countries. What emerges from this review is that, for most people, health becomes a topic of interest only in its absence, and that concepts are greatly affected by country, culture, economics, social class, gender, and other such factors. On the whole, Western popular definitions of health echo medical definitions relating to absence of disease. However, middle-class people tend to include psychological and well-being aspects (for example, strength and energy), and working people tend to emphasize functional aspects (like getting necessary tasks done), although there is also considerable variation within groups, according to Calnan.

Lay concepts of causation tend to reflect strong cultural influences. In France, one study of middle-class people showed that disease is seen as being caused by external factors such as the urban environment and "germs," whereas health is determined by internal factors such as heredity and disposition (Herzlich, 1973). A comparable U.S. study, however, found that health was viewed as the product of self-determined lifestyle, and that "release" or "freedom" (especially from pressure or stress) was an integral part of the concept (Crawford, 1984).

Nevertheless, there is often a strong consistency of views about health across diverse cultural groups. For example, among Native Americans, health is perceived as "living in total harmony with nature and having the ability to survive under exceedingly difficult circumstances" (Spector, 1985, p. 181). Similarly, among Africans, "when one possessed health, one was in harmony with nature" (Spector, 1985, p. 142) and "Chinese medicine teaches that health is a state of spiritual and physical harmony with nature" (Spector, 1985, p. 128).

Medical Definition

For most of this century, medicine has dominated the health arena, and hence also the definition of health. Various medical dictionaries show the following under the entry "health": "The normal physical state, i.e., the state of being whole and free from physical and mental disease or pain, so that the parts of the body carry on their proper function" (Critchley, 1978, p. 784); "Condition of soundness of the mind and all bodily organs" (Wakeley, 1975, p. 200); and "The state of health implies much more than freedom from disease, and good health may be defined as the attainment and maintenance of the highest state of mental and bodily vigour of which any individual is capable" (MacPherson, 1992, p. 265). On the whole, these definitions are relatively positive. However, the rest of the definitions in these large volumes are primarily concerned with disease, and it is generally felt that the standard medical definition of health is "the absence of disease."

A Nursing View

Unlike medicine, nursing takes a more holistic view of health/sickness. Here, the overwhelming impression is one of multidimensionality. For example, one textbook emphasizing health promotion (Murray & Zentner, 1989) provides a table with 25 definitions of health (some historical), and most of these have multiple aspects. Another nursing text (Boddy, 1985) says there are four main conceptual areas of health (intrapersonal, interpersonal, extrapersonal, and metapersonal), and each of these is divided into several subsections. For example, "intrapersonal" is subdivided into biomedical, psychological, eudaimostic[1], and equilibrium concepts of health. Presumably, these concepts reflect the variety of levels at which nurses work.

WHO/Ottawa Charter

Next to medical definitions of health, undoubtedly the most influential definition in this century has been that of the World Health Organization (1947): "Health is a state of complete physical, mental, and social well-being and not merely the absence of disease and infirmity." This definition is perpetuated in that most influential of health promotion documents, the *Ottawa Charter for Health Promotion* (1986; hereafter, the Ottawa Charter or the Charter), which adds to it an ecological dimension.

There is no doubt that this definition has profoundly affected many people working in the health field, especially those in health promotion, community health, and public health. It has paved the way for the social model, which arguably may be the dominant one in Canadian health promotion at present.

However, the WHO definition has been repeatedly criticized. Some criticisms have been academic, questioning the use of the term "state" rather than "process". Others have pointed to the impossibility of ever achieving a "complete" or perfect state of health. But the most significant criticisms relate to this definition's generalization that "health is more than the absence of disease."

The heart of these criticisms is that such a definition puts no boundaries on what it is possible to encompass by the term health (hence, there is no limit on expenditure). Here are a few examples: ". . . a most unrealistic definition which has bedeviled societies ever since. . . . This definition is patently absurd and unattainable" (Bates & Lapsley, 1985, p. 227); "While there is no single source of our present [health system] troubles, the 1947 World Health Organization (WHO) definition of health is a good candidate, providing the first ingredient, that of an open-ended understanding of the concept of health" (Callahan, 1990, p. 34); "All kinds of problems now roll to the doctor's door, from sagging anatomies to suicides, from unwanted childlessness to unwanted pregnancy, from marital difficulties to learning difficulties, from genetic counselling to drug addiction, from laziness to crime. . . ." (Kass, quoted by Fox, 1977, p. 10); "Critics of this. . . all-inclusive approach point out that this is precisely the kind of thinking that raises expectations that medicine cannot meet" (Harron, Burnside, & Beauchamp, 1983, p. 115). It should be noted, however, that most of these critics come from traditional health care settings, not from health promotion or public health.

The effect of all this is, according to some, to help turn the concept of health into a battleground over rights and resources. For example, a 1975 report of the Organization for Economic Co-operation and Development

---

¹Eudaimonism is a theory that the highest ethical goal is happiness and personal well-being. Hence, a eudaimostic concept of health would be one in which health — as personal well-being — is the supreme value.

(OECD), called *Health, Higher Education and the Community* (Centre for Educational Research and Innovation, 1977), says: "Health has ceased to be a traditionally neutral sector and become a battlefield for a sometimes acute social conflict" (p. 97). This shift is not entirely due to the WHO definition, but it has certainly helped to raise the expectations of both consumers and health professionals as to what can be labelled "health" as an activity on which public funds can be spent.

Although the WHO definition is often regarded as a universal one, it is more correctly a product of the particular set of social and political circumstances that occurred after the Second World War. According to Daniel Callahan, one of the definition's harshest critics, when WHO came into being between 1946 and 1948, many saw the problems of the world as a "sickness." For example, Dr. Brock Chisholm of Canada, the first Director-General of WHO, said, "The world is sick and the ills are due to the perversion of man: his inability to live with himself. . . . The scope of the task before the Committee [setting up WHO] knows no bounds" (Callahan, 1990, p. 35). The irony of this is, of course, that the definition which is so often seen as liberating health from the thrall of medicine appears to have arisen originally as a medical solution to the ills of the world, as seen immediately post-war! This desire to change the world through doing something in the arena of health seems to live on in the Ottawa Charter, which talks of peace, justice, ecology, income, etc. as health issues. Undoubtedly these things affect health. But are they primarily matters for the health sector?

Academic Concepts

Many academics are involved in the health field, and academics are typically strong on definitions and concepts. This chapter is not the place to do full justice to this topic, but one or two examples may be useful.

Two of the major non-medical academic areas involved in health are psychology and sociology. Indeed, the fastest-growing applied area in U.S. graduate schools of psychology is "health psychology." In health psychology, the current favoured view of health is a "biopsychosocial" one, which, as in nursing, is construed as "adding the person to the biomedical model." "This new perspective," says Sarafino (1990, p. 16), "involves the interplay of biological, psychological, and social aspects of the person's life." True to psychology's individual-oriented roots, in the biopsychosocial approach, the social aspect is not greatly elaborated beyond the immediate social context.

Sociology, on the other hand, gives greater emphasis to the role of the social environment in relation to health. According to the editors of the book, *Health and Canadian Society,* which presents sociological perspectives on the topic (Coburn et al., 1981, p. 2): "Sociology is ultimately based on the premise of societal determinism, the assumption that to some extent, social factors determine observed patterns of attitudes, values and behaviour. . . ." Consequently, sociologists working in the health field have tended to concentrate their efforts on examining health phenomena at the interpersonal level, the level of health institutions, and the level of relationships between health institutions and the wider society. With one notable exception (Antonovsky, 1981), they have also tended to focus on the determinants of illness rather than health.

In addition to these explicitly discipline-related academic views of health, there have also been many attempts to build models or "representations" of health. One enduring issue is whether health is on a continuum with disease (e.g., Goodstadt, Simpson, & Loranger, 1987), or whether it is some independent phenomenon. As we discuss in the next section of this chapter, Labonté (1993) has developed a model with three interrelated circles labelled health/wellness, illness, and disease.

Another important general academic model comes from biologically oriented systems-theory approaches, which use such concepts as homeostasis, balance, feedback, cybernetics, and others. Perhaps the best-known proponent of this approach is René Dubos (1959), who sees health as a homeostatic and constantly modulated organismic state produced by the continuing demands of adaptation. Dubos, however, is a biomedic, and does not stray far from the negative view of health. He says: "The nearest approach to health is a physical and mental state fairly free of discomfort and pain which permits the person concerned to function as effectively and as long as possible in the environment where chance or choice has placed him" (quoted in Stone, 1979, p. 8).

Allied to systems concepts are concepts of ecology as they relate to health. These emphasize the importance of environmental, adaptational, and overall contextual interplay between the organism and his or her biosphere, and have been important for influencing the view of health taken by WHO, in a document such as the Ottawa Charter.

Overall, these academic definitions of health largely reflect the corner of the learned world to which their proponents' disciplines relate. They also tend to be rather complex, as is the way with matters academic.

Holistic Concepts

An especially influential non-academic force in modern thinking about health has come from what can be characterized as the "holistic health movement," a popular middle-class phenomenon with strong American overtones. In one sense, the holistic concept of health is a natural progression of the WHO view of health as being "more than the absence of disease." But its analysis of the determinants of health is quite different.

The holist typically represents health as a highly valued goal in its own right, and that goal is one of relatively unattainable body-mind perfection, often characterized as "high-level wellness." For example, Brallier (1978) says,

> Holistic health is an ongoing sense of finely tuned wellness, which involves not only excellent care of the physical body but also care of ourselves in such a way that we nurture our capacity to be mentally alert and creative as well as emotionally stable and satisfied. . . (quoted in Alster, 1989, p. 78).

According to Alster (1989) in her critique of the holistic movement, this concept results in "health-conscious citizens" who "anxiously. . . monitor their pulses, nutritional intakes, bowel patterns, sleep habits, exercise levels, social lives, and sexual activities" and who "actively seek to maintain health by engaging in a stupefying variety of 'health-promoting' behaviour," but who for all this remain uneasy, "never certain of remaining well" (pp. 73-74). As many other critics have noted, unlike the WHO view, the holistic concept puts the responsibility for health directly on the individual, rather than looking to social conditions, and thus creates a climate for victim-blaming. On the whole, it is not a concept favoured by those in Canada who work in the public health sector. So, what concepts *are* favoured by Canadians?

Canadian Concepts

Although the dominant concept of health in Canada in this century probably has been and continues to be the "absence of disease or illness," in the past two decades, people working in the public health field have increasingly shifted their thinking about health towards an expanded concept consistent with those put forward by the World Health Organization in its founding charter and in the *Ottawa Charter*. A number of factors have contributed to this shift.

One was *A New Perspective on the Health of Canadians* (Lalonde, 1974; hereafter, the Lalonde Report). Although it did not define health explicitly, and implied it in terms of the absence of sickness and disease (Raeburn & Rootman, 1989), the promulgation of the health field concept significantly shifted attention to non-medical determinants of health which have become critical to an expanded view of health. Unfortunately (as is pointed out elsewhere in this book), the programmatic response came to emphasize the lifestyle, rather than the environmental, determinants of health. Nevertheless, there was a shift away from traditional biomedical notions (see the chapter by Lavada Pinder later in this book).

Another contribution toward the shift was the conference in Toronto in 1984 called Beyond Health Care. That conference was important in shifting Canadian and international public health thinking towards the idea of health as a collective concept. It was there that a Canadian public health physician, Trevor Hancock, with an American psychiatrist, Len Duhl, put forward the concept of "healthy cities." This concept clearly conveyed the idea that it was possible to apply the notion of health to aggregates of people, such as cities. This idea was reinforced two years later in the Ottawa Charter (1986), which suggested that either an individual or *group* (our emphasis) could reach a state of "complete physical, mental and social well-being." In any case, the 1984 conference did give birth to a worldwide movement to establish healthy communities, which movement emphasizes many of the notions about health put forward by the World Health Organization.

One year after the conference, Trevor Hancock and Fran Perkins, a colleague in the Toronto Department of Public Health (Hancock & Perkins, 1985), made another contribution toward shifting the thinking about health in Canada by publishing an article, "The Mandala of Health," in a journal then called *Health Education* (subsequently *Health Promotion*), a widely distributed publication of Health and Welfare Canada. As shown in Figure 1, the Mandala portrays the individual at the centre of a set of environments including the family, the community, the human-made environment, the culture, and the biosphere. The model also shows four key factors that influence the health of both the individual and the family — human biology, personal behaviour, the psychosocial environment, and the physical environment. The term lifestyle is also used to connote "personal behaviour *as influenced and modified by*, and *constrained by*, a lifelong socialization process, and by the psycho-social environment, including cultural and community values and standards" (p. 8). Finally, the medical system is included as a system concerned with human biology and personal behaviour. This conceptualization of health has become widely used in educational and public health settings in Canada, and has helped people working in the health field to adopt a holistic perspective on health.

A fourth contribution to the shift was *Achieving Health for All: A Framework for Health Promotion* (Epp, 1986; hereafter, the Framework). Although it did not cite the definition of health used in the Ottawa Charter, it was clearly consistent with the thinking contained therein and adopted

Figure 1   The mandala of public health.

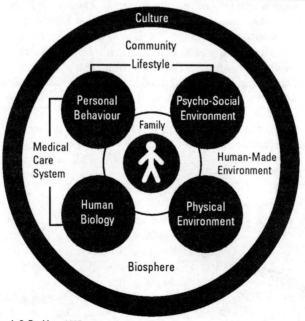

Source: Hancock & Perkins, 1985.

the same definition of health promotion used in the Charter, which had been previously specified by the European Office of WHO in a 1984 discussion document on health promotion. As noted in the chapter in this book by Pinder, the Framework was distributed across the country and discussed widely by governments, professional and voluntary organizations, the academic community, and others. As a result, it has had an enormous influence on thinking about health, consistent with the ideas put forth by the World Health Organization.

Perhaps another small contribution to the shift was the paper that we published (Raeburn & Rootman, 1989) in the journal that was then called *Health Promotion* (now *Health Promotion International*). Titled "Towards an Expanded Health Field Concept: Conceptual and Research Issues in a New Era of Health Promotion," it built on the thinking contained in the Lalonde Report (1974) and linked it with more recent thought, notably, that contained in the Ottawa Charter. Specifically, it put forward an expanded health field concept (Figure 2). As shown, it slightly recast the five action areas of the Charter as inputs or determinants. On the output side, it identified measurable health outputs. The paper suggested that the "input segments provide guidelines for planners when changes or developments in health systems are being contemplated" and "the output segments cover the main dimensions of interest in any modern view of the measurement of health status" (p. 389). The paper also made a preliminary attempt to link the concept of health with that of quality of life. It concluded by inviting comment and discussion. Unfortunately, it has not stimulated much reaction, at least to date. Nevertheless, we believe it has made some contribution toward drawing attention to output aspects of the health promotion process, positive and subjective aspects of input and output, and social and environmental input — all of which are consistent with and complement the ideas contained in the Ottawa Charter.

Finally, Ron Labonté, whose chapter follows this one, has made a more

Figure 2 Expanded health field concept.

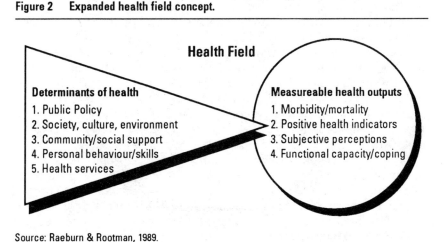

Source: Raeburn & Rootman, 1989.

Figure 3   Health, illness, and disease may overlap, but they are uniquely different facets of experience.

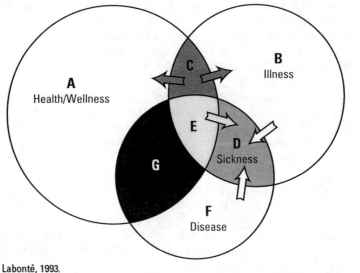

Source: Labonté, 1993.

recent contribution to our thinking about what health is and how it relates to illness and disease (Labonté, 1993). As shown in Figure 3, he suggests that health is not on a continuum, as many others have suggested. It is rather a domain that overlaps in varying degrees with two other domains — illness and disease. According to Labonté, the circle of health/wellness represents persons who, when asked, would say that they are healthy. Those who fall into area A would be people who have a commitment to important values, a sense of control over their life, an ability to see change in one's life as a challenge rather than a threat, and who are not experiencing illness or do not have a medically diagnosed condition. Perhaps they would be people who are at the high end of the scale on physical, psychological, social, and personal health.

The illness circle, on the other hand, represents the experience of feeling ill or out-of-sorts, the clear area being illness that cannot be explained by conventional medicine — as Labonté (1993) puts it, the "'well, dear, it's all in your head' stuff." The third circle, labelled disease, represents diagnosed or diagnosable pathologies, the clear area covering undiagnosed or "silent" disease such as high blood pressure, various STDs, and so forth.

The shaded area D represents the situation where people are diagnosed as having a disease and they actually feel sick. E is where people feel sick as a result of being given the diagnosis. The shaded area G refers to the case of people who are diagnosed with diseases but consider themselves to be quite healthy. An example might be older persons with some disability who consider themselves to be in excellent health for someone of their age — a not-uncommon occurrence. Finally, shaded area C is the grey zone of feeling "so-so," where it doesn't take much to be tipped into feeling well.

Although Labonté's conceptualization has not as yet been widely discussed in Canada or elsewhere, it should stimulate considerable discussion once it becomes disseminated more widely. Moreover, this conceptualization of health is likely to enrich our understanding considerably in a way that constructively builds on thinking to date.

Implications

We have only begun to show the complexity and variety of possibilities in conceptualizing health. And we have not even started to address health as qualified by such terms as "mental" or "social". Nor have we looked at health as an adjective. Indeed, one writer, after reviewing the array of concepts of health, observed, "Perhaps because it is so difficult to arrive at a fully satisfactory definition of health, most contemporary discussions slip quickly from attention to health as a noun to consideration of health as an adjective" (Stone, 1979, p. 9). And it is, of course, as an adjective that the word health appears in the term "health promotion."

Given the variety and difficulty in this area, is there any point in trying to define health at all? We would argue that it is important to make the effort, simply because concepts tend to drive the enterprises with which they are associated. If we don't know what we are talking about, how can we do it properly?

It is clear from the above discussion that although it is almost impossible to arrive at a universally acceptable concept of health, there is often broad consensus within sectors of the health field. These concepts can be important for determining the direction of that field. For example, much of WHO's activity is guided by its concept of health; psychologists base hundreds of studies around the biopsychosocial concept; holistic health people eat and exercise according to their view of things; and so on. So what implications can one draw from the above? We would like to suggest the following.

A Multilevel, Multidimensional Concept

First, the concept of health as used historically and by many groups in many countries actually encompasses a range of concepts. However, all these concepts are related to a *domain of life that has to do with the human organism's condition, well-being and functioning*. As such, they can be set against other domains of human interest, such as the purely economic or political on the one hand, and the purely social-structural/environmental

Figure 4   Simple representation of the domain of health concepts with its two chief dimensions.

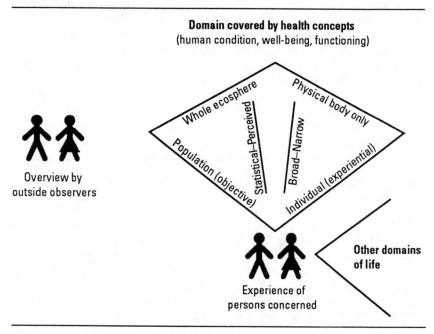

on the other, although these matters clearly impinge on health. Having established this common domain, then within it one can identify variation along at least two principal dimensions, which are shown in Figure 4.

One of these dimensions could be called narrow – broad. At the narrow end, we have a focus on the physical body and disease, and at the broad end, we see an expansion to the whole ecosphere. As we move along the scale from the narrow end, we see added to a purely body-based concept of health such factors as those described by the terms psychological, social, societal, cultural, environmental, economic, and political. We also see an expansion from a preoccupation with disease to a broader domain that encompasses such aspects as well-being, quality of life, social health, and so on.

The second dimension within the broad domain conceptualizing health could be called perceived – statistical. This is a bit more subtle, and may often be the cause of conflict between different disciplines because of a failure to articulate it clearly. That is, at least among academics and bureaucrats, health can refer either primarily to the condition and well-being of the human organism as such, or it can refer primarily to a population or statistical view, where what is of interest are incidence and patterns of health over geographic areas or in sectors of the population. The latter is the concept of health favoured by planners and policy makers, and hence has political power. The former is that used more by those who work directly with people, and its power is perhaps more emotional. Each is important, and each presumably should inform the other. But often they are seen as conflicting points of view.

This issue was discussed in a keynote paper at the 1990 Toronto conference on health promotion research (Raeburn, 1992). There it was argued that health promotion has two main constituencies among professionals and researchers — those who are mainly policy-oriented and favour statistical, social-structural, environmental, economic, political science, and population views, and those who work with the experiential or "real" lives of people, in clinical, group, domestic, family, community, cultural, and other settings. At the research level, these two camps are typically characterized by their positivist and qualitative stances, respectively.

Admittedly, this is an overly simplistic analysis, and many professionals and researchers combine both dimensions or describe cases that are otherwise not "pure." Still, we believe there remains a real and often unacknowledged tension between those who value working primarily with individuals, groups, and communities in an empowering way, and those who want to have maximal impact on as many people as possible by mass or political (and hence non-empowering) means. We see this as a continuing issue in health promotion, especially as it tends to lead to conflict between professional groups such as nurses, health educators, and community developers (the "people workers") on the one hand, and managers, public servants, academics, and politicians on the other (the "policy people").

A Concept in Context

The second general implication we draw about the concept of health is that *its definition is relative to the context in which it arises.* That is, how the concept will be defined will depend on who is doing the defining, why they are defining it, and the setting in which they are operating. For example, lay and professional concepts of health will differ because the domain is being addressed from entirely different perspectives. By the same token, health in an impoverished developing nation has entirely different imperatives from those of an affluent industrialized country. The way an individualistically oriented doctor sees health in the clinic is different from the perspective of the politician or public health activist. And so on. Each will define this huge domain individually, in a way that suits and guides her or his efforts in that domain.

A related conclusion here has to do with the economics of health. It is probably true to say that internationally — and Canada is no exception — the major current political preoccupation related to health is cost containment. In general, it is likely that the narrower the definition, the cheaper health is perceived to be, whereas the broader the definition, the more expensive it is. This idea is reinforced by the feeling that because most countries devote relatively large sums of public money to health, many people try to jump on the health bandwagon and justify what they do in "health" terms. But one now sees a political effort to remove these people from the bandwagon. This issue obscures the argument that expanding the concept may end up to be cheaper than the narrow, medicalized approach. This presumably is the reason why a government would contemplate funding something called health promotion. But to the extent that health promotion is not demonstrably cost-effective in the crudest of terms (understandable to the simplest of politicians!), then it may be in jeopardy as a publicly funded enterprise.

The conclusion we draw from these implications is that, from the point of view of this book, the concept of health of most interest is that expressed in the context of Canadian health promotion. That is, what does health mean as discussed by Canadian health promoters in Canada? In the next and final section of this chapter, we attempt to answer this question, drawing on the material presented so far and our perceptions of the state of thinking in health promotion in this country.

Health in the Context of Canadian Health Promotion

The following elements would seem to be important for a concept of Canadian health promotion (CHP health):

- There is a strong social, community, and self-reliance element, given that the overall model of health promotion is centred around the concepts of self-help, mutual aid, and citizen participation.
- The history of CHP health comes via the Lalonde Report, so that there are overtones of lifestyle and behaviour. However, this emphasis on lifestyle has, of more recent times, been balanced by the influential social model of the Ottawa Charter.
- As far as Canadian academic representations of health in a health promotion context are concerned, CHP health is multidimensional, going well beyond the narrow end of the health definitional dimension. That is, it typically involves subjective and objective components, includes both humanistic and statistical aspects, and has individual as well as environmental and policy components. From the point of view of research, it has both qualitative and quantitative aspects.
- Publications relating to health promotion from across Canada reflect a common tone, but also display the considerable diversity that comes from different regions and population groups: West and East, French and English, urban and rural, Aboriginal and non-Aboriginal, and so on. Therefore, CHP health has a strong cultural and equity aspect, and recognizes the significant contribution of the diverse groups and communities that make up this country.
- Priorities in health promotion have often been focussed upon

such sectors of the population as the elderly, women, the disabled, children, and others. In each case, one consideration has been that population's power vis-à-vis the rest of society. Therefore, there is a strong implicit element of empowerment in CHP health.

- A major philosophical centre of health promotion has been Ottawa, and the view from there is not only one of diversity and equity across the country, but of intersectoral considerations, involving housing, mental health, education, drug policies, and so on.

- Relatively few medical people work in health promotion, or have been influential in its conceptual development in Canada. Therefore, the CHP health concept has a strongly non-medical tone, which (according to our previous observation) tends to remove it from the narrow end of the conceptual dimension. A consequence of this is that the biological aspect does not necessarily figure all that prominently. At the same time, given the power games of money allocation, the justification for funding inevitably falls back on biomedically oriented prevention arguments (in terms of "killers" such as heart disease and cancer), so that the general tenor of CHP health tends to be preventive rather than wellness-oriented.

- Because so many aspects and dimensions are involved in CHP health, the concept of quality of life is increasingly invoked. This broad concept encompasses the positive goals of health promotion, while taking into account the narrow–broad, as well as the perceived–statistical, components of the health field. It also encompasses a view of health in terms of its determinants as well as the final product.

If we were pressed for a succinct definition of CHP health, then perhaps it would go something like this:

> Health as perceived in the context of Canadian health promotion has to do with the bodily, mental, and social quality of life of people as determined in particular by psychological, societal, cultural, and policy dimensions. Health is seen by Canadian health promoters to be enhanced by sensible lifestyles and the equitable use of public and private resources to permit people to use their initiative individually and collectively to maintain and improve their own well-being, however they may define it.

In the pages that follow, it will be for the reader to decide whether such a definition rings true.

References

Alster, K.B. (1989). *The holistic health movement.* Tuscaloosa: University of Alabama Press.

Antonovsky, A. (1981). *Health, stress and coping.* San Francisco: Jossey-Bass.

Bates, E.M., & Lapsley, H.M. (1985). *The health machine: The impact of medical technology.* Ringwood, Australia: Penguin.

Boddy, J.M. (ed.) (1985). *Health: Perspectives and practices.* Palmerston North: Dunmore Press.

Brallier, L.W. (1978). The nurse as holistic health practitioner. *Nursing Clinics of North America, 13,* 643-655.

Calnan, M. (1987). *Health and illness: The lay perspective.* London: Tavistock.

Callahan, D. (1990). *What kind of life: The limits of medical progress.* New York: Simon & Schuster.

Centre for Educational Research and Innovation (1977). *Health, higher education and the community: Towards a regional health university.* Report of an International Conference at OECD, Paris, 1975. Paris: Organization for Economic Co-operation and Development.

Coburn, D., D'Arcy, C., New, P., & Torrance, G. (eds.) (1981). *Health and Canadian society.* Toronto: Fitzhenry & Whiteside.

Crawford, R. (1984). A cultural account of "health": Control, release and the social body. In J. McKinlay (ed.), *Issues in the political economy of health care (pp. 60-103).* London: Tavistock.

Critchley, M. (ed.) (1978). *Butterworths medical dictionary.* London: Butterworths.

Dubos, R. (1959). *Mirage of health.* New York: Harper & Bros.

Epp, J. (1986). *Achieving health for all: A framework for health promotion.* Ottawa: Health & Welfare Canada.

Fox, R.C. (1977). The medicalization and demedicalization of American society. In J.H. Knowles (ed.), *Doing better and feeling worse: Health in the United States* (pp. 9-22). New York: W.W. Norton.

Goodstadt, M.S., Simpson, R.I., & Loranger, P.D. (1977). Health promotion: A conceptual integration. *American Journal of Health Promotion, 1*(3), 58-63.

Hancock, T., & Perkins, F. (1985). The mandala of health: A conceptual model and teaching tool. *Health Education, 24*(1), 8-10.

Harron, F., Burnside, J.W., & Beauchamp, T.L. (1983). *Health and human values.* New Haven: Yale University Press.

Herzlich, C. (1973). *Health and illness.* London: Academic Press.

Labonté, R. (1993). *Community health and empowerment.* Toronto: Centre for Health Promotion.

Lalonde, M. (1974). *A new perspective on the health of Canadians.* Ottawa: Health & Welfare Canada.

MacPherson, G. (ed.) (1992). *Black's medical dictionary* (37th ed.). London: A. & C. Black.

Murray, R.B., & Zentner, J.P. (1989). *Nursing assessment and health promotion strategies through the lifespan* (4th ed.). Norwalk, CT: Appleton & Lange.

Raeburn, J.M. (1992). Health promotion research with heart: Keeping a people perspective. *Canadian Journal of Public Health, 83*(Suppl. 1), 20-24.

Raeburn, J.M., & Rootman, I. (1989). Towards an expanded health field concept: Conceptual and research issues in a new age of health promotion. *Health Promotion International, 3,* 383-392.

Sarafino, E.P. (1990). *Health psychology: Biopsychosocial interactions.* New York: John Wiley.

Spector, R.E. (1985). *Cultural diversity in health and illness.* Norwalk, CT: Appleton-Century-Crofts.

Stone, G.C. (1979). Health and the health system. In G.C. Stone, F. Cohen, & N.E. Adler (eds.), *Health psychology — A handbook* (pp. 1-18). San Francisco: Jossey-Bass.

Sykes, J.B. (ed.) (1982). *Concise Oxford dictionary* (7th ed.). Oxford: Oxford University Press.

Wakeley, C. (ed.) (1975). *Faber medical dictionary* (2nd ed.). London: Faber & Faber.

World Health Organization (1984). *A discussion document on the concept and principles of health promotion.* Copenhagen: European Office of the World Health Organization.

World Health Organization (1986). *Ottawa charter for health promotion.* Ottawa: Canadian Public Health Association.

Death of Program, Birth of Metaphor: The Development of Health Promotion in Canada

Ronald Labonté

A few years ago, in a seminar crowded with health workers in Adelaide, South Australia, I declared health promotion dead, and proceeded to count the many ways: the proliferation of senior government departments; of journals and academic chairs; of new credentialling associations and research institutes; and bureaucracy's iron law of oligarchy, which transforms health promotion practitioners into health promotion managers, often at their own status-driven requests. But cynicism is the luxury of the well-off, with our big mouths and bigger vocabularies. That is to say, I was wrong in Adelaide. Health promotion is indeed dead, if we regard it as a social movement comprising all of society's ills and from which a new momentum will emerge towards peace, shelter, education, food, income, a stable ecosystem, sustainable resources, social justice, and equity (to name only the officially sanctioned causes within public health). There are some who argue convincingly that, in these terms, health promotion never in fact lived, but merely and dangerously appropriated the language of social activism within the controlling corridors of bureaucracy (Stevenson & Burke, 1991).

On the other hand, health promotion is very much alive if we regard it more modestly as a cultural space within those corridors, a new "knowledge challenge" (Eyerman & Jamison, 1991) to sedimented professional paradigms and institutional norms. Health promotion in this sense is a professional/institutional *response* to the knowledge generated over the past two decades by many groups or movements — women, environmentalists, those seeking social justice or occupational health and safety. It is a conceptual lens through which those in the health sector might review (or review) their practice.

In tracing the development of health promotion concepts in Canada, as well as the interrelationships between them, I will take as my analytic device their proponents and social movements. My conceit will be to weave this analysis into my own biography as a health educator/health promoter, whose work began the year before publication of *A New Perspective on the Health of Canadians* (Lalonde, 1974; hereafter, the Lalonde Report or the Report) and as one who has struggled to push the practice behind the concept of health promotion to its political limits. Though the first person rings singularly throughout this chapter, my struggles were (and are) not unique, and I do not tell my story for reasons of self-aggrandizement. Rather, my experiences may help to contextualize the more abstract arguments of the development of health promotion as a concept and as a professional practice.

This essay is structured around what I consider to be milestones in Canadian health promotion:

- The Lalonde Report, which gave birth to the social marketing of lifestyles. This approach to health promotion essentially extended behavioural health education programs (which originated in school health programs) into popular health education via mass media.
- The Shifting Medical Paradigm Conference, held in 1980 and which gave rise to the Canadian critique of lifestyles. Two opposing perspectives emerged from this conference, one stressing self-responsibility for health, the other claiming that health was primarily grounded in social structures and conditions.
- The Beyond Health Care Conference, held in 1984, which vaulted the issues of healthy public policy, healthy cities, and the activist advocacy of the Toronto Public Health Department into international view. This represented the entry of politicized health promotion into the mainstream of practice.
- The *Ottawa Charter for Health Promotion* (1986; hereafter, the Ottawa Charter or the Charter) and *Achieving Health for All: A Framework for Health Promotion* (Epp, 1986; hereafter, the Framework), the great bureaucratic watershed that placed community at the centre of everything. These reports took a politicized health promotion into the mainstream, with all the inherent contradictions of the state appropriating the rhetoric of social movements that have arisen in opposition or challenge to it.

In discussing the Charter and the Framework, I will also ruminate on the post-watershed era, a time marked less by any striking focal point than by a steady and quiet absorption of the flood of new ideas into routine professional and institutional practice.

1974: The Lalonde Report

Health Promotion as Behavioural Health Education and Social Marketing

The Lalonde Report, named for then Health and Welfare Minister Marc Lalonde, was essentially a state response to three crises that have come to characterize the Canadian health care system:

- Medical intervention had passed its margin of utility in producing population health. Growth in sick-care expenditures did not match gains in life expectancy; many interventions were scientifically unproven and/or iatrogenic; and, in theory at least, the shifting of illness expenditures to other programs or policy areas (e.g., health education, environmental protection, income maintenance) would yield proportionately greater gains to population health.

- Sick-care expenditures increased rapidly in the late 1960s and early 1970s as a result of the open-ended, fee-for-service universal medicare program, which created budgetary problems for both federal and provincial governments.

- Medical interventions were proving unsuccessful in curing chronic diseases, notably cancers and heart disease. Meanwhile, knowledge of preventive practices was increasing.

Seen generously, the Report was an attempt to break free of the medical approach to health and to return to a more holistic perspective (Hancock, 1986). Viewed less generously, the Report was an off-loading of responsibility for escalating health care costs from service providers (hospitals and doctors) and their insurance brokers (the state) to individuals and their unhealthy lifestyles (Labonté & Penfold, 1981a, 1981b; Vayda, 1977).

The Report's argument was simple. Health, implicitly defined as the absence of disease or disability, did not result solely from health care, but from the interplay of determinants from four health field elements: human biology, lifestyles, the environment, and health care. The Report aimed explicitly to break the public perception that the health field was synonymous with professional medical care, graphically portraying how little that sector contributed to health, yet how much the cash-strapped government was spending on it relative to the other three elements. The Report preached an intersectoralism that "disregard[ed] questions of jurisdiction which may be important to governments but are not of primary concern to the people of Canada when their health is at stake" (Lalonde, 1974, p. 63), and made a modest attempt to articulate a comprehensive set of strategies.

The Report was seriously flawed in several respects. It challenged the fact of medical monopoly, but not its paradigm; it failed to mention well-being, and described mental health only in terms of psychiatric jargon. It defined the environment in narrow physical terms, with little reference to the social environment of poverty, unemployment, inequity, and the sundry "-isms" of discrimination. It espoused a health promotion strategy for the environment that was little more than a patronizing injunction to trust government to regulate. It acknowledged the women's movement and the trade union movement, not for the knowledge or policy challenges they presented to government, but as vehicles to communicate healthier lifestyles to "housewives. . . and sedentary employees" (Lalonde, 1974, p. 68). Brought forth in a context of rising expenditures for sick care, the Report mandated health promotion with the task of curbing such costs, a task that might make sense if the costs of sick care bore a sufficiently strong relation to people's experiences of disease and disability (and they do not). Most importantly, the Report subsequently gave rise to health promotion as social marketing, an approach resoundingly criticized for "blaming the victim."

There are many possible interpretations for the Lalonde Report's failure to fulfill its conceptual potential, and for its becoming a text better known abroad than at home. One interpretation lay blame on cautious or conservative policy which emphasized one element (i.e., lifestyles) over the others. Another interpretation faulted the two-tiered Canadian system of government, in which the federal tier can generate good ideas that the provinces may ignore for any of a myriad of reasons, not the least of which may be protest over transfer payment reductions for health services or encroachment upon provincial autonomy. I believe that the principal reason for the Report's minor influence lies in its intrinsically narrow conceptualization of health promotion as a "strategy aimed at informing, influencing and assisting both individuals and organizations so that they will accept more responsibility and be more active in matters affecting mental and physical health" (Lalonde, 1974, p. 66). This singularly top-down view of health was deeply resented by many of those individuals and organizations whom the health educators and promoters sought to influence.

The above account represents the Greater Tradition of health promotion at that time. In Chinese thought, there is also a Lesser Tradition, belonging to those too poor to claim the attention of the official historians. Lesser Traditions are more modest stories, and field-level health promotion in the mid-1970s was less concerned with philosophical issues of power and control than it was with clarifying the difference between health education and health promotion. Health education in the 1970s was the dominant non-medical public health practice, an offspring of school health programs and the sanitary health crusades that persisted through the 1950s. The bottom line of health education, as Palko wrote in 1982, was "to influence the behaviour of people when there is sufficient evidence that such behaviour is harmful to health," and to avoid being "given responsibility for looking after audio-visual equipment and preparing pamphlets" (Palko, 1982, pp. 4-5). Behavioural influence took the form of exhortations regarding lifestyle. Avoiding a job description as Ms. or Mr. Projector Fix-it took the form of endless attempts to create health education as a credentialled profession, an endeavour I thought smacked of the same elitism and power-overing that health educators themselves experienced by dint of being the lowest-ranked members of the junior team in the medical leagues.

Power and politics, though not yet explicit in the discourse of health promotion, were never far away in practice, as I learned in one of my early health promotion jobs with the provincial Alcohol and Drug Commission, a new body created in the wake of the LeDain Commission on the Non-Medical Use of Drugs. The Alcohol and Drug Commission was strapped with the impossible task of producing information on marijuana that would be acceptable to politicians. Twelve months were spent drafting a manual on alcohol and drug information for professional use, carefully reviewing scientific studies to ensure accuracy. Time and integrity did not prevent the legislature from erupting into head-hunting condemnations when the section on marijuana implied that the drug was not solely responsible for heroin addiction, street gangs, theft and violence, rising unemployment, and the declining popularity of the ruling political party.

In practice, the science of health promotion espoused by the Lalonde Report was just smoke and mirrors, used as a vehicle for the biases of primarily White, male, middle-aged, middle-class conservatives. The Division of Venereal Disease Control, where I worked next, promoted a poster showing a woman-as-temptress leaning against a lamppost, declaring that "four out of five pick-ups have VD." Yet health department statistics at the time showed that fewer than one in five prostitutes were infected, much less "pick-ups," an ambiguous term defined by one pamphlet as "good-time girls lacking the good sense to charge for their favours." VD health education was less about disease prevention than about monogamous marriage and fundamentalist sexual values, justified through the exaggerated threat of disease (Labonté, 1981). This same moralism reared its head again in the early 1980s, when herpes was constructed as a media event and was claimed to represent the price of the sexual revolution, and again in the first years of the HIV pandemic, when the term "innocent" was used to demarcate persons who acquired the virus through blood transfusions from all others with the syndrome, who presumably had brought it upon themselves. Perhaps more innocently, but no less unscientifically, a mid-1970s advertisement comparing the fitness level of the average 30-year-old Canadian to that of the average 60-year-old Swede was designed more by what would make a catchy slogan than what reflected proven fact.

There would be nothing neutral about health promotion. Health promotion was about power: who had it, who did not, how that power was reinforced in certain ideologies (including health beliefs), and how the tables could be turned. Then lacking the permissive statements of the Charter and Framework, I attempted to turn the tables by enlisting groups in the political vanguard to design the educational and social-marketing materials I produced. The Vancouver Women's Health Collective assisted in producing, or reviewed, all the material prepared on sexuality and family planning used by the provincial Ministry of Health. Feminist artists were contracted to create the visual statements. Messages of women's emancipation were entwined with messages on contraception. One poster, the first produced by any government department in the province portraying women of colour, showed women of various ages in both traditional and non-traditional occupations with the slogan: "These women all have something in common... they all practise a method of birth control."

This approach, though modest, sought to contextualize the message of health promotion within that of social activists. Accepting that health statements (which we now call health discourses) are never neutral or simply factual, but are highly complex structurings of "reality" and social relationships, I worked with those groups who were struggling to transform the dominant discourse into one that was more emancipatory. I then believed (and still maintain) that health promotion as an empowering practice begins with the legitimizing support that health professionals and organizations give to those social movements that challenge disabling social beliefs and practices.

This approach to health promotion, in which some elements of empowerment glimmered through its work with social movements, nonetheless stumbled over four hurdles:

- It remained centred on the individual practitioner; little or no institutional change occurred.
- It remained locked within a disease-prevention approach. The disease-based issues of health professionals were still paramount in the exchange with social-activist groups.
- It remained boxed within the schematic of social marketing, a rigidly defined approach to social change in which knowledge and attitudes are influenced through communications programs. Despite their sophistication, these programs are predicated on a passive consumer whose only action of interest is that which the marketing program attempts to sway.
- It remained fixed within institutional and biomedical forms of problem solving. Sexism or heterosexism in medical practice might be criticized, but not the foundations of medicine itself. Self-help and alternative constructs of health held little currency.

1980: Shifting Medical Paradigm Conference

Health Promotion as Self-Responsibility and the Structuralist Critique

British Columbia has long held the reputation of being Canada's crunchy-granola province, the portal through which Eastern philosophies, mysticism, and drugs would enter, and the region that had more in common with the meditative solipsism of Esalen in California than with the acquisitive grubbiness of Bay Street brokers in Toronto. The Shifting Medical Paradigm Conference (March 20-21, 1980), sponsored by the University of British Columbia Continuing Education Department, the Vancouver Health Department, the British Columbia Ministry of Health, and the federal Health Promotion Directorate, was subtitled "From Disease Prevention to Health Promotion." It had less to do with health promotion as we now understand it than with challenges to the healing paradigm of Western biomedicine. It was, in west-coast fashion, a testament to the self. This testament took two forms.

One form criticized iatrogenic Western medicine, its construction of the passive role of "patient," its denial of the importance of preventive practices, and the inability of its reductionist physico-chemical science to account fully for people's experiences of illness, recovery, and health. This form came in many hues: spiritual philosophies of holism and health achievable through guided meditations; Eastern healing arts based on different concepts of physiological functioning and built more upon inductive empiricism than upon

deductive testings of hypotheses; a resurrection of Western traditions of
herbalism and marginal therapeutics such as homeopathy and chiropracty.
Common to all of these was a belief that Western medical science was suffering a deserved crisis in confidence, expressed most strongly in Illich's
Medical Nemesis (1977) and the spate of subsequent exposés on how doctors and medicine were actually bad for your health.

At its best, this challenge created a space where the individual could
reclaim "well-being" from the categorical definitions of disease and sickness, along with the subsequent dependence upon professionals and their
institutions. The power to name one's experience, and to have that naming
acknowledged by others as legitimate, is considered the *sine qua non* of
empowerment (Fay, 1987; Freire & Macedo, 1987). The importance placed
on self-help affirmed the potential healing powers that individuals could
claim for themselves. At its worst, this challenge degenerated into a number of cult-like groups or organizations espousing a simplistic view of the
power of positive thinking, and a marketplace of competing alternative
therapies (vitamins, herbs, specific treatments) no less reductionist than
the Western medicine they stood against. In either situation, analysis of the
structuring of social power relations was scant or non-existent, apart from
trenchant critiques of the power of the Western medical monopoly. (The
vitality of these alternative health and self-help/human potential groups in
the late 1970s and early 1980s was partly due to the scant attention paid
by both traditional and New Left political movements to the desire for personal growth and development. At their worst extreme, the former looks
inward without recourse to external context, while the latter looks out-
ward with no recourse to inner guidance.)

The second form that this testament took remained grounded within
Western medicine. Two voices predominated: the growing surge of gov-
ernment-generated lifestyle marketing campaigns already discussed, and
the primarily U.S.-based "wellness movement" with its emphasis on peak
self-in-body achieved through "proper" nutrition, exercise, and stress management. The line between lifestyle campaigns and wellness programs
blurred, although the latter tended to emphasize a more individualistic, by-
one's-own-bootstraps approach to well-being (consistent with its U.S.
parentage), while the former preached the social as well as personal benefits of avoiding disease (consistent with its Canadian parentage). Both
approaches shared, in common with other groups critical of the Western
medical paradigm, a belief in self-responsibility and the self-capacity for
health. They disagreed on the finer points of just what determines the
healthiest lifestyle choices (macrobiotic foods blessed by crystals, or one
serving per day from each of the four food groups).

The Shifting Medical Paradigm Conference was important for the legitimization it gave to the alternative health movement and for its emphasis on
different healing modalities, spirituality, and the individual's role in moving
from illness to wellness. It was also important for introducing a wellness paradigm, in which the individual's experiences are more important than the
strictures of medical diagnoses. But the absence of any reference to poverty,
gender, race, or environmental issues irritated several delegates, myself

included. Was this "new" health promotion paradigm simply a different version of the old one, in which the individual was still constructed in isolation from society — free, perhaps, from medical dominance but hardly free from the dominance of economic or patriarchal oppression?

One lone speaker delivered the curmudgeon's address. Susan Penfold asked, "What is more important: providing fitness programs for a few middle-aged male executives to improve their business acumen, or day-care facilities for the thousands of women whose double duty of work in and out of the house is making them sick?" It was pungent stuff, a feminist slap in the face of the conference's self-congratulatory tone.

As a member of the conference committee, it was my responsibility to facilitate a workshop on the ideas presented by one of the plenary speakers. I quickly adopted Susan's theme for my workshop; it had given me the legitimacy I felt I needed to introduce the missing political dimension into the health promotion debate. The workshop produced a five-page manifesto and a plea to the conference committee to expand these ideas further. The task fell upon Susan and me, and resulted in an invitation in 1981 to the First National Conference on Health Promotion, held in Ottawa. The conference name signalled the shifting winds from health education to health promotion.

Susan gave the keynote address. I sat nervously in the front row making notes for what later became an article, "Canadian Perspectives on Health Promotion: A Critique" (Labonté & Penfold, 1981a), and subsequently a monograph, *Health Promotion Philosophy: From Victim-Blaming to Social Responsibility* (Labonté & Penfold, 1981b). The ideas contained in these works were not new; they had germinated in Marxist, feminist, and budding environmentalist social critiques, including many directed at medicine and the health care system. They had been given some voice in the United States, in response to the *Healthy People* report (the American response to the Lalonde Report), by Brown and Margo (1978), and Crawford (1977), among others. The eventual significance of the health promotion critique, as raised in our article and monograph, derived from the practitioner's perspective of naming commonly experienced frustrations and concerns that no one had yet addressed in print.

The argument was simple. The health of oppressed peoples (the poor, women, persons from minority cultures, workers, and others) was determined at least as much, if not more, by structural conditions (poverty, hazards, powerlessness, pollution, and so on) than by personal lifestyles. Moreover, personal lifestyles were not freely determined by individual choice, but existed within social and cultural structures that conditioned and constrained behaviour. Behavioural health education, social marketing, or wellness approaches to health promotion fostered victim-blaming by assuming that individuals were entirely responsible for their choices and behaviour. They also blamed the victim indirectly by ignoring the structural determinants of health, those causes that are embedded within economic, class- and gender-based patterns of social relationships.

The tone of the critique was unabashedly polemical. I recall the excitement of writing the two pieces, bringing to them the certainty of the social vision and solidarity still being enjoyed by "the Movement" — leftist, feminist, gay/lesbian, health and safety, anti-poverty, and environmental groups. It was a certainty born of opposition to a prevailing ideology, and to a unity in that opposition that was soon to fracture into a cacophony of competing and often exclusive groups. The critique essentially incorporated the knowledge challenges of social movements as they might apply to health. Health promotion was defined well away from behaviourism, marketing, or wellness; it was "the process of empowering people to take greater control over, and responsibility for, their health" (Labonté & Penfold, 1981b, p. 45).

Although the critique was primarily a reaction against the lifestyle fetish, it did attempt to chart an empowering course of action. Empowerment in health promotion would occur through:

- critical awareness of society's pathogenic issues and structures (e.g., pollution, economic and sexual inequality, etc.);
- organization around social issues identified by different disadvantaged groups and other "health consumers" as health-endangering;
- awareness of lifestyle choices that are hazardous to personal health, and how such choices relate to larger social and environmental health issues;
- visible and financial commitment on the part of governments, corporations, medical and other professionals, and other large social institutions to redress the social inequalities and policy contradictions that lead to poor health.

During this early-1980s phase of health promotion, the focus of health educators and promoters was beginning to shift. Rather than bring a social-activist perspective to disease prevention (e.g., working with women's and gay health groups on contraception or STD programs, or with anti-poverty groups on making nutrition education more relevant to the poor), they declared the core issues of these movements (sexism, male violence, homophobia, poverty) to be health promotion issues in their own right.

Again, this construction of health promotion had certain limitations. Firstly, as a critique, it existed in opposition to then current health promotion practices, yet failed to articulate an alternative practice. Critiques are always easier to provide than alternatives. They may be necessary initially to break through sedimented ideas, but they are insufficient in themselves. The cry for health promotion as social responsibility (as opposed to victim-blaming) stood in need of ideas for professional practice and strategies for institutional change.

Secondly, it was a structuralist critique. Structuralism in social theory appears in both leftist and rightist political camps (neo-Marxist or conflict sociology, and functionalist sociology, respectively). The structuralist position of the health promotion critiques was clearly neo-Marxist. As post-structuralist and feminist theorists have "deconstructed" in recent years (e.g., Foucault, 1979; Poster, 1989; Nicholson, 1992), structuralist theories have led to untenable notions of social change (e.g., communism is the driving force of history; the working class is the privileged engine of revolutionary change). There is an unpalatable determinism about it, in which the phenomenological self — lost in the behaviourism of early health education and social-marketing programs and recovered in the alternative and wellness paradigms — becomes lost once again in the attack against the victim-blaming, apolitical individualism of the lifestyle or wellness approaches. This point was made in an important response to the Labonté/Penfold Critique (as it became known) by Ken Allison (1982). Allison argued that we had lost sight of the role and responsibility of the individual, and referred to the Brazilian educator Paulo Freire and his theory of critical consciousness as a basis for developing an empowering form of health education. Freire's work was to have considerable and persisting influence on the development of health promotion concepts, particularly that of empowerment, from the mid-1980s onwards.

1984: Beyond Health Care Conference

Political Health Promotion Enters the Mainstream

Publication of the critiques, and my own growing outspokenness on such matters as occupational health and safety, strained my relationship with the B.C. Health Ministry. A politicized health promotion practice was not yet possible in that province, which had been dominated for years by a fundamentalist conservative government. I resigned my position under less than amicable terms, learning a powerful lesson about the powerful: when challenged directly, they snap back. A politicized health promotion would require professional risk-taking; but if politicized health promoters remained marginal within their organizations, then the health-compromised powerless would be condemned to token support and constant struggle against "the system." The critiques, though drafted from a practitioner's vantage, were voiced from the "outside" with little concern for how they would be heard from the "inside." Was it possible to work, in a non co-optive way, towards some rapprochement between the inside-out approach (the we-know-best tone of behaviourism and social marketing) and the outside-in approach (the rejection of professionals, institutions, and the state by both the "bootstraps" wellness movement and the left-leaning, health promotion structuralists)? I was to begin answering that question when I left British Columbia to join the Toronto Department of Public Health in 1982.

The Department of Public Health had slowly been gaining a reputation for innovation through its Health Advocacy Unit. A magnet for some of the most progressive professionals in the country, the Unit had entered public debates on pollution and health in the workplace, garnering media headlines; a report had been drafted deeming poverty, among other social conditions, a major health blight; and when the Department decentralized its services, several community development and health promotion positions had been created that were unique for *not* being defined by specific mandates of disease prevention programs. My job description was particularly

large and vague, two terms that were to become synonymous with the
developing "new" health promotion, i.e., anything that would improve the
health and well-being of the citizens of Toronto. My political reputation
being known in advance, it was assumed that I would work on the "structural" problems: poverty, unemployment, workplace health and safety,
powerlessness. I did so (once again), by seeking those groups and organizations who were already working on such issues and who were committed to some notion of empowerment. Rather than presume that public
health had any great insights to offer activist groups, I posed the question:
"If the health department were to do something about (fill in the health-
determinant blank) that would assist you in your objectives, what might
that be?"

This community development approach bred several important lessons:

*   It was easier to tackle smaller pieces of the big problems than to
    assume that health departments could, or should, claim the whole
    problem (and its solutions) for themselves. I spent months trou-
    bling over how the health department could intervene in unem-
    ployment before planning modest educational and support-group
    programs, on the advice of unemployment service and political
    action groups themselves.
*   There was considerable distrust of the Department of Public Health
    by many groups, particularly those representing the least powerful.
    This distrust was usually overcome only through direct action, i.e.,
    the willingness of health workers to take risks in supporting these
    groups, and the willingness of the Department to take risks by pub-
    licly endorsing the aims of such groups. My own work with a group
    of sole-support mothers in a low-income housing project might
    never have gotten off the ground had the Department not publicly
    declared welfare benefits inadequate to maintain health (Labonté,
    1986).
*   A public health voice on social justice issues, by virtue of its pro-
    fessional "authority," was an important complement to the more
    politically stated demands of social justice groups. When welfare
    reform reached the level of provincial government policy making,
    briefs by public health bodies were important factors in winning
    all-party support for the proposed reforms. A public health voice
    could be powerfully legitimizing. When a citizens' group in anoth-
    er province suffered a legal setback in their struggle to prevent use
    of a toxic herbicide, the Department and the Board of Health advo-
    cated on their behalf. This raised the group's media and political
    profile (Labonté, 1984).
*   There existed a tension between the linear, bureaucratic need to
    manage programs (objective setting, prediction, accountability)
    and the spiral flow of community development processes, in which
    objectives changed and groups external to the Department rejected
    any claim by the Department to account for their decisions and
    actions. This tension was so ubiquitous that it virtually defined the
    community development process. The Department was stumbling

along the learning curve of negotiating authentic partnerships with less powerful, and often more politicized or conflictual, groups.

- There was opposition within the Department to new forms of professional practice. Despite its policy statements supporting more political health promotion, there was little consensus on what this practice should look like, or whether it even had merit. Many health promoters[1] found themselves engaged in a struggle with the bureaucratic style that often typifies large, complex organizations and makes them conservative. Sometimes we would assume the culture of the organization, and at other times the culture of groups opposed to big bureaucracies. At all times, we struggled against the possibility that community development and empowerment — two of the key concepts just entering politicized health promotion — would degenerate into a situation where the organizationally powerless met the socially powerless.

These lessons remain as true, and as unresolved, in health promotion today as they were a decade ago. In this dynamic there is a "them" (big bureaucracy) versus an "us" (the empowerers, the allies of the oppressed communities and groups), in which — as John McKnight influentially aphorized — "services do not empower; only resources empower" (personal communication, Prevention Congress III, Waterloo, Ontario, 1987). This sentiment was often regarded in either-or terms that pitted community against bureaucracy and citizens against professionals. It spoke eloquently to a professional rejection of past constraints, i.e., the paradigmatic constraints of a reductionist biomedical approach to health; the elitist contraints of a we-know-best professionalism; the hierarchical power-overing constraints of institutions and bureaucracies. But it denies the role that services and professionals often play in community development processes; leads to a devaluing of professional direct-service providers; obscures the role of community; and ignores the continuing, real presence of bureaucracies and political governing processes.

The rapprochement between the outside-in and inside-out approaches began to take a clearer form only with the Beyond Health Care Conference organized by one of Canada's leading health promotion conceptualists, Trevor Hancock, with the support of the Toronto Board of Health, the Health Promotion Directorate of Health and Welfare Canada, and the Canadian Public Health Association. Two of the many ideas discussed at this international think tank were to become synonymous with the "new" health promotion: healthy public policy, and healthy cities/communities. Both ideas have generated considerable professional and academic discussion, most of which ignores what I believe to be their essence: a new language through which the politicized structuralist analyses of health promotion and health determinants (derived from the knowledge challenges

---

[1] I use this term generically. Although few persons in the Department of Public Health were called health promoters, many staff (some called health educators, others called community health workers, public health nurses, some managers, many front-line staff) were working according to norms wholly consistent with the yet-to-come Charter and Framework.

of social movements) can enter bureaucratic and mainstream political debate. Healthy public policy — a clever play on words — essentially posits a new role for public health professionals and their agencies: that of engaging in policy debates with those bureaucratic and political sectors which govern the structuralist domains known to influence health in both its negative and positive aspects (i.e., disease and well-being, respectively). At their core, Healthy Cities/Communities projects seek two objectives: to improve citizen participation in these debates at the level of political governance most immediately accessible to them, and/or to improve the degree to which local government sectors co-operate in their planning and policy development.

1986: The Charter and the Framework

Political Health Promotion Becomes the Mainstream

The Charter and the Framework are both well known, internationally as well as to Canadian health promoters. Indeed, the Charter quickly became the shot heard round the world as far as public health practitioners were concerned. During a series of training workshops in New Zealand and Australia in 1991, I was amused and troubled by the reverence with which the organizers would "set the stage" by hanging framed, large-script versions of the Charter's five strategies, as if they were a new mantra for practice. The same quiet desire for specific how-to's persists in the desire among public health practitioners to identify the one, *real* strategy for empowering communities, a strategy that always slips from our grasp: popular education (Freirian critical consciousness raising) in 1988; community development in 1989; empowerment in 1990; self-esteem in 1991.

The Charter and the Framework sent me into a period of profound identity crisis, one that still resonates. I had lived my life, and developed my practice, as a critic and a partial outsider to the political and bureaucratic structures that I believed were disempowering. Now these same structures had adopted the rhetoric that had cost me my job in British Columbia scarcely five years earlier. My political antennae were beeping madly: Was this progress? Was this co-optation? Would my work become easier, or more difficult? Should I believe that senior mandarins actually took the concepts of equity, social justice, and empowerment seriously, or was this merely a convenient mouthing of platitudes? When asked to speak to the issue of community health promotion strategies at the 1987 Canadian Public Health Association, I found it difficult to ignore the huge legitimizing space that the Charter and the Framework had created for practitioners such as myself. But I also found it hard to take the sound and the fury seriously, fearing that, as Shakespeare decried, it would come to "signify nothing."

I have already argued that the shift in health promotion concepts, codified in the Charter and the Framework, are a response to social movements, and not a new social movement in themselves. I have also argued that they invite us to embrace the new social knowledge that these movements have struggled to create. This argument leads to a number of structural conflicts, contradictions, or tensions. While it is beyond the scope of this chapter to discuss these practice problematics in any depth, brief comments on each of the Charter's five strategies are offered below. (For a detailed discussion, see Labonté, 1993.)

Create Supportive Environments

Rather than exhort individuals to change individually, health professionals have an equal responsibility to act upon the environmental conditions that shape behaviour, doing so in such a way as to remove structural barriers that prevent individuals from making healthy choices. The major difficulty encountered here is one of avoiding a social-engineering approach to health promotion, in which external environments are manipulated for some "right" choice as determined by persons in positions of technocratic power (Grace, 1991). In making "healthy choices the easy choices," whose concept of health are we following?

Develop Personal Skills

Most health professionals still see their role in terms of encouraging healthier lifestyles, and believe that this goal requires certain educational and therapeutic skills unique to their profession (Labonté, 1988/89). The very notion of developing personal skills smacks of residual paternalism: professionals provide information, resources, and programs to individuals or groups who are presumably deficient in ways that professionals are not. Through this exchange of professional "wisdom," people become empowered — i.e., "we will empower this or that unhealthy group." Through the intractable logic of the English language, this phrase constructs individuals and groups in the passive voice, those who are being "done to" while never doing.

Reorient Health Services

There are many stumbling blocks to this particular strategy. Some are evident: the inertia of an institutionalized, biomedically grounded sick-care system that still commands most of the resources in the health sector and much of the media coverage on health; the opportunity costs of *not* investing in alternative policy areas such as the environment, housing, or welfare reform. But there are more subtle problems. How do we (health professionals, health agencies) communicate effectively with the public on the "prevention paradox" (Rose, 1985)? This paradox concerns how costly medical procedures often result in a direct gain to individual patients, yet have no measurable effect on population health; while alternative investments in population health strategies (including environmental protection, welfare reforms, and actions on other socio-environmental risk conditions) may show improved indicators for aggregate health, yet have only indirect and minimal individual gain. Another difficulty arises in the use of community-based services to replace more costly (and, as many critics have argued, iatrogenic and dehumanizing) forms of institutional care. However, many feminist scholars (e.g., Walker, 1990) caution that community-based services, in the absence of well-funded community supports, may well result in transferring the responsibilities of care from state-funded organizations to women (mothers, wives, daughters).

Build Healthy Public Policy

This strategy, more than any other, represents the inside-out approach. *If* public health practitioners accept a broad analysis of health determinants, and *if* they adopt a political or advocacy framework of choosing to align with less powerful groups in their struggles for greater political equity (Watt & Rodmell, 1988), then healthy public policy represents the language through which the bureaucratic agenda might be altered. But does health (however defined) become a superordinate goal, a kind of imperialism that other policy sectors must "buy in to"? We in the health sector have created a new set of concepts and metaphors to help us grapple with challenges from social movements. Such concepts and metaphors are not necessarily shared by persons in other sectors, who may think more in terms of housing rights, sustainability, safety, human development, or other ideational touchstones. We must not colonize other sectors with our own problematical namings, or our own brand of solutions.

Can one prevent the unquestioned biomedical definition of health from dominating health concepts that may be utilized in other policy sectors? The Charter and the Framework have clearly removed health promotion from the natural-science paradigm of biomedicine, and placed it within the more pluralistic (and messier) social-science paradigm of human and social relations. But the health sector itself has yet to accept fully the implications of a non-reductionist approach to health (i.e., one concerned with well-being, or quality of life). On the one hand, if health becomes so broadly constructed that it encompasses most of human experience, it loses any utility as a variable in policy discourse, or in most other realms bureaucratic. But if health is constructed narrowly in biomedical terms, the empowering potential of the Charter and the Framework grinds to a halt, the notion of socio-environmental health determinants reduces to a matter of disease prevention, and the knowledge challenges of the social movements disappear into the *technos* of disabling institutions. Good qualitative research can remove health practitioners from between this rock and a hard place, but such research is still poorly understood within the health sector and looked upon somewhat · condescendingly.

Strengthen Community Action

This strategy may be the most problematic one facing contemporary health promoters, for it leaves unanswered three key questions: What is community? Which community groups should be supported? and, How do we understand power-relational issues?

Community, however else we understand it, bridges conceptually the small groups of kin/friends/co-workers and our larger social institutions and structures. However, when community is defined bureaucratically, it tends to be given geographic or demographic attributes — e.g., community as housing project, community as neighbourhood, community as municipality; or, the "poor community," the "women's community," the "aging community," the "disabled community," the community of this or that ethnoculture. Geographic definitions of community define people's informal and formal interrelationships by political jurisdictions; demographic definitions of community define these interrelationships by how data are collected. This distinction may be useful administratively, but it also may have little to do with how people actually structure their social relationships.

There is growing acceptance of a framework of action based on advocacy, which explicitly recognizes that priority community groups are those whose income, educational, occupational, and general social-class positioning places them low within the hierarchy of political and economic power (City of Toronto, 1991; Watt & Rodmell, 1988). Stating this is easy; acting upon it remains difficult. There has been a polyphony of competing claims by such community groups in recent years. Available resources for community organizing and support have also declined through all sectors. Which groups merit support over others? What criteria are used in making choices? How do we continue to work from a vaguely leftish agenda of social change and analysis in an era of increasingly conservative, market-driven politics? More importantly, how do we develop authentic partnerships with community groups and organizations, most of whom lack the resources and legitimizing power that accrue to health professionals and agencies?

This last question is currently assuming greater importance in health promotion thinking, as the rhetoric of the Charter and the Framework leads some bureaucrats to conclude that they shouldn't even sneeze without first holding a community consultation. This raises the whole other matter of just what it is we are asking community groups to become partners in — our own tedious and often conservatizing bureaucratic process, or some larger project of social change in which we recognize the strengths of our differences, rather than collapse them into a singular strategy or voice?

Conclusion

My cursory critique of the post-watershed health promotion era is not intended to declare the concept's emancipatory potential null and void. Health promotion is not a specific practice, and it is certainly not a particular program. Nor is health promotion an "evolving concept," as one often hears it described. This notion implies that, at some future time, health promotion will become fully reified and transparent in meaning.

As I stated at the outset of this chapter, I view health promotion as a metaphor, as a professional and bureaucratic lens through which past practices can be revalued. I do not claim that this definition describes what health promotion *is*. Rather, it is how I find health promotion to be conceptually useful within its somewhat explicit project of empowerment. Health promotion is unavoidably a contested concept, meaning various things to the various persons who use it. Indeed, one might say that the term itself is a serendipitous label attached to the empowerment project because, at the time when the social-movement critiques of health entered the main business of bureaucracy and policy, health promotion was the "minority" construct in the "minority" discipline of public health. What better label could be used to incorporate the marginalized challenges from without?

My fascination with health promotion as a potential lever to institutional and organizational transformation derives from my reluctant abandonment of neo-Marxist theories of social change (though not of social critique) and my irritation with community romanticism. To state my view simply, I believe that institutions and organizations will neither wither away nor be overthrown; therefore, they must be transformed. Health promotion may represent a cultural or new "public space" (Melucci, 1989) in which health professionals seek to transform their institutions. The questions of what they will seek to transform them into, and how they will do this, are still very much part of the new (emerging) practice, although the institutional transformation may well be a shift from *what* institutions do, to *how* they do.

Conceived as an emancipating revaluation of professional practice, health promotion exists between two dialectically entwined perils: that of co-opting or neutralizing social struggle/conflict within the conservatizing *ethos* of institutions, and that of denying its bureaucratic parentage and naively proclaiming "the community" as the solution to all our sociopolitical and economic health woes. These risks are not intractable; they can be mitigated, if not overcome. The mitigatory means lie in how we answer the one question fundamental to the "new" health promotion practice: How can professionals working under its rubric engage in specific actions that are empowering, that ameliorate inequitable social relationships?

The empowering essence of any answer to this question lies in the professional's authentic commitment to hearing the experiences of people's lives, understanding these experiences in the words that people use to express them, and negotiating mutual actions to improve those situations that people would like to alter. The authenticity of this commitment is contained in the challenge made by Lily Walker, an Australian Aboriginal woman: "If you are here to help me," she said, "then you are wasting your time. But if you come because your liberation is bound up in mine, then let us begin" (cited in Valvarde, 1991).

References

Allison, K. (1982). Health education: Self-responsibility vs. blaming the victim. *Health Education, 20,* 11-13, 24.

Brown, E.R., & Margo, G.E. (1978). Health education: Can the reformers be reformed? *International Journal of Health Services, 8,* 3-26.

City of Toronto (1991). *Health inequalities in the City of Toronto.* Toronto: Department of Public Health.

Crawford, R. (1977). You are dangerous to your health: The ideology and politics of victim-blaming. *International Journal of Health Services, 7,* 663-680.

Epp, J. (1986). *Achieving health for all: A framework for health promotion.* Ottawa: Health & Welfare Canada.

Eyerman, R., & Jamison, A. (1991). *Social movements: A cognitive approach.* University Park: Pennsylvania State University Press.

Fay, B. (1987). *Critical social science.* Ithaca: Cornell University Press.

Foucault, M. (1979). *Discipline and punish: The birth of the prison.* Middlesex: Peregrine Books.

Freire, P., & Macedo, D. (1987). *Literacy: Reading the word and the world.* South Headley, Massachusetts: Bergin & Garvey.

Grace, V. (1991). The marketing of empowerment and the construction of the health consumer: A critique of health promotion. *International Journal of Health Services, 21,* 329-343.

Hancock, T. (1986). Lalonde and beyond: Looking back at A New Perspective on the Health of Canadians. *Health Promotion (International), 1,* 93-100.

Illich, I. (1977). *Medical nemesis: The expropriation of health.* London: Penguin.

Labonté, R. (1981). The perils of promiscuity: VD and victim-blaming. *Canadian Family Physician, 27,* 1928-1932.

Labonté, R. (1984). Chemical justice. *This Magazine, 17*(6), 4-12.

Labonté, R. (1986). Social inequality and healthy public policy. *Health Promotion (International), 1,* 341-351.

Labonté, R. (1988/89). Healthy public policy: A survey of Ontario health professionals. *International Quarterly of Community Health Education, 9,* 321-342.

Labonté, R. (1993). *Health promotion and empowerment: Practice frameworks.* Toronto: Centre for Health Promotion, University of Toronto and ParticipAction.

Labonté, R., & Penfold, S. (1981a). Canadian perspectives in health promotion: A critique. *Health Education, 19*(3/4), 4-9.

Labonté, R., & Penfold, S. (1981b). *Health promotion philosophy: From victim-blaming to social responsibility.* Vancouver: Health Promotion Directorate, Western Regional Office.

Lalonde, M. (1974). *A new perspective on the health of Canadians.* Ottawa: Health & Welfare Canada.

Melucci, A. (1989). *Nomads of the present.* Auckland: Radius Books.

Nicholson, N. (1992). "On the postmodern barricades: Feminism, politics and theory," in Seidman, S., & Wagner, D. (eds.), *Postmodernism and social theory* (pp. 82-100). Oxford: Blackwell.

Palko, M. (1982). Perspectives of the past: Twenty years of health education in Canada. *Health Education, 21*(1), 2-5.

Poster, M. (1989). *Critical theory and poststructuralism.* Ithaca: Cornell University Press.

Rose, G. (1985). "Sick individuals and sick populations," in Buck, C., Llopis, A., Naajera, E., & Terris, M. (eds.), *The challenge of epidemiology* (pp. 829-837). Washington, DC: Pan-American Health Organization.

Stevenson, H.M., & Burke, M. (1991). Bureaucratic logic in new social movement clothing. *Health Promotion International, 6,* 281-290.

Valvarde, C. (1991). *Critical theory in health education.* Montréal: Montréal DSC (mimeo).

Vayda, E. (1977). Preventive programs and the political process. *Modern Medicine in Canada, 32,* 260-264.

Watt, A., & Rodmell, S. (1988). Community involvement in health promotion: Progress or panacea? *Health Promotion (International), 2,* 359-368.

World Health Organization (1986). *Ottawa charter for health promotion.* Ottawa: Canadian Public Health Association.

NATIONAL
PERSPECTIVES

The Federal Role in Health Promotion: Art of the Possible

Lavada Pinder

For nearly two decades Canada has enjoyed, and to a great extent earned, the reputation of being the country that introduced health promotion and went on to help shape it on a global scale (Kickbusch, 1989). Throughout this period the federal government has played a central role. Internationally, the federal government is applauded as the publisher of the ground-breaking documents, *A New Perspective on the Health of Canadians* (Lalonde, 1974; hereafter, the Lalonde Report) and Achieving Health for All: A Framework for Health Promotion (Epp, 1986a); as host of the First International Conference on Health Promotion, which produced the *Ottawa Charter for Health Promotion* (1986; hereafter, the Charter); and as organizer of the Health Promotion Directorate, the first of its kind in the world.

Nationally, response to the federal government's role in health promotion has been mixed: the government has been commended in some quarters and criticized in others. Detractors say that challenges have been set out without accompanying changes in policy and resource allocation (Farrant, 1991). Others have been impressed with the conceptual leadership the federal government has given, and are more aware of the difficulties in following through (Last, 1986). The fact is that the federal government is an exceptionally complex environment in which to introduce and implement new ideas. To do so requires an understanding of the political and bureaucratic process and a knowledge of what can and cannot be done in a federal system of government. Furthermore, the radical conceptual and definitional changes that health promotion has undergone in a relatively short time have not made the federal government's role an easy one. In the end, however, health promotion, like most innovations, has tended to reflect the commitment and skills of the major players and the times in which they live.

In any case, the federal government has played a unique role in the development of health promotion in Canada and elsewhere. This chapter attempts to assess this contribution fairly by putting health promotion into perspective, describing federal government activity from the Second World War to the present, and analyzing the factors that have influenced events and outcomes.

The Policy Environment and Its Effect on Health Promotion

If policy is defined as an agreement for action, then it must be concluded that currently the federal government has no declared policy on health promotion. If, however, a wider net is cast and public policy is viewed as a set of guiding principles and values within which decisions are taken on action or inaction, then the federal government has adopted a lively approach to health promotion policy (O'Neill & Pederson, 1992). The problem is that the latter approach can leave health promotion in a continual struggle to maintain its position, heavily dependent on support from the political and senior bureaucratic hierarchy of the day and, consequently, very vulnerable to resource reductions. The question is: Why has the Canadian government taken such a laissez-faire approach when it has gained such respect and recognition for its efforts in health promotion?

Part of the answer may be found in trying to come to grips with the federal government's failure to lead the development of an overall health strategy that includes health goals. National health goals, derived from contemporary notions of what creates health, would put health care in perspective and demand a comprehensive, far-reaching health promotion policy. The federal government's reluctance may also reflect the limitations in its health mandate, federal – provincial relations, and the overriding preoccupation with health care costs.

The statutory basis for the federal involvement in health promotion can be found in the Department of National Health and Welfare Act (1944). Under this statute, the duties and functions of the Minister include all "matters relating to the promotion or preservation of health. . . of the people of Canada. . . ." However, it is the 1867 British North America Act which sets constitutional limits on federal power by assigning responsibility for health and welfare to the provinces and municipalities. At the same time, the Act made no provision for resources, although it gave the federal government significant taxation powers. The result of this constitutional dilemma is that the federal and provincial governments expend extraordinary energy and effort in coming to agreement on the use of the federal government's spending power (Charles & Badgley, 1987). Needless to say, federal influence can dwindle when transfer payments are reduced.

Federal – provincial co-operation is hard won, and sometimes it is not won at all, despite a variety of mechanisms. Over past years, the Ministers of Health have met from time to time, while the Conference of Deputy Ministers meets on average twice a year. Various advisory committees report to the Deputy Ministers for the stated purpose of identifying needs of national importance, recommending policy options, and developing collaborative strategies. In practice, however, differing agendas and lack of resources can make consensus difficult and follow-up even more so.

Exceptions to this can be found in such areas as drug abuse and the recent children's initiative, Brighter Futures, where the federal government has invested resources. In such cases, negotiations may be difficult but they are taken very seriously.

Canada's reputation for being on the leading edge has always been somewhat diminished by the absence of an overall health strategy and, in particular, national goals. While many provinces have got on with their own goal-setting exercises, the federal government has tended to flirt with the issue. In 1974 the Lalonde Report established goal setting as one of the five key strategies to improve health. In 1982 the Ad Hoc Committee on National Health Strategies produced a report for the Ministers of Health advocating priorities and goals (Canada, 1982). In 1984 and in 1987, the Canadian Public Health Association (CPHA) passed resolutions calling on the Department of National Health and Welfare and the provincial Ministries of Health to work together to establish health strategies and goals (CPHA, 1984; CPHA, 1987). Both times, the CPHA offered to develop and co-ordinate the exercise and in 1988 got so far as presenting a proposal to one of the federal – provincial advisory committees (CPHA, 1986). In 1989, it seemed the time had come when then Deputy Minister of Health, Dr. Maureen Law, in addresses to two national conferences, indicated that the federal government was receptive to national goal setting (Law, 1989a; 1989b). Again in 1992, the Canadian Public Health Association made the establishment of a national health strategy with clear goals the number one recommendation in its Issue Paper on Federal/Provincial/Territorial Arrangements for Health Policy (CPHA, 1992).

Still, there is no health strategy; there are no goals. Arguments that health goals can be arbitrary and narrow, and can set an inflexible direction, are no longer valid given the agreement that contemporary health goals must be broad and multisectoral. What is more likely is that the timing and political climate have not been appropriate. Canada has gone through periods when the right circumstances have enabled bold policy moves. For example, during the period following the Second World War, nationalism was high, co-operative federalism was a reality, the economy was thriving, and expansion was possible. The notion of institutional welfare took precedence over residualism, i.e., the least possible government intervention. Canada saw the introduction of the Canada Assistance Plan, old age assistance, and medicare (Yelaja, 1987). However, with economic decline and changes in ideology, fiscal policy and deficit control have taken priority. Broad policy responses to social and health issues are not, with few exceptions, the order of the day. Rather, there are shorter-term, smaller-scale initiatives (Splane, 1987). Single issues such as drugs, AIDS, and family violence dominate the social policy agenda along with health care reform. Health care reform may not only control the health policy agenda for some years to come but could, in doing so, draw health promotion into its orbit — first by taking away scarce resources, and secondly by making health promotion a function of cost containment.

Entrenching the Medical Model, 1944 - 1974

The thirty-year period before the publication of the Lalonde Report saw far-reaching changes in social and health policy in Canada. The adoption of a national health insurance scheme that would remove financial barriers to medical and hospital care had been an aim of the federal government for a good part of the century. The first proposals were made as early as 1919, but it was not until after the Second World War that federal influence was really felt by the provinces. Grants for hospital construction were made available in 1948. A national hospital insurance plan was introduced in 1958 and the national medicare program in 1968. To finance these programs, the federal government paid fifty percent of costs to cover medical and hospital services with no limit and no plans for cost containment. Where there had been shortages in treatment beds and numbers of physicians, Canada became well (if not over) supplied (Charles & Badgley, 1987). The outcome of this was felt in two ways. First, there was soon little money for anything else associated with health but care and treatment. Community services, prevention of disease and disability, and promotion of health were poorly financed. Second, "medicare reflected the uncritical belief that scientific medicine could solve most of society's health problems," and the public came to believe that health was a product of institutional care and medical intervention (CPHA, 1992).

Meanwhile, the federal government was active but more low-profile in its efforts to promote child and maternal health, immunization, dental health, good nutrition, and mental health. In those days the Department of Health and Welfare made a practice of hiring experts in their fields who provided consultative services to the provinces and developed and distributed information resources. Health education was considered the link between public health issues and the average citizen. In 1961, the Department of Health and Welfare hired its first health educator, Michael Palko, to co-ordinate health education activities. Palko has stated that, initially, health education consisted of "doing things *to* and *for* people." The notion of working *with* people came later, as learning and behaviour theory became part of health education practice (Sgro, 1982).

During the 1960s and early 1970s, more health educators were hired throughout the Department of Health and Welfare as well as in the provinces. One concrete action to stimulate health education and create a forum for the exchange of ideas was the bimonthly newsletter, *Health Education*, which Palko launched in January 1962 with a mailing list of 200. Thirty years later, this newsletter — now *Health Promotion* — is a quarterly, serving the field in the two official languages with a circulation of 20 000. But health education did not become a major force to improve health. This may have been because, unlike the United States, there was no network of schools of public health graduating health educators. Only two universities provided training, and there was no strong advocacy for the profession. Also, there existed no framework setting out issues and strategies, which could have positioned health education as an essential element.

As long as the medical model of health was pre-eminent, health education would be marginalized.

By the end of the 1960s, medicare financing was an issue. The federal – provincial Committee on the Costs of Health Services (Canada, 1969), the Hastings Report (Canada, 1973), the Mustard Report (Ontario, 1974) and many more all pointed to the need for a shift to less expensive community care, for organizational and structural changes, and for health promotion and disease prevention.

Cancer, cardiovascular disease, respiratory illnesses, and accidents were some of the health problems that were being treated but not prevented by the health care system. Environmental and behavioural threats to health were being viewed as new challenges not appropriately addressed by the health care system. This situation demanded a new approach.

The Lifestyle Decade, 1974 – 1984

The Lalonde Report (1974) was the first major government paper to declare publicly that the health care system was not the most important factor in determining health. By introducing the health field concept — human biology, environment, lifestyle, and health care organization — the federal government established Canada as a conceptual leader in advancing thinking about health.

The Lalonde Report was the product of the Long Range Health Planning Branch, a small organization set up within the Department of Health and Welfare in 1971 as a think tank. The document was developed without internal or external consultation. The result is a largely uncompromised paper. Acceptance was ensured by publishing its ideas in the *Journal of the Canadian Medical Association* in February 1973, presenting the health field concept to the Conference of Deputy Ministers in December 1973, and the fact that virtually every conceivable interest group, organization, and profession could find itself mentioned in the text. Once the decision was made to proceed, the process was completed in six months. Only the highest authority was sought. Cabinet approved the paper in February 1974, and it was tabled in Parliament by the Honourable Marc Lalonde in April of that year (Laframboise, 1990).

In Canada, there was a low-key response to the release of the Lalonde Report. Although the federal government wanted the document to "stimulate interest and discussion on future health programs for Canada," it did not actively promote the Report beyond distributing about 40 000 copies (over the years, 400 000 were printed) and mentioning it in speeches. Elsewhere, it was praised and followed by similar reports in the United Kingdom, the United States, and Sweden (Hancock, 1985).

There were no announcements, no new resources, and no implementation plan. The originator of the document, the Long Range Health Planning Branch, was clearly a policy analysis group, not a program planning and coordination unit. For its part, the Branch worked on developing strategies in four areas — smoking, occupational health, physical activity, and nutrition — and producing reports on health field indicators. More visible was Operation Lifestyle, developed by the Information Directorate and launched in March 1976. From that time until 1978, Operation Lifestyle delivered lifestyle messages to Canadians, provided resources such as the FIT-Kit for use in the workplace and a computerized Lifestyle Profile, and presented Lifestyle Awards. Elsewhere in the Department there was some organizational relabelling, and new federal – provincial committees and working groups were struck. For example, the Health Education Division in the Health Programs Branch was renamed the Health Promotion Division and a Subcommittee on Health Promotion was established, reporting to the federal – provincial Advisory Committee on Community Health. However, the upshot was that, both here and abroad, the Lalonde Report and follow-up on it became most closely identified with the lifestyle element of the health field concept (McEwen, 1979).

In December 1977, the first significant structural change occurred with the establishment of the Lifestyle and Health Promotion Directorate. This was an effort to develop capacity for planning and co-ordinating health promotion. Six months later, in the summer of 1978, organizational changes in the Department saw the reorganization of the Health Programs Branch into the Health Services and Promotion Branch and the formation of the Health Promotion Directorate in the summer of 1978. Ron Draper was named the first Director-General.

Six organizational units were brought together with a view to integrating alcohol, tobacco, drug, nutrition, family planning, and child health programs into a comprehensive health promotion program. Each unit had its own priorities, client groups, commitments, and style of working. Fitness was not included in the new Directorate, either as an issue or as an organizational unit, likely owing to the fact that Fitness Canada had its own Minister and legislative authority. The Non-Medical Use of Drugs Directorate was the largest organization and was seen to dominate integration activity. To a large extent this was true, as its issues remained central and its senior managers became the new directors. Needless to say, there was a good deal of trepidation among the 140-odd staff who found themselves expected to work together. This was exacerbated by the fact that the new Directorate came into being in the midst of fiscal crisis which required staff and budget reductions (Draper, 1982).

The Health Promotion Directorate was clearly set up to act on the health promotion strategy outlined in the Lalonde Report, and that strategy reflected what was at that time understood to be health promotion. It is somewhat ironic that, at about the same time, the limitations of the lifestyle approach were starting to be seriously examined. Articles appeared that not only took the federal government to task for lack of action on all elements of the health field concept and all five strategies, but also equated the focus on personal responsibility with victim-blaming (Labonté & Penfold, 1981).

This is the environment in which Ron Draper took on the task of organizing the first Health Promotion Directorate. There were organizational challenges, resource limitations, and increasing criticism of a health promotion strategy based on the lifestyle approach. But Draper was a long-time public servant experienced in developing and negotiating social policy. He was one of the last of the "reformist bureaucrats," a term used by Richard Splane to describe like-minded officials committed to social welfare advancement and reform (Splane, 1987). He was also a student of the Lalonde Report, and not in the least intimidated by the challenges ahead.

Initiating a new health promotion program demanded a unique organization. The Health Promotion Directorate brought together staff with analytical, planning, research, education, training, community development, and social-marketing skills to design and deliver national programs. In the early 1980s the staff numbered just over 100 — 70 in Ottawa and 30 located in five regional offices (Atlantic, Québec, Ontario, Prairies, Western). The budget was about ten million dollars annually.

Not quite two years after the new Directorate was formed, the Department approached Cabinet to clarify direction and resources. A Cabinet decision in March 1982 provided the program with a comprehensive mandate by virtue of its aims, issues, target groups, and strategies, but few new resources. The budget was increased by about five million dollars and some staff were added. The aims of the program were: (1) to promote wellness or good health; (2) to encourage the avoidance of unnecessary health risks; and (3) to assist those with handicaps or chronic diseases to learn skills for coping with their circumstances. The issues were virtually all major lifestyle concerns with the exception of fitness — nutrition, smoking, alcohol and drug use, safety, and mental health. The population groups were children and youth, women, the elderly, the handicapped, Native people, and people with low incomes. Four strategies were laid out to guide action. These were: (1) informing and equipping the public to deal with lifestyle issues; (2) promoting a social climate supportive of healthy lifestyles; (3) supporting self-help and citizen participation; and (4) promoting the adoption of health promotion programs and practices within health care, social welfare, and other established programs (Draper, 1989). With only a quarter of the resources needed for full implementation, the scope was reduced to focus mainly on national tobacco, alcohol, drug, and nutrition programs, although developmental work continued on school and workplace health, heart health, child health, and the national health promotion survey. The Health Promotion Contribution Program, with a budget of approximately four million dollars per year, was administered by the five regional offices and supported community projects developed by and for women, the disabled, and Native people.

Contact with the provinces was formalized through a federal – provincial Committee on Health Promotion. This Committee, established in 1979, was co-chaired by the Director-General of the Health Promotion Directorate and the Director of Health Promotion for Saskatchewan. There was one representative, and sometimes two, from each of the provinces and territories. Subcommittees in alcohol and drugs and nutrition reported to it. The Committee was dissolved in 1984 when it was absorbed into the federal – provincial Advisory Committee on Community Health during one of the periods when the Conference of Deputy Ministers became concerned about the number of federal – provincial committees. At the time, some felt it should have been reversed — that Health Promotion as a broader future-oriented issue should have absorbed Community Health. The fact that many members of the Health Promotion Committee tended to be fairly low in the hierarchy of their departments likely accounted for the decision as much as lack of vision.

In the mid-1980s, there was increasing concern with the narrowness of the federal health promotion strategy. This concern found expression through work with the World Health Organization European Regional Office in redefining health and health promotion. At the same time, the government changed, a new Minister took office, and a new Assistant Deputy Minister, fresh from the provinces, took over the Health Services and Promotion Branch.

Shifting the Paradigm, 1984 and On

The Honourable Jake Epp arrived in his new office as Minister of National Health and Welfare with a stated interest in health promotion and disease prevention. His interest coincided with Health Promotion Directorate concerns. The 1984 WHO European Region discussion document on health promotion concepts and principles had made considerable impact and a need was being expressed to redirect health promotion in a fundamental way (WHO, 1984). The new Assistant Deputy Minister, Dr. Peter Glynn, responded by assigning the Director-General of Health Promotion to begin preparing a policy review, thus linking political will with bureaucratic capacity. By 1985, two decisions had been taken that would usher in the modern era of health promotion for Canada and the world. The Minister requested that a policy paper on health promotion be prepared, and agreed to host the First International Conference on Health Promotion in Ottawa in November, 1986. The Conference, in collaboration with WHO and the Canadian Public Health Association, provided both a platform and a deadline (Pinder, 1988).

The development of the 1986 discussion paper on health promotion, published under the title *Achieving Health for All: A Framework for Health Promotion* (Epp, 1986a; hereafter, the Framework), was similar to that of the Lalonde Report in at least one important aspect: the Framework was developed with little internal consultation and virtually none with the provinces, the national non-governmental organizations, or professional associations. Like the Lalonde Report, the Framework's ideas were tested in speeches. An address by the Minister on health promotion and aging in Hamilton in May 1986 (Epp, 1986b) and another entitled "National Strategies for Health Promotion" at the CPHA Conference in June 1986

(Epp, 1986c) contained most of the new concepts and met with very favourable response. As with the Lalonde Report, lack of significant participation within the Department (or from other departments) did not, in the short term, present an obstacle, as the document had senior bureaucratic and political support.

The 1984 WHO-Euro definitions of health and health promotion provided the underpinning for the concepts and strategies outlined in the Framework. The conceptual consistency with the Ottawa Charter is therefore not surprising. The Framework presented three challenges to the health of Canadians: reducing inequities in health, increasing prevention, and enhancing coping with chronic disease and disability. It outlined three health promotion mechanisms to address these challenges: self-care, mutual aid, and healthy environments; and three implementation strategies to operationalize the mechanisms: fostering public participation, strengthening community health services, and co-ordinating healthy public policy.

Unlike the Lalonde Report, the release of the Framework was followed by intensive promotion. In 1987 Department seminars were held with all branches, and meetings also took place with senior staff of several federal departments. Meetings were organized with every province and with most national non-governmental organizations and professional associations. The Framework was cited in speeches made by the Minister and officials. There were presentations and displays at conferences, workshops, and symposia. Nearly 800 000 copies were distributed with special inserts in professional journals such as the *Canadian Journal of Public Health* and the *Journal of the Canadian Medical Association*. No avenue was overlooked in the effort to get the word out, and the response was favourable. The Framework was greeted by a mixture of hope and cynicism by public health groups who wanted goals and next steps (e.g., Ontario Public Health Association, 1987; Canadian Association of Social Workers, 1988). Medically oriented groups felt that the role of health professionals had been overlooked, and wondered how the health care system could be made more responsive to the needs expressed in the paper (McWhinney, 1987; Squires, 1987).

Like the Lalonde Report, the Framework offered no specific strategy for implementing its new ideas. It was always made clear during the promotional period that the Framework was intended to stimulate debate and discussion, and that there were no new resources. But ideas are powerful, and the Framework was seized upon by public health workers in governmental and non-governmental organizations alike.

Whatever new resources were available for health promotion resulted from special initiatives related to drugs, driving while impaired, and AIDS. In 1987-88, the Health Promotion Directorate budget nearly tripled as funds were made available for Canada's Drug Strategy, the National Strategy to Reduce Impaired Driving, and AIDS in order to conduct social-marketing, educational, and research programs and to support community action. Efforts to develop a broader mandate and obtain resources to make the new ideas practical were clearly on a collision course with single issues of more immediate political and public concern.

Given this reality, the Health Promotion Directorate took a two-pronged approach in an effort to reflect the new health promotion. First, delivery responsibilities for federal programs related to drugs, impaired driving, AIDS, nutrition, and tobacco were shaped to health promotion principles. All were examples of intersectoral co-ordination, bringing together many federal departments, provincial governments, voluntary and professional organizations, and the private sector. Social-marketing campaigns set a positive, non-judgemental tone; educational materials were developed to train professionals and augment school programs; qualitative research explored living and working conditions; and community action funds responded to locally defined needs.

Secondly, a decision was taken to use as much of the core funds as possible to support health promotion development. School and workplace health continued to be a fundamental part of the program. Of particular importance was the knowledge development strategy initiated by Dr. Irving Rootman, who sought and obtained the collaboration of the National Health Research Development Program (NHRDP; see the chapter later in this book by Rootman and O'Neill). Rootman, presently the Director of the Centre for Health Promotion at the University of Toronto, was then a Director in the Health Promotion Directorate. Under his leadership, a series of literature reviews was organized to explore the concepts set forth in the Framework; workshops held with universities across the country resulted in health promotion research priorities and a network of researchers; NHRPD, with the Social Sciences and Humanities Council, set up a program to support health promotion research centres; the second Health Promotion Survey was completed in 1990; and there was support for the First National Conference on Health Promotion Research.

During this same period the Health Promotion Contributions Program supported the Healthy Communities and Strengthening Community Health projects (from 1988 to 1991) and *Health Promotion* magazine continued as the principal national vehicle for both health promotion leaders and workers to put their ideas and programs out to the field.

Support for the development of health promotion globally has been primarily through involvement in the international conferences following the Ottawa Conference. Individual staff have been active in health promotion research and global school and workplace health activities, as well as bringing a health promotion perspective to Canadian participation in international programs related to drugs, tobacco, nutrition, heart health, and AIDS. In 1988, a large contingent attended the Second International Conference on Health Promotion: Healthy Public Policy, held in Adelaide, Australia; a Canadian case study was presented, and a special issue of *Health Promotion* was published, subtitled "From Ottawa to Adelaide." In 1991, there was less support available to send participants to the Third International Conference on Health Promotion: Creating Supportive Environments, held in Sundsvall, Sweden. Nevertheless, a large contingent of Canadians attended. The Health Promotion Directorate supported the preparation of *Creating Educational Environments Supportive of Health*, one of five briefing books that provided the basis for Conference discussions.

Conclusion

There can be little dispute that the federal government has been influential in the development of health promotion in Canada and, for that matter, in the world (Canada, 1989; Cunningham, 1993). The amount of health promotion activity in all parts of the country can be attributed, in no small way, to the role played by the federal government. There has been openness to ideas, and these ideas have been articulated and promoted. The Lalonde Report and the Framework are hard evidence of this fact. Politicians have committed publicly to the need for change in our approach to health, and federal bureaucrats have been ready with ideas about which changes are needed. Statements in 1974 about the limitations of health care in improving health and in 1986 about inequities in access to health are of fundamental importance to the health field and beyond it. The federal government can be counted on to play its part internationally: it has done so in the three international conferences on health promotion held to date and in countless technical meetings and consultations.

The federal government led the way in setting up the Health Promotion Directorate — the first of its kind in the world. It was unique because of its size, but also because of its leadership. It drew together skilled, creative staff and put together a program that reached deep into the country through its regional offices. This is the organization that brought a health promotion perspective to the federal government's priority issues. This is also the organization that has striven diligently to balance its role in risk reduction with efforts to support health promotion leaders and further the development of the field.

The fact remains, however, that these efforts have taken place in the absence of a coherent policy that would position health promotion as a serious strategy to improve health and protect it during times of restraint. The Honourable Marc Lalonde, in his 1987 Andrew Patullo lecture to the Association of University Programs in Health Administration, calls health promotion "the poor cousin of health policy" (Lalonde, 1988). Has this been because of a lack of national health goals? Is this simply a feature of our times and values, when it is unrealistic to expect visionary social policy? It has been said that "without lobby pressures, health ministers are powerless to act even if they want to" (McEwen, 1979). Is the absence of an organized lobby or coalition fuelling health promotion and ready to protest cutbacks a major factor? The answer to these queries is likely a resounding yes, but they lead to other equally intriguing questions. Was the process of developing new concepts too isolated from the stakeholders? Have the conceptual shifts come so quickly that the public and politicians have lost touch with what health promotion means in practical terms? Is Canada doomed to a preoccupation with health care rather than with health? The Lalonde Report and the Framework were both developed internally by a few people with the support and approval of the Minister in office at the time. Neither paper was given the status or high profile that might call for wide debate either with the provinces or with the public. There were no hearings that might have engaged interest groups, and there were no resources at stake that might have demanded negotiation with the provinces. Because each paper was closely identified with a particular Minister, there is no guarantee that future incumbents will be equally interested. Both documents were put forth to stimulate discussion with the implicit understanding that, depending on the response, there would be concrete follow-up. But clearly, neither was part of an overall strategy for redirecting policy. By way of contrast, the Hall Commissions on health care made provision for public participation and served to reinforce the importance of health care policy in the public mind (Hall, 1964, 1980).

Conceptually, health promotion has moved quickly. In the late 1970s and early '80s, health promotion was concerned with lifestyle change to prevent disease and disability. The beginnings of an infra-structure were being put in place to assist programs designed to support, educate, and involve people in the adoption of healthy behaviours. Moreover, politicians, professionals, and the public had a sense of health promotion that they understood and could act upon. It was narrow and it was middle-class, but it was concrete. Accompanying these profound, and needed, changes in health promotion has been a lack of understanding of exactly what health promotion is and what it does. It takes time to shift a paradigm; it takes even more time to demystify it and make it real to people.

Coming to grips with the federal role in health promotion means facing up to the national preoccupation with health care. In the 1950s and 1960s, and again in the 1980s, the federal government negotiated prepaid medical care with the provinces. Now in the 1990s, it is one of the flagships of national unity, and health care reform (often a euphemism for cost containment) is the principal concern of Ministers of Health. Is there a danger that the development and maintenance of health care has sapped almost every bit of energy, leaving little with which to pursue other promising health strategies?

In the final analysis, it can be safely concluded that the federal government has made a significant contribution both here and abroad to earning Canada its reputation as a leader in health promotion. Closer examination of the role played by the federal government reveals creativity and innovation with regard to conceptual and program development. What detracts somewhat from this picture is that in terms of policy, strategy, and resources, the necessary inroads have not been made for health promotion to be acknowledged alongside health care as an "equally important cornerstone" of our health system. But the pursuit remains worthwhile. The twentieth anniversary of the Lalonde Report is upon us — and this could be the opportunity for reflection, learning, and renewal.

References

Canada (1969). *Task force reports on the costs of health services in Canada.* Ottawa: Queen's Printer.

Canada (1973). *The community health centre in Canada.* Report of the Community Health Centre Project to the Health Ministers. Ottawa: Information Canada.

Canada (1982). *Report of the Ad Hoc Committee on National Health Strategies.* Ottawa: Health & Welfare Canada.

Canada (1989). *Evaluation of the health promotion program.* Unpublished report prepared by the Program Audit & Review Directorate, Health & Welfare Canada, November.

Canadian Public Health Association (1984). CPHA 1984 resolutions and motions. *CPHA Health Digest, 8*(4), 61.

Canadian Public Health Association (1986). *Establishing health objectives and strategies for Canada, phase 1.* Unpublished proposal prepared by the Working Group on Establishing Health Objectives and Strategies for Canada. Ottawa: Author.

Canadian Public Health Association (1987). CPHA 1987 position paper/Resolutions and motions. *CPHA Health Digest, 11*(3), 19.

Canadian Association of Social Workers (1988). A position paper on *Achieving health for all: A framework for health promotion.* Ottawa: Author, June.

Canadian Public Health Association (1992). *Caring about health.* Issue paper on federal/provincial/territorial arrangements for health policy. Ottawa: Author.

Charles, C., & Badgley, R. (1987). Health and inequality: Unresolved policy issues. In Yelaga, S. (ed.), *Canadian social policy* (pp. 47-64). Waterloo: Wilfrid Laurier University Press.

Cunningham, R. (1991). *Promoting better health in Canada and the USA: A political perspective.* Unpublished paper prepared for the Department of Politics, University of Glasgow.

Draper, R. (1982). *A Canadian perspective on health promotion.* Paper presented at the Joint Annual Meeting of the Society of Public Health Education and the Canadian Health Education Society. Montréal, November 13.

Draper, R. (1989). *The WHO strategy for health promotion.* Paper presented at the Community Participation and Empowerment Strategies in Health Promotion Workshop, Bielefeld, Germany, June 5-9.

Epp, J. (1986a). *Achieving health for all: A framework for health promotion.* Ottawa: Health & Welfare Canada.

Epp, J. (1986b). *An address to the Conference on Health Promotion and Aging,* Hamilton, May 1.

Epp, J. (1986c). *National strategies for health promotion.* An address to the 77th Annual Conference of the Canadian Public Health Association, Vancouver, June 17.

Farrant, W. (1991). *Building healthy public policy: The healthy communities movement as an entry point.* Paper prepared for the Social Planning & Research Council of British Columbia.

Hall, E. (1964). *Royal Commission on Health Services.* Vol. 1. Ottawa: Queen's Printer.

Hall, E. (1980). *Canada's national – provincial program for the 1980s.* Ottawa: Health & Welfare Canada.

Hancock, T. (1985). Beyond health care: From public health policy to healthy public policy. *Canadian Journal of Public Health,* 76(3) (Supp. 1), 9-11.

Kickbusch, I. (1989). Moving public health into the '90s. In P. Wolczuk, J. McDowell, & K. Ainslie (eds.), *Proceedings of the National Symposium on Health Promotion & Disease Prevention* (pp. 1-15). Victoria: Office of Health Promotion, British Columbia Ministry of Health.

Labonté, R., & Penfold, S. (1981). Canadian perspectives in health promotion: A critique. *Health Education,* 19(3), 4-9.

Laframboise, H. (1990). Non-participative policy development: The genesis of *A new perspective on the health of Canadians. Journal of Public Health Policy,* 11, 316-322.

Lalonde, M. (1974). *A new perspective on the health of Canadians.* Ottawa: Information Canada.

Lalonde, M. (1988). Health services managers or managers of health? *Journal of Health Administration Education,* 6(1), 71-83.

Last, J.M. (1986). Achieving health for all. *Canadian Journal of Public Health,* 77(6), 384-385.

Law, M. (1989a). *An address to the First National Conference on Chronic Diseases in Canada — Challenges and opportunities.* Toronto, April 21.

Law, M. (1989b). *Opening address at the 80th Annual Conference of the Canadian Public Health Association.* Winnipeg, June 20.

McEwen, E. (1979). Whatever happened to the Lalonde Report? *Canadian Journal of Public Health, 70* (1), 13-16.

McWhinney, I. (1987). Fine words, but will he deliver? *Journal of the Canadian Medical Association, 136,* 473-474.

O'Neill, M., & Pederson, A.P. (1992). Building a methods bridge between public policy analysis and healthy public policy. *Canadian Journal of Public Health, 83*(2) (Supp. 1), 25-35.

Ontario (1974). *Report of the Health Planning Task Force.* Toronto: Ministry of Health.

Ontario Public Health Association (1987). *A response to Achieving health for all: A framework for health promotion.* Toronto: Author, May.

Pinder, L. (1988). From *A New Perspective* to the *Framework. Health Promotion, An International Journal, 3*(2), 205-212.

Sgro, F. (1982). Perspectives of the past: Twenty years of health education in Canada. An interview with Michael Palko. *Health Education, 21*(1), 2-5.

Splane, R. (1987). Further reflections: 1975-1986. In Yelaja, S. (ed.), *Canadian social policy* (pp. 245-265) Waterloo: Wilfrid Laurier University Press.

Squires, B. (1987). Medical education to achieve health for all. *Journal of the Canadian Medical Association, 136,* 474-475.

World Health Organization (1984). *Concepts and principles of health promotion.* Copenhagen: WHO Regional Office for Europe.

Yelaja, S. (1987). Canadian social policy: Perspectives. In Yelaja, S. (ed.), *Canadian social policy* (pp. 1-26). Waterloo: Wilfrid Laurier University Press.

The Canadian Healthy Communities Project: Creating a Social Movement

Sharon Manson-Singer

The Context for Change

A variety of events and developments prepared the way for the Healthy Communities movement in Canada. These developments included important policy statements, ground-breaking conferences, and the adoption of Healthy Cities as a key health promotion project by the European Regional Office of the World Health Organization (WHO-Euro).

The landmark document released by Health and Welfare Canada, *A New Perspective on the Health of Canadians* (Lalonde, 1974), set forth the concept of the health field and expanded the health domain to include the environment, personal lifestyle, and human biology, in addition to the organization of health care. This document led the way for the world community. In 1977, the World Health Organization adopted the slogan Health for All by the Year 2000 (WHO, 1978, 1981) in an effort to promote health in all member nations. In that process, the fostering of health was integrated into social and economic development.

In Canada, the Beyond Health Care Conference (see "Beyond Health Care," 1985) was convened to explore the concept of "healthy public policy" as opposed to "public health" policy (Hancock, 1985). The four objectives of the conference included conceptualizing, raising awareness, lobbying, and developing proposals for action for improving healthy public policy. A workshop following the conference was specifically devoted to discussing the idea of a "healthy city."

The following year, WHO launched the Healthy Cities movement in Europe (WHO, 1988b). The city-based approach emphasized starting where people live and built upon the primary care model employed by WHO in which health care is provided by locally based practitioners. While the Healthy Cities movement in Europe was not concerned with the delivery of primary care per se, the influence of the primary care model was evident. For instance, health was conceptualized as more than medical treatment and hospitals; it was also about the creation and encouragement of healthy environments where citizens had adequate social, economic, and political resources to secure health and health care (WHO, 1988a).

The focus on cities was a reintroduction of the municipal role in public health. This role had been integral to mid-nineteenth century public health when improved sanitation, clean water, and better living conditions were regarded as key factors in reducing mortality rates. McKeown (1976), for example, in a historical review of the medical task, asserts that some of the greatest advances in reducing death rates came from precisely these public health measures.

Housing and health had been addressed by municipal and town planners in Canada for some time. Dr. Hodgetts, an Advisor on Public Health in the first decade of the twentieth century, was adamant that better housing conditions and attention to urban planning issues could do much to improve the quality of life by preventing disease. As a result, the Committee on Public Health of the Commission on Conservation took up issues related to urban planning (Commission of Conservation, 1911). These ideas permeated the public health profession and shifted the definition of health from a strictly individual focus to a broader one that included community issues. For example, in 1923, Dr. Winslow claimed that public health was the science and art of preventing disease and promoting health through organized efforts for sanitation, control of communicable diseases, education for personal hygiene, and the organization and delivery of medical and nursing services (in Brown, 1991) — all of which could be influenced at the municipal level to ameliorate the health status of urban residents.

In the mid-1980s, then, municipalities re-emerged as primary actors and stakeholders in the promotion of healthy cities. The Canadian Healthy Communities Project (CHCP) emerged from this background. A key factor in the initiation of the project in 1986 was the switch in name and emphasis from Healthy Cities to Healthy Communities. In Canada, there are many communities and relatively few major cities. Renaming the project ensured a broader base of participation and a uniquely Canadian approach to the Healthy Cities movement, because all sizes of community were welcome.

This chapter chronicles the development of the Canadian Healthy Communities Project from the point of view of one participant in the process. The author was a member of the Steering Committee for the Canadian Healthy Communities Project from 1989 to 1992. Hopefully, this chapter will spur a more comprehensive evaluation of the Healthy Communities movement in Canada.

Creation of the Canadian Healthy Communities Project

The idea for a Healthy Communities network was described at the Beyond Health Care Conference held in Toronto in 1984 ("Beyond Health Care," 1985) in a series of workshops devoted to Healthy Cities. Participants recommended, among other things, integrating urban planning with public health agencies, developing community support networks related to public health issues, recognizing the links between health and housing, and increased government funding for non-governmental organizations to achieve community care goals ("Beyond Health Care," 1985, pp. 76-78). The conference was an important milestone in creating a climate for change and a critical mass of people in the health care arena devoted to creating the changes required to achieve health for all.

The actual genesis of the CHCP followed some time later in 1986 when Trevor Hancock, a British-trained physician with Canadian experience as a medical officer of health, was funded by the federal government's Department of Health and Welfare to participate in the European-based WHO Healthy Cities movement (Kickbusch, 1985). Hancock was to inform Canada of lessons learned and to develop a proposal for Healthy Cities in Canada (T. Hancock, personal communication, January 1993).

Hancock (1992) describes the CHCP proposal as quintessentially Canadian in that it was housed in a tripartite coalition of non-governmental organizations (NGOs) including the Canadian Public Health Association (CPHA), the Federation of Canadian Municipalities (FCM) and the Canadian Institute of Planners (CIP). The federal government has consistently used non-governmental organizations to launch new programs in health and social services in the provinces. The involvement of NGOs is more than a philosophical stance in that the federal government of Canada has no jurisdiction over health or social services, nor over municipal governments, as defined by the Canadian constitution. The involvement of NGOs in developing or implementing federal initiatives has been a necessity, not necessarily a goal of inclusion. Using NGOs to spearhead federal programs in areas where it had no jurisdiction has allowed the federal government to pursue national goals without having to negotiate entry into the area with each one of the provinces and territories — a difficult, if not impossible, task given recent and past constitutional history.

The stage for NGO involvement was set in 1986 when leaders of the Canadian Public Health Association gathered with Jake Epp, then Minister of Health and Welfare, to discuss the concept of health promotion. In 1987, the Federation of Canadian Municipalities' fiftieth anniversary celebrations centred on the Role of Municipalities in Promoting Health. Jake Epp spoke again at that conference of the need for involvement at the local level in achieving the goal of health for all. The third partner to join was the Canadian Institute of Planners, a professional group whose members are influential within city and community administrations and who were willing to be enlisted in a new community development strategy designed to improve the health of communities. In the fall of 1987, a joint proposal was forwarded by these three organizations to the Health Promotion Directorate of Health and Welfare Canada and received funding for a three-year demonstration project starting in fiscal year 1988 (T. Hancock, personal communication, January 1993). The project was to be located at the Canadian Institute of Planners' office in Ottawa and managed by a Steering Committee with representatives of the three sponsoring organizations and members from across Canada. The involvement of municipal government as an explicit partner was what made the Canadian Healthy Communities Project unique and differentiated it from other community-level health promotion programs at the time. Thus, the Canadian Healthy Communities Project was formed and ready to be launched in every community in Canada. The next task was to empower the vehicle designed to carry forward the idea.

Expansion

The members of the CHCP Steering Committee were chosen for their political praxis and their knowledge of social action. Membership consisted of five Steering Committee members (Joan Anderson, a public health worker in Edmonton; Louise Gosselin, Directrice, Sherbrooke, une Ville en santé; Dan Leckie, Executive Assistant to Jack Layton, Councillor for the City of Toronto; Sharon Manson-Willms, Professor of Social Work, University of British Columbia; and John Savage, Mayor of Dartmouth, now Premier of Nova Scotia); representatives from each of the three sponsoring agencies (CPHA representative Réal Lacombe of Villes et Villages en santé in Québec City and, from time to time, Janet McLachlin from the staff of CPHA; FCM representative Pat Hunsley at the end of the project; CIP representative Dave Witty, Chair of the Steering Committee and President of CIP); staff (Susan Berlin, Co-ordinator of CHCP; Dave Sherwood, Executive Director of CIP); and Trevor Hancock, who was a consultant to the project.

Understanding how to start a *national* social movement in the abstract was slightly more difficult and demanded more time than each member had previously experienced in beginning a community development strategy. All Steering Committee members had to learn how to understand the concept from a variety of regional perspectives, in two languages, and from the structural constraints of the three sponsoring agencies who were funded by the federal government.

An information kit (CHCP, 1989), logo, and newsletter were all developed during the start-up period in 1989. Relationships between the Management Committee, which included the Co-ordinator of CHCP, the Executive Director of the Canadian Institute of Planners, and staff from the other sponsoring agencies, were negotiated and renegotiated. The policy-setting role of the Steering Committee was clarified and refined as well as the role of the management group, who were to implement the policy directives given by the Steering Committee.

The focus was to be clearly Canadian despite the pressure from international colleagues in the Healthy Cities movement, in Europe and Australia in particular, to become more involved at the international level. There was agreement that international involvement was to wait until at least the second year of the project in order to allow the CHCP to proceed as clearly Canadian. There was concern that, because the movement in Europe was ahead of the Canadian project, the problems extant there (Council of Europe et al., 1988) would dominate Canadian efforts rather than allow the emergence of a uniquely Canadian project.

Issues that were challenging the international movement were nevertheless also important in Canada. Who could become a Healthy Community? How would a Healthy Community be recognized? What were useful and appropriate Healthy Communities indicators (Hancock, 1986, 1989; Hayes & Manson-Willms, 1990; Manson-Willms & Gilbert, 1991; O'Neill, 1991; Stevenson & Burke, 1992)? These questions were to prove important in the development and downfall of the CHCP.

The membership model adopted by the CHCP was inclusive: there was to be no test or evaluation of a municipality seeking designation as a Healthy Community. All that was required was that a municipality initiate an interdisciplinary Healthy Communities committee and pass a council resolution to that effect. Membership in CHCP was fifty dollars, regardless of the size of the municipal budget. The low fee was a tangible demonstration of the CHCP commitment to inclusiveness and accessibility.

The Mission Statement for CHCP was created in the spring of 1989:

> to enhance the quality of life for all Canadians, by involving municipalities and their citizens in ensuring that health is a primary factor in political, social and economic decision-making (CHCP Steering Committee, Minutes, May 12, 1989).

This statement recognized a definition of health that was adopted by the CHCP which, in line with conceptual developments in health promotion, viewed health as a resource for everyday living and recognized the linkage between health and economic, social, and political factors affecting individuals in their communities. In the view of the Steering Committee, health should not be a separate item on the agenda of municipal council meetings. Instead, it should be used as a template for decision making in all regular council activities.

For example, engineering decisions regarding sewer lines would be reviewed from the perspective of health. If a municipality were considering the need for new sewers, the CHCP model would have the engineers and city planners review the decision from the perspective of a Healthy Communities initiative. They would question how expenditures on a sewer line might affect health and whether there were other ways to achieve an outcome that would create (more) health. For example, would it be more efficient and healthier to have the community move to four-gallon toilet tanks, a reduction of 20% on average from existing toilet tanks, as a possible solution rather than invest in an expanded sewer system? How would these expenditures on sewer lines affect health? Are there other ways to improve sanitation that also create health? Questions such as these would be asked to determine the best possible action at the local level.

The statement of intent by the Steering Committee was a further development of the Mission Statement, and was both ambitious and inclusive of many social goals. The Committee pledged to be

> at the forefront of major evolutionary change in the nature of social organizations, as they adapt to the challenges of political and social equity and ecological integrity (CHCP Steering Committee, Minutes, May 12, 1989).

The Steering Committee explicitly committed itself to creating a social movement with this statement. There was no doubt that the goal was idealistic, and yet there was a collective sense among Steering Committee members that moderating the intent would be dishonest when in fact what we were trying to create was a new paradigm for defining and understanding the effect on health of local actions by municipal governments. The goal was to introduce a new vocabulary into the everyday language of citizens. The development of the newsletter, the Mission Statement, and a defined model for working together within the first year of funding were important foundational blocks in the CHCP movement. The shared understanding of health as a resource for everyday living and a Mission Statement that reinforced that message were critical to the initiation of the CHCP movement.

Demonstration

The next phase was to deliver on the promise made in the first phase of CHCP to involve Canadian communities from every region in Canada and to assist them to become participating Healthy Communities. It became evident that communities were seeking instruction and legitimization for their efforts and activities designated as Healthy Communities projects. The open-ended nature of the definition of health and the instructions contained in the Mission Statement, which seemed more about the pursuit of ideals rather than concrete goals, created a need to illustrate the concept.

The seven newsletters (see CHCP, *Challenge Change*, 1989, '90, '92) contributed to a national understanding of the project by profiling successful community initiatives and provincial networks of Healthy Communities. Among the projects illustrated were those in Rouyn Noranda, Dartmouth, Sherbrooke, Toronto, Edmonton, and Saanich, B.C. The emerging networks of Healthy Communities were also described, such as Villes et Villages en santé in Québec; the Healthy Communities Network in B.C. under the auspices of the Office for Health Promotion and the B.C. Strengthening Healthy Communities Network; and the early stirrings of a network in Alberta under the Alberta Catalyst Group. (Ontario continues to work toward establishing a Healthy Communities network, while Manitoba established a Healthy Communities co-ordinator and Saskatchewan took a slightly different route, establishing networks around health promotion themes that included, but were not restricted to, Healthy Communities.) These profiles of individuals, programs, and network characteristics in the newsletter allowed nascent groups to compare themselves with established projects and to contact groups and key individuals across the country.

There was a continuous demand across the country for the CHCP Co-ordinator to perform motivational or inspirational workshops, which she did with missionary zeal. There was, however, a limit to the number of places she could be at one time and still manage the day-to-day affairs of the CHCP. Consequently, the Steering Committee determined that there was a need for more explicit materials to guide communities in establishing

Healthy Communities projects and for a process to follow in securing a council resolution to become a Healthy Community. The solution was to create a workbook, which was envisioned as a practical orientation to the concept and to the tasks that could be undertaken in the name of Healthy Communities (see CHCP, 1991). The workbook was conceived as an inter-active tool to assist community groups to move ahead. Part of the concept of the workbook was to build a series of case examples to demonstrate suc-cess in Healthy Communities projects — to build on the competence and strength of local communities in creating their own projects. These case studies would encourage local action and validate community efforts.

Like the demands of eager social change agents in potential communi-ties in the field, the workbook too was a demanding project. The desire to create a guide that was both inspirational and practical meant that it was not easily or quickly accomplished.

What became clear through experience was the need for face-to-face con-tact with eager communities and for community projects to have linkages with one another. The CHCP was, after all, a "people" project. A national con-ference was born out of this desire and need, the purpose of which was

> to facilitate local community action by education and promoting networking opportunities (CHCP Steering Committee, Minutes, October 19, 20, 1989).

The conference was a major demonstration vehicle for the CHCP con-cept. It brought together almost 300 community leaders — professionals from public health offices, city planners, community developers, grass-roots organizers, and some international figures in the Healthy Communities movement — and others who were anxious to see what Healthy Communities was all about.

The three-day Toward a Common Future Conference was held in October 1990 in Montréal to coincide with the city's 350th anniversary. It featured the best Healthy Communities examples that Canada could offer, and brought together people from all sectors around the Healthy Communities and Healthy Cities movements. The program (CHCP, 1990) included site visits to nearby communities to demonstrate the effectiveness of the Villes et Villages en santé initiative in Québec (see CHCP, 1990b). Unfortunately, part of the value of the visits may have been lost for Anglophone visitors, as the program was in French in the smaller communities. Nevertheless, the enthusiasm was contagious and there was a general feeling that the combination of discus-sion, demonstration, opportunities for networking, and great food made the conference memorable, if not outstanding.

The Conference was the beginning of the swan song for the CHCP. Several factors contributed to the demise of the national project, which began with the conference itself and then ricocheted into other key aspects of the CHCP.

Dissipation

There were several bullets that brought down the CHCP, some of which were deliberately aimed and others self-inflicted. The armoury may be categorized as inexperience, lack of resources, lack of definition of the concept of

Healthy Communities, a desire to "give the idea away," competition from other movements, and difficulties in the relationship with the funders.

Inexperience in conference planning allowed the budget for the Toward Our Common Future Conference to be underfunded, and outright miscalculation of expenditures resulted in overspending. The consequence was a deficit that accounted for the remainder of the final fiscal year budget for the project and thus effectively curtailed further meaningful activity on behalf of the CHCP Steering Committee.

Related to this lack of experience with conference planning was a lack of resources which led to underestimating the personnel time required to produce the handbook on how to create a Healthy Community. The workbook project, conceived in early 1989 and contracted out later in the same year, proved to be more consuming of the national office staff time than anticipated. The draft required revision, according to the subgroup of the Steering Committee charged with its review, and the necessary revisions were sacrificed to the more pressing demands of the national conference. Consequently, there was no tangible product to give to communities and funders until mid-1991, well past the original deadline. The draft, once produced, was further handicapped by a lack of adequate resources to fund printing and distribution.

The lack of a concrete product such as the workbook exemplified the difficulties experienced by the lack of definition of Healthy Communities generally. Noack and McQueen (1988) have argued that the field of health promotion — and by inference, we would say of Healthy Communities — requires greater definition before an understanding of measurement issues can be tackled. This argument has been repeated, expanded, and refined over the years. Some have suggested that the definition of a Healthy Community demands a subjective interpretation (Hunt, 1988). Others argue that the search for a standardized definition was doomed to failure, as the "one size fits all" schema (Hayes & Manson-Willms, 1990) would prove an impossible task as long as the local meaning of a Healthy Community was different in each municipality in Canada. In fact, some argued that Healthy Communities must be planned locally in order to demonstrate health (Boothroyd & Eberle, 1990). Healthy Communities, as understood at the local level, could therefore be interpreted as all things to all people, with the result that the concept came to be regarded as meaningless. In the worst scenario, this openness of definition bred cynicism about health promotion generally and Healthy Communities initiatives in particular (Hayes, 1993) instead of nurturing new ideas. Many saw the movement as a black hole of ambiguity and feared involvement lest they disappear into a great void.

For the Steering Committee, the lack of definition arose from an attempt to maintain an inclusive rather than exclusive stance with respect to efforts to improve health. The generosity of the definition had unanticipated consequences, however. Chief among these was the perception that the federal government was attempting to off-load health care costs onto municipalities rather than maintain social and economic structures that promote health, and that self-help and mutual aid, as defined in the health promotion framework (Epp, 1986), were code words for a "pull up your bootstraps" mentality that made health the responsibility of the individual citizen. "Municipalization" of health and social services was one of the terms coined to describe this process; it meant that municipalities were being saddled with responsibilities to respond to problems that were shaped by policies far from their control — whether provincial, federal, or global. The Steering Committee's perception was that there was a maldistribution of power to effect change at the local level, as the conditions negatively affecting health were caused far away from the local level and were immune to local control.

Another unanticipated outcome of the inclusive definition of Healthy Communities was the relationship between the medical profession and the municipal focus of the CHCP. There was fear that the established medical and health professions would take over Healthy Communities projects and reduce them to public health services rather than build on the new view of health as a resource for everyday living. Again, the Steering Committee conceived this as a maldistribution of power between consumers of health and others in the health care system.

The CHCP Steering Committee was clearly on the side of inclusiveness, and stated that the idea of Healthy Communities could not be "owned" and instead should be "given away" (CHCP Steering Committee, Minutes, December 4-5, 1989). Further, the Committee accepted the idea that power to create a healthy community could not be "given"; it could only be "taken" by the community to create its own desired outcome. The Steering Committee's goal of creating a social movement where the ideas could be adopted by local citizens who were empowered to act to improve the health of the community meant that it was necessary to maintain an open selection process. Susan Berlin described it as a "holistic social change process for long-term change" (Berlin, Lacombe, & Martin, 1992, p. 19).

This acceptance of locally defined projects resulted in some disagreement both within and outside the movement regarding the appropriateness of the strategy of inclusiveness. The open selection process meant that there could be no single definition of the vision of a Healthy Community; rather, each community had to define its own vision. But the concept of Healthy Communities was either a gift to be given away or it was a Trojan horse. Without control of the definition of Healthy Communities projects or of the local use of the ideas to create projects, the outcomes were liable to criticism, from friends and foes alike, as either not being true to the goals of the movement or being so broad that their attachment to the movement was negligible.

The fifth problem faced by the CHCP was competition from other social movements with similar goals. Both the environmental movement and the "safer cities" movement had goals congruent with those of the Healthy Communities movement. However, both had two factors that may have sustained the participation of local councils at the expense of the Healthy Communities movement. First, both movements engendered action by building on powerful psychological messages based on primal fears. Second, both had access to statistics that could be used as indicators of success or failure.

For example, pollution is defined in the environmental movement as the end of clean air and water, thus powerfully affecting every citizen's immediate lifestyle and that of their children. Images of choking citizens, burning waste, dirty water, smog-filled air and piles of untreated, stinking garbage evoke the kind of visceral response that motivates action. Furthermore, actions taken are measurable, and the indicators of success are demonstrable and accessible both to voters and municipal councillors. Measurable indicators — such as tonnage of recycled materials, or air and water quality — and fines for non-compliance with anti-pollution bylaws can be used for reporting successes and failures.

"Safer cities" appeals to people's fear of violence as a motivation to become involved. Personal experience with crime, either by oneself, family members, or neighbours, personalizes the issue. Citizens mobilize to protect their property and security, and assess success on the basis of reduced crime statistics, increased convictions, and restitution.

In both cases, even if the indicators can be seen as problematic on their own, they can easily be used as markers of change. Both movements can arouse fear for the future and motivate quick response. The thrust of the environmental and the safety and security movements is reminiscent of the words of Suzanne Keller (1968) in *The Urban Neighborhood* who said it was much easier to describe what one did not want in one's neighbourhood than to describe what one wanted. Yet, Healthy Communities is fundamentally a process of defining what is desirable and working collaboratively to achieve it.

Healthy Communities means *positive* change, creating health rather than eradicating disease. The images created are pleasant, wholesome, and comfortable. It does not promise greater wealth and better health for the *individuals* who participate in the movement; it promises better health and wealth distribution among all in the community, and may mean that some members of the community may have to relinquish some of their comfort to benefit others. The CHCP movement demanded that participants think about health in a collective sense, rather than in the sense of self-interest or self-protection. Head-to-head competition with other movements sharing similar goals was deemed by the Steering Committee to be inappropriate. Yet, Louise Gosselin (personal communication, April 24, 1993), a Steering Committee member, reflected that by ignoring other movements with common interests, the CHCP suffered.

There was a desire to support the development of these other movements, as their objectives were congruent with the CHCP's goals. Certainly, clean and safe environments are a part of a healthy community, and it was not feasible for CHCP to argue that the Healthy Communities movement should be bigger than either one of the other movements. Success from CHCP's perspective would be defined by both the competing movements' adoption of Healthy Communities as a way of framing their own actions to improve the environment and safety of communities. This non-traditional approach of collaborating rather than competing with other like-minded groups and of not asking for recognition or acknowledgement of shared goals was highlighted as a problem by Berlin, Lacombe, and Martin (1992) in their analysis of Healthy Communities and Canada's Green Plan. They stated that traditional measures of success were not those used by the Steering Committee. Working at the grass-roots level rather than focussing on major organizations, universities, or national associations has meant that the phrase "healthy communities" has become virtually a household word in Canada, and yet the project was not renewed for funding (Berlin, Lacombe, & Martin, 1992).

These factors had a cumulative effect on the relationship with the funding agency. In the world of federal government grants, resources were decreasing while demands for accountability were increasing. The CHCP posed particular difficulties for the federal bureaucrats, because officials could not easily point to a single product or comparable developments across the country as evidence of accomplishment to justify continued funding. The time frame for evaluating the success or failure of the CHCP was too short for the systemic change and community development process sought by the Steering Committee. The project was concerned with changing attitudes — the premise being that changed attitudes eventually result in changed behaviours. The desire to acknowledge the development of individual Healthy Communities as a credit to the communities themselves may have been a philosophically appropriate behaviour; however, it did not work pragmatically to demonstrate the accomplishments of the CHCP. In the end, money to further the goals of the project was unavailable, and the CHCP staff were laid off in the spring of 1991 after three years of funding.

The project continues to have an address in Ottawa at the Canadian Institute of Planners' office; the CIP Executive Director handles inquiries and responds to requests for existing information. There have been three subsequent meetings of some members of the CHCP Steering Committee, with some members of the Strengthening Healthy Communities Project (Canadian Healthy Communities Project & Strengthening Community Health, 1992a, 1992b & 1993) to maintain contact and discuss each other's projects. A joint proposal, *Action for Better Communities*, proposed a merger between the two groups, but was turned down by Health and Welfare Canada in 1991.

An Evaluation of the Movement

The CHCP launched an important idea in municipalities across Canada, namely, that decisions could be evaluated according to their effect on the health of local citizens. Further, the project argued that health was not only the purview of public health officers, but an issue that should and could be considered by all members of the city staff and citizens. It is as old as public health itself, although it is a new way of thinking about health from a community perspective, and asks citizens to look at their community and locally determine whether it is "healthy." Provincial governments in British Columbia, Ontario, Québec and to some extent in Alberta, Saskatchewan,

Manitoba, New Brunswick, and Nova Scotia, have promoted Healthy Communities programs through grants which have stimulated local action. The Yukon Territory is engaged in promoting Healthy Communities projects (see the chapter by Matthias later in this book for a more comprehensive discussion of health promotion in the Yukon).

Provincial governments in Canada have a direct fiscal incentive to attempt new models to achieve health for all as a result of the passage of the federal government's Government Expenditures Restraint Act (1991). The Act reduces the amount of federally shared money for actual expenditures in health care and demands that the provinces either find new sources of revenue by raising taxes or cut expenditures in order to fund health care. Alternative solutions that involve municipalities and citizens in programs of self-help and mutual aid to solve local problems, and at the same time promise to reduce expenditures, are thus welcome innovations to provincial Ministers of Health. Consequently, some have viewed the development of the Healthy Communities movement as an indicator of a neo-conservative agenda that seeks only to downshift the burden of the federal and provincial deficits to municipalities, thus making it the local taxpayers' role to pay for health and social problems.

This interpretation of the movement did not assist in the further development of Healthy Communities examples. Municipalities feared that becoming involved would mean that they would be forced to take responsibility for health without the requisite dollars to meet the demand effectively. Given that health care is viewed by Canadians as a fundamental right of citizenship, breaking this sacred trust by reducing access or service to health care is considered political suicide. Securing participation at the municipal level is made more difficult by existing fiscal realities, and yet at the same time offers the opportunity for developing exciting new models for change in the way in which we describe, define, and organize services to achieve health for all. John Savage, a former CHCP Steering Committee member, writing in 1993 as the leader of the Liberal Party in Nova Scotia but prior to his election as Premier, stated: "Wait and see what happens with Healthy Communities if we can do it provincewide, given the alarming lack of money in Nova Scotia" (J. Savage, personal communication, April 5, 1993).

Giving the idea of Healthy Communities away to any community that would take up the challenge meant that there was no national control over the idea nor over the effect of the gift on the recipients. Creating a social movement ensures that there will be change, and the desire was clearly to create change! As Higgins (1992) has noted, local action is limited in its ability to affect conditions that are created provincially or nationally. Her conclusion is that the movement is "strong in vision, but light in theory and power" (Higgins, 1992, p. 176).

The creation of the Canadian Healthy Communities Project has resulted in a self-sustaining universe of Healthy Communities activities across Canada. The pathways and relationships to larger social structures have yet to be determined, and the exact influence of the movement remains unknown. However, Healthy Communities has become a legitimate part of the health and municipal discourse in Canada and continues to be used to focus attention on health and social conditions that need to be changed at the local level. It will continue to evolve as is needed in the local communities, where the concept is now firmly rooted.

Acknowledgements

The author is grateful to David Witty, Janet McLachlin, John Savage, Louise Gosselin, and Trevor Hancock, former Steering Committee members of the Canadian Healthy Communities Project, for their helpful comments; and to Leanne Dospital for her very capable research assistance.

References

Berlin, S., Lacombe, R., & Martin, S. (1992, December). *Healthy communities and Canada's green plan.* Unpublished manuscript. Ottawa: Consulting & Audit Canada.

Beyond health care: Proceedings of a conference on healthy public policy. (1985). *Canadian Journal of Public Health, 76*(Supp.1).

Brown, M.C. (1991). *Health economics and policy.* Toronto: McClelland & Stewart.

Boothroyd, P., & Eberle, M. (1990). *Healthy communities: What they are, how they're made.* Vancouver: University of British Columbia, Centre for Human Settlements.

Canadian Healthy Communities Project (1989). *Challenge Change* (Newsletter), *1*(1, 2, 3).

Canadian Healthy Communities Project (1990). *Challenge Change* (Newsletter), *2*(1, 2, 3).

Canadian Healthy Communities Project (1992, Fall). *Challenge Change* (Newsletter), *3*(1).

Canadian Healthy Communities Project (1989). *Information kit.* Ottawa: Author.

Canadian Healthy Communities Project (1989; May 12, October 19 & 20, December 4 & 5). *Minutes of Steering Committee.* Ottawa: Author.

Canadian Healthy Communities Project (1990). *Toward a Common Future Conference Program,* Montréal, October 28-31.

Canadian Healthy Communities Project (1991). *Workbook*. Ottawa: Author.

Canadian Healthy Communities Project & Strengthening Community Health (1992a, February 1 & 2). *Minutes of Canadian Network Meeting*. Ottawa: Author.

Canadian Healthy Communities Project & Strengthening Community Health (1992b, October 16-18). *Minutes of Canadian Network Meeting*. Ottawa: Author.

Canadian Healthy Communities Project & Strengthening Community Health (1993, March 19-21). *Minutes of Canadian Network Meeting*. Ottawa: Author.

Commission on Conservation (1911). *Second annual report*. Montréal: John Lovell. Quoted in C.R. Smith & D. Witty (1970), *Conservation, resources and environment: An exposition and critical evaluation of the Commission of Conservation, Canada*. PLAN, *11*(1), 55-71.

Council of Europe, World Health Organization, and Stadt Wien (1988). *The Vienna recommendations on health in towns*. Vienna: Author.

Epp, J. (1986). *Achieving health for all: A framework for health promotion*. Ottawa: Ministry of Supply & Services.

Hancock, T. (1985). Health in transition. *Canadian Home Economics Journal, 35*(1), 11-13, 16.

Hancock, T. (1986). *Indicators of a healthy city: Issues and approaches*. Paper presented at the healthy cities Indicator Workshop, Barcelona, March 1987.

Hancock, T. (1989). *Information for health at the local level: Community stories and healthy city indicators*. Revised version of paper presented at the Health in Towns Conference, Vienna, May 1988.

Hancock, T. (1992). The development of the Healthy Cities project in Canada. In J. Ashton (ed.), *Healthy cities* (pp. 43-48). Buckingham: Open University Press.

Hayes, M.V. (1993). The rhetoric of health promotion and the realities of the Downtown Eastside: Breeding cynicism. In M.V. Hayes, L. Foster, & H. Foster, *Community environment and health*. Western Geographic Series #27. Victoria, B.C.: University of Victoria Press.

Hayes, M.V., & Manson Willms, S. (1990). Healthy community indicators: The perils of the search and the paucity of the find. *Health Promotion International, 5*(2), 161-166.

Higgins, J.W. (1992). The Healthy Community movement in Canada. In B. Wharf (ed.), *Communities and social policy in Canada* (pp. 152-180). Toronto: McClelland & Stewart.

Hunt, S.M. (1988). Subjective health indicators: The general health policy model. *Health Promotion (International)* 3, 23-34.

Keller, S. (1968). *The urban neighborhood: A sociological perspective.* New York: Random House.

Kickbusch, I. (1985). *Health promotion: The move towards a new public health.* Copenhagen: WHO Regional Office for Europe.

Lalonde, M. (1974). *A new perspective on the health of Canadians.* Ottawa: Ministry of Supply & Services.

Manson-Willms, S., & Gilbert, L. (1991). *Healthy community indicators: Lessons from the social indicator movement.* Vancouver: University of British Columbia, Centre for Human Settlements.

McKeown, T. (1976). *The role of medicine: Dream, mirage, or nemesis?* London: Nuffield Provincial Hospitals Trust.

Noack, H., & McQueen, D.V. (1988). Health promotion indicators: Current status, issues and problems. *Health Promotion (International),* 3, 117-125.

O'Neill, M. (1991). *Building bridges between knowledge and action: The Canadian process on healthy communities indicators.* Québec: Laval University.

Stevenson, H.M. & Burke, M. (1992). Bureaucratic logic in social movement clothing: The limits of health promotion research. *Canadian Journal of Public Health,* 83(Supp. 1), S47-S53.

World Health Organization (1978). *Alma Ata 1978: Primary Health Care.* Health For All Series, No.1. Geneva: Author.

World Health Organization (1981). *Global strategy for Health for All by the Year 2000.* Geneva: Author.

World Health Organization (1988a). *Five-year planning framework.* Healthy Cities Papers, No. 2. Copenhagen: Author.

World Health Organization (1988b). *Promoting health in the urban context.* Healthy Cities Papers, No.1. Copenhagen: Author.

Additional Readings

Canadian Healthy Communities Project (1988; November 22, December). *Minutes of Management Committee*. Ottawa: Author.

Canadian Healthy Communities Project (1989; January 12, February 15, April 15, May 16, August 22, September 26, November 23). *Minutes of Management Committee*. Ottawa: Author.

Canadian Healthy Communities Project (1990). *Information pamphlet*. Ottawa: Author.

Canadian Healthy Communities Project (1990; January 9, March 23, June 12, August 3, October 11). *Minutes of Management Committee*. Ottawa: Author.

Canadian Healthy Communities Project (1988, November 4). *Minutes of Steering Committee*. Ottawa: Author.

Canadian Healthy Communities Project (1989; January 9, 10). *Minutes of Steering Committee*. Ottawa: Author.

Canadian Healthy Communities Project (1990; March 31, April 1). *Minutes of Steering Committee*. Ottawa: Author.

World Health Organization (1988). *Framework for health promotion research and the role of the network of WHO collaborating centres for health promotion research*. Report of a Consultation on the Co-ordination of Research in Health Promotion. Copenhagen: Author.

World Health Organization (1988). *A guide to assessing healthy cities*. WHO Healthy Cities Papers, No. 3. Copenhagen: Author.

World Health Organization (1989). *The new public health in an urban context*. WHO Healthy Cities Papers, No. 4. Copenhagen: Author.

The Strengthening Community Health Program: Lessons for Community Development

Ken Hoffman

The Canadian Public Health Association's program, Strengthening Community Health (SCHP), was a national initiative to assist communities in the process of defining the health issues that affect them most directly, and in organizing to take action on those issues.

SCHP began as a simple concept — that strengthening community health means strengthening communities — and for a three-year period, the participants in the program worked to turn that concept into reality in innovative and creative ways across the country.

What Is "Strengthening Community Health"?

Strengthening community health is a group of seniors in Lambton County in Ontario who organized to conduct their own study of how housing and transportation issues affected them, and what action they could take to address these issues.

Strengthening community health is the Nova Scotia Health Action Coalition, which brought together representatives from over 20 groups and organizations to ensure that citizens have an effective role in the provincial health planning process.

Strengthening community health is the British Columbia Healthy Communities Network, linking together over 80 communities across the province to share information and take joint action.

Strengthening community health is an initiative in which Newfoundland communities learned to use video as a tool to stimulate discussion and mobilization regarding local health concerns.

These and many other initiatives across Canada illustrate what "strengthening community health" meant, at the local level, when it was put into practice through SCHP.

Together with the Canadian Healthy Communities Project, SCHP occupied a unique place in the development of health promotion in Canada. For the first time, it emphasized strengthening the way communities work, as opposed to strengthening community health services, in order to enhance the health of communities. SCHP was a national initiative that served as a catalyst for a wide range of activities and initiatives at the provincial and local levels. It brought groups and organizations that had never worked together before into partnership in a common agenda of strengthening communities. It created a forum where participants from across the country supported, strengthened, and challenged each other through sharing their experiences.

SCHP was, in many ways, a prototype. It was an attempt to integrate a health promotion approach into the *process* of strengthening community health, rather than simply viewing health promotion as an outcome. The experience of SCHP provides useful lessons to government policy makers, public health professionals, and members of community organizations who wish to establish a process for working together on issues of common interest.

This chapter outlines the evolution of SCHP, and describes examples of some of its achievements in different provinces. The way in which SCHP developed, and how it operated, is just as important as its specific achievements at the community level. The chapter closes with a reflection on the contribution of SCHP in the areas of healthy public policy, community development, public health, and the Healthy Communities Project.

Background

The Strenghtening Community Health Program had its roots in the *Ottawa Charter for Health Promotion* (WHO, 1986; hereafter, the Ottawa Charter) and *Achieving Health for All: A Framework for Health Promotion* (Epp, 1986; hereafter, the Framework), both released in the same year. The Ottawa Charter provided an internationally recognized definition and elaboration of the elements of health promotion. The Framework was a policy document issued by Health and Welfare Canada that described three key strategies for addressing the main health challenges facing Canadians: (1) fostering public participation, (2) strengthening community health services, and (3) co-ordinating healthy public policy.

To help translate the policy directives of the Framework into action, Health and Welfare Canada funded the Canadian Public Health Association (CPHA) to co-ordinate a series of cross-Canada consultations on strengthening community health services in 1987-88. The most important conclusion to emerge from this process was the following:

> The consultation workshops were set up to identify issues, needs and gaps in community health services, and strategies to strengthen them. What emerged in the workshops, however, was the realization that one couldn't talk about community health services without defining what community health is.

Furthermore, as we examined the interaction between community and health, we realized that in order to strengthen community health we were talking about strengthening the community itself. (Siler-Wells, 1988, p. 3.)

The participants at the consultations identified five cornerstones that would form the basis for strengthening community health in Canada:

• Create a policy focus and orientation that supports increased access to health (to shift the focus of health policy from sickness treatment towards a focus on the determinants of health);

• Mobilize political and community will (to assume greater ownership and control at the community level over the decisions affecting community health and community health services);

• Support new partnerships (to encourage consumers to increase their self-determination and empowerment, and to assist the shift in the role of the professional from that of "expert" to that of enabler of community and individual health actions);

• Adopt a "co-active" approach (to develop better ways of working together in the process of making community health decisions, choosing priorities, and providing services. These strategies involve better co-operation, collaboration and co-ordination between all the players involved);

• Nurture our strengths (to recognize and build on the existing resources in communities).

The report of the consultations (Siler-Wells, 1988) included recommendations to government, as well as to the voluntary and private sectors, on ways to incorporate the principles of health promotion and healthy public policy into programs, policies, and services. These recommendations formed the foundation on which SCHP was built.

Development of SCHP: Putting the Idea into Practice

Establishment of the Program

In 1988, CPHA received approximately one million dollars from the Health Promotion Contributions Program of the Health Promotion Directorate of Health and Welfare Canada to operate SCHP for a three-year period.

The operational structure to support SCHP consisted of three main elements:

• A small Community Health Secretariat, within the national office of CPHA, to provide overall administration and co-ordination for SCHP and to facilitate networking and communication;

• A program Advisory Committee to provide advice to the CPHA Board and the Community Health Secretariat; and

• Provincial and territorial Steering Committees to co-ordinate and to support action at the local and provincial levels.

The role played by each of these program elements evolved over the course of SCHP.

Guiding Principles

A major challenge faced by the participants in SCHP was to define what was meant by "strengthening community health." The first step in that process was to describe a healthy community. The Secretariat and the Advisory Committee for SCHP developed three guiding principles as a way of initiating discussion about the process of strengthening communities (Bhatti, 1989, p. 6):

- Healthy communities value the dignity and worth of every member. Each person is a resource who can make a significant contribution to the community.
- Healthy communities are health enhancing. They provide opportunities for individuals to protect and to promote their well-being. Such communities ensure access for all members to the basic necessities of life. Supports are made available to help individuals cope with major life events. Investments in human resources, "people places," and events are considered a priority.
- Healthy communities are ones in which members feel integrated, and over which they feel they have control. Members have a sense of belonging. Participation in decision making and in the planning of community activities and services is encouraged. Healthy communities have the capacity to provide their members with the skills and knowledge required for active and informed participation.

Provincial and Territorial Workshops and Steering Committees

The provincial and territorial Public Health Associations acted as catalysts in starting the process of strengthening community health. They organized workshops that brought together a wide variety of organizations to discuss what strengthening community health might mean for that province or territory. The participants at each workshop interpreted the guiding principles in light of issues affecting their communities at that time. They identified priority issues and discussed how they might work together to put the concept of strengthening community health into action.

Most provinces and territories developed a Steering Committee to co-ordinate their activities. These committees proved to be pivotal to the evolution of SCHP. Their members came from organizations that had a broad interest in improving community health. Groups that were involved included university extension departments, social planning councils, various health-related associations (e.g., nurses' and hospital associations), the regional offices of the federal Health Promotion Directorate, some provincial health departments, and organizations that focussed on such specific issues as community mental health, women's health, and the environment. As there were no standard criteria for membership in the Steering Committees, their composition reflected local priorities and interests, and differed from province to province.

Each Steering Committee prepared a yearly action plan for its area. The National Secretariat provided each Steering Committee with seed funds to carry out these activities. Funding was allocated to each province on a roughly equal basis, ranging from nine to thirteen thousand dollars per year for the three years of the project. The Steering Committees developed their activities with considerable independence. As no two provinces shared the same conditions, it was important that each committee develop a strategy to address its needs and utilize its strengths to the fullest extent possible. The emphasis in this process was to strengthen the Steering Committees, enabling them to test their ideas in the community and to build partnerships in some common projects.

The Steering Committees developed a wide range of activities during their first year of operation, including the following three examples:

- Newfoundland's priority was to stimulate broad interest and discussion about the concept of Healthy Communities. The Steering Committee oversaw the development of a video highlighting examples of initiatives from five different communities across the province.
- In Québec, the Steering Committee developed an information package and a consultation process to stimulate discussion among community-based organizations regarding the anticipated impact of reforms to the health and social services system.
- British Columbia combined the Strengthening Community Health and the Healthy Communities initiatives under a single committee, and organized a series of regional workshops to help launch the process throughout the province.

Through such activities, the Steering Committees learned what strengthening community health meant in a practical sense, as well as the challenges involved in working together in broad, diverse coalitions.

Mission Statement

After one year of practical experience in their provincial and territorial projects, representatives of the Steering Committees, the Secretariat, and SCHP's Advisory Committee articulated their vision for SCHP through the following Mission Statement and Areas of Emphasis:

> To contribute to the development of healthy communities by recognizing and encouraging community identification of health issues and by supporting and linking co-operative efforts to take action. (Strengthening Community Health Program, 1989, p. 1)

The areas of emphasis were:

- Co-action (collaborative action to foster collaboration among groups and organizations in strengthening community health);
- A community agenda for health (to stimulate public and political action based on a broad concept of health);
- Community control (to promote collective action for community control over decisions that affect health).

The development of the Mission Statement and the Areas of Emphasis was important in the evolution of SCHP because it helped clarify the concept of strengthening community health and assisted the national and provincial/territorial groups in focussing their activities.

Further Program Activities

In the two years that followed, the Steering Committees worked at three main areas. First, they consolidated and strengthened themselves as working groups. Given the diverse experiences of the committee members and the dynamic nature of SCHP, time was needed to develop a common understanding of the program and to learn how to make decisions together.

Second, the Steering Committees and the Secretariat continued to develop new initiatives, stimulated by activities occurring in other parts of the country. For example, the success of the Newfoundland video spawned similar initiatives in at least three other provinces. The sharing of information and experiences across the country was a major function of the Secretariat, and this was accomplished through three main methods: (1) the production of a regular newsletter (appropriately titled *The Multiplier*), (2) a series of cross-Canada audio teleconferences, and (3) an Annual Program Consultation. Of these three, probably the most significant were the Annual Consultations, where participants from each province and territory met with the national Program Advisory Committee and the Secretariat staff to exchange information and to plan for the future. The Consultations were important, not only for sharing information, but for decision making. The Steering Committee representatives from the provinces and territories assumed more of the responsibility for setting direction and policy for SCHP with each of the three successive Annual Consultations. These meetings were also important in democratizing the program, and in moving it closer to the participatory approach that it was promoting at the community level.

Third, the committees explored other sources of funding for their activities, building on the seed funding from SCHP. Some committees were successful in obtaining support in cash or in kind from their own members, from provincial governments, and from private sources such as community businesses. These new resources allowed the committees to expand their activities and to broaden their base of support.

Program Evaluation

Although SCHP, as originally funded, did not include a budget for program evaluation, the Secretariat, the Program Advisory Committee, and Health and Welfare Canada felt that it should be undertaken. A consultant was hired to conduct an external evaluation of SCHP at the national level. At the provincial and territorial levels, both the Secretariat and the Steering Committees felt strongly that, given the nature of the program, a participatory evaluation process was appropriate.

Each Steering Committee conducted its own self-evaluation, using a methodology based on that developed by the Women's Research Centre (Ellis, Reid, & Barnsley, 1990). These evaluations provided valuable insights into how SCHP was perceived by the people who had invested many volunteer hours to translate the ideas of strengthening community health into action.

Merging of Strengthening Community Health and Healthy Communities

Funding for SCHP and the Canadian Healthy Communities Project ended at the close of March, 1991, and the SCHP Secretariat concluded its operations. A proposal to bring SCHP and the Canadian Healthy Communities Project together and to continue funding for the joint initiative was rejected by the federal government, which cited budget cutbacks.

Despite the lack of federal funding and a National Secretariat, SCHP continues to have a presence, in some form, in at least six provinces. In most cases, SCHP and the Healthy Communities initiatives have joined together at the provincial level. In Nova Scotia and Québec, however, these two initiatives have maintained separate identities for historical reasons.

In Québec, the focus of SCHP was primarily on the strengthening of community-based health and social services organizations in the face of a major reorganization of the health system in that province. Although the activities of the project in Québec expanded beyond this initial focus, the key participants were the members of the provincial bodies representing these organizations. Therefore, the thrust of this group was distinct from that of Villes et Villages en santé (the Québec version of the Healthy Communities project), which was developed from a municipal base. The two projects agreed that although their activities were often complementary, they were not common enough to warrant a merger.

Nova Scotia was a different situation. In this case, because Healthy Communities caught on only in Dartmouth, there was really no provincial presence for this initiative. In contrast, SCHP developed (and continues to involve) a broad provincial base of groups and organizations interested in supporting active citizen participation in decision making on health issues. There was no real consideration of a merger of the two projects, as there was really only a single, active provincial network.

At the national level, key representatives from both SCHP and the Healthy Communities initiatives have developed a network for information sharing and consultation. The Canadian Institute of Planners has contributed considerable time and effort to the co-ordination of this network, and the federal government has funded meetings and conference calls. The relationship between Healthy Communities and SCHP is discussed further in the section later in this chapter headed Reflections on the Program.

Program Achievements

The major achievement of SCHP was its role as a catalyst. Under SCHP, a wide variety of agencies and organizations came together, in many cases for the first time, to identify issues and to implement concrete strategies designed to strengthen the health of their communities. SCHP spawned a rich variety of initiatives and activities, and enabled people to form new partnerships, some of which have continued long after the formal program has ended.

The main achievements of SCHP can be related to its three Areas of Emphasis:

Collaborative Action

In virtually every province and territory, SCHP brought together groups and organizations that had never worked together before, under the broad mandate of strengthening community health. They had to define what strengthening community health meant for them, develop a common agenda, and find a way of working together. The partnerships varied from one part of the country to another.

In Nova Scotia, an important partnership was formed between the extension departments of St. Francis Xavier University and Henson College to organize training in community development.

In British Columbia, the Steering Committee for the B.C. Healthy Communities Network included the B.C. Public Health Association, the Social Planning and Research Council, the B.C. Nurses' Association, and the B.C. Hospital Association. Not only did they jointly organize workshops, but they used their combined influence to put community health issues on the province's health reform agenda.

In Québec, the proposed reform of the health and social services system brought together many community-based organizations that were concerned about how the reforms might affect them. The Québec Steering Committee included representatives from the Québec Public Health Association, as well as groups representing women's centres, cultural communities, community mental health, retired and semi-retired persons, and community employment services, with the additional support of the regional office of the Health Promotion Directorate and the provincial Ministry of Health and Social Services. The focus of SCHP in that province was to strengthen the community-based organizations so that they could work more effectively with their communities, and also be more effective in dealing with government.

Seven provincial or territorial governments became important partners with the Steering Committees, making significant contributions in cash or in kind. This demonstrated that the SCHP initiatives had achieved a measure of credibility at the political and bureaucratic level. It also showed that a nationally co-ordinated process could successfully address provincial and territorial concerns, if the agenda could be set at the local level.

The collaborative work of the Steering Committees generated other important benefits, including increased access to resources to support joint initiatives. For example, participating organizations volunteered time and office space, contributed to telephone and mailing costs and, in some cases, provided funding. The Steering Committees were able to use the seed funds they received from SCHP to leverage resources effectively from other sources. In the national evaluation of SCHP, 77% of the respondents estimated the value of in-kind contributions to the program to be equal to, or greater than, the seed funding received.

A Community Agenda for Health

Many innovative strategies were used to place a broad approach to community health on the public and political agendas. In Nova Scotia, Québec, Alberta, and British Columbia, the development of SCHP coincided with major reviews of the health care system. The Steering Committees in these provinces used these reviews as an occasion to speak about the need to strengthen and support the community in order to make real and sustained improvements to community health.

In British Columbia, the members of the B.C. Healthy Communities Network convinced the provincial Royal Commission on Health Care and Costs to focus on community health issues for an entire day. The Network organized a comprehensive presentation that included a discussion on the determinants of health, and the links between health and the social environment. There was also a discussion on the importance of self-help and citizen control as part of an overall strategy to improve the health of communities. The presentations stimulated a good deal of discussion among Commission members, and received considerable media coverage.

In Nova Scotia, SCHP was a catalyst in the development of a Health Action Coalition of individuals from across the province. They came together to monitor the provincial health planning process that was being conducted at that time. The Coalition wanted to ensure that there would be adequate citizen participation at the planning, implementation, and evaluation stages. It organized a series of forums across the province to discuss the proposed changes to the health system. The Coalition succeeded in generating considerable public interest and participation, and secured the involvement of several senior politicians.

Other provinces used a variety of techniques to stimulate broader discussion of a "healthy community" approach. The most widely used example was the Newfoundland video, which featured citizens from five communities talking about what made their communities "healthy." The video was a useful way to stimulate discussion about how the idea of healthy communities could be translated into action. It spawned similar projects in several other provinces. It also serves as a good example of how a low-budget video can serve as a tool to explain and stimulate interest in a subject that was considered abstract and difficult to understand.

Community Control

Several initiatives were directed towards strengthening the capacity of community members to define, organize, and take action on health issues of concern to them. The Seniors Strengthening Community Health Project, in Lambton County in southwestern Ontario, was one of these. Local seniors representing 60 different groups came together, with the support of the local health unit, to explore ways in which senior citizens could play active and contributing roles in the health of their community. The seniors identified the five issues that they considered to be most important for them: housing, transportation, loneliness, health, and involvement. In the area of housing and transportation, the seniors reached an agreement with Central Mortgage and Housing Corporation (CMHC) to participate in a pilot study to identify the needs and services in the county. Although the methodology for the study was developed by CMHC, the seniors implemented the study themselves. Approximately 100 seniors were involved in co-ordinating and administering a survey to a representative sample of seniors throughout the county. These volunteers promoted the survey, answered telephones, collected completed questionnaires, and recruited support from local industry to cover the costs of printing, advertisement, computer rentals, and clerical support. They hired two masters-level students in gerontology to assist in the analysis of the data. The seniors prepared a report which they presented to the 60 seniors' groups and to various levels of government. The most important part of this process was that the seniors were in control at all times: *they* defined their needs, *they* decided how the survey would take place, and *they* determined how the results would be used. The process had a positive effect on the seniors' community in Lambton County. To quote Stewart Duncan, Chair of the Housing and Transportation Committee, "It makes a difference having seniors co-ordinating the project because seniors in the community know the information will be used for their benefit. It's seniors working for seniors" (Hoffman, 1991, p. 4).

In Nova Scotia, emphasis was placed on leadership development and how community health workers could support citizens in achieving greater control over decision making regarding health. Several workshops brought community health workers and leaders of community initiatives together to discuss how this could be done.

Manitoba's Steering Committee organized a Community Exchange Day in a lower-income area of Winnipeg. The event was held in a building that was a focal point for the local community. More than 120 community members participated and took advantage of the opportunity to meet with people who provided health and community services in the area. A popular education approach was used to help the participants from the community realize that they already had many of the skills necessary to take action on community issues. The "exchange" occurred when community members had a chance to discuss their issues and concerns with the groups and organizations in attendance. The event was a useful one for the organizations as well, since they learned how they could work together more effectively in the community.

A further example of community control was the way in which the participants in the program, especially the members of the Steering Committees, began to exercise greater control over, and to feel greater ownership for, SCHP. Over time, they demanded and received a greater voice in the direction and operating style of SCHP, within the limits established by CPHA. While the first Annual Program Consultation saw relatively limited participation and discussion, by the third Consultation the participants had assumed ownership for SCHP. The program had been successful in strengthening its own community in some ways.

Reflections on the Program

Was SCHP a success? What kind of impact did it have on health promotion in Canada? What can be learned from the experience of SCHP? It is difficult to answer these questions conclusively or objectively. Nevertheless, it might be useful to assess the contribution of SCHP in the following areas: (1) SCHP as an instrument of healthy public policy, (2) SCHP as a national initiative in health promotion and community development, (3) the effect of SCHP on the public health community, and (4) the relationship between SCHP and the Healthy Communities Project.

SCHP as an Instrument of Healthy Public Policy

Although it was by no means the largest national initiative in health promotion ever undertaken in Canada, the way in which SCHP was implemented makes it particularly interesting from a public policy perspective. By funding SCHP through a non-governmental organization (CPHA), the government assumed the role of catalyst rather than program manager. CPHA approached the implementation of SCHP in a similar catalytic fashion. Unlike many government initiatives, SCHP did not approach communities with a predetermined agenda. Instead, it supported a process where the provincial and territorial Steering Committees identified and addressed the issues that were most relevant to them, under the broad mandate of strengthening community health. Perhaps the best proof of the effectiveness of this approach is the fact that two years after the closure of the national program, SCHP or its successors are still active in at least six provinces.

SCHP was a successful strategy for mobilizing significant community resources across the country in order to address broad issues affecting community health at a reasonable cost. It was also effective in shifting the agenda from improving the services being delivered to communities, to strengthening the communities themselves. However, three years was not long enough for this type of process to become self-sustaining. If governments wish to assist communities to develop new capacities and greater independence, they must be prepared to commit themselves for at least five years in order to give the initiatives a chance to take root.

It is unfortunate that the government that introduced the Framework, and funded both SCHP and the Healthy Communities Project, did not seem to appreciate how successful these initiatives were. One of the features that had contributed to the success of SCHP — the fact that it was perceived by its participants as being "their" program rather than a federal government initiative — may have made it vulnerable politically. The federal government could not easily claim credit for the success of SCHP, since putting a federal stamp on the program would have made it difficult to achieve the type of collaboration that occurred at the community and provincial levels.

Health promotion in general, and initiatives like SCHP in particular, present a new challenge to governments. Community groups and organizations are more willing to come together when they can establish their own priorities, but most government initiatives come to the community with a pre-determined agenda. Governments must be prepared to renounce their ownership of these initiatives and find satisfaction in acting as a catalyst in a community process. But this may be seen as a threat to both the political and the bureaucratic systems that exist today, since neither system rewards this type of behaviour. However, as governments are forced to re-examine the way they work in light of the current pressure for deficit reduction, they may be more inclined to consider this catalytic approach to working with communities to be a legitimate and cost-effective strategy.

SCHP and Community Development

One of the most significant features of SCHP was the way in which the program's philosophy evolved over time. Rothman (1974) identifies three main approaches to community work which, while theoretically distinct, are not mutually exclusive in practice:

- Community development, where the focus is on the process of empowering communities and citizens to increase control over and to improve their health;
- Social planning, where the focus is more on the gathering and analysis of information on health issues by formal agencies and organizations; and
- Social action, where the focus is on mobilizing people to advocate for a shift in power relationships and resources, as well as basic institutional change.

The proposal that led to the funding of SCHP was based on a social-planning approach, with a focus on community health organizations. However, as SCHP was implemented, this approach shifted away from social planning and towards community development, with some social action. This shift in emphasis is important in understanding what happened in SCHP. One part of the community development process took place in communities themselves, through initiatives that strengthened community control. An equally important part happened when the participants in SCHP took more ownership and control over the initiative.

Program participants pushed the Secretariat and CPHA to practise the community development philosophy espoused by SCHP. This desire to assume greater control over the program was a challenge to both Health and Welfare Canada as the funder, and to CPHA as the organization responsible for administration of SCHP. It was also an issue for the provincial and territorial Public Health Associations, as the main catalysts for the process in each province. These organizations were more accustomed to administering programs in a hierarchical fashion, where they were in control and assumed complete responsibility for the operation of the program. SCHP called for a completely new model, in which participants asked for (and received) much greater information about how the program was managed, and actively participated in setting the directions for it.

The evolution of SCHP towards greater control by its participants raised a number of issues. As the program was not initially designed as a community development initiative, most of its resources were concentrated in the central CPHA office. This was a source of contention for SCHP participants in the provinces and territories who felt that they were underresourced. Of a total program budget of one million dollars, approximately one-third went directly to the provincial and territorial Steering Committees to support their activities, approximately one-third to support the operation of the Secretariat, and one-third was spent on program support functions such as the newsletter and the Annual Program Consultations. What is the optimal balance needed to stimulate and support program activities in the field (in this case, across the country), while maintaining some national identity, focus, and contact? What should be the role of a central office or Secretariat in a program based on community development principles — catalyst, co-ordinator, or clearinghouse?

The increasing desire of SCHP participants to set their own course inevitably placed some strain on the relationship between SCHP and CPHA. The role of CPHA as a catalyst in helping the program to get started cannot be underestimated. If it had not been for the support of the CPHA and its willingness to act as a program sponsor, it is likely that SCHP would never have been implemented. Nevertheless, as SCHP matured, it became apparent that the vision of its participants was diverging from that of its sponsor. The main issue was how much independence SCHP participants could have in setting the direction and operation of the program while it remained a part of CPHA.

The relationship between the Steering Committees and their provincial and territorial Public Health Associations was also strained in some parts of the country. In those provinces where the Public Health Association was prepared to participate as an equal member of the Steering Committee, SCHP generally thrived. In provinces where the Public Health Association tried to maintain tight control over the initiative, true partnerships did not develop, and SCHP never really prospered.

The experience of SCHP helped to highlight some issues for organizations (provincial or national) that wish to support initiatives based on a community development approach: Are they prepared to work as catalysts? Are they ready to give up control over the initiative, when necessary? Can they work as equal partners in a coalition with other organizations and with community members?

SCHP and Public Health

As mentioned in the previous section of this chapter, SCHP posed major challenges for some public health associations. At the heart of these challenges was the readiness of public health units to move from a traditional position of "control" over the field of community health to become catalysts for change in communities. Many of the same issues were faced by individual public health workers. Trained to be "experts" (primarily nurses and physicians), and working within hierarchical organizations (public health units headed by physicians), many public health professionals found it difficult to shift their own thinking from how to deliver a better service to how to support a community-driven process, or how to work effectively as a member of a coalition.

Workshops and meetings were held in various provinces to explore this issue, and to provide training to front-line staff in health units, the better to understand a community development approach. However, it soon became evident that this training had a limited impact. When these people returned to their health units and attempted to implement this approach, they were often hindered by their managers, who were still using a service-oriented approach. Making the transition in health units from strengthening community health services to strengthening the community will require a major shift in attitude at every level of the organization. Through SCHP, there are now good examples of how some community health organizations have been able to support this shift. These should be useful as a guide for other health units attempting to move in this direction.

Relationship with the Healthy Communities Project

It was unfortunate that both SCHP and the Canadian Healthy Communities Project were founded at the same time, and as separate initiatives. Although there was close collaboration between the programs from their inception, a great deal of energy was spent in discussing what made them different from each another. The focus of Healthy Communities was on the planning and policy-making process of municipal governments. This orientation was defined from the start of the program, and was consistent across the country. SCHP, on the other hand, concentrated more on issues of citizen participation and community control, at the provincial and local levels. The character and focus of SCHP developed over time. It had a different look and feel in each province, depending on local priorities and the membership of each Steering Committee. This made SCHP harder to describe and harder to characterize than the Healthy Communities initiative.

Although the work of the two programs was complementary, the existence of separate national offices, newsletters, and operational styles was confusing, and sent mixed messages to the public. Alberta and B.C. decided not to spend time organizing separate initiatives, and combined SCHP and Healthy Communities from the start. In other provinces, the initiatives merged gradually, encouraged by the merging at the national level. In Québec and Nova Scotia, the two initiatives remained separate.

At the national level, the two networks that existed under SCHP and Healthy Communities have merged, and this development has helped to preserve a national identity for both processes, despite the loss of funding from the federal government. Because of the clearer identity of Healthy Communities, both in Canada and around the world, this new national network has tended to adopt the Healthy Communities focus on healthy public policy at the municipal level. The SCHP experience, however, has made Healthy Communities in Canada look significantly different than it does in other countries. In particular, the Canadian initiative places strong emphasis on community participation in and community control over the process. Many of the European and American initiatives, on the other hand, tend to emphasize the role of professionals in urban planning and public health. As Healthy Communities continues to grow and to flourish across Canada and around the world, perhaps one of the legacies of SCHP will be to legitimize and to strengthen the role of community members in this major health promotion initiative.

Conclusion

The most remarkable thing about SCHP is that over two years after the conclusion of the national program, its spirit remains very much alive across the country. This is a tribute to the people who had the vision to give meaning to the concept of strengthening community health in their own provinces, territories, and communities, and their commitment to keep it alive. This is the greatest measure of success of any initiative, and an indication that strengthening community health was more than just another program, in the usual sense of the word.

SCHP and Healthy Communities represent a fundamentally different way of working with communities — a process based on social transformation rather than social services. Ferguson (1980, p. 205) made these observations about social transformation in *The Aquarian Conspiracy*:

> *At first glance, social transformation seems a foolhardy, even perilous ambition for any group to undertake. There is a necessary and critical chain of events. First, profound change in individuals who care deeply about social change. . . . They must then devise ways to foster paradigm shifts in others; they must perturb, awaken and recruit. This aligned minority, knowing that changes of heart and not rational argument alone will sway people, must find ways of relating to others at the most human and immediate level.*
>
> *If they are not to fall into the old traps (power plays, desperate compromises, self-aggrandizement), they must live by their principles. Knowing that means must be as honourable as ends, they go into political battle stripped of conventional political weapons. They must discover new strategies and new well-springs of power.*
>
> *And this aligned, principled, sophisticated, committed and creative minority must also be irrepressible. It must make waves large enough to set off a reordering of the whole system. . . . Difficult? Impossible? Seen another way, the process cannot fail because it is also the goal.*

References

Bhatti, T. (1989). *Strengthening community health program: Operational framework.* Ottawa: Canadian Public Health Association, April.

Ellis, D., Reid, G., & Barnsley, J. (1990). *Keeping on track: An evaluation guide for community groups.* Vancouver: Women's Research Centre.

Epp, J. (1986). *Achieving health for all: A framework for health promotion.* Ottawa: Health & Welfare Canada.

Ferguson, M. (1980). *The Aquarian conspiracy.* Los Angeles: J.P. Tarcher.

Hoffman, K. (1991). Seniors working for seniors. *The Multiplier: The Newsletter of the Strengthening Community Health Program,* January, p. 4. Ottawa: Canadian Public Health Association.

Rothman, J. (1974). Three models of community organization practice. In Fred M. Cox et al. (eds.), *Strategies of community organization: A book of readings.* Chicago: F.E. Peacock.

Siler-Wells, G. (1988). *Strengthening community health means strengthening communities.* Ottawa: Canadian Public Health Association.

Strengthening Community Health Program (1989). *Mission and goals.* Ottawa: Canadian Public Health Association.

World Health Organization (1986). *Ottawa charter for health promotion.* Ottawa: Canadian Public Health Association.

Developing Knowledge for Health Promotion

Irving Rootman and Michel O'Neill

From 1974 to 1986, knowledge for health promotion in Canada developed in an *ad hoc*, unplanned way, both inside and outside academia. One possible exception to this pattern was the National Health Promotion Survey which, when carried out in 1985, was (to our knowledge) the first of its kind. This survey was carefully planned over a three-year period and was innovative in many respects, including the way in which its findings were marketed (Rootman, 1986a). However, as was pointed out by Robin Badgley in the 1970s (see the first chapter of this book), most of the research pertaining to health promotion in Canada has been limited in many respects (Badgley, 1978). This situation still continues to some degree, but federal efforts since 1986 to develop knowledge for health promotion have led to some improvements and, hopefully, will lead to others.

Specifically, over the past seven years Canada has been involved in a unique effort to develop knowledge for health promotion. Initiated by Health and Welfare Canada, this project has had significant impact on the organization of research in health promotion in this country. The purpose of this chapter is to describe and analyze this initiative, to consider its impact to date, and to speculate about its future.

Origin of the Knowledge Development Project

In June 1986, Canada's then Minister of National Health and Welfare, the Honourable Jake Epp, addressed the 77th Annual Conference of the Canadian Public Health Association (CPHA) on "Strategies for Health Promotion" (Epp, 1986a). Drawing on an internal working paper (Draper & Stern, 1985) prepared by Ron Draper, the Director-General of the Health Promotion Directorate, and Rita Stern, the Directorate's Western Regional Office Director, Mr. Epp suggested several strategies, including research.

Acting on this pronouncement, a number of staff of the Health Services and Promotion Branch of Health and Welfare Canada initiated a project to develop health promotion knowledge for Canada. One of the first steps was the establishment of an internal working group, co-ordinated and managed by one of us (Irving Rootman) who was at the time a Director in the Health Promotion Directorate of the Branch. This committee decided that it should use the term "knowledge development" rather than "research" because the Draper and Stern paper had used that term to convey the idea that academically based "scientific" research was only one way to develop knowledge. Another important way is to synthesize the practical experience of practitioners and/or lay people. In the end, the project emphasized research in the scientific sense of the term, probably because most of the people on the internal working group, and the external group which was formed shortly thereafter, were academic researchers (or at least sympathetic to scientific research).

Phase I: Defining the Problem

After deciding on the term to use, the internal working group decided to commission three working papers to help define the scope of the enterprise: (1) a review of health promotion research carried out by the Branch to that date (Rootman, 1986b); (2) a review of recommendations for health promotion research made in international documents (Magwood, 1986); and (3) a paper identifying and synthesizing needs for health promotion knowledge put forward by staff of the Health Services and Promotion Branch (Storm & Petrasovits, 1986). These materials were compiled in the summer and fall of 1986 and were used as background information for both the internal and external working groups.

The external working group was established in collaboration with the Branch's Extramural Research Programs Directorate which is responsible for administering the National Health Research Development Program (NHRDP) that funds externally conducted public health research at the national level in Canada. (This arrangement is perhaps another reason why the knowledge development effort came to focus on research rather than other forms of knowledge development.) The external group consisted of nine members from various parts of the country with different disciplinary backgrounds chosen by the Health Promotion and Extramural Research Programs Directorates. It was charged with two tasks: (1) to contribute to the development of a research strategy for health promotion consistent with the directions outlined in the Minister's address at the June CPHA Conference, and (2) to identify priorities for the NHRDP in the field of health promotion.

The first meeting of the group took place in October 1986, one month prior to the First International Conference on Health Promotion at which the Minister would release the now-famous document, *Achieving Health for All: A Framework for Health Promotion* (Epp, 1986b; hereafter, the Framework). At this meeting the group agreed to accept its terms of reference and to use the Framework as the basis for its work. It should be noted that, in contrast to the CPHA address, research was no longer identified in the Framework as a leading strategy (Figure 1). However, it was clear that research was seen as an underlying strategy for health promotion and therefore, both the internal and external working groups felt they had a mandate to proceed.

Figure 1   A framework for health promotion.

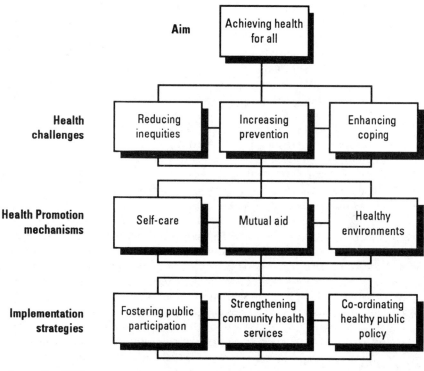

Source: Epp, 1986b.

Following the November International Conference, the external group met for the second time. In that meeting, the group drafted an interim statement that was used as the basis for inviting applications for health promotion research as part of the general annual solicitation of research projects of the NHRPD. The group also recommended commissioning literature reviews on elements of the Framework as well as one on experiences in combining research and action. A request for proposals was issued in February 1987, and over 40 were received.

At a combined meeting of the internal and external groups, the proposals were reviewed and 16 were recommended for funding. This was more than originally intended, but because there were more high-quality proposals than anticipated, it was felt that it would be worthwhile to support more. Generic reviews were funded in all of the areas covered by the Framework with the exception of two. One was the cell in Figure 1 called "Achieving health for all," representing the overall goal of health promotion efforts in Canada. This was an oversight, and in retrospect probably should have been the basis for one or more reviews. The other was the cell called "Increasing prevention," for which no satisfactory proposal for a generic review was received. Instead, several more focussed reviews and mini-papers were commissioned on this topic.

Immediately following the selection of the reviews to be underwritten, a meeting was held involving all those whose proposals had been chosen. The purposes of this meeting were: (1) to present the background of the project; (2) to introduce reviewers to each other and to Branch contacts who had been designated to facilitate their work; (3) to establish a foundation for networking among reviewers; and (4) to establish guidelines for final reports. After a summer of working on the reviews, the reviewers were assembled once again in the fall of 1987 to report on their progress, enhance further linkages among themselves, and suggest future directions for their work.

The reviews and mini-papers were completed in January 1988, and were distributed to members of both working groups as well as to internal contact persons in the Department of Health and Welfare. In addition, a list of recommendations contained in the reviews and mini-papers was compiled and distributed to the members of both groups who were asked to rate them as high, medium, or low priority.

These ratings were then tabulated and provided to the members of the external working group at their next meeting. At this meeting, they were asked to formulate research priorities and strategies based upon these ratings, their own experiences, and the various papers and reviews. The internal working group was asked to do the same. Based on these recommendations, both groups prepared reports which were submitted to the Branch. As this completed the tasks assigned to the external working group, it was then disbanded.

Phase II: Consultation

Using these two reports, a discussion paper representing a synthesis of views of the two groups was prepared (Health & Welfare Canada, 1988). This paper was used as the basis for a national consultation conducted between September 1988 and March 1989. Thirty-two workshops involving several hundred knowledge users and producers were held across the country during this period. Each workshop was organized by a local host chosen because of his or her involvement in health promotion research and familiarity with other interested researchers and practitioners in that locale. Hosts were instructed to invite no more than fifty people to their workshop. They were also asked to invite some researchers who were working in areas not associated with traditional health promotion research in Canada, and most were able to do so. Staff of the Health Promotion Branch presented the discussion paper and set the stage for its consideration in both large and small groups.

Following the workshops, each host submitted a report. These were synthesized into a national report, which was subsequently reviewed in a national workshop of the local hosts or their designates held in May 1989 in Ottawa. The discussion at that workshop was used to produce a revised report (Health & Welfare Canada, 1989a), which was then sent to all national workshop participants and any local hosts who had been unable to attend.

Phase III: Implementation

One of the recommendations of the national workshop was that the Branch appoint a national Advisory Committee, which it did following the meeting. This committee consisted initially of five members (one for each region of Canada as defined by the regional office mandates of the Health Promotion Directorate); it was later expanded to include "alternates" for each region, as well as the five Health Promotion Directorate regional directors, in addition to a number of people from other parts of the Branch. The group met about twice a year between August 1989 and July 1991. Early on, the group suggested that the Branch take the following priority actions to implement the recommendations of the consultation phase:

- Develop health promotion indicators;
- Develop and legitimize methods for health promotion research;
- Organize a national conference on health promotion research;
- Support the development of regional and national networks of health promotion researchers;
- Disseminate relevant publications and reports; and
- Lobby funding agencies to support health promotion research.

To date, the following has occurred in relation to each of these proposed actions:

With regard to indicators, a national workshop took place followed by five regional workshops, which focussed mainly on the topic of indicators for the Healthy Communities movement. The results of these workshops were presented in November 1990 in two sessions at the First National Conference on Health Promotion Research and are analyzed elsewhere (O'Neill, 1993).

As for methods, to date the only federal knowledge development action (that we are aware of) that is directly related was the First National Conference on Health Promotion Research. Held in Toronto in November 1990, it focussed on expanding the repertoire of research methods in health promotion. The results of this conference were published as a supplement by the *Canadian Journal of Public Health* (Maclean & Eakin, 1992).

The national conference was held as planned, as were two series of regional workshops: a first series on indicators in 1989-90, and a second series, with no specific topic, in 1990-91. All of this supported the development of national and regional networks, especially in the prairies (see the chapter by Joan Feather later in this book). Moreover, in Québec, the seed money for the second workshop was used, in collaboration with the Québec Public Health Association, to trigger a provincewide consensus-building process on health promotion, aimed at strengthening and linking the various networks of health promotion researchers and practitioners.

In addition, in Ontario, the Regional Office of the Health Promotion Directorate supported two projects to enhance the development of the network of researchers there. The first was a project carried out by the Ontario Prevention Clearinghouse to construct a computer-based provincial inventory of health promotion researchers and practitioners. The second was a project carried out by the Centre for Health Promotion at the University of Toronto to identify community health promotion knowledge needs and capacities. The Centre was also involved in organizing an invitational conference on Behavioural Research and Health which obtained support from NHRDP as well as the Ontario Ministry of Health and several health-related voluntary agencies (Centre for Health Promotion, 1992). Although this last event was not formally linked to the national knowledge development initiative, it helped to foster the networking sought by the Knowledge Development National Advisory Committee.

Health and Welfare Canada published several issues of a newsletter on health promotion knowledge development as well as two issues of an inventory of health promotion researchers in Canada (Health & Welfare Canada, 1989c, 1991), all of which were intended to contribute to the development of the network as well as help to fulfill the dissemination requirements identified by the Committee. A number of other publications were disseminated as well, usually in Canada's two official languages, including a summary of all the literature reviews (Health & Welfare Canada, 1989b), a summary of the consultation report (Health & Welfare Canada, 1989a), and several papers based on the literature reviews (e.g., Jutras, 1988; Powell, 1988; Small, 1989), some of which (e.g., Pederson et al., 1988) have received international attention.

Finally, as a result of lobbying granting agencies, the NHRDP conducted a special competition on health promotion research in 1990. Moreover, NHRDP and the Social Sciences and Humanities Research Council (SSHRC) held a competition to fund health promotion research centres across the country.

Thus, it appears as if there have been a reasonable number of actions taken to implement the recommendations that emerged from the consultation process. However, the momentum of the project slowed considerably during 1991 and 1992, when several Health and Welfare staff responsible for the knowledge development initiative left and the funds allocated to it were reduced. On the other hand, it also appears as if the momentum were picking up again, in that the University of Toronto Centre for Health Promotion was asked to develop a plan for continuing the knowledge development effort. Funding has just been announced for six health promotion research centres. Moreover, a second national research conference was held in March 1993 in Vancouver, where, among other activities, a workshop was held to analyze and rekindle the knowledge development dynamic.

In addition, there have been a number of positive developments bearing on the development of knowledge for health promotion in Canada which were not the direct result of federal efforts. Independent of the NHRDP – SSHRC competition, research groups or centres of health promotion have been started — like the University of Toronto Centre for Health Promotion, which obtains its core funding from the University; the Institute for Health Promotion Research at the University of British Columbia, and the Centre for Well-Being in Alberta, which obtain much of their core funding from their respective provincial governments; or the Groupe de recherche et d'intervention en promotion de la santé de l'Université Laval, in Québec City, which is a less formal structure.

The North York Community Health Promotion Research Unit obtains its core funding from the provincial government in Ontario. Ontario also allocated funds to establish a Behavioural Research Unit in Tobacco as part of the provincial tobacco strategy, and the National Cancer Institute of Canada has provided funds to establish a Behavioural Research Unit in Cancer. The B.C. provincial government has begun funding health promotion research through a major granting program. As mentioned, several voluntary associations in the health field, as well as provincial and federal governments, have also provided financial support to hold conferences on behavioural and social science research in health which have some implications for health promotion knowledge development. Moreover, a major federal – provincial initiative on heart health has been launched, involving between three and nine sites in each province where demonstration projects are held and evaluated, using a similar methodology defined by the NHRDP. These are but a few examples of the knowledge development activities going on outside the realm of the federal initiative.

Reflections on the Past

Although no formal overall evaluation has yet been undertaken of the federal government's health promotion knowledge development effort, we can nevertheless reflect on its accomplishments and failures with the benefit of hindsight. As mentioned earlier, one of us (O'Neill, 1993) has assessed the regional workshops held in 1990–91, and we have both given considerable thought to what has happened so far — and what might happen in the future.

On the positive side, it is clear that the federal knowledge development project has stimulated the development of various health promotion research processes in Canada. If it had not taken place, it is extremely unlikely that two national conferences on health promotion research would have occurred, that the literature on health promotion would have been synthesized and publications based on these syntheses distributed widely, that six new health promotion research centres would have been funded, that the network of health promotion researchers in Canada would have been identified explicitly, and that collaborative working relationships between researchers and practitioners would have developed to the extent that they have. At the present time, there is something of a spirit of co-operation and common identification among researchers in Canada interested in health promotion which probably would not exist had the federal effort in knowledge development not occurred.

In our view, a number of factors contributed to this success. One was the release of the Framework in 1986. Not only did it provide some legitimization for knowledge development for health promotion, but the conceptual framework that it contained helped to guide the literature reviews and the definition of priorities for research.

Another element in the success of the knowledge development initiative has been the attempt to involve many people and to keep the process open. This has helped to build a constituency for the future and allowed new ideas to enter.

A third factor in the success of the project to date, in line with the overall federal strategy on health promotion, was the production and wide distribution of useful products. The literature reviews, in particular, appear to be appreciated by researchers and others working in health promotion, and have built good will and understanding for the initiative which should continue to be helpful.

Another important factor was the fact that the project had champions within the federal government who had some access to resources to support it. In particular, the fact that it was managed by one of the Directors of the Health Promotion Directorate and was strongly supported by the Director-General of the time (Lavada Pinder) meant that it was able to maintain momentum. The importance of this became apparent when these two people left and the project fell to others who had less power to influence resource allocation, leading to a period in which activity slowed appreciably.

Finally, the willingness of people to give their time and effort to the process without remuneration contributed enormously to its success. In particular, efforts of the Health Services and Promotion Branch staff, above and beyond the call of duty, have helped the project to accomplish what it has to date. The efforts of external committee members, reviewers, local hosts, and others have also been enormously important.

On the negative side, it is clear that others working in health promotion may not have benefitted to the same extent as academic researchers, and that some networks of researchers have been more involved than others. As mentioned earlier, although the term knowledge development was used intentionally to encompass more than university-based scientific research, in the end the activities that have been carried out to date have focussed almost entirely on such research. That is, the process has not given significant legitimization to the synthesis of practical experience as an important form of knowledge development for health promotion. Nor has it developed any mechanisms to support this kind of knowledge development. In addition, although attempts were made to disseminate the results of the process to professional and grass-roots practitioners, the extent to which they received and used this information is uncertain.

It is also clear that, so far at least, the amount of actual research stimulated and funded by the process has not been substantial. Although NHRDP initiated a special competition for health promotion research in 1990, very few applications were actually supported because most failed to meet the criteria of the review committee. This has also been the case for projects reviewed annually by the Health Promotion Committee (#61) of NHRDP, which was created in 1987. This might have created a certain disenchantment within the research community, which has been extensively solicited from 1986 to 1989 with very little actual project funding since then.

On the other hand, there was tremendous interest in the competition to fund health promotion research centres, with over 50 letters of intent and 15 proposals being submitted. However, the process of this competition was somewhat chaotic (it was the first joint venture of two major funding bodies, and the federal government was in the midst of significant efforts to reduce expenditures). It remains to be seen how the funded centres will succeed in producing high-quality research, in legitimizing multiple knowledge development approaches, and in making strong connections with people in the field.

A third possible limitation of the process so far has been the extent to which it has been able to foster inter- and multidisciplinary efforts and to bring in people from fields not normally associated with health. Although an attempt was made to do so through the workshops, it was only partly successful. As O'Neill (1993) argues, the workshops demonstrated the significant barriers to interdisciplinary work more than they contributed to building new interdisciplinary bridges. We think that one of the key barriers is the fact that the reward systems and promotion mechanisms of academia are organized so as almost to preclude any kind of interdisciplinary exchange (O'Neill, 1993).

A fourth limitation of the process up to now is that it was directed almost entirely by Health and Welfare Canada without any significant collaboration by other federal ministries, by other levels of government, or by the voluntary or private sectors. Although this in some ways made it simpler to proceed in a single-minded fashion, it meant that there has been almost no "buying in" from other organizations in Canada that have an important stake in developing knowledge for health promotion. Thus, even though provincial, voluntary, and private research funding agencies were invited to participate in the 32 workshops held across the country (and in some cases did so), we see relatively little evidence of new or revised funding priorities, although the Medical Research Council has recently indicated an interest in funding "population health" or health promotion research. Perhaps if they had been partners from the beginning, more success in this regard would have been achieved.

Finally, it is possible that even though the Framework was a useful stimulus and organizing schema for the work carried out under knowledge development in Canada, it also may have limited its development by directing researchers away from areas of equal or greater importance to health promotion, such as some suggested by the Ottawa Charter but not highlighted by the Framework (e.g., skill development) or by other theoretical frameworks. In fact, it was rather surprising that there was not more critical comment and analysis of the Framework by those involved in the process. Perhaps this would have led to a more dynamic review of the literature and experience and to a more useful research agenda.

Looking Forward

Recognizing both the successes and limitations of the process to date, how would we advise proceeding with the development of knowledge for health promotion in Canada? While we do not pretend to have all the answers, we do have a few suggestions.

First, we should build on what has been accomplished so far. As noted, this has not been insignificant. Moreover, the leadership role of the federal government has, by and large, been helpful. The federal government is, in fact, still in an ideal position to support the development of knowledge for health promotion in Canada. There is no other body that we know of that has as its mandate an overview of health promotion throughout the country, or the resources to be able to stimulate activity in this field from coast to coast and from the U.S. border to the arctic. Thus, the federal government should be encouraged to continue its efforts and to invest more resources in doing so, given that the investment to date has been surprisingly modest (probably less than one million dollars over the seven years reviewed) for a return that has been nationally and internationally recognized, as several chapters of this book testify.

Having said that, we think the federal government should pursue knowledge development in health promotion in closer collaboration with the other players in the field — particularly, other levels of government and the voluntary sector. Hopefully, the political climate in Canada will permit such collaboration. In such an enterprise, the federal government would be wise not to try to impose a single organizing framework, but rather to build on frameworks developed and used by others as well as on the strengths of the networks it has helped to stimulate.

Now that six research centres in health promotion have been funded by the federal government and several others have been established with other resources, it would make sense to encourage these structures to play an active role in knowledge development. This would include building bridges to practitioners, communities, voluntary organizations, the private sector, and various levels of government. However, in doing this, it is important to recognize that there may be as much interest and talent in health promotion research in centres not funded by the NHRDP – SSHRC competition. An organized effort should be made to involve them in the process, along with other members of the research community in health and related fields.

In this regard, perhaps more effort and resources need to be expended in supporting interdisciplinary and multidisciplinary research. Although the funded centres are encouraged to engage in this kind of research, it is difficult to do, and there is therefore a need to make examples of successes widely known and provide opportunities to develop the required skills.

In general, more effort needs to be expended in education and training in health promotion. There is a great deal of training going on in health promotion/health education in Canada, but much of it has been *ad hoc* and lacks co-ordination with other efforts in Canada (Rootman, 1993). There is a need to review such initiatives and to integrate them with knowledge development efforts.

Finally, there is a need to give more legitimacy to the collection and sharing of practical experience as an acceptable mode of knowledge development in Canada. This means researchers must treat as equals people who practise health promotion, and must try to bring them into the process of developing knowledge at all stages — providing them with, among other things, access to academic channels for disseminating knowledge. Moreover, researchers should realize that in many health promotion endeavours (as is the case with the Healthy Communities movement in particular), they are but one interest group — and not always the most powerful — in the process of knowledge development (O'Neill et al., in press).

Conclusion

This chapter has provided an overview of a key initiative to develop knowledge for health promotion in Canada over the past eight years and has suggested some directions for future efforts. It is interesting to realize that currently there is a significant interest in health promotion research in this country, as exemplified by a decision of the Royal Society of Canada to explore the possibility of assessing the status of this body of research in Canada (Green et al., 1992). The fact that this prestigious independent body of scholars is even considering such a possibility is, in our own view, significant. Finally, we think that the conceptual haziness of health promotion creates all kinds of theoretical, but even more importantly, political problems for health promotion research; indeed, if it is difficult to agree on the content of health promotion, what kind of specific research can we expect to be funded under its name in a period of shrinking funds (O'Neill, 1988)? Perhaps the suggestion made by O'Neill and Cardinal later in this book — i.e., to separate the philosophical from the practical dimensions of health promotion — can help resolve this dilemma.

We have made a good beginning in knowledge development for health promotion. Let us ensure that we do even better in the future.

Acknowledgements

The authors gratefully acknowledge the efforts of the many people who have contributed to the Health Promotion Knowledge Development project in Canada, including the members of the internal and external working groups and the Advisory Committee, local workshop organizers, co-op students from the University of Waterloo, support staff, and especially Lavada Pinder and Michael Nelson, whose support of this initiative made it possible.

References

Badgley, R.F. (1978). Health promotion and social change in the health of Canadians. In *Proceedings of the Seminar on Evaluation of Health Education and Behaviour Modification* Programs. Toronto: CHES/Canadian Council on Health Education, pp. 20-43.

Draper, R., & Stern, R. (1985). Proposals for health promotion and disease prevention program. Internal working document. Ottawa: Health & Welfare Canada.

Epp, J. (1986a). National strategies for health promotion. Address to the 77th Annual Conference of the Canadian Public Health Association, June 17, 1986.

Epp, J. (1986b). *Achieving health for all: A framework for health promotion.* Ottawa: Health & Welfare Canada.

Green, L.W., et al. (1992). Prospectus for a study of research on health promotion in Canada for the Royal Society of Canada (discussion document). Vancouver: University of British Columbia, Institute for Health Promotion Research, and the Royal Society Research Evaluation Unit, December 1992.

Health & Welfare Canada (1988). *Priorities and strategies for research to promote the health of Canadians: A discussion paper.* Ottawa: Health Services & Promotion Branch.

Health & Welfare Canada (1989a). *Developing knowledge for health promotion in Canada: National report on research priorities and strategies.* Ottawa: Health Services & Promotion Branch.

Health & Welfare Canada (1989b). *Knowledge development for health promotion: A call to action.* Ottawa: Health Services & Promotion Branch.

Health & Welfare Canada (1989c). *Health promotion research directory.* Ottawa: Health Services & Promotion Branch.

Health & Welfare Canada (1990). Developing knowledge for health promotion in Canada. *Health Promotion, 28* (3), insert.

Health & Welfare Canada (1991). *Health promotion research directory.* Ottawa: Health Services & Promotion Branch.

Jutras, S. (1988). Formal and informal caregivers: Towards a partnership in prevention. *Health Promotion, 27* (2), 9-12.

Maclean, H., & Eakin, J. (eds.) (1992). Health promotion research methods: Expanding the repertoire. *Canadian Journal of Public Health, 83*(Suppl. 1), March-April.

Magwood, K. (1986). *Health promotion research needs identified from the literature.* Ottawa: Health Services & Promotion Branch, Health & Welfare Canada.

O'Neill, M. (1988). What kind of research for what kind of health promotion? *Health Promotion International, 3,* 337-341.

O'Neill, M. (1993). Building bridges between knowledge and action: The Canadian process on healthy communities indicators. In Davies, J., & Kelly, M., *Healthy cities: Research and practice*. London: Routledge & Kegan Paul, pp. 127-147.

O'Neill, M., et al. (in press). Academic partners of the movement: The Laval University research program on healthy cities. In E. de Leeuw, M. O'Neill, & M. Goumans (eds.), *Proceedings of the Maastricht expert seminar on healthy cities research*. Maastricht, The Netherlands: University of Limburg.

Pederson, A.P., Edwards, R.K., Kelner, M., Marshall, V.M., & Allison, K.R. (1988). *Co-ordinating healthy public policy: An analytic literature review and bibliography*. Ottawa: Minister of Supply & Services.

Pinder, L. (1988). From *A new perspective* to the *Framework*: A case study in the development of health promotion in Canada. *Health Promotion International, 3*, 205-212.

Powell, M. (1988). Fostering public participation. *Health Promotion, 27*, 5-8.

Rootman, I. (1986a). Development of a national health promotion survey: The Canadian experience. *Health Promotion International, 1*, 393-399.

Rootman, I. (1986b). *Review of past and current Health Promotion Directorate research*. Ottawa, Health Services & Promotion Branch, Health & Welfare Canada.

Rootman, I. (1989). Knowledge for health promotion: A summary of Canadian literature reviews. *Health Promotion International, 4*, 67-72.

Rootman, I. (1993). Health promotion in Canadian universities. *Proceedings of Health Promotion Institute* sponsored by North American Regional Office, International Union on Health Education, Toronto, August, 1992.

Small, B. (1989) Healthy environments for Canadians: Making the vision a reality. *Health Promotion, 27*, 2-7.

Storm, T., & Petrasovits, A. (1986). *An assessment of knowledge development needs by program components in relation to the health promotion framework*. Ottawa, Health Services & Promotion Branch, Health & Welfare Canada.

PROVINCIAL

PERSPECTIVES

Health Promotion in British Columbia

Jack L. Altman and Sharon M. Martin

This chapter will attempt to review the status and some of the history of health promotion in British Columbia. It is not an exhaustive report, but one that focusses on the most salient features of health promotion in the province, from both a conceptual and an applied perspective. Beginning with a description of the setting and historical context, we move on to consider the major developments in health promotion over the past ten years and end depicting the link between the evolution of health promotion in B.C. and the province's recent efforts to restructure and reform its health system.

We have chosen a descriptive, somewhat anecdotal style rather than an academic format, the better to portray a community perspective. Readers who wish to pursue specific topics in greater detail may consult the Bibliography at the end of the chapter.

Context

The B.C. Experience

British Columbia is Canada's westernmost province, rich in natural resources, culturally and ethnically diverse. B.C. has one of the country's highest growth rates as immigrants continue to stream in from other parts of Canada and the world. British Columbians are often viewed as "laid back" inhabitants of "lotus land," apparently different in attitude from other Canadians. In fact, residents of B.C. find it easy to disregard central Canada because of the physical separation (distance, rugged mountain chains) and the three-hour time difference. The various provincial regions represent extremes of climate and terrain ranging from rain forest to desert. But, like other parts of Canada, most of B.C.'s 3.25 million people live in metropolitan areas in the south. The remaining population occupies smaller, sometimes isolated, communities in the interior, the north, and the coast.

While British Columbia has undergone much change in the past decade in both its population base and its institutions, the Ministry of Health in Victoria has continued to control health sector activities in a "top-down" fashion. Unlike other provinces, B.C. has no history of community health or social service boards. Few municipalities have experimented with wards or neighbourhood councils. While quasi-regional health boards (Union

Boards of Health) do exist to provide some public input into regional health service delivery, they have no significant authority and very limited resources. Hospital or residential facility boards are also in place, but their primary responsibility is to the institution rather than the community.

As a result, communities have had little power and few resources to establish any significant infrastructure. This has made it difficult for them to address local concerns effectively. Activities that institutions take for granted — research, priority setting, marketing, implementing programs — have been beyond the capacity of most communities. It has been a frustrating dilemma: without local control there has been no infrastructure, and without an infrastructure, communities have been unable to take control.

The Service Base

Like health systems in other provinces, B.C. health services[1] have emphasized professional help for people who are sick or at risk of becoming ill. Support has focussed almost exclusively upon the delivery of clinical care, with three distinct purveyors of services or programs. First, there are the health organizations run directly by government (public health, continuing care, etc.). Second, there are providers at "arm's length" from government, but ultimately dependent on public funding (physicians, hospitals, etc.). Finally, small grass-roots agencies that also receive public monies have sprung up in neighbourhoods or communities.

The grass-roots organizations have had the most difficult time over the years owing to their uncertain financial base. Paid to deliver specific services and unable to secure core funding, they quickly learned that one-to-one service delivery was both their best route to survival and the most opportune way of responding to community needs. Furthermore, "living on the edge" with no budget flexibility, they have been in an awkward position to advocate for change to overall policy.

Consequently, there has been a proliferation of local organizations as new groups, with no other funding sources, have formed to provide services to increasingly specific populations. This growth of neighbourhood agencies has also posed difficulties for community cohesion, because the various groups have operated in isolation from each other. With no overall community plan, duplication or redundant services were often as severe a problem as service gaps. Two or three separate organizations might receive funding from different government sources to provide essentially the same program.

Ironically, the centralized bureaucracy in Victoria has dealt with the government-run health organizations in essentially the same manner as the grass-roots community groups. Although their meagre funding base was

---

[1] The term "service" used in this chapter denotes a continuum of potential staff activities ranging from one-to-one clinical care to family or group support, to health education, to community development. It represents the various types of "interventions" available in providing support to the public.

secure, government health staff have had little decision-making power at the local level. Ministry of Health officials have controlled both the amount of funding and the content of programs, with little meaningful citizen participation in either.

The health care — or, more accurately, sickness-care budget — has been directed almost exclusively at the arm's-length providers. Unfortunately, the more independent arm's-length health providers have also ignored public involvement as an element in their operation. While closer to the people they serve, they have typically developed services for individuals they believe to be in need and have restricted themselves to the clinical service model as the sole intervention strategy. Consequently, at the community level, there are often many services (government, local health agency, and grass-roots) competing with one another for "customers," and few mechanisms for citizen participation. Health has been basically equated with services and care.

Response to the Epp Framework

The decade of the 1980s was a seminal period for health promotion in B.C. Initially, the province's formal health organizations demonstrated little interest in the new definitions of health[2] and health promotion[3] promulgated by the World Health Organization (WHO) in 1984. (Despite the lack of support from the official health system, isolated health promotion activities — under such different titles as community organizing, community development, or social development — had been occurring for years.) Some sparks, however, were beginning to appear. For example, the Public Health Department in Vancouver established "Seniors' Wellness" positions in 1985 to work with the city's "older" population. The innovative twist to this service was the expectation by the Vancouver Health Department that instead of simply focussing on individual lifestyle (e.g., diet, exercise), the new staff were to work in partnership with the community in program development.

The publication of the Epp document, *Achieving Health for All: A Framework for Health Promotion* (hereafter, the Framework), and the Ottawa Charter in 1986 suddenly provided a powerful boost to the credibility of health promotion. Such processes as community involvement, advocacy for healthful public policy, and collaboration across community sectors benefitted from a substantial dose of legitimacy. A year later, Health and Welfare Canada funded the B.C. Public Health Association (BCPHA) to

---

[2] Health is the extent to which an individual or group is able, on the one hand, to develop aspirations and satisfy needs; and, on the other hand, to change or cope with the environment. Health is therefore seen as a resource for everyday life, not the object of living. It is a positive concept emphasizing social and personal resources as well as physical capabilities.
[3] Health promotion is the process of enabling people to increase control over, and to improve, their health. To reach a state of complete physical, mental, and social well-being, an individual or group must be able to identify and to realize aspirations, to satisfy needs, and to change or cope with the environment.

hold a provincial health forum on the Framework. In convening the meeting, BCPHA made a special effort to go beyond health professionals and seek broad community representation. Among the participants were care professionals, community organizers, old and young consumers, and volunteers from housing, urban planning, and social service groups.

Meeting participants identified five key obstacles to implementation of the Framework:

- inadequate planning at all levels;
- little political will;
- the absence of links among agencies and between agencies and community;
- minimal consumer participation; and
- resistance by health care professionals to changing their role.

To broaden their support in addressing the barriers, the group recommended that the first post-forum action should be the organizing of similar workshops across the province.

To that end, Health and Welfare Canada (the Western Region of the Health Promotion Directorate — WROHPD), the Vancouver Urban Core Workers, and BCPHA co-sponsored a session in the Downtown Eastside of Vancouver. Again, participants came from diverse fields, but identified similar concerns and actions. They concluded that it was essential for people from different community sectors to work together in identifying health concerns and solutions. Such a process was deemed to have critical implications for the individuals and communities involved. Most significantly, it was understood that this approach would strengthen communities by improving their understanding of issues and expanding their role in addressing problems. This strategy reflected the new WHO definitions and focussed on the factors increasingly acknowledged as important to the health of communities (i.e., the broader determinants of health).

In summary, the workshops identified critical obstacles to the success of health promotion in B.C. Most of these described deficits: in planning, political will, collaboration, and consumer participation, but one was an excess, namely, the dominance of professionals and bureaucrats in the system. On the positive side, it was also clear from the meetings that community residents were ready to become more informed, involved, and co-operative in addressing community health concerns.

The B.C. Healthy Communities Network

Following the success of the two workshops, the B.C. Public Health Association and the Western Regional Office of the Health Promotion Directorate convened a meeting with other provincial organizations interested in community participation and the new WHO definitions: the Social Planning and Research Council, the Registered Nurses Association, the B.C. Health Association, the Institute of Planners, the University of British Columbia, and the provincial Ministry of Health. The purpose of the meeting was to discuss how to continue the process of public involvement begun by the two workshops.

Participants quickly perceived their overall goal to be one of preparing the way for a community health coalition or network. However, the group confronted a number of prior tasks: clarifying objectives, addressing the differences and the self-interests of participating organizations, and explaining two nationally funded community strategies (Strengthening Community Health and Healthy Communities). After further meetings, it was decided that the provincial groups would form a Steering Committee, the B.C. Healthy Communities Network (BCHCN), to recognize, promote, and link community actions for health across the province.

This new coalition or Network was intended to assist communities in developing partnerships, mobilizing political will, and planning local initiatives. One of the first actions taken by the Steering Committee was to merge the two national initiatives, Strengthening Community Health and Healthy Communities. Both projects were implementation strategies of the Framework, with the former directed at the political and corporate structures of municipalities and the latter aimed at involving citizens and local organizations at the neighbourhood or community level. The BCHCN believed that to retain two such similar initiatives as separate would be confusing, redundant, and would dilute the committee's efforts.

In March 1989, the BCHCN Steering Committee invited community leaders from across the province to a workshop to respond to its drafted goals and purpose. Participants, with different backgrounds and interests, agreed that the key elements to building a healthy community were community involvement and partnership. They all supported the continuation and expansion of the BCHCN and recommended finding funds for a full-time co-ordinator. The presence of a paid staff member would make it easier to share information, provide consultation, build links among communities across the province, and promote the concept of healthy communities to uninvolved sectors.

The workshop participants also identified some specific barriers facing the BCHCN. These included vested interests and "turf," the resistance of the predominant health care system to change, and the lack of community control over decision making. There were also two references to "education." First, participants objected to the formal education process in which professionals were taught to become "experts" who expect to furnish the answers and make the decisions. Second, participants were concerned that public education was failing to create informed consumers.

Throughout the workshop, participants had opportunities to meet other people from their region who were committed to the Healthy Communities process. They realized that there was a great deal of "healthy community" activity across the province and that they had the capacity, that is, the skills and experience, to organize their own community networks. As noted above, this type of community work was not new; it had been occurring for years under different names, though in an unco-ordinated manner.

This was the beginning of an iterative process: community leaders returned to their communities to organize local workshops to identify health concerns, and develop action plans, while the BCHCN continued to stage an annual provincial workshop where leaders could discuss their local issues, describe the resources required to continue the process, and establish links across B.C.

Provincial and Federal Initiatives

In March 1989, the provinces and territories of Canada organized a National Conference on Health Promotion and Disease Prevention in Victoria, B.C. This event brought together high-level civil servants, politicians, grass-roots organizations, and service providers to examine the topics of health promotion and disease prevention and their relevance to provincial health systems. The meeting was "to act as a catalyst for nationwide planning on co-ordinated initiatives in health promotion and disease prevention to balance the attention. . . being directed towards the treatment of disease." At that conference, the B.C. Ministry of Health announced the opening of an Office of Health Promotion (OHP). The national conference and the establishment of the OHP gave health promotion in B.C. considerable recognition and credibility.

The subsequent decision by the Office of Health Promotion to adopt WHO's definition of health promotion was especially significant, as it established a community-oriented framework for the Office and its activities. Stemming from that conceptual base was OHP's decision to create the Healthy Communities Initiatives Fund to support "healthy community" projects around the province with $30 000 grants. The Fund used criteria of citizen participation, partnerships, municipal commitment, and the development of healthful public policy. These criteria further enhanced the understanding and image of health promotion in the province, while the projects themselves contributed to the lengthy process of building community infrastructure.

Such diverse communities as Port Alberni, Prince George, and the West End of Vancouver received funds to develop a community health plan. For example, in the West End, residents and community organizations conducted a telephone survey of 600 households about major health concerns. The health issues identified were safety, transportation, and inadequate support to people with mental illness. A subsequent community forum allowed service providers and citizens to devise community solutions such as a Neighbourhood Watch and The Nest, a safe place for people with mental illness to come for meals.

By 1990, funding for health promotion activities in B.C., essentially nonexistent in the past, was expanding rapidly. Besides the OHP's Healthy Communities grants, the B.C. Health Care Research Foundation began supporting health promotion research activities. The BCHRF inaugurated competitions for research in health promotion aimed specifically at women, children, culturally diverse populations, and Aboriginal people. Submission criteria included improving "the individual's, family's or community's ability to take control of their health and the factors that affect it" and establishing "effective links with the community."

Funding for community health promotion activities also came from the Federal Government through the Western Regional Office of the Health Promotion Directorate. In addition, the WROHPD addressed the theoretical framework of health promotion through a series of workshops with researchers, practitioners, and educators on Knowledge Development in Health Promotion ("Taking the ideas forward, making them real," "From rhetoric to reality").

Paradoxically, because it focussed on "care," another provincial initiative that resulted in a major advance for health promotion in B.C. was the province's Royal Commission on Health Care and Costs. The Commission operated from 1990 to 1991, providing the public and service providers an opportunity to review the sickness-care system. The Commission and presenters, however, found themselves occasionally "thinking about what health is" and how disease could be avoided in the first place, drawing additional attention to health promotion and disease prevention.

The Ministry's response to the Royal Commission's report, *Closer to Home*, came a year later, with two sections, "Better Management" and "Regionalization," emphasizing health promotion. This response to the Royal Commission served as the basis for the Ministry's 1993 policy document, *New Directions for a Healthy British Columbia*. With this report, Elizabeth Cull, the Minister of Health, acknowledged the broader determinants of health and called for a new approach to the province's health system — one that embodied public participation, local control, and regionalized services.

In another gesture of support for health promotion, the federal government and the B.C. Ministry of Health provided most of the funding for the second National Conference on Health Promotion Research in Vancouver in March 1993. Again, the conference helped focus public attention on health promotion and brought together researchers from all sectors — academic institutions, community, government, and service organizations.

Federal and provincial funding was extremely important to the development of health promotion in B.C. Not only did it provide resources for community initiatives, but it also reinforced the credibility of public participation, advocacy, and planning. By mid-1993, it was apparent that the two senior levels of government had become definite supporters of health promotion. The backing was genuine, even if communities suspected that health system cost containment and potential financial off-loading were the hidden agenda. What was less clear was the commitment of the bureaucracy and other institutions to the health promotion process.

Institutional Shifts

The Bureaucracy

Historically, health administrators and professionals not only failed to support health promotion initiatives in the community; they actively blocked them. The clinical service model was predominant, and control over programs remained with staff. In the past five years, however, there has been a slow but perceptible change among program administrators, researchers, and front-line staff.

Owing to the increasing emphasis on health promotion at the political and community levels, program managers have moved to examine the implications of health promotion from at least three perspectives. First, they have had to determine whether health promotion should be a component of the services they are currently delivering. Second, if health promotion is not a feasible service intervention for their organization, they have had to consider whether they should work in partnership with other agencies that do possess explicit health promotion mandates. Third, managers have had to judge the impact that health promotion principles might have upon their internal operations (shared governance at the worksite, employee participation models, etc.).

Although it is apparent that a shift towards health promotion is occurring among administrators and professional staff, it is not clear how pervasive and profound the change really is. Managers and health care professionals are considerably more aware of the need for community involvement in policy and program development, but there is much debate about what form that involvement should take. While most managers support community input, few are prepared to go as far as community ownership, either full or shared. Many believe that health promotion is a temporary phenomenon that will dissipate over time. Moreover, the introduction of health promotion as a significant service element is difficult, requiring organizational change skills and a high degree of commitment from the manager.

Despite the difficulties and variable levels of commitment, B.C. health organizations are beginning to blend health promotion activities successfully into their operations and demonstrate that it is possible for health promotion to become "mainstream." Sectors include public health (e.g., Skeena Health Unit, Vancouver Health Department), mental health (Greater Vancouver Mental Health Services), and even hospitals (e.g., Mount St. Joseph's and St. Paul's in Vancouver). For example, the staff at the West-Main Unit of the Vancouver Health Department have been able to incorporate health promotion fully into their work. Community health nurses, nutritionists, physicians, and other professionals have shifted their attention to the community and collective action rather than relying exclusively upon one-to-one service delivery.

The process may have been easier in public health, given its traditional focus on the overall health of the population and its early endorsement of the WHO definitions. The adoption of health promotion as an acceptable intervention approach in public health has occurred despite the emphasis of professionals over the past two decades upon individual risk factors and deficits. Critical to this change has been the recognition that clinical service is not the only, nor necessarily the best, means of providing support to the public. It has also meant that the community, rather than managers and professionals, should "own" its problems and solutions.

The Research Sector

Researchers in B.C. have also embraced (well, at least hesitantly hugged) health promotion in the past five years. In 1990 the University of British Columbia established an Institute for Health Promotion Research (IHPR) to support interdisciplinary research and graduate education in the field. "The research agenda of the institute seeks to examine the social, behavioural, and environmental determinants of health" and actions related to the determinants. Even before the creation of the IHPR, the Centre for Human Settlements at UBC had become a participant in the Healthy Communities process and advocated urban planning that was community driven. Simon Fraser University (Departments of Geography, Education), the University of Victoria (Gerontology), and various colleges and technical institutes have also offered courses and supported research in health promotion.

In dealing with health promotion, the research community has had some of the same hurdles to overcome as the bureaucracy. There has been the question of the relevance of health promotion as a substantive area of research and the role of health promotion or control in how investigators actually conduct their research. Traditionally, researchers have enlisted people as study subjects rather than as partners in research. Scientists have decided the areas and the methods of investigation without input from the population under scrutiny. Most importantly, results have usually not been shared with subjects nor with the larger community.

As with the bureaucracy, however, there is reason for optimism in the research community. Investigators are shifting to qualitative methods of research that make it easier both to conduct research in health promotion and to include the public as partners. Front-line health professionals who have returned to school for graduate degrees are selecting research topics of interest to the community. The BCHRF is even exploring the possibility of funding staff to work in community settings and help researchers undertake applied community issues.

Generally speaking, administrators, researchers, and service providers alike appear to be in an early phase of adopting health promotion as part of their operations. There is growing recognition of the importance of health promotion, but staff are still struggling with its conceptual framework and overall relevance to the health of the population. Broad acceptance and implementation of health promotion in both the applied and research settings are yet to come.

New Directions

As noted before, much of the material behind B.C.'s New Directions for a Healthy British Columbia came from two sources: the Closer to Home report produced by the province's Royal Commission on Health Care and Costs, and the Ministry's subsequent response to the report. The New Directions document released by Elizabeth Cull, then Minister of Health, on February 2, 1993 clearly acknowledges the broad understanding of health used by the WHO. It recognizes that health care is but one determinant of health and that more attention must be paid to such factors as income, education, housing, and the natural environment.

Report recommendations include the creation of a Provincial Health Council to develop health goals for the province and to monitor B.C.'s overall health status. There is recognition that equity is a serious concern and that a coherent policy be developed for persons with physical or mental disabilities, Aboriginal people and visible minority groups, and persons living in poverty, particularly children, women, and seniors. Significantly, it also recommends the establishment of a process to determine the health impact of all new government policies, programs, and legislation.

Cull also acknowledged the importance of public participation in the management of the health care system. She called for a decentralized, regional system of health care management through the creation of publicly controlled regional health boards and community health councils. Funds have been set aside to support skill and knowledge development of citizens to allow them to participate with confidence in this process. There is an emphasis upon equipping the public with sound information about the health care system and its operation.

New Directions provides a strong, cohesive framework for the change of the health care system and the advancement of a broader understanding of health, but it faces immense barriers. B.C.'s health care system consumes almost one-third of the provincial budget and employs about ten percent of the population. New Directions represents massive organizational change and significant public involvement. Not only is there a need for clear outcomes, but there has to be clear understanding of the process of change. How and why should the public get involved? For most, the current system works well. How and why should the bureaucracy and other professionals give up control? Many jobs are linked to the current system. There are issues affecting unions, professional associations, municipal governments, health care providers, health care institutions, and regional economies.

The challenge is to have enough time to involve the vested interests and the average citizen in the process. Ultimately, the most important aspect of New Directions may be that it concentrated on the development of the community infrastructure. This, in turn, facilitated the participation of the public. To date, much of the impressive rhetoric of New Directions has remained just that, although there are indications (e.g., a recent reorganization of the Ministry bureaucracy, appointment of regional directors) that genuine change is near.

Conclusion

A number of distinct, but converging, factors have shaped the evolution of health promotion in British Columbia. These forces have originated in communities, different levels of government, and various institutional sectors.

The events described above were seldom independent of one another; in fact, they were often interrelated.

Health promotion has made substantial progress in British Columbia since 1986. The province has a flourishing Healthy Communities movement involving approximately 100 municipalities. The current provincial government is committed to health promotion and has embarked on major systemic change. There have even been shifts among administrators, researchers, and service providers with almost everyone at least acknowledging that some form of public involvement is necessary in policy and program development.

The broad notion of health and its determinants have also gained acceptance. People are more aware that housing, economics, social support, and education are important to their health, and that control over issues that matter to them is crucial. Health professionals have learned about the capacity of communities and the benefits of partnerships, especially when making decisions about health. Within public health, there is an increased appreciation that clinical service delivery and health promotion are different. While not rejecting the importance of care in specific situations, staff are beginning to recognize that involving communities as partners in addressing their underlying health issues produces better outcomes than continuing to add professional one-to-one services.

The Healthy Communities process has been extremely significant for British Columbia. Not only has it supported the theory that community consultation is important, but it has also demonstrated one way of genuinely involving the community. This co-operative model has engaged citizens, politicians, and professional staff in a collective planning exercise that links agencies to one other and to the community, thus strengthening the community infrastructure. While lacking the power of the large institutions, its rapid growth has brought it to the attention of the "system."

Despite the progress in health promotion to date, some major hurdles remain. Much of the bureaucracy and institutional sector is still far from being completely "on board" and continues to wield disproportionate power compared to that of the community. Citizens and grass-roots organizations reiterate that health promotion is a slow process and one that requires basic resources — primarily, long-term (though not necessarily large) funding and information. Resources are particularly important if the process is to be truly representative and include those groups traditionally excluded. Finally, there are critical questions about the eventual destiny of New Directions. While the current government is unquestionably supportive, it is not clear how deep the support runs within the civil service.

On balance, there appears to be room for optimism because the B.C. experience is so heavily community based. Citizens and communities have awakened to their appropriate role; ultimately, it will be extremely difficult for any sector to resist that pressure.

Acknowledgement

The authors wish to acknowledge and thank Rita Stern. Rita was very help-ful in the initial discussions of this chapter and, as the Regional Director of the Western Regional Office of the Health Promotion Directorate, Health and Welfare Canada in the late 1980s, was a key contributor to many of the breakthroughs that occurred in health promotion in B.C.

Bibliography

British Columbia Healthy Communities Network (1989). *Strengthening healthy communities.* Vancouver: Author.

British Columbia Healthy Communities Network (1990). *Submission to the British Columbia Royal Commission on Health Care Costs.* Vancouver: Author.

British Columbia Healthy Communities Network (1990). *Telling our sto-ries/Addressing the future.* Vancouver: Author.

British Columbia Ministry of Health (1989). *National symposium on health promotion and disease prevention.* Victoria: Author.

British Columbia Ministry of Health & Ministry Responsible for Seniors (1993). *New directions for a healthy British Columbia.* Victoria: Authors.

British Columbia Public Health Association (1991). *Creating healthy public policy: Everybody's business.* Vancouver: Author.

British Columbia Royal Commission on Health Care and Costs (1991). *Closer to home* (The Report of the British Columbia Royal Commission of Health Care and Costs). Victoria: Author.

Epp, J. (1986). *Achieving health for all: A framework for health promotion.* Ottawa: Ministry of Supply & Services.

Health & Welfare Canada (1992). *From rhetoric to reality.* Vancouver, 1992.

Health & Welfare Canada & Canadian Public Health Association (1987). *Strengthening community health means strengthening communities.* Ottawa: Authors.

World Health Organization (1984). *Health promotion. A discussion docu-ment on the concept and principles.* Copenhagen: Author.

World Health Organization, Health & Welfare Canada, & Canadian Public Health Association (1986). *Ottawa charter for health promotion.* Ottawa: CPHA.

Alberta: A Haven for Health Promotion

Nancy Kotani and Ann Goldblatt

Health promotion is at a critical point in Alberta. In the midst of the province's unprecedented struggle to reform the health delivery system, health promotion is viewed by some as the conceptual torch to lead the provincial policy makers out of the wilderness created by the medical model.

For those who hold this view, health promotion represents the shift in focus away from the treatment of disease, toward the elements that cause health. Health reform is not just an exercise in fiscal restraint, albeit an increasingly significant force. It represents a much larger agenda to create and sustain health.

Others are of the mind that health promotion is a luxury that Alberta can do without in these tough times. Now is the time to consolidate our existing medical system, and re-emphasize basic health education instruction in our public institutions. Characteristic of Alberta, these opposing views are often manifest along urban and rural lines.

Poised on the brink, the real impact of health promotion in Alberta has yet to be determined. To date, the ideas of health promotion have been at once front and centre in the dialogue on health reform in Alberta, and relegated to fringe activity supported by scant resources.

There is a recurrent theme in the history of health promotion in this prairie province. The very infrastructure that other regions of the country are now attempting to build for health promotion has been in place for over 25 years in Alberta: it is the infrastructure developed in preventive social services, without formal participation of the health sector. Yet, the ideas at the core of this infrastructure are consistent with the goals and orientation of the emerging health promotion field.

The formal health sector has only quite recently found a foothold for health promotion in public health units, having been preoccupied with expanding and protecting the medical care system in urban and rural Alberta. Health promotion, in the eyes of public health reformers, represents the revitalization of public health principles.

At this time, the real impact of health promotion in Alberta has yet to be determined. The authors carry a hope for health promotion that belongs to the people of "next year country," a phrase that, during the Depression years, described the prairie sentiment of veiled optimism that next year in Alberta would be better.

This chapter is written from the perspective of two Edmonton-based public health practitioners. We see the true value of health promotion in the critique it offers of the biomedical model of health, with its dependence on technology, and the critique of behavioural change as the mechanical product of information. Health promotion's emphasis on context brings social movement theory into the institutionalized health sector (Poland, 1992; Stevenson & Burke, 1992).

Context

Right-Wing Haven for Health Promotion

Popular mythology revels in the image of "red-neck" Alberta. Few would expect the right-wing political culture to create the environment for a progressive movement for health promotion. But at the core of conservative philosophy is the belief in local autonomy and community self-sufficiency. Sixty years of conservative government, beginning with the Social Credit Party of Alberta in 1935, have shaped policies and programs designed to fend off welfare dependency. While other provinces were intentionally building the welfare state, Alberta was putting services in place that would ensure independence at the community level.

Alberta's political economy of the 1930s was "quasi-colonial," as described by C.B. Macpherson (Macpherson, 1953). The province was dominated by federal policies, and its largely agricultural base was indebted to the eastern-based banks.

In this climate, Alberta elected Social Credit, a grass-roots party that would stand up to Ottawa and eastern interests. Their deep and abiding mistrust of any power base outside the province endeared them to the electorate.

Social Credit enjoyed huge pluralities, from 1935 through the 1971 election of their political heirs, the Alberta Progressive Conservatives, under the leadership of Peter Lougheed. With a third consecutive election victory in May 1993, the Tories led by Premier Ralph Klein still set a populist agenda.

The political culture of Alberta continues to be characterized by a strong monetarist policy dating back to the reforms of William Aberhart's Social Credit philosophy. Anti-statism, the antithesis of the CCF/NDP party's thinking in neighbouring Saskatchewan, stands for a belief in the individual and the free enterprise system. There is also a strong Christian-based humanitarianism intended to support people in need and foster family values (Bella, 1981).

Political scientist Leslie Bella (1981) in her doctoral thesis, "The Politics of the Right-Wing 'Welfare State'," argues that the innovative social policies of preventive social services introduced in Alberta in the mid-1960s were intended to prevent rather than introduce the welfare state. The Social Credit government, Bella argues, recognized the growing pressure to be part of the halcyon days of social policy that existed in the early 1960s, but added its own twist:

- Public policy in this area should reflect a commitment to independence and *less* government intervention;

- Local people can identify issues before they become problems and they can work together to prevent them (Bella, 1981).

Hence, unique in Canada, Family and Community Support Services (FCSS), originally named Preventive Social Services (PSS), enabled local authorities to identify community issues and develop local responses in over 250 centres, reaching 95% of Albertans. Established just slightly in advance of the Canada Assistance Plan, FCSS is a partnership between the federal, provincial, and municipal governments. The program was and remains focussed on the prevention of individual, family, and community breakdown. From the outset, the model included regionally based community development consultants, initially to help PSS boards get started, and more recently to offer support and direction.

Community development was instrumental to PSS. As a result, a fairly sophisticated infrastructure of community-based services developed. Many of Alberta's community day-care centres, community resource centres, and parent support programs stem from the program.

Perhaps it was in an attempt to wash away the "next year country" association that the Alberta of the 1970s began to build a large and powerful public sector and in so doing relegated its historical ideological roots to the realm of mythology. Conceivably, a provincial treasury enriched by seemingly endless oil and gas revenues simply knew no bounds or discretion. There was no apparent need for restraint, and along with the availability of cost-shared federal dollars, Alberta's welfare state continued to grow.

In fact, the small-c conservative governments of Alberta have proceeded to build one of the largest public infrastructures in Western Canada. Under Lougheed, the state became heavily involved in the private sector, and in the guise of preventing welfare dependency, built a huge health and social service bureaucracy.

The social policy statement, Caring and Responsibility (Alberta Social Services, 1988), reiterated Alberta's philosophy of promoting self-sufficiency.

PSS/FCSS represents one of the better-known Alberta social policy initiatives. The model was "centralized decentralization," predicated on a strong, centralized resource of professional support, and a locally accountable delivery system. From a community perspective, the Alberta government supported an effective public sector infrastructure.

"Centralized decentralization" was not limited to this sector. Throughout the Lougheed years, from 1971 to 1985, Alberta embarked on a number of similar ventures.

Alberta Recreation and Parks adopted a community development approach, helping local communities establish a base for sports and leisure. Similarly, services for disabled persons worked on a regional model and focussed on helping individuals, families, and communities create the resources they would need to remain independent.

The University of Alberta had one of the few Canadian graduate-level programs in community development between 1968 and 1983. During this period, many community development graduates came to Alberta from other provinces, attracted by the progressive orientation of the policy espoused by the government of the day.

However, as the boom years faded into the recession of the 1980s, even Alberta's economic base softened, and government began to dismantle the infrastructure. Like the late-arriving party guest, health promotion's arrival in Alberta found that pickings were lean, though the menu was to their liking.

So What Was Going On in Health?

During the times of plenty when Alberta was building a network of preventive social services, the health sector was preoccupied with construction of a different ilk. Massive dollars were poured into building hospitals in urban and rural communities where the Conservative government held wide popular support. For more than a decade, Alberta was embroiled in federal – provincial disputes over what was seen to be the imposition of the federal medicare agenda. Only with the passage of the Canada Health Act in 1984 was Alberta able to focus its attention on broader questions of health policy.

Health services consumed an ever-increasing proportion of the provincial budget. At the same time, there was growing uncertainty about the ability of the medical model to effect improvements in health status. Major health reforms in other provinces faced with similar conditions seem to have been accelerated by a change in government. Newly elected governments were prepared to broach the task of significantly shifting resources towards health, away from a preoccupation with the treatment of illness, because they were unencumbered by past commitments. However, there has not been such a catalyst in Alberta to force a radically new agenda for health. Six decades of conservative governments in this province have solidified a mind-set about health. As a consequence, most changes have been cosmetic in nature.

The first Public Health Act of 1907 set the precedent for the public health role of controlling the spread of disease. As the threats of infectious and communicable disease diminished, awareness of the social determinants of health re-emerged. Over the 1970s and '80s, epitomized by the common understanding of the Lalonde Report (Lalonde, 1974), lifestyle and behaviour-change strategies to remedy non-infectious diseases dominated public health work.

Centralized resources within the provincial government were almost exclusively oriented to supporting health education. In 1987, following the release of the *Ottawa Charter for Health Promotion*, Alberta's health units had begun to adopt the language of health promotion, but in fact still focussed on individually oriented educational campaigns designed to modify risk behaviours (Community & Occupational Health, 1987).

The development of a more contemporary view of public health suffered from the lack of a permanent home. During the 1980s, provincial responsibility for public health changed three times. Only since 1991 has there been a permanent Assistant Deputy Minister for Public Health and, after a long gap, a permanent director of health promotion. The Alberta Health Promotion Branch has outlined the first strategic plan for health promotion for Alberta and has a significant role in the planning discussions on reforming the health system.

During the 1980s, public health units in Alberta did not move far afield from established programs. Instead, the units seemed to stagnate, isolated from the locality-development infrastructure being created by the social health practitioners, and philosophically different from the institutional and acute care sectors. The slow erosion of the centralized professional support left the 27 health units without a great deal of direction or vision. The public health sector that advocated health promotion in other parts of Canada was not in a strong position to do so in Alberta.

Just prior to the creation of the first Ministry of Health, the Minister responsible for Community and Occupational Health, Jim Dinning, released a small document entitled, "Moving into the Future for the Health of Albertans" (Community & Occupational Health, 1988). It did not garner much attention, but was an indicator that the thinking about health and illness was beginning to shift within government circles. This document pushed the principle that health was more than the absence of disease. The strategic directions of promotion, prevention, and community care were identified as the ways to improve and reorient the health system in Alberta.

During the late 1980s, three health units were pilot sites for "global funding." The province fully funds Alberta's health units, through an envelope system. The experiment opened the possibility of reorganizing the delivery of public health along the lines of health promotion. Lacking provincial leadership, the pilot languished, and its full potential remains untapped.

Alternative models for delivering health services, outside the formal institutions, have received little attention. Three community health centres (one in Edmonton and two in Calgary) deliver primary care services and advocate on behalf of low-income, culturally diverse communities. The model has yet to capture wide public interest in Alberta. Integrating primary health care and public health may emerge as a comprehensive response to community health issues.

Health Promotion's Arrival

Movements "in Sync"

Striking similarities exist between the political philosophy that has dominated Alberta and the 1980s discourse on health promotion. It should be of little surprise, then, that the new health promotion is readily understood by the community development workers trained in the PSS/FCSS environment. The emphasis on community action and control and on minimalist service intervention is the language of both movements.

While health promotion represented the light at the end of the tunnel for many reform-minded health practitioners, community development workers in other sectors took the introduction lightly, since for them there was nothing apparently new in *Achieving Health for All: A Framework for Health Promotion* (Epp, 1986) or the Ottawa Charter.

The experience of trying to establish the Healthy Communities movement in Edmonton is a testament to this lack of enthusiasm for health promotion, and variations of this experience were repeated in trying to build
an Alberta-wide movement. Adopting a model imported from the east was
looked upon with scepticism by the "alienated" west. Further, the principles were not breakthrough thinking for people who had long seen themselves as proponents of community development. Healthy Communities
was built on problematic assumptions. At one level, health professionals
were increasingly interested in broadening their definition of health and in
engaging partners whose activity also promoted health, perhaps more so
than their own. Often, those partners saw the formal health promoters as
latecomers with an unclear agenda. After the rhetoric of common aims, the
difficult issues that block substantive change remain unmoved.

Without a track record for partnership building across sectors, the
health promoters, largely working in public health or academic institutions, hoped that a common interest in creating healthier environments
would translate into collaboration. People already engaged in social and
environmental health issues — e.g., in housing, employment, community
support services, independent living, environment versus development
battles — did not have energy left over to figure out how the health players could become involved.

Some communities in Alberta used the support of the national
Strengthening Community Health and Healthy Communities projects to
begin unravelling difficult turf issues. The support was channelled through
the Alberta Catalyst Group, led by Val Wiebe. Bringing together catalysts
from public health, environment, preventive social services, and the wellness movement, the group was stretched in its capacity to offer resources
to communities, depending entirely on federal dollars in the absence of
provincial buy-in to sustain the project.

Perhaps more evident in Edmonton, suspicion of bureaucrats' and large
institutions' becoming enmeshed in community decision making inhibited
partnerships. Professionals accustomed to and comfortable in the role of
"experts" found sharing power with communities to be a difficult transition.

Snuffed or Spawned by Health System Reform?

Alberta did not have a Ministry of Health until 1988. The formally powerful and separate Ministry of Hospitals and Medical Care was combined
with lower-profile Departments of Community Health, including Public
Health and Occupational Health and Safety. Nancy Betkowski was named
the first Minister of Health. For a period of time, Family and Community
Support Services (FCSS) was also included in her Ministry.

In 1988, the government formed the Premier's Commission on the
Future of Health Care in Alberta.[1] The Commission solicited and received

---

[1] Announced in the Alberta Legislature Throne Speech in March, 1988.

voluminous input, using such tools as town hall meetings throughout the province, to gauge public opinion. In December 1989, the Commission completed *The Rainbow Report* (Premier's Commission on Future Health Care for Albertans, 1989). The Commissioners urged Albertans to think, not spend their way into the future.

Often misunderstood, the controversial report offered few of the recommendations of conventional Royal Commission reports. Rather, the Rainbow Commission created a conceptual vision for health, embodying the five principles of choice, opportunity, decisions, people, and change. Despite the Commission's strong vision, principles, and historical perspective of the ecological role of public health, it missed the opportunity to liberate health from its institutional, individual, medically dominated preoccupations.

The bulk of the report centres on how to improve the efficiency of the system of medical treatment. Instead of taking the more contemporary view of health promotion, which understands health to be a resource for daily living, socially located, and maintained through individual effort and healthy standards of community life, the Commission reduced health promotion to health education for the purposes of lifestyle modification. This brought the thinking full circle back to the rhetoric of the health bureaucrats.

Yet a positive spin-off of *The Rainbow Report* was a commitment to three related provincial health initiatives for long-term planning and the introduction of management principles to the health system. The Accountability and Role Statement Projects pushed the major health sectors to define roles and responsibilities and the relationships between the sectors. Concurrently, Alberta Health brought together representatives from stakeholder groups to develop Health Goals for the province.

Trends in Health Promotion

Active Living

Today, the two parallel streams of health promotion in Alberta, namely, promoting healthy lifestyles and addressing health determinants, are in dynamic tension. Leadership for promoting healthy living lies within the recreation and leisure field. Health determinants, on the other hand, are beginning to be addressed through the focussed efforts of reform-minded public health practitioners.

In the late 1980s, Alberta Recreation, Parks and Wildlife Foundation, funded by provincial lottery funds, became the backer for the Active Living movement. The idea of creating a provincial centre for well-being originated with the first Canadian Summit on Fitness in 1986. Through individuals with a particular vision in the University of Alberta's Faculty of Physical Education and Recreation, the Alberta Centre for Well-Being came into existence in 1989.

The Centre received a substantial grant to undertake education and research, and to bring together people with a shared vision of promoting healthy lifestyles in the general population. Dr. Judy Sefton was the founding Executive Director. The centre maintains a base in Edmonton and research associates in universities in Calgary and Lethbridge.

The Alberta Centre for Well-Being established alliances with hospitals, the Premier's Council on Persons with Disabilities, the Premier's Council for Alberta Families, Alberta Recreation and Parks, workplaces, and rural municipalities. Their burgeoning networks and partnerships are attributed, in part, to the fact that they are not identified with the "all-knowing" health sector.

Intellectual tension centres on the philosophical underpinnings of Active Living and social determinant interpretations of health promotion. The Alberta Centre for Well-Being drew largely from U.S. field experience to support research and sponsor educational forums on approaches intended for mainstream society. The Centre entered into the Healthy Communities—Alberta movement, offering technical support for a computerized data base of health roles and activities, known as the "network of networks."

The New Public Health

The other stream sees health promotion as the revitalization of fundamental public health principles. Dr. James Howell, Medical Officer of Health for the Edmonton Board of Health, in his 1993 paper, "The Modern Role of Public Health," recounted the impact of the Ottawa Charter.

The document recognized "the need for considered action by communities, by governments, by all forms of organizations and all sectors of the economy" towards the goal of health for all. "This is surely a restatement of the actions that were demanded by Chadwick and Shattuck and others who vilified living and working conditions in the latter half of the nineteenth century and demanded reforms on a large scale." Community action, then, is the basis for all public health (Howell, 1993).

The Edmonton Board of Health, influenced by national and international papers on health promotion, formed a Health Promotion Division to take a community approach to creating supportive environments for health. This first prototype in Alberta brought together health education, nutrition, and mental health promotion.

From its early experimentation with striking up linkages with every sector whose activity touched on health, the Division moved to a more focussed approach. The 1990 Strategic Plan consolidated the integration of health promotion and public health ideology. Reducing inequities in health became the primary thrust for the 1990s. The strategies embraced the key principles of Healthy Communities — community participation, intersectoral action, and healthy public policy.

The Edmonton Board of Health also expressed its interest in a community-driven strategy by forming and providing ongoing funds to the Boyle McCauley Health Centre to address the primary health care needs of inner-city residents.

Knowledge Development

The Health Promotion Division of the Edmonton Board of Health initiated four Summer Schools between 1987 and 1990, drawing on participant groups of about 25 people and international faculties. From a broad look at the concepts in the Ottawa Charter, through Heart Health, Equity and the Environment, the Summer Schools on Health Promotion were organized to expand and influence thinking and build a network of players and sectors across Alberta.

Invitations went to decision makers, service providers, government officials, and community representatives. It was hard to attract people from outside the conventional health institutions. Participants from Edmonton, Calgary, and several smaller centres in Western Canada were exposed to leading-edge thinkers from Canada, the United States, England, Wales, and Finland in an intensive learning environment.

The objectives were consistently to "move from theory to practice," using case examples in Western countries to demonstrate a health promotion approach. The outcome was mostly at the level of articulating principles for practice.

People emphasized public participation in decision making and intersectoral action above all else. An advocacy platform emerged with the assumption that people would carry the directions for change back to their respective networks.

The summer retreats connected people who had already begun to think beyond the narrow boundaries that "health" had defined. Over time, other centres across Canada emulated the summer school approach; the knowledge development network continues to expand.

In retrospect, the gains in health promotion knowledge development in western Canada are largely due to the leadership and support of the Health Promotion Directorate, set up within Health and Welfare Canada. Its decentralized Pacific Regional office provided a window to advance health promotion practice and theory. Their contribution to the development of health promotion in Alberta is immeasurable. Grants for innovative initiatives, and support for knowledge development in the field, resulted in increased capacities and stronger infrastructures.

Conclusion

Lessons Learned

In the decade since health promotion was first introduced in Alberta, many lessons have been learned. It is clear now that simply importing ideas and concepts from elsewhere is of minimal value. Early attempts to introduce health promotion by way of Healthy Communities projects overlooked the experience that already existed in Alberta. Models from other communities have to be examined in light of the context in which they were developed.

The key to health promotion is the application of a rigorous critical analysis of the context, issues, barriers, capacities, and positions of those affected to achieve intended outcomes. Without the analysis, health promotion is simply health education dressed up.

Health promotion proponents had to refocus from trying to change the policies of other sectors that affect health to influencing their own practice settings. Securing commitment to work toward the achievement of health rather than the resolution of illness then opens the opportunity to build partnerships with other stakeholders beyond the formal health system.

Effective partnerships recognize the diverse agendas present at the table, and are equally sensitive to the need for those agendas to be met. Building partnerships is more than muddling through; they require an analysis at the outset with clear statements of purpose.

The final lesson rests with the observers. The full impact of health promotion in Alberta can only be assessed in Alberta. In seeking to understand others' experiences, we emphasize the importance of reserving judgement based on our own perceptions and values. As is the case in other parts of the country, the future for health promotion in the province of Alberta largely depends upon the ability of local practitioners to be relevant to regionally specific social, political, and economic conditions.

Acknowledgements

The authors wish to thank several people who assisted in the preparation of this chapter: Lloyd Bentz, Recreation, Parks & Wildlife Foundation, Edmonton; Katherine Caine, Alberta Health, Edmonton; Hildegard Campsall, Peace River Health Unit, Edmonton; Joel Christie, Consultant, Edmonton; Sandi Darrell, Alberta Health, Edmonton; Georgeann Hancock, Minburn-Vermilion Health Unit, Edmonton; James M. Howell, Edmonton Board of Health, Edmonton; Judy Sefton, Alberta Centre for Well-Being, Edmonton; and Val Wiebe, Alexandra Park Community Health Centre, Calgary.

References

Alberta Community Health & Social Services (1983). *Health promotion programming in local authorities in Alberta* (A discussion paper, Community Health Promotion Standing Committee). Edmonton: Author.

Alberta Community & Occupational Health (1987). *Health promotion programs in Alberta health units.* Edmonton: Author.

Alberta Community & Occupational Health (1988). *Moving into the future for the health of Albertans.* Edmonton: Queen's Printer.

Alberta Health, Health Promotion Branch (1991). *Promoting health for all Albertans. A strategic plan.* Edmonton: Author.

Alberta Health, Advisory Committee on Health Goals & Objectives for Alberta (1991). *A strategy to develop health goals and objectives For Alberta* (draft). Edmonton: Author.

Alberta Premier's Commission on Future Health Care for Albertans (1989). *The rainbow report: Our vision for health.* Edmonton: Queen's Printer.

Alberta Social Services (1988). *Caring and responsibility.* Edmonton: Queen's Printer.

Bella, L. (1981). *The politics of the right-wing "welfare state."* Unpublished doctoral dissertation, University of Alberta, Edmonton.

Burnet, J. (1951). *Next year country: A study of rural social organizations In Alberta.* Toronto: University of Toronto Press.

Epp, J. (1986). *Achieving health for all: A framework for health promotion.* Ottawa: Supply & Services Canada.

Goldblatt, A., & McGuire, D. (1988, January). *Summer school on community health promotion* (Proceedings of Summer School held August 16-21, 1987). Edmonton: Edmonton Board of Health.

Howell, J.M. (1993). *The modern role of public health.* Edmonton: Edmonton Board of Health.

Irving, J.A. (1959). *The Social Credit movement in Alberta.* University of Toronto Press.

Kickbusch, I. (1989). Back to the future. In J. Wolczuk, J. McDowell, & K. Ainslie (eds.), *Proceedings of the National Symposium on Health Promotion and Disease Prevention* (March 12-15, 1989) (pp.1-15). Victoria: B.C. Ministry of Health, Office of Health Promotion.

Lalonde, M. (1974). *A new perspective on the health of Canadians.* Ottawa: Supply & Services Canada.

McDowell, J.A. (1992). *From rhetoric to reality: A walk on the practical side.* (Notes, Symposium on Knowledge Development in Health Promotion, Yukon, February 27-March 1, 1992.) Victoria: Health Promotion Directorate B.C./Yukon Region.

Macpherson, C.B. (1953). *Democracy in Alberta.* Toronto: University of Toronto Press.

McQ Enterprises Ltd. (1988). *Summer school on community health promotion: Effective heart health programs* (Proceedings of summer school held August 22-26, 1988). Edmonton: Edmonton Board of Health.

McQ Enterprises Ltd. (1989). *Summer school on community health promotion: Towards equity in health* (Proceedings of summer school held August 20-25, 1989). Edmonton: Edmonton Board of Health.

McQ Enterprises Ltd. (1990). *Summer school on community health promotion: Health and the environment* (Proceedings of summer school held June 10-15, 1990). Edmonton: Edmonton Board of Health.

Poland, B.D. (1992). Learning to walk our talk: The implications of sociological theory for research methodologies in health promotion. *Canadian Journal of Public Health, 83*(Supp. 1), 31-46.

Stevenson, H.M., & Burke, M. (1992). Bureaucratic logic in new social movement clothing: The limits of health promotion research. *Canadian Journal of Public Health, 83*(Supp. 1), 47-53.

World Health Organization, Health & Welfare Canada, & Canadian Public Health Association (1986). *Ottawa charter for health promotion.* Ottawa: CPHA.

Promoting Health in Saskatchewan

Joan Feather

T his chapter will examine how the concept and practice of health promotion evolved in Saskatchewan as a product of interaction between
community needs and political agendas over the past decade and a
half. In that period, the province experienced dramatic shifts in philosophy
within its provincial government. Economic prosperity in the 1970s gave
way to serious recession, mounting provincial debt, and increasing poverty in the 1980s. Meanwhile, Saskatchewan's Aboriginal community, among
the poorest of the poor, moved slowly but with increasing determination
toward settlement of outstanding land claims and self-government. These
conditions are part of the social environment influencing well-being for
Saskatchewan's people. They provide the framework essential for understanding the formal policies and program structures created in the name of
health promotion by the provincial government. Finally, they set the stage
for the response of communities and non-governmental organizations
(NGOs) to provincial policies and to perceived community needs.

Provincial Government Policies and Programs

Early Approaches to Health Promotion

On the eve of the publication of *A New Perspective on the Health of
Canadians* (Lalonde, 1974; hereafter, the Lalonde Report), Saskatchewan
unveiled a major lifestyle change program. Following the recommendations of an all-party committee of the Legislature examining liquor regulations, in March 1974 the provincial Health Department announced a program called AWARE to "raise the level of public awareness of drinking patterns which are harmful, and to reinforce social attitudes which will have
a positive effect in changing such drinking patterns" (Whitehead, 1975,
p. 3). The program used mass media; the aim was to change attitudes
among social drinkers, make them aware that alcohol is a drug, and help
them to recognize factors in the social context that tend to encourage
immoderate drinking behaviour (Saskatchewan Health, 1974).

Although aimed at the problem of alcohol misuse, the program had no
direct link with the provincial Alcoholism Commission, a government
agency with community education, treatment, and rehabilitation staff.
Instead, AWARE was amalgamated with the Health Education and Information
Branch of the Health Department in 1975 to form a Health Promotion

Branch. This Branch was "to place greater emphasis on health promotion in general, and to recognize the need for public education in those areas where health problems are associated with today's lifestyles" (Saskatchewan Health, 1976, p. 10). Evaluation of the AWARE program showed that attitudes were indeed changed in a desirable direction. Another mass media program, Feelin' Good, followed in November 1977, with the aim of promoting healthy lifestyles, beginning with an emphasis on physical fitness and nutrition (Saskatchewan Health, 1978). Then, as part of a major restructuring of the Health Department, the Health Promotion Branch and its lifestyle programs were absorbed into the Community Health Services Branch as a division. Specialists from community health in such areas as nutrition and family planning became part of the Health Promotion Division, liaising with the community health field staff in health regions throughout the province. This structure remained in place until 1985.

Children and youth received special attention. In 1979, the International Year of the Child, the province conducted a survey of health knowledge, attitudes, and behaviour of Saskatchewan youth (Weston, 1980), and in 1981 released a major report calling for renewed emphasis on child and family health services (Saskatchewan Health, 1981). Within the Health Promotion Branch the result was targetting of lifestyle education programs to children and adolescents (Saskatchewan Health, 1982). Outside of government, the Institute for the Prevention of Handicaps was created with funding from both Saskatchewan Health and the Department of Social Services as well as the Saskatchewan Association for the Mentally Retarded. Its purpose was to educate the public and professionals on prevention of developmental disorders and handicaps in children (Institute on Prevention, 1982). It became a major information clearinghouse, and has been highly creative in its mass media products to promote awareness and understanding concerning effective preventive measures.

In effect, in the provincial Health Department and in agencies like the Institute in the late 1970s, health promotion meant social marketing through the mass media, coupled with health education and disease prevention programs. Professional staff of the Community Health Services component of the Health Department and their counterparts in the two cities of Regina and Saskatoon were central to the delivery of these programs. The idea of lifestyle as a major health determinant, introduced in the Lalonde Report, was the driving force in health promotion. This focus was based on the belief that

> a significant proportion of illness in the last quarter century is the result of inactive and faulty lifestyles. Heart attacks, cancer, and motor vehicle accidents are the three leading causes of death in Saskatchewan. These causes could be significantly reduced by improvements in lifestyle habits affecting diet, exercise, stress, smoking, alcohol and drugs. The Health Promotion Branch is responsible for developing programs which will help Saskatchewan residents attain healthier lifestyles. (Saskatchewan Health, 1977, p. 15)

The term "healthy public policy" had not yet been coined, but there were notable examples of healthy and empowering public policies introduced in the 1970s and early '80s in Saskatchewan. For example, the province reduced barriers to dental health through a landmark school-based children's dental program, and established a prescription drug insurance program.

Perhaps the most intriguing development from the point of view of empowerment was the creation of the Department of Northern Saskatchewan in 1972. The aim was to give this disadvantaged region higher priority in all spheres of provincial government programming, and to increase Northerners' participation in and control over decisions in such areas as education, local government, and economic development. Northern branches and programs from all provincial government departments were combined into a single organization, to improve co-ordination of public policy affecting the North. Community development workers helped to strengthen local communities and facilitate their taking control of government functions. The demonstrated effects of this activation alarmed bureaucrats in the Department and elsewhere in government. Communities put new skills to the test in organized protests against certain policies of the Department itself. As a result, the community development program of the Department drew fire from critics of these attempts to end socio-economic colonialism in the North. The community developers were dismissed, on the pretext that

> the work of the Community Development section in providing motivational stimulus and the organizational assistance provided by the area co-ordinators was becoming less and less necessary. . . . people of Northern Saskatchewan had reached a level of participation in the development process which reduced the need for services from [the Field Services Section]. (Saskatchewan, 1976, p. 6)

But there remained a legacy of local government organization, and the North was physically transformed with the development of roads, schools, health centres, sewer and water systems (Gruending, 1990). Saskatchewan had taken a step toward greater equity between north and south.

Health Promotion in the 1980s

The New Democratic Party (NDP) government was defeated in the provincial election of 1982, and the Progressive Conservatives swept into power with a large majority. Over the next decade, Saskatchewan witnessed what has been described as the aggressive pursuit of a "new right" agenda (Pitsula & Rasmussen, 1990). The direct effects on the Health Promotion Branch in the Health Department were less obvious than effects in other sectors.

During its first term in office, the new government eliminated a food subsidy for remote northern communities, putting nutritious food beyond the reach of many northern low-income families (Joseph, 1985). The Department of Northern Saskatchewan was dismantled, as was the Women's Division of the Department of Labour. Reform in the welfare system began to undermine the already precarious safety net for the poor and disabled (Riches & Manning, 1989). Capital projects such as hospital and nursing home construction proliferated. There were tax breaks and royalty cuts for resource industries, and homeowners enjoyed home improvement grants and mortgage interest subsidies. By 1986, Saskatchewan had accumulated a significant public debt.

Re-elected in 1986 for a second term, the government "raised a hue and cry about the debt, cut back drastically on government spending, and began to privatize aggressively" (Pitsula & Rasmussen, 1990, p. 121). Although it was the privatization of the natural gas utility that may have ultimately rallied the strongest opposition, the cuts in health and social sectors had widespread negative repercussions for the government as well.

The funding cuts effected in the spring and summer of 1987 ("Tory budget," 1987) were especially ironic in view of the newly released federal health promotion document, *Achieving Health for All: A Framework for Health Promotion* (Epp, 1986; hereafter, the Framework), which advocated actions to reduce inequities, increase prevention, enhance coping, and develop supportive social and public policy environments and strong community health services. In Saskatchewan, funding cuts hit transition houses for battered women and children, family planning services, community mental health programs, human rights advocates, crisis intervention services, organizations for the handicapped, legal aid services for the poor, the Native court worker program, and municipal capital programs including sewer and water works, among others (Brown, 1987). The school-based children's dental program was dismantled, with parents being directed to private dentists where such could be found (Saskatchewan Health, 1988a). A deductible was imposed in the prescription drug plan that put access to needed medications beyond the reach of some families ("Parents feel," 1987).

Funding and program cuts contributed to an unsupportive social environment for the poor and disadvantaged. Their plight was exacerbated by public rhetoric originating with Cabinet ministers who took a dim view of many of the poor as undeserving, the homeless as homeless by choice, and the unemployed as refusing to work (Saskatchewan Legislative Assembly, 1989). What came to be referred to as "workfare" replaced welfare, in violation of the spirit of the Canada Assistance Plan (Riches & Manning, 1989). Welfare rates were reduced and benefits cut; policies were infused with moralizing, and the poor were further humiliated by the actions of a "fraud squad" intent on eliminating welfare abuse ("Fraud squad," 1987).

Provincial government popularity dropped dramatically following these funding and program cuts ("NDP doubles," 1987), especially those affecting the children's dental and prescription drug plans. Minor adjustments were made to soften the effects of the cuts, for example by eliminating the long wait for rebates from the prescription drug plan for people who had paid more than their deductible. But the weight of the provincial debt was undeniable, and the government could not buy its way back into the public's favour.

The provincial Health Promotion program was directly affected by the political ill-fortune of the government of the day. In terms of structure, in 1985 the Health Promotion Branch had once again become a separate branch of the Health Department, but this time combined with Communications. One of its objectives was to "continually reassure and reinforce the positive aspects of the health system to the Saskatchewan

public." It was to "integrate communications and health education closely with executive decision-making processes within the department"
(Saskatchewan Health, 1985, p. 83). As the cuts of 1987 progressed, however, the government paid a high price in popularity ("NDP doubles,"
1987). The need for skillful public communication to minimize fallout
became more urgent, and the communications function was removed from
Health Promotion and relocated closer to the office of the Minister.

As for health promotion programming, in June 1988 came the
announcement of a major new health promotion initiative, called Everyone
Wins. Its expressed aims were "to motivate individuals, communities and
organizations to make responsible decisions on personal health and
lifestyle; to increase public awareness of the advantages of healthy lifestyle;
to instill motivation and commitment to improvement; and to foster community, NGO, private-sector and government support for health promotion initiatives" (Loewen, 1988, p. 2). It focussed on seven areas of
"lifestyle enhancement": nutrition, physical fitness, accident prevention,
coping with stress, non-smoking, responsible use of alcohol and drugs, and
communicable disease. Major components of the program were mass
media campaigns, production and distribution of literature and audio-visual materials, mammoth health "fairs," a community resource package to
help groups identify needs and plan related activities, community grants of
up to one thousand dollars for such activities, a resource kit for workplace
health promotion programs for employees, and encouragement for private
sector sponsorship of lifestyle enhancement programs in the community.

These aspects of the Everyone Wins program were greeted with cynicism in some quarters because of the contradictions of the program in view
of the recent health and social service cuts, the "glitz" of the new campaign, its outdated and narrow focus almost exclusively on lifestyle modification, and the use of community grants to spread token amounts of government largesse to communities and groups across the province.

Under the broad umbrella of the Everyone Wins initiative, other steps
were taken. A Health Status Research Unit was established at the University
of Saskatchewan to undertake research into the health status of the
Saskatchewan population and to provide technical advice related to certain
aspects of the Everyone Wins program. A provincial Advisory Committee to
the Minister was appointed in the fall of 1988, representing 14 major stakeholder organizations such as the Medical Association, the Registered Nurses
Association, and the College of Medicine. The Committee would "provide
advice and recommendations on strategies and opportunities for enhancing
the effectiveness and impact" of the program (Saskatchewan Health, 1988b,
p. 1). It would also "identify achievable health promotion targets and goals
for the province" (p. 1). The Advisory Committee's goal-setting process
began in early 1989. At the urging of the Health Status Research Unit in its
technical advisory capacity, the committee agreed to incorporate as much
stakeholder participation as possible (Health Status Research Unit, 1989a).
But this consultation process was hampered by the unrealistic time frame
imposed by the province. Some stakeholder representatives balked at the
constraints they encountered: the goals were to relate only to the seven

lifestyle areas of the Everyone Wins program. Many of those consulted argued successfully for broadening the goals to include equity, environmental concerns, and mental health (Advisory Committee on Health Promotion, 1989). Work on measurable objectives and associated strategies followed, with the Health Status Research Unit urging the adoption of a comprehensive array of strategies consistent with the Ottawa Charter (Health Status Research Unit, 1989b). In January 1991, Saskatchewan's Healthy Living Goals were unveiled (Saskatchewan Health, 1991). The Health Status Research Unit proceeded to develop a plan for establishing baselines and monitoring progress on all the objectives (Feather, 1991a).

Although widely distributed, the goals were not formally endorsed or adopted by the provincial government. Indeed, it became increasingly unlikely that they would be seriously considered as the province moved through the spring and summer of 1991 toward an election call.

The Everyone Wins program and its goal-setting process, while still centred on lifestyle change objectives, did include new opportunities for communities, workplaces, and other groups to plan and carry out modest health promotion projects. The program may have served another purpose as well: it enabled the province to demonstrate a positive response to health issues.

Another positive initiative was the appointment of a six-member commission (known as the Murray Commission after its chair, R.G. Murray) in July 1988 to examine the future directions of health care in the province. Reporting in the spring of 1990, the Commission dealt mainly with service reorganization, decentralization, and the consolidation of governance of health services under division councils in large geographic units across the province (Saskatchewan Commission on Directions in Health Care, 1990).

Health promotion was not a major theme of the Commission's report. It acknowledged the health vulnerability of the poor, children, Native people, Northerners, teenage mothers, and the physically disabled. It recognized the public interest in reducing health risk, protecting the environment, and enacting appropriate public policies. But it concluded merely that "these examples emphasize the unbreakable bond that links behaviour and lifestyle and health. The more recognition there is of that bond, and acceptance of the personal and community responsibility it demands, the less will be the demands on the health care system" (Saskatchewan Commission on Directions in Health Care, 1990, p. 16).

Health promotion would be included as a function of the new health divisions' community health and supportive living services, a large collection of responsibilities including public health, chiropody, community therapy, home care, community mental health services, support for family care givers, and aids to independent living. Divisions would have five dollars per capita to spend on health promotion. Health promotion programs should be "targeted at increasing people's sense of responsibility for preserving the health of their community and their personal good health" (Saskatchewan Commission on Directions in Health Care, 1990, p. 59). This would be achieved by increasing the number of traditional public health staff, particularly in education and nutrition, and appointing a health education officer to serve as a resource person to other professionals. The Commission made no reference to the Framework.

The need for intersectoral planning and action received scant attention in the Commission's report. A special commission would monitor government policies and report to the Legislature but have no authority. It could only "refer to, and where appropriate, express caution about industrial, commercial and public undertakings which could undermine good health" (Saskatchewan Commission on Directions in Health Care, 1990, p. 55). Only with regard to northern Saskatchewan was there explicit recognition of the social determinants of health and the need for actual intersectoral policy co-ordination.

The provincial government went further to demonstrate its concept of public consultation and participation. The throne speech in March 1990 announced that there would be a group called Consensus Saskatchewan appointed as a think tank and consultation panel to make recommendations concerning the "growth and well-being" of Saskatchewan's people, security and stability of communities, expansion and diversification of the economy, and responsible and efficient management of resources. Appointed in May 1990, the 95 members of Consensus Saskatchewan worked at record pace to hold 108 public meetings and to report in September. The group acknowledged that growth and prosperity would depend on strong local communities, better employment opportunities, better education, adequate housing, food and clean water. But an underlying theme pervaded many of the wide-ranging recommendations, including those related to health: Saskatchewan should move "toward the development of independent, responsible individuals who are accountable for their actions" (Consensus Saskatchewan, 1990, p. iii). Explicitly, "the people of Saskatchewan must accept that good health is an individual responsibility" (Consensus Saskatchewan, 1990, p. 43). Promotion of healthy lifestyles and prevention of illness would contribute toward this goal.

These consultations and their products did little to dampen criticism or reduce cynicism about the government's programs and intentions. A climate of fear and suspicion pervaded the civil service because of job cuts and firings (Biggs, 1991). This demoralization, combined with actual staff shortages, drained creativity in the ranks of government employees. Innovation would have to come from communities and organizations where needs were visible and urgent, and where the concept of health promotion as enablement and empowerment could take root.

Community Needs and Response

The Coalition Strategy

Coalitions have been a popular social action strategy in Saskatchewan for decades. They are an effective vehicle for public participation in issues affecting health. Early in the 1980s, when federal and provincial governments seemed prepared to retreat from the principles of medicare, a national Health Coalition formed to fight to preserve cost-shared, universal, and accessible health care. A Saskatchewan Health Coalition joined in, with strong union support and, eventually, over 20 member organizations and more than 150 individuals. The Coalition critically analyzed the Murray Commission Report, held public forums, and arranged all-party meetings to challenge candidates on health issues in the 1991 provincial election.

Welfare rights groups organized in response to the government's welfare reform program in the mid-1980s, and grew into a provincewide network. A Social Justice Network emerged out of solidarity with welfare rights groups and related concerns about the disintegrating social, employment, and health service climate. One group organized a "summer school of social justice" to train members of the public in the fine art of protest. Concerns about racial tensions in urban centres spawned a Coalition Against Racism. Action Now, and the Saskatchewan Seniors Association, are vocal proponents of the needs and views of older citizens.

There are formal coalitions among health agencies to tackle specific health problems: for example, the Interagency Council on Smoking and Health, a provincial AIDS Coalition, urban coalitions to address the problems of child hunger, and an interagency coalition to improve and co-ordinate services for pregnant and parenting teenagers. A network of urban core workers in Saskatoon, meeting to develop consistent approaches to the issue of poverty and its consequences, led to the establishment of the Saskatoon Social Planning Council. A provincial Literacy Network, a coalition on bicycle safety, and the Saskatchewan Heart Health Coalition are further examples. Federal funding has played an important role in many of these initiatives.

Municipal Initiatives and the Healthy Communities Project

There are fewer examples in Saskatchewan to illustrate what has been termed the Healthy Communities approach to health promotion. However, one example of intersectoral action for well-being at the municipal level predates the formal Healthy Communities Project by several years. In 1977 a concerned city councillor in Saskatoon, Helen Hughes, was instrumental in establishing a "community liaison committee" with municipal and Native organization representation to improve interracial communication and build opportunities for Native people in education, housing, employment, recreation, and health. Support expressed by the media, community agencies, and individuals persuaded Council to overcome its reservations about becoming "involved in a matter of social concern" (Fisher & McNabb, 1979, p. 23). The Community Liaison Committee functioned until 1982 with funding from the city, the province, and the federal government. It hired a development worker, organized workshops and interracial communications conferences, and supported task forces discussing such specific issues as housing, law, and enforcement. The provincial government helped by providing research data and other information from its Social Planning Secretariat, which had targeted urban Native issues as a high priority for the province. But Hughes, the project's driving force, left the province in 1979, government funding priorities changed with the election of 1982, and the Community Liaison Committee was disbanded.

Five years later, the idea of Healthy Communities was being promoted nationally and internationally. Regina declared itself committed to the concept in 1988. In 1990 the Saskatchewan Public Health Association urged the provincial Department of Urban Affairs to provide funding for a central staff position and start-up grants to communities. But at the time of writing, the Regina project remains in its infancy, and the province has yet to indicate willingness to provide leadership and financial support. In 1992, federal grant support through the Health Promotion Directorate, Winnipeg, made it possible for a major Healthy Communities project to get under way in Saskatoon with sponsorship by the Saskatoon Social Planning Council and the Colleges of Nursing and Extension at the University of Saskatchewan. This project may play a key role in promoting the concept elsewhere in the province.

Interest in the Healthy Communities idea is strong in some quarters. The Saskatchewan Public Health Association co-sponsored a major workshop on "health and action" in the fall of 1991 (Feather, 1991b), with Evelyne de Leeuw, a leading proponent from the Netherlands. Workshop organizers made follow-up plans for increasing awareness of the concept, building public support, and using informal networking processes to encourage communities where action is already occurring.

One example of such action is illustrative. People around Davidson, a town in the midst of the grain belt, were shocked to realize that some of their farmer neighbours, threatened with loss of their farms because of debt and the cost-price squeeze, were depressed and suicidal. Farmers turned to church leaders who helped rally service clubs, businesses, municipal governments, helping professionals, and others to form the Davidson Farm and Town Self-Help Group. A psychologist employed by the Centre for Agricultural Medicine at the University of Saskatchewan, and later another working with the provincial Mental Health Services Branch, were instrumental in providing training and resources for the farmers in this area and elsewhere in combatting farm stress. Not only has the town changed its approach to attracting and keeping families in the community, but farmers now get practical advice, information, and moral support in their struggles with the banks and credit corporations (Brotherton, 1992).

Other examples could be cited (Finney, 1991; Morin & Britton, 1991). They illustrate that Healthy Communities action is alive and well, in substance if not in name, in Saskatchewan. Without support from the provincial government, however, prospects for promoting the concept in other communities are limited.

The Strengthening Community Health Project

The second national health promotion initiative to seek provincial endorsement was called Strengthening Community Health. The Saskatchewan Public Health Association (SPHA) acted as provincial sponsor for this program. The initial consultation workshop hosted by the SPHA took place in May 1987. The timing is significant: the province was entering its "summer of discontent" (Pitsula & Rasmussen, 1990) as health and social service program cuts accelerated and the province appeared to be turning its back on the disadvantaged. In this context, 25 participants from a broad range of community health interests and agencies identified challenges to community health services: for example, to overcome the vested interests and territoriality of health professionals that stand in the way of empowerment, and to focus on the root causes of ill health by attending to basic needs, e.g., food, shelter, employment, and security (Siler-Wells, 1987). Among the actions needed to meet these challenges, the group identified as a fundamental requirement training in the skills of community development, adult education, and popular education for health professionals. The participants protested that "slick mass media campaigns," the "standard government practice in health promotion" (Siler-Wells, 1987, p. 50), did little more than raise the profile of the sponsoring government. They argued that without a local network of resources to build on the increased public awareness, little would be achieved.

At a second workshop in March 1988, with more participants from formal public health practice, discussion centred around the need for a health goal-setting process, and for changes to the health service system to increase public "participation"; actual popular mobilization through community development received little attention (Saskatchewan Public Health Association, 1988).

The final workshop in this series took place in January 1989. By this time the provincial Everyone Wins program was under way, and the province had appointed its Advisory Committee on Health Promotion with the announced intention of setting provincial health promotion goals. The Murray Commission was at work on proposals for changes to the health care system. The latter two issues dominated the discussion, concerns centring around the extent and form of public input into these two processes. The workshop also debated ways to create public demand for access to both health promotion services and an environment that is health promoting (Saskatchewan Public Health Association, 1989). It discounted the notion that health promotion could be successfully marketed on the basis of increasing personal responsibility. Instead, the Saskatchewan Public Health Association should sponsor training in the community development process, for the public and health professionals alike, and try to create commitment to community development as a basic principle.

Taking up this challenge, the Association organized a training workshop on community development with Godwin Eni[1] in December 1989, for SPHA members and invited individuals from the members' communities, with emphasis on recruitment from rural Saskatchewan. Although the Association was unable to lend significant support to these trainees in their community-based work, it has maintained an interest in community

---

[1] Division of Health Policy & Management, Department of Health Care & Epidemiology, University of British Columbia.

development training, and in 1992 passed a resolution calling on the provincial government to establish a self-help/community development clearinghouse.

Native Community Health Development

Meanwhile, community development in practice has played an important role in northern Saskatchewan Native communities. Some individuals who had been part of the Department of Northern Saskatchewan in the 1970s were still to be found working with Native communities to transfer control of health services from the federal government to First Nations. An outstanding example is the William Charles Health Centre operated by the Montréal Lake Band north of Prince Albert. This was the first health service in Canada controlled by a single Indian band. The Band undertook a needs assessment that revealed the roots of most disease and trauma in poverty, overcrowding, and substandard living conditions, alcohol abuse, poor self-care, and inaccessible treatment services (Mitchell, 1991). It negotiated with the Medical Services Branch of the federal government an agreement that provided for a community-controlled health program to be housed in a new building constructed by Montréal Lake's own development company. The Band defined a comprehensive array of services to be offered from the Centre, and negotiated a unique funding arrangement based on the commitment of the Band to reduce medical transportation costs and thereby recover some of the needed money. The community wanted and got control of its service. It established a team approach within the Centre with a distinctly Native atmosphere surrounding the services. As a result, Band members are more aware of health as an issue, feel more competent to engage in self-care and to make lifestyle changes, accept preventive services more readily, come earlier for needed treatment, and make dramatically fewer demands on medical transportation to southern centres (Moore, Forbes, & Henderson, 1990).

More recently, two large tribal councils, encompassing all bands in the northern half of the province, have signed transfer agreements that include highly innovative programming. Community developers, health educators whose jobs centre on community health mobilization, and Band health service administrators who will have training in community development and health promotion as well as management, are part of the new wave of First Nations health service staff (Prince Albert Tribal Council, 1990).

The challenging health problems in many northern communities (Feather, 1991c; Tan, et al., 1992) warrant additional comment with respect to strategies for health promotion. Many communities paralyzed by alcoholism have seen and heard the story of Alkali Lake, a reserve in British Columbia that successfully overcame its communitywide alcohol problem. Encouraged by this example, some have achieved remarkable recovery and sobriety rates, thanks to key individuals becoming role models and pushing strategically for changes in behaviour and expectations. Taking control of education and health services produces self-confidence, pride, and the skills that make other challenges less daunting. Where once only a few learned to read and write, now dozens of young adults graduate from high schools staffed by Northerners, trained in an off-campus teacher education program based in the North, and employed by a Northern school board or Band council. Dependency on welfare payments is recognized for its demoralizing effects; instead, communities engage in sophisticated economic planning projects and call for control of the lands surrounding their communities and of the resource development projects that once drained northern wealth into southern corporations. Processes of personal healing, human resource development, and community development are fundamental to these changes. The result is health promotion.

Conclusion

The form and substance of health promotion efforts by the provincial government in Saskatchewan have been a vivid reflection of opposing political philosophies. Formally, health promotion within the provincial Health Department from the mid-1970s until the present has been characterized by lifestyle programming and health education. But in other policies affecting health and well-being, the contrast between the government initiatives of the 1970s and those of the 1980s is dramatic. Partly in response to health and social service cuts, and inattention to the needs of the disadvantaged during the 1980s, community coalitions and networks emerged as a significant force for social justice. While the Canadian Healthy Communities Project and the Strengthening Community Health Program have had relatively little impact in this province, there are outstanding examples of innovative local action to promote health and well-being. There are places in Saskatchewan where community health development has been dramatically effective in enabling people to achieve their goals.

Nurturing the concept of health promotion in Saskatchewan continues to be a challenge. But several key factors should be noted for their contribution to this process. Federal government health promotion initiatives have played a key role here. Although not widely used in government during the 1980s, the Framework was invaluable as an expression of the aspirations of many individuals committed to reducing inequities and struggling for policies that would create more supportive environments for health. At critical junctures, federal grant funding, especially from the Health Promotion Directorate, made it possible for innovation to occur. Networks and coalitions have supported people in their struggles against hostile social policy, lack of funding, and service cuts. The examples of specific communities that have overcome major obstacles to health are an inspiration to others. Lessons to be learned from the healing of northern and Native communities are slower to be appreciated but no less important. The community development skills refined in the crucible of First Nations empowerment are being recognized more widely.

Epilogue

In late 1991 the Tory government went down in a resounding defeat as the NDP swept back into power. For several months the new government was totally preoccupied in analyzing the scope of the provincial debt and assessing its room to manoeuvre. Concerns about the extent of the deficit were blamed for premature announcements of changes in health care policy; these were not encouraging (e.g., increased fees for users of prescription drugs, chiropractic, and optometric services). In a more positive light, in August 1992, the government unveiled a major health reform initiative, outlined in a document, *A Saskatchewan Vision for Health* (Saskatchewan Health, 1992).

The reform is based on two principles: the concept of "wellness" as the goal of health services, and community control of health service delivery. Three strategies will be used to achieve these goals: public policies that promote good health; health promotion and disease prevention; and integration and co-ordination of health services. The Framework is prominent in the *Vision* document, as is the World Health Organization's new definition of health.

Legislation has been introduced to support the formation of new health districts, in which attention is initially focussed on integrating and rationalizing hospital, long-term care, ambulance, and home care services. In Saskatoon and Regina, interim boards appointed by the province have moved quickly to take control of services and make changes to adjust to reduced funding overall. In Saskatoon, one million dollars has been shifted from acute care to community health and home care services. In smaller cities and across the sparsely populated southern half of the province, progress is very uneven toward defining district boundaries and rationalizing services. In many rural areas, anxieties over losing institutional beds and jobs overshadows all other considerations. The province is providing facilitators to assist communities to form districts; subsequently, they will help districts determine health needs and develop health plans. Ultimately, all district boards will manage community health, mental health, and addiction services. But current guidelines are vague and, for the moment, outside major centres these services are marginalized in the turmoil over district formation and funding reductions.

In the North, at a more realistic pace, municipalities and tribal councils are discussing with provincial and federal governments how more co-ordination can be achieved in addressing the pressing health issues of Métis and First Nations communities. Without the inertia generated by an oversupply of beds and treatment services, and with the self-confidence developed through recent political maturation, these communities have good prospects for improving health through health reform.

It is unclear how the government's own Health Promotion Branch will fare in the new context, or how effectively public policies will be co-ordinated between sectors at the provincial level. The 1993 budget (Saskatchewan, 1993) unveiled more drastic cuts to established health insurance programs, including the drug plan and the children's dental program. While most of the financial news for health care was bad, there was increased financial support for poor families and low-income seniors, and more money for regional economic development. A provincial Health Council — to monitor the impact on health of public policies — has been promised for months, but has yet to be announced.

The fiscal credibility of the NDP government rests on its ability to adhere to a long-term plan of reducing the deficit and balancing the budget. The credibility of its wellness reform initiative is inextricably linked to the larger fiscal dilemma. Is Saskatchewan on the verge of a new era in health promotion? Out of the present confusion, many here in the heart of "next year country" hope that with determination and creativity we can create new strategies and programs that will enable Saskatchewan's people to achieve a higher level of well-being.

Acknowledgements

I am grateful to many who spent time talking with me about events and issues associated with health promotion in Saskatchewan, or commenting on early drafts: Georgia Bell Woodard, Pat Bell, Bruce Chamberlin, Gerri Dickson, Loretta Ebert, Kathryn Green, Brian Habbick, Joanne Hader, Lynn Hainsworth, Gary Ledoux, Barbara Mathur, Meredith Moore, Diana Ralph, Kathy Seaman, and Mark Stobbe. The responsibility for interpretation and conclusions in this chapter is mine alone.

References

Advisory Committee on Health Promotion (1989, October). *Report of first consultation meeting*. Regina, Saskatchewan. Unpublished.

Biggs, L. (1991). Building binges and budget cuts: Health care in Saskatchewan, 1982-1990. In L. Biggs & M. Stobbe (eds.), *Devine rule in Saskatchewan* (pp. 177-202). Saskatoon: Fifth House.

Brotherton, L. (1992, April). *Davidson farm and town self-help group*. Paper presented at Annual Conference of Canadian Mental Health Association in Saskatchewan and Saskatchewan Public Health Association, Saskatoon.

Brown, C. (1987). *Profile of reductions in health care in Saskatchewan*. Regina: Saskatchewan Public Health Association. Unpublished manuscript.

Consensus Saskatchewan (1990). *Leading the way: A blueprint for Saskatchewan*. Regina: Author.

Epp, J. (1986). *Achieving health for all: A framework for health promotion.* Ottawa: Health & Welfare Canada.

Feather, J. (1991a). *Monitoring Saskatchewan's health living goals: A discussion paper.* Saskatoon: University of Saskatchewan, Health Status Research Unit. Unpublished manuscript.

Feather, J. (Ed.) (1991b). *Saskatchewan communities: Health and action.* Saskatoon: University of Saskatchewan, Health Status Research Unit.

Feather, J. (1991c). *Social health in northern Saskatchewan.* Saskatoon: University of Saskatchewan, Northern Medical Services.

Finney, P. (1991). Prince Albert Mayor's Committee for Community Development: A comparison with the Healthy Community concept. In J. Feather (ed.), *Saskatchewan communities: Health and action* (pp. 30-36). Saskatoon: University of Saskatchewan, Health Status Research Unit.

Fisher, R., & McNabb, H. (1979). *A social services planning approach to Native/non-Native relations in Saskatoon.* Saskatoon: Community Liaison Committee.

'Fraud squad' skulker upsets victim (1987, May 15). *Star Phoenix,* p. A8.

Gruending, D. (1990). *Promises to keep: A political biography of Allan Blakeney.* Saskatoon: Western Producer Prairie Books.

Health Status Research Unit (1989a). *Goal setting initiatives in health promotion.* Saskatoon: Author.

Health Status Research Unit (1989b). *Intervention strategies for health promotion.* Saskatoon: Author.

Institute on Prevention of Handicaps (1982). *Annual report 1981-82.* Saskatoon: Author.

Joseph, R. (1985). *Assessment of food costs in northern Saskatchewan.* Regina: Medical Services Branch, Health & Welfare Canada.

Lalonde, M. (1974). *A new perspective on the health of Canadians.* Ottawa: Supply & Services Canada.

Loewen, G. (1988, May). *Health promotion campaign.* Regina: Saskatchewan Health. Unpublished memorandum.

Mitchell, D. (1991). *The William Charles Health Centre, part II.* Regina: Saskatchewan Indian Federated College.

Moore, M., Forbes, H., & Henderson, L. (1990). *The effects of providing primary care services under band control to a previously poorly served commu-*

nity. Paper presented at the 8th International Congress on Circumpolar Health, May, Whitehorse, Yukon.

Morin, M., & Britton, S. (1991). *Community health development in Ile à la Crosse*. Paper presented at Annual Conference of the Canadian Public Health Association, June, Regina, Saskatchewan.

NDP doubles Tories in voter opinion poll (1987, June 25). *Leader Post*, p. A1.

Parents feel children will suffer (1987, June 12). *Leader Post*, p. A3.

Pitsula, J.M., & Rasmussen, K. (1990). *Privatizing a province: The new right in Saskatchewan*. Vancouver: New Star Books.

Prince Albert Tribal Council (1990). *Directional health development plan*. Prince Albert: Author.

Riches, G., & Manning, L. (1989). *Welfare reform and the Canada Assistance Plan: The breakdown of public welfare in Saskatchewan 1981-1989*. Regina: University of Regina, Social Administration Research Unit.

Saskatchewan (1976). *Annual report, 1975-76. Department of Northern Saskatchewan*. Regina: Author.

Saskatchewan (1993). *Securing our future: Budget address, March, 1993*. Regina: Author.

Saskatchewan Commission on Directions in Health Care (1990). *Future directions for health care in Saskatchewan*. Regina: Author.

Saskatchewan Health (1974). *Annual report, 1973-74*. Regina: Author.

Saskatchewan Health (1976). *Annual report, 1975-76*. Regina: Author.

Saskatchewan Health (1977). *Annual report, 1976-77*. Regina: Author.

Saskatchewan Health (1978). *Annual report, 1977-78*. Regina: Author.

Saskatchewan Health (1981). *Saskatchewan health for children and youth*. Regina: Author.

Saskatchewan Health (1982). *Annual report, 1981-82*. Regina: Author.

Saskatchewan Health (1985). *Annual report, 1984-85*. Regina: Author.

Saskatchewan Health (1988a). *Statistical report on the Children's Dental Program, September 1, 1987 to August 31, 1988*. Regina: Author.

Saskatchewan Health (1988b). *News release on Advisory Committee on Health Promotion*, November 16.

Saskatchewan Health (1991). *Healthy living goals.* Regina: Author.

Saskatchewan Health (1992). *A Saskatchewan vision for health: A framework for change.* Regina: Author.

Saskatchewan Legislative Assembly (1989). *Debates and proceedings 32* (77A, July 14), p. 2661.

Saskatchewan Public Health Association (1988, March). *Second workshop on strengthening community health services.* Regina: Author.

Saskatchewan Public Health Association (1989, January). *Third workshop on strengthening community health services.* Regina: Author.

Siler-Wells, G. (1987). *Strengthening community health means strengthening communities.* Ottawa: Canadian Public Health Association.

Tan, L., Irvine, J., Habbick, B., & Wong, A. (1992). *Vital statistics in northern Saskatchewan, 1974-1988.* Saskatoon: University of Saskatchewan, Northern Medical Services.

Tory budget cuts bring charges of betrayal (1987, June 18). *Leader Post,* p. A1.

Weston, M. (1980). *Youth health and lifestyles.* Regina: Saskatchewan Health.

Whitehead, P.C. (1975). *Drinking practices and attitudes in Saskatchewan.* Regina: Saskatchewan Alcohol Commission.

Health Promotion in Manitoba

John English

According to Mr. Don Orchard, currently Minister of Health of the province of Manitoba, "We need a health care system that focusses more on health promotion and disease prevention rather than primarily on restoration" (personal communication, October 15, 1992). This comment, made during a speech to health care workers, characterizes the reorganization being brought about by reform of the Manitoba Ministry of Health (Manitoba Health). It will restructure health services as we know them in the early 1990s. The proposed reform of Manitoba's health system could have significant impact on the health of Manitobans and the practice of health promotion in this province.

The reform strategy document, Quality Health for Manitobans (Manitoba Health, 1992b), identifies several major personal, social, cultural, and economic factors strongly associated with the health of the population. These factors include: productivity and wealth (i.e., people in affluent societies are inclined to be healthier than those in poorer ones); genetic endowment; environmental factors; socio-economic factors (including interpersonal relationships); lifestyle; and the health services system. In the past we have tended to view health in the context of physicians and hospitals and have ignored these other determinants of health, even though, as we now know, they are crucial to averting illness and to developing the energy, vitality, and zest for life that characterize health.

Health promotion in Manitoba is primarily the responsibility of Manitoba Health. Although in its widest sense, health promotion is practised through many avenues, this chapter will focus largely on the undertakings of Manitoba Health over the past 20 years. The Manitoba Public Health Association (MPHA) and the federal government's Regional Office of the Health Promotion Directorate deserve a fuller description of their enterprises than can be given in these few pages.

Demographics

Manitoba, often considered one of the "have-not" provinces in Canada, is the most easterly prairie province and lies geographically at the centre of Canada. It is predominantly plains country, bordered by Ontario to the east and Saskatchewan to the west. The Northwest Territories border its subarctic north; the American states of North Dakota and Minnesota lie to the south.

Waves of settlers, starting in the 1600s with English and French fur traders, joined Manitoba's original Native population. They were followed by agricultural settlers from Scotland, Iceland, Russia, and the Ukraine, and in the early 1900s, from Ontario and various European countries. Immigration from Asia and Central and South American countries continues today.

The 1991 census recorded the population as one million people, about half of whom reside in Winnipeg, the capital. A further 20% live in smaller urban centres. Most of the population is concentrated in the south in a triangular agricultural area stretching from Lake Winnipegosis in the west to the southeast corner of the province.

Of the nearly 500 000 jobs in the province, about 37 000 are in agriculture, 63 000 in manufacturing, 87 000 in trade, and 163 000 in services. Thirty-nine thousand people are employed in all levels of public administration.

Historical Overview of Health Promotion in Manitoba

Health promotion has been an issue in Manitoba for decades. The current Manitoba Health reform document quotes a former provincial Director of Nursing, Elizabeth Russell, in about 1924:

> Every city, town and rural municipality should be adequately provided with means for health conservation and health education. The money advanced through the tax rates for such work cannot be used for a better purpose.
> Why? Health conservation and health education mean health promotion and disease prevention. Health promotion and disease prevention are the only means of curtailing the enormous expenditure for the maintenance of institutions for the sick. . . (Manitoba Health, 1992b, p.1).

Aspects of Miss Russell's advice have been implemented since that time, but nearly fifty years passed before a division specifically responsible for health promotion was organized within Manitoba Health. In the interim, various governments built health care institutions to provide services through the use of expensive technology. But we now know something that was clearly evident to Miss Russell in 1924: that these strategies did little to increase our life span or significantly improve the overall health status of the population. Manitobans continue to die of chronic diseases — some brought about by genetic problems or habits engendered by our affluent society, others associated with poverty and environmental conditions — all of which could be addressed by a broader concept of health promotion.

Dr. Dexter Harvey, Professor of Health Education at the University of Manitoba, maintains that the strategies of community activation, community involvement, and public participation were practised as far back as the end of the Second World War: "Anybody who. . . is past 40 can recall that these concepts were very much applied after the war, especially during the 1950s and 1960s" (personal communication, 1992).

By the early 1970s, the health education practised by staff in the Department of Health and Social Services, a forerunner to Manitoba Health, was consistent with some of the conclusions later noted in the *Alma Ata Declaration* of the World Health Organization (WHO), which established the goal, "Health for All by the Year 2000."

Manitoba Health organized an Education Services component at this time. The responsibility of its central office was to act as a resource to health educators in the newly formed, autonomous health regions. Harvey believes that during the mid-1970s the reputation of the Manitoba Health Education Service was excellent:

> Manitoba was considered to be the leader in that area across Canada. It was health promotion as we have come to understand it today. They were not calling it that, but it was certainly health promotion activities with a high degree of community involvement and programs delivered at community level. (Personal communication, 1992)

Despite this reputation, the practice of health promotion was not influencing decisions made in the larger system of health care. The intersectoral involvement so necessary in effective health promotion endeavours did not exist in the health education service of the day.

In the mid-1970s, the federal document, *A New Perspective on the Health of Canadians* (Lalonde, 1974), identified lifestyle as a significant factor affecting health. This document precipitated a shift away from the medical model toward a much broader concept of health and was a driving force behind the formation of the Manitoba Health Promotion Directorate.

In what was seen by some to be an arbitrary political decision, Manitoba Health reorganized the Health Education Services into the Health Promotion Directorate under the leadership of Dr. Dale Gelski in 1981 (D. Gelski, 1992, personal communication). Lottery funds were made available to supplement the Directorate's budget. Gelski reported:

> During the early stages of its development there were meetings between the provincial Directorate staff and the Federal Prairie Region Health Promotion Directorate office. These meetings allowed for a free exchange of ideas and philosophy about the nature of health promotion. Working also with concepts from the Lalonde document and material from the World Health Organization, a theoretical framework for health promotion in Manitoba was created during the Directorate's first eight months. (Personal communication, 1992)

Some sources speculate that the overbearing nature of the decision to establish the Provincial Health Promotion Directorate gave rise to resistance which slowed the planned change. Gelski, reflecting on these difficulties, commented:

> Social forces in 1982-83 presented a tremendous challenge to developing health promotion. We were competing with so many other high-profile health issues, such as sexually transmitted diseases, and mental health was very prominent at that time, as well as the curtailing of resources in our hospitals. It was very difficult to establish a platform for health promotion. The challenge was to get politicians, voluntary agencies, the health department itself, and the university to listen, and to take health promotion seriously.

It was believed that change should be introduced gradually

. . . because health promotion was a quantum leap from the medical model which prevailed at that time. After a review of epidemiological evidence from the Manitoba Health Services Commission, it was decided to embark on a diabetes education program. This project was the pilot demonstration of the Health Promotion Directorate using health education in rural communities and including the professional community as part of the project. (D. Gelski, 1992, personal communication)

The original plan was to build on a previous experience (a diabetes education resource) and address chronic diseases in general; the focus would then shift from secondary prevention to primary prevention (i.e., measures taken to prevent the occurrence of health problems). Dr. Gelski stated:

Our main objective was to provide the patients with knowledge of the diabetes disease process and to help motivate them and change their lifestyle. Here is where we really started to get into the behavioural change process without really knowing the difficulty of the challenge. To take these people and to encourage them not only to be knowledgable about their situation, but also to internalize it and go on to do something about it; to make some changes in their lifestyle that would change the course of the disease — we really got back to the disease prevention methodology. (Personal communication, 1992)

Dr. Gelski's statements clearly indicate that the planned change had its roots firmly established in primary prevention of disease. Unfortunately, with new leadership, the initiative lost much of its focus and did not move beyond secondary prevention. A diabetes education project in each of the regions throughout Manitoba is a legacy of this initiative. Clearly, this project adhered firmly to the old paradigm of health education to prevent complications in people already diagnosed, but failed to move significantly beyond this approach.

Emerging Trends

The WHO definition of health promotion was introduced in 1984: "Health promotion is the process of enabling people to increase control over, and to improve, their health. . . . It represents a mediating strategy between people and their environments, synthesizing personal choice and social responsibility in health to create a healthier future" (World Health Organization, 1984). In retrospect, it was probably difficult to make the paradigm shift — to ascribe greater importance to social rather than medical influences on health — despite this rhetoric. Yet the WHO definition facilitated the emergence of a broader perspective on health problems, as illustrated in the federal discussion document, *Achieving Health For All: A Framework for Health Promotion* (Epp, 1986; hereafter, the Framework). This landmark document, along with the *Ottawa Charter for Health Promotion* (World Health Organization, 1986), laid the groundwork for what was to come in Manitoba.

Following the government's lead, MPHA made a conscious decision to concentrate its efforts on the Strengthening Community Health Project (discussed by Ken Hoffman earlier in this book). This project, described in the Framework, was redefined to include Healthy Communities enterprises.

MPHA organized a Healthy Communities Network to support members who were encouraging initiatives in their communities. Much of the detailed work of the Network was done by subcommittees that addressed network organization, advocacy, promotions, and education; their efforts were co-ordinated by an Executive Committee. At this writing, a sophisticated and cost-effective organization has emerged. Many members manage to weave aspects of community development into their jobs because they strongly believe in the efficacy of a broad approach to health promotion.

The Network meets regularly to share ideas, vent frustrations, solve problems, and think creatively about healthy communities. Inspiration is drawn from similar work being done in communities across Canada.

A brochure with a provincial focus links local Healthy Communities projects with the larger provincial movement. In Manitoba there are seven Healthy Communities projects under way in Winnipeg, Gimli, Flin Flon, Brandon, Virden, Riverton, and The Pas. Some of these would have foundered for lack of personnel and fiscal resources, had it not been for the support of the federal Health Promotion Directorate, which sponsored competitions for funding innovative projects.

Individual initiatives also arose from universities. For example, Dexter Harvey of the University of Manitoba was involved in community health promotion at the regional level in partnership with Manitoba Health promotion personnel: "We worked in the interlake health region with community groups, organizations, and agencies to help interpret the kind of activities that were going on so that there would be a better fit between them and the community's needs" (personal communication, 1992).

Another network originated under the sponsorship of the Federal Health Promotion Directorate (Prairie Region), composed of representatives from the Prairie Region Federal and Provincial Health Directorates, the University of Manitoba, and the University of Saskatchewan. This group — Knowledge Development for Health Promotion — is interested in the pithy problems posed by the need to develop a methodology for investigating health promotion in communities. (For a fuller discussion, see the chapter by Irving Rootman and Michel O'Neill earlier in this book.) Knowledge development is a particular challenge to researchers who find traditional Cartesian methodologies inadequate to study the complexities of the phenomena under scrutiny. The group's mandate is to organize seminars to foster interest in studying the effectiveness of communitywide health promotion projects, especially Healthy Communities initiatives.

All of these collaborative initiatives illustrate a deliberate and concentrated effort to make the paradigm shift necessary to address the scope of health promotion as defined by WHO.

At the beginning of the 1990s, the provincial Health Promotion Directorate, as part of Community Health Services, was still involved in several major disease prevention programs, in addition to the diabetes education program mentioned above. Such programs as smoking reduction, fitness, and nutrition supported a central program concerned with cardio-vascular health. The nutrition program targetted pregnant women, particu-larly high-risk prenatal groups and Aboriginal people, to establish healthy eating habits for their children early in life. Another program was concerned with the early detection and rehabilitation of hearing difficulties.

The Services to Seniors program was originally integrated into the Directorate because some seniors' centres were operating health programs without a mandate. Funds and staff consultation, especially in health pro-motion, were provided by Manitoba Health to develop community councils whose purpose is to co-ordinate Services to Seniors. The Department reported that in 1988-89 alone (the latest public data available), seniors' centres were developed in four communities outside Winnipeg, and project staff participated in 85 support services projects, 63 of which were rural.

The fitness program also made a significant contribution to the health promotion activities of the Directorate. Its objective was to raise the pro-portion of Manitobans participating in regular exercise from 55% to 60% over four years. This required a change of strategy from public education about the benefits of exercise to one of social marketing. A threefold strate-gy was designed, consisting of (1) training and accreditation of fitness lead-ers, (2) support of community-based activities, including consultation to the community on request, and (3) support of small businesses for health promotion in the workplace.

With a few exceptions, the overall picture indicates a continuation of the old health education paradigm. Still needed was an intersectoral component or a co-ordinating strategy, and more community involvement in addressing social issues affecting health.

A New Direction

In May 1989, Manitoba Health published a policy paper, *Partners for Health: A New Direction for the Promotion of Health in Manitoba* (Manitoba Health, 1989). This policy had two main goals: (1) to encourage every Manitoban to take personal responsibility for her or his own health and (2) to involve the entire community in a more active and focussed effort at identifying and correcting risks to health in the environment, at work, in legislation, and in lifestyles. This initiative not only involved everyone but, most importantly, it addressed the co-ordinating strategy missing in earlier initiatives and included an action plan with five major components.

The first goal was to set up Manitoba's Health Advisory Network, com-prising representatives from all parts of the health services system. The Network's mandate was to "identify areas where better integration of health services can contribute to improved health outcomes throughout. . . Manitoba" (Manitoba Health, 1989).

A second component was to increase efforts by Manitoba Health to promote health by working with community groups, business, and industry across the province. These efforts were to concentrate on healthy lifestyles and services to such special target groups as multicultural, Aboriginal, and seniors' organizations.

The third strategy was to exercise leadership in the area of healthy public policy. Under the direction of the Minister of Health, an eighteen-month review of "healthy public policy" was planned. The goal was to review "high-priority government programs, activities and legislation to identify where reforms could contribute to better health and a safer, healthier environment" (Manitoba Health, 1989).

The fourth action was to extend Partnership for Health by recruiting other community groups into the provincial health promotion efforts of Manitoba Health. As an enticement, lottery funds were suggested as a possible source of seed money.

The fifth initiative — Health Promotion at Work — was designed to reduce compensation claims and absenteeism, as well as improve productivity and the health of individual employees. Prevention was its focus. By emphasizing the importance of fitness, adequate nutrition, and smoking reduction, it encouraged healthy lifestyles.

At last a stronger movement toward the new health promotion paradigm was growing through the establishment of real consultative processes with communities across Manitoba. Still, the Partners for Health policy initiative has had its critics. One source, who asked to remain anonymous, complained:

> They put many constraints and demands on community initiatives, especially when it came to following a process that seemed to come into being out of the bureaucrats' own perception of the way things should be done. Even community participation was no guarantee that the disenfranchised would be heard. (Personal communication)

The idea behind Partners for Health was to develop a partnership between the province and a community. To enter into this partnership, the community had to come up with a health promotion idea that fit the agenda set by the province. If it did not, the project was rejected. Bureaucrats who judged which partnerships would be approved thus held considerable power over those who were trying to make a contribution to the total health promotion effort, but whose agenda or methods did not coincide with the agenda of the government. Scepticism developed and anger arose when the expectation of an equal partnership was not fulfilled.

As in preceding decades, Manitobans today are very concerned with the economic conditions of Canada as a whole and Manitoba in particular. There remains tremendous pressure on government at all levels to control spending. This means cuts in programs. The health budget in Manitoba consumes almost one-third of the revenue and is an obvious target for restraint. To curtail its monumental expenditures, Manitoba Health has more recently devised a strategy for health reform that has been endorsed in principle by every political party in the province.

Health Reform

The first Partnership for Health policy paper laid the groundwork for more extensive reform designed to cut deeply into accepted practices of the health care system, including health promotion. *Quality Health for Manitobans: The Action Plan* was the title of Manitoba's health reform blueprint (Manitoba Health, 1992b). The subtitle, "A strategy to ensure the future of Manitoba's health services system," concisely describes its focus. The impetus for this plan arose from the Ministers of Health Conference held in Winnipeg in 1991 at which the First Ministers directed provincial Ministers of Health to "initiate work to apply the broad principles of the Canadian health care system to the objectives of sustainability, affordability, flexibility, responsiveness, and effectiveness of the system, funded without destabilizing provincial and federal finances" (Manitoba Health, 1992b).

In his introduction, the Deputy Minister of Health identified the plan as having six themes: (1) co-operation among a number of government departments, agencies, and Manitobans, all working collaboratively with Manitoba Health; (2) recognition of the need for services closer to communities where people live and work; (3) education of Manitobans to enable informed choices about matters affecting their health; (4) evaluation to ensure that services benefit Manitobans; (5) the opportunity for innovation in developing new roles for health workers; and (6) better allocation of resources on the basis of cost effectiveness.

The newly identified major determinants of health (productivity and wealth, genetic endowment, environmental factors, socio-economic factors, lifestyle, and the health services system) are now seen as critical to deterring illness and to developing the vim, vigour, and vitality for living that exemplify health. To accommodate this new direction, Manitoba Health was reorganized. Ironically, both the fitness program and the Services to Seniors program, which exemplified a broader approach to health promotion, have been moved to other parts of the provincial bureaucracy. The Directorate has been renamed Health Promotion, Protection and Disease Prevention, and finds itself as part of the Healthy Public Policy Programs Division. In the words of the health reform document:

> Today we understand that it is not good enough simply to provide physicians and hospitals to care for people once they become ill or disabled. Government has an obligation to work with people to promote health, prevent illness and postpone disability. The healthy public policy approach provides us with a means of meeting that obligation across the whole spectrum of public policy in Manitoba. (Manitoba Health, 1992b, p. 11.)

The current Health Promotion Directorate brings together staff from various programs to address a wide variety of health issues, including such current concerns as accidents and violence in all its forms.

A Healthy Public Policy Steering Committee, first identified in the *Partners for Health* policy document, heads the new division. Chaired by the Deputy Minister of Health, this potentially powerful committee, comprising other Deputy Ministers, is responsible for evaluating every major government action and policy for its impact on the health of Manitobans. However, it is widely believed that this committee has not reviewed new policy in the four years since it was constituted. Because policy is made at all levels of the government, plans are under way to develop a method for review that could be implemented throughout the system. Hopefully, it will be ready when the health system has been restructured. The committee will need to have power and to adhere strongly to the principles of health promotion if it is to weather the storms that could result from trying to influence decisions in other sectors of the provincial government. The danger is that no matter how well intentioned the members, personal survival in the bureaucracy could take precedence over the need to act as a strong advocate for necessary changes in policy.

The Future of Health Promotion in the New Health System

In the proposed health care system in Manitoba, all health professionals will be asked to redefine their role. For example, physicians will be asked to share their gate-keeping role with nurses who will be redeployed into community health centres. A philosophy of primary care will prevail in these centres. Staff, predominately nurses, will be responsible for responding to the needs of the community, not just for managing and treating acute and chronic illness, but also for health promotion. Psychiatric nurses will serve similar functions in mental health. The Acts governing the health disciplines will need revising to ensure legislation enabling nurses to fill new responsibilities. For Registered Nurses these responsibilities will include prescribing medication, midwifery, and the administration of anaesthetics — all of which will require further education (Manitoba Health, 1992a). Such endeavours may be difficult to accomplish in this time of fiscal restraint, yet without such support, there could be serious consequences.

As a result of consultation with consumers, a priority action strategy of the new health system will be public education and patient empowerment in two "dramatic and creative reforms" (Manitoba Health, 1992b, pp. 42-46). The first reform concerns childbirth and is the direct result of influence by the women's movement: pregnancy and childbirth are recognized as states of health. "Hospitals and public health programs will join forces to provide the best support to new and growing families once women leave the hospital after childbirth" (p. 42). Hospital delivery for low-risk pregnancies will be at local community health facilities, saving the high-technology facilities for high-risk populations. Unfortunately, the government seems to have missed the point made by the women's movement, which argues that hospital deliveries per se are disempowering. Instead, many women are advocating birthing centres or home deliveries by midwives.

The second reform arises from consultation with recipients of mental health services, and is based on the assertion that "most people with mental illness could remain in the community" (p. 43). Crisis services, supportive housing options, and psychosocial rehabilitation are being developed in communities to reduce dependency on institutions. In facilitating empowerment of this traditionally marginalized group, the reform will seek to develop viable alternatives to current services (e.g., home care as opposed to institutional care) and to provide clear, accurate information about these options, enabling people to make informed choices.

The Minister of Health expects health reform to be in place by the end of four years (1996), a rapid pace for change of such magnitude. One can expect that health professionals will need to expend much energy coping with changing expectations of their role and will initially respond to that part of their role which is the most urgent and easiest to fulfill. There is a very real danger that until community health centre staff develop sufficient community skills, a hiatus will occur in community-focussed health promotion. However, it is believed that the new structure will eventually produce a health organization at the community level that can best respond to people's health needs in a comprehensive, holistic way.

Conclusion

This chapter has considered provincial health promotion as seen through the lens of health reform in Manitoba. Almost a decade has passed since the social component of health promotion activities was identified. However, not until the recent advent of health reform in the province has Manitoba Health been able to make the paradigm shift from the old illness prevention model. The government health reform documents consider the impact of complex interactions in the social system on the health of its citizens. In the 1980s, we began to see progressive collaborative initiatives, some of which were supported by Health and Welfare Canada's Prairie Region Health Promotion Directorate.

The new emphasis by the province on healthy public policy provides a theme for more comprehensive health promotion endeavours than in the past. It is encouraging that Manitoba Health is subscribing to the view that by managing the key determinants of health a "tremendous amount of human suffering can be averted" and a great deal of money can be saved (Manitoba Health, 1992b). However, lack of strong support and tangible commitment from the entire Cabinet for the development of healthy public policy could render the committee responsible for its development impotent. It is now up to the government, health professionals, and Manitobans to work together to meet the challenge.

Acknowledgements

I would like to recognize all those who responded to my requests for information in order to write this chapter, and also those who show their dedication to health promotion in their daily work in the field. These people often put their heart and soul into a job that shows few immediate changes.

References

Epp, J. (1986). *Achieving health for all: A framework for health promotion.* Ottawa: Health & Welfare Canada.

Lalonde, M. (1974). *A new perspective on the health of Canadians.* Ottawa: Supply & Services Canada.

Manitoba Health (1992a). *Proceedings of round table on nurse-managed care.* Winnipeg. Unpublished manuscript.

Manitoba Health (1992b). *Quality health for Manitobans — The action plan: A strategy to assure the future of Manitoba's health service system.* Winnipeg: Author.

Manitoba Health (1989). *Partners for health: A new direction for the promotion of health in Manitoba.* Winnipeg: Author.

World Health Organization (1984). *A discussion document on the concept and principles of health promotion.* Copenhagen: European Office of the World Health Organization.

World Health Organization (1986). *Ottawa charter for health promotion.* Ottawa: Canadian Public Health Association.

Health Promotion in the Yukon Territory

Sharon Matthias

ealth promotion in the Yukon is framed by the meanings that Yukon people ascribe to health and by the social and physical characteristics of this Territory. To help situate this discussion of health promotion strategies, a brief history of the Yukon, an explanation its governance, and an overview of Yukoners' health are provided.

The choice of health promotion strategies considered in this chapter is based on a broad perspective of the determinants of health. The primary focus is on recent health promotion activities, though trends are also considered. Specific health promotion activities are classified as either collective or individual strategies; it is in the collective approach that the Yukon excels.

Historical, Physical, and Social Characteristics

History provides an important social basis for health issues and for the perspectives on health of Yukoners. People have lived on what is now called the Yukon for perhaps 30 000 years, during which time both the climate and the landscape have changed. European explorers are believed to have reached Yukon in the early 1800s. The Gold Rush of 1898 brought drastic changes in the traditional ways of living, as it drew more than 40 000 White men and a few White women into a country where before there had been only a handful of Whites and a few thousand First Nations people. The building of the Alaska Highway during the Second World War had a further profound social impact because it affected those First Nations that had not been exposed to the Gold Rush settlers (McClellan, 1987).

Today, the Yukon Territory covers about 200 000 square kilometres in the northwest corner of Canada, with a population of approximately 30 000. Most of the Territory is high country, separated from the Pacific coast by the still higher Coast Mountains. Whitehorse, the capital, has a population of about 21 000. Other communities range in size from Dawson City (population 1700) to Elsa (population 33). There are fourteen First Nations and seven First Nations languages (Yukon Bureau of Statistics, 1993b).

Historically, the Yukon has had a relatively young population, and the present proportion of citizens over 65 (3.7%) is still much smaller than in the rest of Canada. There are slightly more males overall (53% compared to 47% females), and this holds for all age groupings except ages 25 to 34, where females marginally outnumber males.

There are a number of ethnic groups in the Yukon. Francophones constitute 4% to 5% of the total population. Most available information, however, distinguishes only two groups: Native (or First Nations) and non-Native. The proportion of First Nations people is about 25% or 30%. [1]

The Yukon is considered part of the circumpolar zone. As such, it exhibits the same "Fourth World" characteristics as other northern countries:

- Small populations occupying vast and largely undeveloped areas of land;
- Economies driven largely by the exploitation of minerals, oil and gas, and other natural resources;
- High transportation and energy costs, and high costs for imported goods, all of which render many traditional forms of business activity uneconomic;
- Heavy reliance (50% and more) upon transfer payments from "remote and condescending southern governments, with a corresponding vulnerability to political winds in far-off places";
- Heavy reliance upon imported capital; and
- Native cultures struggling to preserve a land base and traditional way of life, despite overwhelming population influx (Sulton, 1992).

Social inequities challenge health promotion in the Yukon. These are demonstrated in many ways, e.g., the distribution of income, or of people of Aboriginal ancestry holding government positions. Efforts towards self-government among Yukon First Nations have further highlighted perceived inequities in self-determination, a phenomenon that has been linked to health status by various authors (e.g, Evans [1992).

Scott and Conn (1987) have described the socio-political pathogenesis of disease, showing the interrelationship and progression from economic, political, and socio-cultural alienation to environmental precursors (e.g., poor housing, contaminated water, poverty) that ultimately lead to the "medical" presentation of depression, violence, substance abuse, suicide, family breakdown, obesity, etc. They note, "If he is truly interested in promoting Native health, the physician must recognize the limits of prescription, and he must acknowledge the profound importance of autonomy and self-determination." This theory appears relevant to both Native and non-Native Yukoners, as recent data demonstrate a distinct gradient when comparing self-reported health and income sufficiency (Yukon Bureau of Statistics, 1993c).

Arising from its history, the Yukon's system of governance differs from those of the provinces in Canada. Some knowledge of these complex arrangements is important in appreciating the health promotion achievements and challenges in the Territory. Because initiatives toward health transfer and First Nations self-government are in the

---

[1] Estimates of the proportion of First Nations persons in the population vary greatly, depending on the source. The proportion of 25% to 30% is used for those considered a beneficiary under the Land Claims settlement. Note that this will not include those Yukoners of First Nations ancestry from elsewhere in Canada (Yukon Executive Council Office/Council of Yukon Indians 1990, *The Umbrella Final Agreement*).

process of altering these structures and processes, what is described here reflects the arrangements during a transitional period in the history of governance in the Yukon.

Governance

The Yukon Act (Revised Statutes of Canada, 1985) sets out the powers of the Yukon Territorial Government: it has primary jurisdiction in health matters, but the federal government has jurisdiction in some of the areas relating to the determinants of health. Since the 1950s, Yukon has contracted with the federal government (Health and Welfare Canada, Medical Services Branch) to provide medical care services, but has gradually supplemented these with direct provision of additional services (e.g., home care, speech language and audiology, family life programming).

As of April 1, 1993, Whitehorse General Hospital has been transferred to a hospital corporation. This was the outcome of a 20-year process generally termed Phase 1 Transfer. Community health services (e.g., nursing stations and community hospitals), mental health and environmental health services are still delivered by the federal government under contract to the Yukon government. These are the subject of Phase 2 of Health Transfer.

The federal Department of Indian and Northern Affairs has jurisdiction in many of the areas affecting the determinants of health for First Nations, including social services. But some federal government programs (Health and Welfare Canada, Medical Services Branch or Department of Indian and Northern Affairs programs) are delivered through local First Nations Councils. Thus, on any given issue, one could easily find representatives from all governments around the table. Resolution of an environmental health issue, for example, might include the Yukon Department of Health and Social Services, Health and Welfare Canada, the Council of Yukon Indians, the relevant First Nations chief or band council representative, Yukon Renewable Resources, Yukon Justice, Yukon Community and Transportation Services, the federal Departments of Indian and Northern Affairs and Fisheries and Oceans, as well as the relevant municipal government.

Health promotion initiatives thus must be developed in a complex political environment. Health promotion is also shaped by the health status of Yukoners and by what Yukoners understand by the term "health." The latter has been important in the development of the 1993 Health Promotion Survey, part of the Yukon Health Promotion Research Program (see Yukon Bureau of Statistics, 1993c). This innovative research program involved three pre-survey phases, during which a literature review was conducted on what the experts understand health to be (see Yukon Bureau of Statistics, 1992b), intensive interviews were conducted with Yukoners to discover what health meant to them (see Yukon Bureau of Statistics, 1992a), and discussions were held with stakeholders on various aspects of health (see Yukon Bureau of Statistics, 1993a). These data were then used to develop a Health Promotion Survey which was administered to a random sample of 1453 Yukon residents in early 1993. Much of the data reported in this chapter are derived from the survey and the developmental studies that preceded it. Over time, the data will be used to shape health policies and programs.

Yukoners' Definitions of Health

First Nations bring an understanding of the crucial importance of culture and spiritual practice to health, and the importance of community healing to the health of individual community members. Thus, there is a compelling rationale for strategies rooted in social, emotional, and spiritual bases as well as the traditional physical or medical model. An appreciation of how Yukoners view health is important for developing and implementing those strategies.

In *An Accounting of Health: What the Individuals Say*, Yukoners describe their sense of health and well-being in physical, psychological, sociological, or metaphysical terms, or in some combination (Yukon Bureau of Statistics, 1992a). Concepts of health are filtres through which "the pieces and associations of one's world are assembled" and provide "a reference point for researchers that policy makers must acknowledge" (p. 9). For example, a Yukoner assessing her health through a physical filtre might describe herself as confident in her body's capacity to perform the things she enjoys doing or as "bursting with energy." Another person, who sees health from a sociological perspective, might describe a sense of well-being when his relationships with friends and family are smooth. Psychological or emotional filtres might mean that health is understood in terms of the freedom to express feelings and to accept expressed emotion from others, "thinking positive rather than negative," or "to be excited by life," or "having control over [one's] own life." Those who perceive health in metaphysical terms might describe an "inner peace" or "being in tune," states providing "pride and determination."

In the Health Promotion Survey, Yukoners were asked to rate the importance of the various filtres (Yukon Bureau of Statistics, 1993c). Eighty-four percent rated the physical dimension as very important to health, compared to 83% for the psychological dimension, 63% for the social dimension, and 47% for the spiritual dimension.

The survey also demonstrated a variety of specific differences regarding the filtres. Gender differences are more pronounced for social, psychological, and spiritual dimensions (more females rated these as very important). Physical health becomes more important with age (72% of those respondents aged 15 to 24 years compared with 90% of those respondents aged 65 years and over). This trend is similar for social and spiritual health. For spiritual health, the importance increases from 49% at ages 15 to 24 years to 73% for those respondents over 65 years. Psychological health is the only filtre that exhibits a decrease in importance with age, from a high of 85% in the ages 15 to 44 years to a low of 77% at age 65 years and over.

Psychological health increases in importance across the income gradient from a low of 72% in the category "poor" to 92% in the "rich" category, while spirituality falls from a high of 59% in the "poor" category to a low of 42% in the "rich" group.

The filtre(s) that a Yukoner uses extend to those factors that influence health. For example, food can be perceived as a sociological phenomenon, a psychological obsession, a physical requirement, or as part of a spiritual health need. Considering food from a physical perspective highlights such factors as nutritional value or caloric and fat content. From a sociological perspective, food can be related to community expectations regarding weight, size, and body proportions, and to important social connections like family dinners, community feasts, or social mixers. A spiritual or metaphysical perspective might interpret food in terms of a spiritual feast, ceremony, or ritual.

The way Yukoners view health varies, to some degree, with place and time. First Nations people talk of influences that cause them to assess their health in different terms in different places — in town, on the land, or with other Native people.

Time also has a powerful influence on the way most people interpret health. The physical and social predominates in youth. Later in life, or following a major event like the death of a spouse, the way in which people see health can change significantly.

The qualitative filtres are also related to other factors. For example, the importance of any form of health except spiritual diminishes with the level of self-rated health. Eighty-nine percent of those respondents with "excellent" health indicate that physical health is "very important," yet 74% of those respondents with "poor" health indicate that physical health is important. Among those respondents for whom psychological health is important, the proportion decreases from 87% for those respondents with "excellent" health to 71% for those respondents with "poor" health.

Yukoners' understanding of health has many ramifications. It has profound implications for health programming and health education strategies. It also has implications for understanding utilization patterns of medical services, and how to influence them.

This information also provides a strong argument for consumer participation in program development, since health professionals tend to share a concept of health that differs from the diverse concepts held by the population as a whole. Specifically, these professionals have usually been influenced by their disciplines to understand health primarily as a physical phenomenon and to focus on those aspects of it that can be diagnosed, repaired, or cured. Therefore, the accounting of health provided by health professionals can be quite different from that provided by lay people (see Yukon Bureau of Statistics, 1992a, 1992b, 1993a, 1993c).

Health Status of Yukoners

When viewed in the aggregate, physical health indicators in the Yukon suggest a pattern more similar to that of southern Canada than of the Northwest Territories. Trends of infant mortality and suicide, historically higher than in the rest of Canada, are now more consistent with southern provinces (Yukon Health & Social Services, 1992a). It is reasonable to assume, however, that the health status indicators for some areas or communities will vary substantially from the overall average. Further, the history of the Yukon, including the resettlement of communities, and the Mission School experience of some First Nation Yukoners, focusses attention on the importance of mental and social health indicators as well as physical health, and on the critical need to consider the socio-economic determinants of physical health problems.

1993 Health Promotion Survey Findings

The 1993 Health Promotion Survey provided provocative information for policy and program development. Some of the findings are reported here.

Self-Reported Health Status

In 1993, 78% of Yukoners rated their health as "excellent", "very good", or "good". Generally, there was little difference between how Yukoners and other Canadians rated their health, although there were some differences by age (if we compare the Yukon data with those gathered in the 1990 nationwide Health Promotion Survey conducted by Health and Welfare Canada). Yukoners rate their health better as they get older, an opposite trend to the rest of Canada. Among Yukoners aged 20 to 24, only 55% rate their health as "excellent" or "very good", compared to 67% in the rest of Canada. Self-rated health exhibits a classic relationship to income. The higher the income adequacy group, generally speaking, the higher the perceived health status, though the "other poor"[2] had a higher rating than those classified as "poor", "lower middle", or "upper middle".

Self-rated health relates to other factors, such as smoking and alcohol behaviour, place of residence, employment, education, and one's "sense of community." Forty-eight percent of smokers and 51% of heavy drinkers rate themselves as having "excellent" or "very good" health, as compared to 61% overall. Sixty-five percent of those living in Whitehorse rate their health as "excellent" or "very good", compared to 53% in all other communities. The employed and unemployed rate themselves the same, but those with post-secondary education (69%) are more likely to rate their

---

[2] This category is not commonly seen, but was created to allow a better fit for Yukon data. Refer to source for specific definitions of all categories, including this one.

health as "excellent" or "very good" than those with secondary education or less. Ninety-two percent of those who rate themselves with "excellent" health state they "have a sense of community," compared to 76% who rate themselves with "poor" health.

Social Relationships and Health

The Health Promotion Survey sought information on how important social relationships are to Yukoners and their health. Ninety-two percent of Yukoners state that their relationships are important to their health. This high level is seen across age, income, and gender. It lessens with age, however, from a high of 92% for those aged 15 to 44 years to a low of 78% for those aged 65 years and over.

Ninety-four percent of respondents state they have someone to confide in (97% female, 92% male), 89% state their partner is supportive (87% female, 91% male), and 86% state their family is supportive. The lowest level of spousal support is linked to the "poor" income adequacy grouping (74%) in comparison to that of the "rich" grouping (94%).

Forty-six percent state they are regularly involved in community activities. Those in the "middle" and "upper income" groupings are the most involved in the community (52%, 49%, 48%) when compared to the "poor" (24%) and "other poor" (35%).

Spirituality and Health

There are few data that portray the relationship between health and spirituality. Because the qualitative component of the research revealed that spirituality and religiosity were important components of health for many Yukoners, a small section of the Health Promotion Survey was dedicated to this area. Fifty-five percent of Yukoners indicated that they are "very" or "moderately" spiritual or religious. Females (61%) exhibit higher levels than do males (50%). The highest level of spirituality is found in the ages 45 to 64 (65%) and the lowest in the ages 25 to 44 years (50%).

Spiritual values play an important role for 52% of Yukoners; again, this was higher in older age groups. Twenty percent of Yukoners state that they are an active member of an organized religion.

Spiritual and religious values appear to be associated with health in a bipolar fashion: Highest values of spirituality and religiosity are found in those respondents with either "excellent" health or those at the other end of the health continuum (63% for those with "fair" health and 62% for those with "poor" health). This relationship is also seen to some degree when spirituality/religiosity is related to levels of stress and to overall quality of life.

Tobacco, Alcohol and Illicit Drug Use

More Yukoners smoke (33%) than other Canadians (28%), and fewer Yukoners have never smoked (31%) compared to the national average (36%). The number of cigarettes smoked daily is comparable to national figures.

A dramatic relationship exists between self-rated health and smoking. Thirty-six percent of those individuals who have "excellent" health are non-smokers who have never smoked, and 39% are former smokers. The ratio of non-smokers drops to 19% in those who have "fair" health. Interestingly, 40% of those who have "poor" health are former smokers.

The Yukon Alcohol and Drug Survey (Yukon Bureau of Statistics, 1990) showed that Yukon had a higher yearly per capita alcohol consumption than the rest of Canada (14.8 litres compared to 9.5 litres). However, there was a lower percentage of current drinkers in the Yukon. The pattern of drinking was also different — half the alcohol was consumed by a small proportion of very heavy drinkers, 6% of Yukoners. Comparison of the Health Promotion Survey with the Yukon Alcohol and Drug Survey of 1990 shows a decline in heavy, frequent drinkers (from 13% to 8%) but an increase in current drinkers (77% to 84%) and in light, infrequent drinkers (28% to 38%). There has been a decline in former drinkers (from 19% to 12%). Further analysis may be able to elicit whether the former drinkers and heavy, frequent drinkers shifted to light, infrequent drinkers.

Perceived Community and Family Health

Yukoners were asked to rate the relative health of their community. Thirty-one percent see the health of their community as "excellent" to "very good", while 36% indicate it is "good" and 22% rate it as "fair" to "poor". Older Yukoners tend to rate the health of their community higher than do younger Yukoners. Also, those in the "rich" category were more likely to rate their community's health as "excellent" or "very good".

The top three important health issues for the community (identified in open-ended questions) were alcoholism and related facilities (24%), mental health (6%), and care for others (5%). The concern for alcoholism and related facilities was greater in the communities outside Whitehorse (30% compared to 21% in Whitehorse).

Yukoners rate the relative health of their family much higher than that of their community. Overall, 60% of Yukoners see their own family as being in "excellent" or "very good" health.

Summing Up

Yukoners' descriptions of their understanding of health provide a complex interweaving of physical, mental, social, and spiritual dimensions to the common indicators of health status. The interconnections between the health of individuals and the health of their families and communities provide an additional level of complexity.

The purpose of the first half of this chapter has been to provide background information to situate the following discussion of health promotion activities in the Territory. As will become evident, not only are the history, geography, and health-related governance different in the Yukon from much of the rest of Canada, but its unique social environment has contributed to a pattern of health promotion activity in recent years that is largely — in contrast to much of the country — collective rather than individualistic.

Collective Health Promotion Strategies

This is an important time in the history of the Yukon, and in the determinants of Yukoners' health. Three major trends in governance are proceeding at this time: the Land Claims/Aboriginal Self-Government process and legislation, Health Transfer, and Health Act Implementation. Each alone could have a profound effect on the determinants of health. Together, and combined with other activities, they have the potential to reshape the long-term health indicators.

It is in the collective strategies that the Yukon shines. The macro influences of Land Claims and Aboriginal Self-Government, Health Transfer, and Health Act Implementation underlie a wealth of collective strategies that are changing the socio-economic context, and which should have an important, long-term impact on reducing health inequities in the Yukon. Important activities have been undertaken in recent years that can be considered under three key health promotion strategies: healthy public policy, community development, and organizational change.

Public Policy

The public policy initiatives related to health promotion cover almost the entire social policy framework. The legislative agenda under Tony Penniket's New Democratic Party government (1985-92) included new statutes in health, education, environment, and workers' health, safety, and compensation. Each has visionary elements that support the concept of "healthy public policy." The principles and philosophy of the Yukon Health Act affect all the statutes administered by the Department of Health and Social Services and so cover health, social services, and juvenile justice.

The Land Claims legislation developed by the Penniket government died on the order paper, and was redeveloped and passed by the Yukon Party government under John Ostashek in March 1993. Implementation awaits federal legislation.

The development of these statutes also supported the concept of healthy public policy: the process incorporated extensive public participation and community involvement, as did the Yukon 2000 initiative to develop an economic strategy.

The public policy activities selected for highlighting in this chapter are the Health Act, Land Claims and Aboriginal Self- Government, and the Interdepartmental Committee on Social Assistance.

Yukon Health Act. The Health Act (1989-90) creates a health promotion framework for all health and social services programming. Passed in December 1990, the Act defines health as "the physical, emotional, social, mental, and spiritual well-being of residents of the Yukon in harmony with their physical, social, economic and cultural environments." This definition was grounded in the public consultation process used in developing the Act, and thus can be taken as fairly representing the views of Yukoners.

Principles for decision making are enshrined in the Act:
- Prevention/promotion
- Partnership of individuals, groups, communities, and governments
- Accessibility
- Cultural sensitivity
- Accountability
- Integration of health and social services.

The Act requires a growing expenditure on prevention and promotion, to reach the equivalent of 5% of the health treatment budget by the year 2000. It also establishes the Health Investment Fund, which was designed to foster community-based health promotion projects. Aboriginal traditional healing practices are recognized and are to be respected. It requires a Yukon Health Status Report every three years, with an annual update. The Act also provides for the creation of local health and social services boards and districts and sets out the process for developing them to ensure they meet community needs. Healthy public policy is mandated for the Yukon government, and the terms of reference for the Health and Social Services Council are established. The language and underlying approach of the Health Act allow an enabling approach, flexible enough to accommodate Yukon Territorial government needs, the unique local community situation, and individual First Nations land claims and self-government agreements.

The development time was very short, taking just under one year from the first cut of the principles to the proclamation date of the new Act. The Minister of the day (also the Premier), Mr. Tony Penniket, and the Deputy Minister generated a first set of six guiding principles to form the foundation of the Act. An initial public document outlined the principles and asked for public feedback. Most responses affirmed the six principles and the broad definition of health. Within government, at both bureaucratic and political levels, there were many discussions about what the Act was supposed to be and do, and the conflicts presented by the desire for both flexibility and control.

A second public document provided an outline of what would be contained in the new Act, with a request for feedback. A third cycle of public input was sought: the senior staff of the Department travelled to all Yukon communities to talk about the Act and any other health issues, and meetings were held with key stakeholder groups. An accelerated drafting and internal review completed the process.

To date, implementation of the Yukon Health Act has been relatively slow. Elements such as the Health and Social Services Council and Health Investment Fund were in place within the first year, and the 1991 Health Status Report (Yukon Health & Social Services, 1991) and 1992 Update (Yukon Health & Social Services, 1992a) were completed. A Social Accounts process is well underway, and administrative data bases continue to be developed and improved. As noted, the Health Promotion Research Program, designed to improve understanding of the attitudes and beliefs of Yukoners toward their health, completed its fourth and final phase in 1993 (Yukon Bureau of Statistics, 1993c).

The Health Investment Fund distributed about $150 000 in its initial year of operation to a wide variety of interesting and creative community health promotion activities, including a series of sweat lodge ceremonies, cross-cultural workshops, a dance group for children and teens, Alive '91 (a two-day breast health conference), youth groups promoting healthy lifestyles and racial harmony, physicians and community groups collaborating for mutual information sharing and education on learning disabilities and FAS/FAE (Fetal Alcohol Syndrome/Fetal Alcohol Effect), wilderness camps for youth, a nutritional study of country foods, cardiopulmonary resuscitation training manuals for the Yukon context, parenting skills workshops, and more. The success of the Health Investment Fund in attracting local community initiatives is likely due to the design of the application package, and the decision to let the funding criteria emerge from the pattern of first applications.

The Health and Social Services Council has begun to consider the success indicators of the principles for decision making, to support evaluation of their implementation. Discussions have continued with a few communities on whether their issues would best be met with local health and social services boards. However, the provisions will be implemented over time, and for the most part will need to await the completion of Phase 2 Transfer and the final form of self-government agreements for First Nations.

The speed and focus of implementation started to change in the later months of 1992. The speed of development left little time for thinking through how to implement the Act, so the implementation process is necessarily slower. Also, attention is now focussed on health transfer and the more complex issues such as self-government — for example, how First Nations will provide services off their settlement lands. Also, the current priority in the Yukon, as elsewhere, is to contain health and social services spending, which leaves little time and resources for long-term planning.

Land Claims and Aboriginal Self-Government. The Land Claims and Aboriginal Self-Government process and legislation is a critical element of "healthy public policy." The roots of the Yukon's Land Claim process go back to 1973, when Elijah Smith and a delegation of Yukon chiefs presented their brief, *Together Today for Our Children Tomorrow* (Council of Yukon Indians, 1973) to then Prime Minister the Right Honourable P.E. Trudeau. This presentation helped to convince the federal government to begin comprehensive land claims negotiations.

An Umbrella Final Agreement (Yukon Executive Council Office/Council of Yukon Indians, 1990) was initialled by all parties on March 31, 1990. It settles such major issues as the total land amount, the financial compensation, and the rights and powers of First Nations. It is not the end of the process, of course, but it sets the framework.

For example, the chapter dealing with Special Management Areas (or conservation areas) provides ways to recognize and deal with important features of the Yukon's natural and cultural environment. It explains how government will embrace the rights and interests of Yukon First Nations when it creates new parks, sanctuaries, wilderness or other special areas, and outlines how renewable resources councils and advisory bodies will be involved in planning and management. The chapter on Access sets out the right of access of Yukon First Nations on Crown Lands, as well as the right of access of the public for commercial and non-commercial purposes, and of the government, on settlement lands.

Negotiators signed a draft Model Self-Government Agreement (Yukon Executive Council Office/Council of Yukon Indians, 1991) on November 29, 1991. This agreement forms the basis for subsequent Self-Government Agreements between each First Nation and the federal and territorial governments. The agreements are precedent setting in a number of ways. They are the first of such agreements in Canada negotiated along with a comprehensive land claims settlement and which empower First Nations to provide programs and services for their citizens off settlement lands.

Each First Nation will determine how they will govern themselves, and negotiate their responsibilities and their relationships with other governments. The negotiations may take place over a period of time. The First Nations do not have to assume responsibilities right away, and it is likely that each will choose to "take down powers" related to program areas within health, social services, cultural and Aboriginal languages, justice, economic development, local government, etc., as each relates to their specific issues and needs.

The Council of Yukon Indians ratified the Umbrella Final Agreement and the model Self-Government Agreement in December 1991, with ratification of subsequent amendments and proposed additional amendments following. The Yukon government has ratified the Umbrella Final Agreement by passing settlement legislation in March 1993 (First Nations [Yukon] Self-Government, 1993 and Yukon Land Claim Final Agreement: Act Approving, 1993).

Some provisions of the Umbrella Final Agreement apply territorywide, to all First Nations. Others allow flexibility so that each Yukon First Nations Final Agreement can reflect its specific circumstances and concerns. First Nations Final Agreements have been completed with four First Nations: Champagne and Aishihik First Nations; Vuntut Gwichin First Nation; Teslin Tlingit Council; and First Nation of Nacho Nyak Dun. The Champagne and Aishihik First Nations ratified their Final Agreement and Self-Government Agreement in October 1992. The other three ratified their agreements in 1993.

Implementation awaits federal legislation. The federal government will introduce legislation as well, to give effect to the Umbrella Final Agreement and the First Nations Final Agreements and Self-Government Agreements. It will also draft legislation to set up the legal basis for some aspects of the claim. For example, a new Surface Rights Act will be prepared and existing mining acts will have to be amended.

Interdepartmental Committee on Social Assistance. An operational example of developing healthy public policy is the work of the Interdepartmental Committee on Social Assistance (Yukon Health & Social

Services, 1992b). This committee was formed in 1992 to examine barriers and strategies to reducing Yukoners' dependence on social assistance. The government recognized that the sharp increase in rate of expenditures would erode the power of government to deliver other programs and services, and also that the rising number of Yukoners on social assistance reflected significant personal distress in the community.

An additional advantage of the committee was the understanding gained by personnel of various departments that social assistance was a safety net. As such, it supported those people who "fell through the cracks" of other government initiatives, and the effectiveness of their programming had an influence, at least to some degree, in the size of the social assistance budget.

The committee was mandated by Cabinet, with membership from seven departments: Health and Social Services, Finance, Economic Development, Tourism, Education, Justice, and the Executive Council Office, Bureau of Statistics. Its major tasks were to review historical expenditures in the social assistance program and to verify projections of future expenditures; develop an understanding of social assistance expenditures — in particular, who is on social assistance and why; identify barriers in the management of the social assistance program, other government programs and the economy to ending dependency on social assistance; to develop strategies (for any and all departments) to contain or reduce social assistance expenditures; and to consider desirable changes to the various funding mechanisms (both federal and territorial) of Yukon Territorial government programs. This Interdepartmental Committee has been mandated by the current government to continue to develop and implement action plans.

Community Development

The community context for health is supported in the Yukon for a variety of reasons. Communities take pride in using internal resources to meet their challenges, consistent with the history and geography of the Yukon. Also, since one department comprises health and social services, the community development aspects of health promotion have a more natural home base, with regional social workers who can incorporate community development approaches in their program delivery. First Nations are moving forward on a community basis, understanding that community healing is a critical element in the success of Aboriginal self-government. This may take different forms, depending on the community, and may show itself through, for example, tribal justice, healing circles, and wilderness camps for alcohol and drug treatment and community-focussed aftercare.

At the same time, there has been no groundswell of activity under the umbrella of the formal Healthy Communities process. There has been a Yukon representative on the federal/provincial/territorial committee, but a community has yet to coalesce under that overall vision. This may be because the energy of the leaders in most communities has been focussed on Land Claims and Self-Government, or on other areas. For example, a "health" committee associated with Whitehorse City has focussed most activity on environmental issues.

Alcohol and drug programming. The Yukon's size assists some other unique occurrences. For example, all communities in the Yukon gathered together in a Community Mobilization workshop for developing community coalitions and action plans for prevention and treatment of alcohol and drug abuse. It appears to be the only Community Mobilization project in Canada, at least of those funded under the Canadian Drug Strategy, that managed a "community of communities" experience. The Liard Basin Task Force is one example of collaborative planning. It brought together representatives of the community of Watson Lake and the Liard Band to assess needs and preliminary strategies for alcohol abuse prevention, treatment, and aftercare for the area. Public consultation is currently underway to review a new Alcohol and Drug Strategy (Yukon Health & Social Services, 1993).

Wildlife management. The requirement for co-management of resources in the Land Claims/Self-Government process is resulting in Wildlife Management Boards which, at a community level, co-manage important natural and environmental resources. These boards also provide a mechanism to identify and carry out approaches that require strong negative community sanctions to prevent problems and where legislation is impractical or impossible because of jurisdictional issues. Forums such as these, which provide a vehicle for local problem solving and conflict resolution on topics important to the community at large, provide significant opportunities for improving community health.

Environmental contaminant control. In some cases, the Territory's complex governance acts as a stimulus to collective, collaborative action. For example, in the area of environmental contaminants, a Contaminants Committee has been formed. Its major function is to bring together Department of Indian and Northern Affairs, Yukon Renewable Resources, Yukon Health and Social Services, Health and Welfare Canada, the Council of Yukon Indians, and any other affected party to discuss and oversee projects conducted under the Arctic Environmental Strategy. At the same time, it provides a useful and productive forum for bringing together all the relevant parties on other environmental health issues, such as toxaphene in lakes and cadmium in caribou. Specific offshoots, such as the Working Group of Kaska Tribal Council/Health and Social Services/Health and Welfare/Renewable Resources to design education strategies and monitor contaminants in caribou and other country foods, bring together people from different backgrounds and perspectives to work collectively to solve a problem. Aside from the specific content of the issue, these groups provide ways for different communities to work together, again offering a basis for improving interpersonal skills and reducing inequities.

Chronic mental illness. An exciting example of community action is the evolution of the Second Opinion Society (SOS). This group, comprising persons who currently or previously suffered from mental illness, has developed strength over the last few years. A recent project sought the perspectives and needs of the community of psychiatric residents.

Conceived, developed, and conducted by the Second Opinion Society, with methodological assistance from Yukon Health and Social Services and Yukon Bureau of Statistics, the results of the survey will assist in developing appropriate community programs for this group of Yukoners (Yukon Health & Social Services/SOS Society, 1992). The Society is also becoming involved in successful delivery of community supports for psychiatric residents.

Organizational Change

Illustrations of current and future organizational change that are related to health promotion or that support a health promotion approach can be found at both the macro and micro levels. At the macro level, initiatives include the Health Transfer process, the devolution of program responsibilities to First Nations, and knowledge development. At the micro level, changes are beginning to be implemented within the structures and departments of government themselves.

Macro developments. In order for Phase 2 of Health Transfer to blend with the requirements of self-government, a comprehensive view will be needed of community needs and design of community services to First Nations and non-First Nations, as well as mechanisms to ensure that they act in concert. Since the funds likely to be available would be too limited to allow two distinct systems of delivery, it should motivate the development of some creative organizational structures and processes.

First Nations' taking over child welfare and other program elements means the organizational structures and decision processes within and between the Yukon Territorial government, individual First Nations, and collective First Nations will change. In part, the specifics will depend on which activities First Nations deliver themselves, and which they decide to purchase from the territorial government.

One element of organizational change is knowledge development. In support of this element at the national level, Yukon Health and Social Services hosted the symposium, From Rhetoric to Reality (and Back to Rhetoric): A Walk on the Practical Side, on February 27-29 and March 1, 1992 in Whitehorse. This symposium, sponsored by the Pacific/Yukon Regional Office of the Health Promotion Directorate of Health and Welfare Canada, was a part of Strategic Directions for Future Development of Knowledge in Health Promotion (Health & Welfare Canada, 1992).

Micro developments. In the last several years, organizational change has included activities to improve the health of the organization. The Ostashek government and the current Minister of Health and Social Services are interested in organizational reform to make departments responsive to communities. While it is too early to forecast what form this might take, some indication was offered by Gaye Hanson, the Deputy Minister of Health and Social Services, speaking to the Health Promotion Conference in Vancouver in March, 1993:

In order to be effective in the implementation of Indian self-government or active in health promotion and community development generally, government must engage in significant change. In the Department of Health and Social Services, the organization that we seek to become is a healthy one that can promote health in its largest sense. As a leader, I cannot ask people to share power if they perceive themselves powerless. I cannot ask people to demonstrate respect and responsiveness if they do not feel respected and nurtured within and by the organization. I cannot ask people to take risks, to create and innovate if they do not see senior management blazing the path and an organizational culture that supports new ideas and continuous improvement. I cannot ask people to see a vision that is not communicated, or to develop a passion about ideas that they do not understand and have no stake in. Community development principles can be turned into action by organizations that practice them internally. A rigid, hierarchical, "cold," linear organization that spends most of its analytical time in a purely quantitative mode will not be capable of making a true contribution to the development of First Nation governments (Hanson, 1993).

Another organizational change of note at the micro level is the Aboriginal Health Committee of the Yukon Hospital Corporation, established as an element of the Phase 1 Transfer Agreements, which will bring an institutionalized mechanism to ensure First Nations influence on design and delivery of hospital services. Lastly, an important micro-level organizational change is the integration of health and social services programming, the first element of which has been the development of the framework and operational principles of a Continuum of Continuing Care. This provides the basis for ensuring, over time, that services to diverse health and social services clients have common operating principles and compatible operational elements. Hopefully, this will prevent unnecessary duplication, ensure the principle of maintaining Yukoners in their own homes and communities for as long as feasible, and limit the need for expensive institutional facilities.

Individual Health Promotion Strategies

Health Education, Marketing, and Mass Communication

Even if less significant than the collective strategies, the Yukon has nevertheless been engaged in activities involving health education, social marketing, and mass communication. For instance, the Yukon Medical Association is keenly interested in socio-economic influences on health, has an active Health Promotion Committee, and actively develops partnerships with other community groups. In addition to their bicycle helmet campaign, physicians have been active with the Yukon Liquor Corporation and local Fetal Alcohol Syndrome/Fetal Alcohol Effect parents' group in developing media campaigns and physician education related to drinking and children with FAS/FAE. A series of diabetes awareness sessions in 1992 involved physicians and local community groups.

Currently, the Yukon benefits from the interest and involvement of a wide variety of groups in addition to the Yukon Medical Association. Non-profit groups such as ASH Yukon (Association for School Health), Yukon Family Services, Yukon Cancer Society, CPR Yukon (originally founded to teach cardiopulmonary resuscitation but now with a wider mandate), Second Opinion Society, Yukon Association for Community Living, Child Development Centre, and others are all heavily involved in a wide variety of individually focussed health promotion strategies. Examples include a School Health Trade Fair, Well Baby Kits for young mothers, Rock Band tours to highlight awareness of substance abuse, Life Skills and Positive Indian Parenting programs. Alive '91 was an extremely successful weekend workshop on breast cancer, sponsored by the Yukon Cancer Society.

There are a variety of examples of self-help and mutual aid strategies. The Collaborators, a group dedicated to collaboration between sectors, has developed the resource guides *Surviving in Whitehorse* and *Thriving in Whitehorse*. Parents of children who have had to be hospitalized "outside" have developed a guide of services and coping strategies for other parents.

The AIDS Program was started in 1990, with shared funding from Yukon Health and Social Services and Health and Welfare Canada. Initially based within the Yukon Department of Health and Social Services, it moved to a community-based program with a community Advisory Committee under the Board of Skookum Jim's Friendship Centre and is now examining the feasibility of standing on its own, with its own governing board. The move to Skookum Jim's allowed more flexible programming, delivered in ways more responsive to the reality of the Yukon than was possible within a government environment. In one issue of note, the AIDS Program and the Medical Officer of Health were resources to the community discussion in 1992 on condoms in the Whitehorse High School, through which parents and students ultimately voted for their availability in the school.

A number of Wilderness Camps are in operation to provide a setting for youth programs or treatment programs. Culture or Healing Camps are also increasing in frequency. Some are focussed on youth; others are for elders.

The frontier spirit of Yukoners includes a strong belief in self-reliance and individual responsibility, and a strong resentment of government interference with individual choice. For example, seatbelt legislation in the Yukon was as much a civil liberties issue as a safety issue. Thus, individual strategies for risk reduction are often much more successful when implemented by community groups rather than government.

Conclusion

Health promotion in the Yukon had a shaky, intermittent history regarding the development of individual strategies in the 1970s and '80s, largely because of Health and Welfare Canada's focus on treatment services in its Northern Health activities. The level of health promotion activity has intensified since the late 1980s. The passage of the Yukon Health Act and the implementation of the Health Investment Fund provided additional resources to support the actions of the non-profit sector and community groups. Now the Health Act provides a model for healthy public policy, as it enshrines the definitions and decision principles essential to health promotion. In addition, its enabling approach to establishing community boards allows the communities to set the role and format for health, rather than the government imposing a "one size fits all" model. The design of programs and strategies is also now more commonly focussed within the Yukon context. There is a long history of programs designed "outside," delivered by professionals trained in a world view that is not applicable to the Northern reality.

When all is said and done, the greatest impacts on health status will likely come from the strategies initiated in other sectors supporting the changes in health services. The extent of collective strategies, and recognition of the critical need for attention to socio-economic and socio-political determinants of health, are perhaps more obvious in the Yukon because of its history and relative size, and the magnitude of inequity.

The parallel forces of a population moving beyond a territorial colony and the moves to self-government for Yukon First Nations underlie the future improvement of health in the Yukon. One is reminded of Scott and Conn's (1987) perspective on the socio-political pathogenesis of disease in what is now a haunting commentary on the underlying social causes of illnesses, and the need for "bottom-up problem definition and design of programs and approaches." At this time, Scott and Conn's comments apply equally well to the benefit of health promotion strategies for all Yukoners: "Education, freedom and welfare can never be fully attained from the outside, in the manner of a present, but from the people's realization of their real needs. The health of a community cannot be prescribed; it must grow from within."

References

Council of Yukon Indians (1973). *Together today for our children tomorrow.* (Available from Executive Director, Council of Yukon Indians, Whitehorse, Y.T.)

Evans, R.C. (1992). *Why are some people healthy and some people not?* Working Paper # 20: Canadian Institute for Advanced Research Program in Population Health.

Health & Welfare Canada (1992). *From rhetoric to reality (and back to rhetoric): A walk on the practical side. Journal of the Proceedings.* (Available from Health Promotion Branch, Health & Welfare Canada, Pacific Region, Vancouver, B.C.)

Hanson, G. (1993). Health promotion activities in the Yukon. Presentation to *Health Promotion — What Works and Why?* March 27, 1993, Westin Bayshore, Vancouver. (Available from Ms. Gaye Hanson, Deputy Minister, Yukon Health & Social Services, Whitehorse, Y.T.)

McClellan, C., Birckel, L., Bunghurst, R., Fall, H.A., McCarthy, C., & Sheppard, J.R. (1987). *Part of the land, part of the water: A history of the Yukon Indians.* Vancouver: Douglas & McIntyre.

Scott, R.T., & Conn, S. (1987). The failure of scientific medicine: Davis Inlet as an example of sociopolitical morbidity. *Canadian Family Physician, 33,* 1649-1653.

Sulton, R.G.M. (1992). Presentation to the Northern Forum, First Annual Board of Directors' meeting, Whitehorse, Y.T. September 2, 1992. (Available from Curragh, Inc., Whitehorse, Y.T.)

Yukon Bureau of Statistics (1990). *Yukon alcohol and drug survey.* Whitehorse: Yukon Territorial Government, Executive Council Office.

Yukon Bureau of Statistics (1992a). *An accounting of health: What the individuals say.* A review of what Yukoners say about the concept of health. Whitehorse: Yukon Territorial Government, Executive Council Office.

Yukon Bureau of Statistics (1992b). *An accounting of health: What the professionals say.* A review of the considerations of the health promotion research program. Whitehorse: Yukon Territorial Government, Executive Council Office.

Yukon Bureau of Statistics (1993a). *An accounting of health: What the groups say.* A review of what the stakeholder groups say about the issues and concepts of health. Whitehorse: Yukon Territorial Government, Executive Council Office.

Yukon Bureau of Statistics (1993b). *Statistical review, 4th quarter 1992.* Whitehorse: Yukon Territorial Government, Executive Council Office.

Yukon Bureau of Statistics (1993c). *Yukon Health Promotion Survey policy source book.* An introductory tour of the data from the 1993 Yukon Health Promotion Survey. Unpublished report.

Yukon Executive Council Office/Council of Yukon Indians (1990). *The Umbrella Final Agreement.* Whitehorse: Yukon Territorial Government & Council of Yukon Indians.

Yukon Executive Council Office/Council of Yukon Indians (1991). *Model self-government agreement.* Whitehorse: Yukon Territorial Government & Council of Yukon Indians.

Yukon Health & Social Services (1991). *Yukon health status report, 1991.* (Available from Deputy Minister, Yukon Health & Social Services, Whitehorse, Y.T.)

Yukon Health & Social Services (1992a). *Yukon health status update, 1992.* Unpublished.

Yukon Health & Social Services (1992b). *Interdepartmental Committee on Social Assistance.* Unpublished.

Yukon Health & Social Services/SOS Society (1992). *SOS survey of psychiatric residents.* Unpublished.

Yukon Health & Social Services (1993). *Alcohol and drug strategy — Public consultation document.* (Available from Deputy Minister, Yukon Health & Social Services, Whitehorse, Y.T.)

Government Initiatives in Health Promotion in the Northwest Territories

Susan Yazdanmehr[1]

Rapid and dynamic political change in the Northwest Territories (NWT) during the past two decades has set the stage for progressive and creative initiatives in health care management. The development of health promotion as a philosophy and process has been inextricably interwoven with the evolution of the management of health care delivery in the NWT. This chapter describes the various characters and situations that have contributed to making health promotion the growing force that it is in the NWT today. This story is interesting because of the unique administrative arrangements for health care delivery, including health promotion, in the territory.

This chapter is based on information derived from a review of various historical accounts and reports of health care in the NWT as well as from personal interviews with many of the participants. It also reflects this writer's experience as a health promotion officer with the Government of the Northwest Territories Department of Health. These sources are acknowledged at the end of the chapter.

Early Days of Health Care in the NWT

The travels and immigration of European and Euro-Canadian peoples to the northern regions of Canada over the past 150 years has radically influenced the health of the first Aboriginal inhabitants of the NWT, the Dene and Inuit. These were strong and hardy peoples with a keen sense of survival born from thousands of years of living in the harsh northern environment. While the cultures of the Inuit and Dene were different from each other, each had developed methods of maintaining health and well-being that reflected their spiritual understanding of themselves and their relationships with others and which were attuned to the seasons and conditions of nature. But these traditional methods of health and healing became insufficient to deal with diseases, hitherto unknown, brought with the influx of explorers, traders, and Christian missionaries.

As a result of the mingling of the Inuit and Dene with the non-Natives,

[1] On behalf of the Government of the Northwest Territories Department of Health.

tuberculosis, influenza, and other communicable diseases devastated their populations. Response to these health conditions issued forth from the various segments of the sparsely populated non-Native group. The Hudson Bay traders, Royal Canadian Mounted Police, and Catholic and Anglican missionaries each provided health care to the Inuit and Dene people according to their own capacity and resources. As the population of the Aboriginal groups was widely dispersed, contact between them and the non-Natives was sporadic. Interchanges were usually based on trade or the Aboriginals' need for non-Native medicines.

In response to the diseases assaulting the Inuit and Dene, the Catholic and Anglican missionaries began to build small hospitals throughout the NWT. These religious groups also put pressure on the federal government for financial and administrative resources to meet the growing need for health care for the Aboriginal populations. This pressure, along with growing political awareness of the health conditions of the Inuit and Dene, eventually brought the federal government into direct involvement in delivering health care in the NWT with the establishment of the Northern Health Services under the auspices of Health and Welfare Canada in 1954.

The Federal Approach to Health Promotion

The aim of the Northern Health Services was to provide a much more organized level of health care to the inhabitants of the North. Over the next twenty years, the federal government developed a network of facilities and supporting health programs across the NWT, including the creation of community health care centres called nursing stations. Because the management and delivery of health care was, and is, a provincial and territorial responsibility based on the Canadian Constitution, federal provision of health care was planned to be temporary; it was only to occur until the territorial government developed the capacity and infrastructure to take on such responsibility itself. The commitment also recognized the special relationship between the federal government and the Aboriginal peoples, according to certain treaties, with particular regard to health needs.

From the mid-1950s to late 1960s, health care in the nursing stations focussed primarily on treating injuries and acute conditions. This treatment orientation and a lack of culturally and linguistically appropriate materials meant that health promotion in the early days of the nursing stations was limited to patient teaching activities, including prenatal and well-child education. Because the non-Native nurses and the Inuit and Dene peoples were usually unilingual in their own languages, communication was difficult. Consequently, the health education efforts of the community health nurses were often hindered by linguistic and cultural barriers. Although local interpreters played a critical role in the diagnosis and treatment of illness, it was unrealistic to expect them to explain health concepts that were not meaningful in the Aboriginal context. Often there simply were no words in the Aboriginal languages for giving health education information.

As more of the Inuit and Dene peoples began to establish permanent residence in the northern settlements (enticed by the housing, trade opportunities, and health care), the socio-economic difficulties that accompanied this transition began to manifest. While the non-Native populations enjoyed relative prosperity through employment in federal or territorial government service, the mining industry, or other forms of commerce, the Aboriginal peoples lost their culture and sense of self-determination.

The move by the Inuit and Dene peoples from living off the land (which had been generally health producing from the physical, social, mental, and spiritual perspectives) to settlement life (with exposure to the differing social norms and values of Euro-Canadian society and the different socio-economic base) fostered a sense of powerlessness. Many found it difficult to cope with the negative effects of the transition. Problems were compounded by alcohol and drug abuse, emotional breakdowns, suicide, family violence, and accidents.

The health of the Inuit and Dene peoples was further challenged by other factors, such as the use of refined, packaged store-bought foods, a reduction in breastfeeding, the introduction of tobacco products, and the adoption of strategies for personal and community sanitation that, while appropriate for a nomadic lifestyle, were inadequate for residential communities. While the incidence of communicable diseases such as tuberculosis, influenza, measles, etc., which had so devastated the Aboriginal peoples was greatly reduced, other diseases such as chronic respiratory infections, asthma, middle-ear infections, dental caries, and sexually transmitted diseases took their place.

Community Health Representative Program and Federal Health Educators

In the 1960s, the Medical Services Branch implemented the Community Health Worker (CHW) program throughout Canada. Recognizing that language and cultural barriers were impeding health education efforts in Aboriginal communities, and acknowledging the importance of community involvement in health issues, this program trained Aboriginal peoples in basic health education and community development. The intention of the CHW program was to develop a core of trained Aboriginal persons as members of the community health team. Their job would be to support and assist the other members of the health team, who were usually non-Native, by providing communication and cultural links with the community. An important component of the CHW job was individual and community health education.

Prior to 1972, the training programs for the CHWs were held in one central location in southern Canada. Some of the Dene and Inuit from the NWT participated in these sessions, returning afterward to their communities to work in the nursing stations as CHWs. After 1972, CHW training was decentralized to allow for the development of training that reflected the cultural and geographical differences of the various Aboriginal tribes and groups. The program was renamed the Community Health Representative

(CHR) program in the mid-1970s in order to dispel community misunderstandings regarding the workers' role.

Along with decentralizing CHR training, health educator positions were established in 1971 for the Medical Services Branch regions across Canada. One of the primary responsibilities of the regional health educators was to support the CHRs as community health educators.

In 1971 the first health educator for the NWT was hired for what was known as the Mackenzie Zone, a region of the western arctic and subarctic. One of the major tasks of this first "official" health educator was to collaborate with other Medical Services Branch personnel in adapting the CHR training program to the culture of the Aboriginal peoples of the North.

As a result, the first CHR training program for the NWT took place in Fort Simpson in 1974. This session was primarily attended by Dene trainees. A training program oriented more to the Inuit took place in the eastern arctic several years later. One of the emphases of this first training program was to develop trainees' skills with audio-visual equipment for health education activities.

This northern-based CHR training program was offered not only to first-time CHR trainees but also as an in-service and peer support to existing CHRs who had received training in one of the earlier courses held in southern Canada. The majority of individuals who attended were recommended as trainees by community nurses and were funded by Canada Employment. Students also came from the Fort Smith Adult Vocational Training Centre from the Home Management Training Program.

Community Health Committees

In addition to developing CHR training programs for northern Aboriginals and supporting CHRs in their communities, the Medical Services Branch health education efforts also focussed on developing community health committees in the Inuit communities of the Kitikmeot region and some of the Dogrib and South Slavey communities of Mackenzie and Fort Smith areas. Because the Inuit CHRs that had trained under the national training programs had become inactive, a special initiative was needed to foster the Inuit communities' involvement in health education. It was determined that health committees could be used as a means of facilitating a sense of community involvement in health issues by giving residents an advisory role in local health issues. Community health committees were to identify health issues of concern that would then be brought to the attention of the community nurses. The nurses, in turn, would either try to resolve the issues locally or pass them on to higher health authorities. The role of the Medical Service Branch health educator was to help communities form and mobilize these local health committees and to encourage and support the CHRs' involvement.

However, neither the CHR program nor community health committees became fixtures of the NWT health care system. Ever-changing federal politics and a lack of funding for such programs contributed to their demise. As well, in southern Canada, the Medical Services Branch was divesting itself of the CHR program by transferring the positions to Native band councils. With no long-term commitment to a national CHR program, commitment at the regional levels of Medical Services Branch was tenuous as well. Infrequent training opportunities for new CHRs, coupled with a lack of regular in-service training and misunderstandings of the CHR role by both communities and other health professionals, led to the eventual attrition of most of the CHRs in the NWT.

One of the major difficulties in developing community health committees was that there was little financial support for their administration or to encourage them to take on activities. In contrast, other community committees were often supported by the territorial government through honoraria for the participants, which encouraged membership. The health committees were further discouraged by the infrequency with which their recommendations were acted upon by any level of government. With only limited support for their structure and function, the committees gradually fell away.

Other Federal Initiatives

The Northern Region Medical Service Branch initiatives in health promotion were not limited to health education, community health committee development, or support for the CHRs. Although they were not necessarily viewed as health promotion initiatives at the time, significant programs were developed in nutrition, alcohol and drug abuse, and to a lesser extent, mental health. These programs were subsequently transferred to the Government of the Northwest Territories in the overall transfer of administrative authority over health care from the federal to the territorial level.

Health Promotion in the Non-Government Sector

During the 1970s, Aboriginal organizations, increasingly concerned about health and social issues, developed some health promotion initiatives. For example, the Dene Nation received funding from the Medical Services Branch Northern Region to hire a Health Co-ordinator and Health Liaison Officers to build a communication link on health and social issues between the Dene communities and the Medical Services Branch, using the administrative structure of the Dene Nation. The Health Liaison Officers, who were usually Dene, kept in regular contact with the Dene communities through the Band Councils. This program continued over the years and was eventually sustained, on a lesser scale, by the territorial Department of Health after the transfer of administrative responsibility for health care from Health and Welfare Canada in 1988.

Non-government health organizations also began to form in the NWT in the early 1970s. The Canadian Mental Health Association NWT

Division (CMHA/NWT Division) and Canadian Public Health Association NWT Branch (CPHA/NWT Branch) were two such organizations.

The CMHA/NWT Division took an active role in advocating for increased mental health services for the NWT, initially from the federal government and later, after the health transfer, from the territorial government. It developed a strong volunteer core and became increasingly involved in mental health promotion. It participated in the inception and growth of a number of health-related community-based groups, such as the NWT Council for Disabled Persons.

In its early years, the CPHA/NWT Branch took on the role of stimulating public awareness of contemporary health issues. The 1974 federal government document, *A New Perspective on the Health of Canadians* (the Lalonde Report) had a significant influence on the philosophy adopted by the Branch. As a result, the Branch became involved in collaborative initiatives with the territorial government on healthy lifestyles. The Branch was also a motivating force behind the formation of Storefront in 1978. Storefront was to provide administrative support to the numerous fledgling non-government groups in the NWT and also act as an advocate on their behalf. The idea was successful, and Storefront continues to provide such services today.

The Territorial Department of Health and the Emergence of Health Promotion

When the federal government officially initiated a program of health services to the NWT in 1954, it did so with the understanding that the territorial government would take over management in the future. By the early 1970s, health matters in the NWT were managed by the territorial Department of Social Development. Over time, as the territorial government grew in its capacity to manage its own affairs, its interest in health issues and management also grew. By 1978, the Department of Social Services was restructured and renamed the Department of Health and Social Services. A year later, the two departments separated, and the Department of Health was formed.

The Department of Health management at the time was acutely aware of the importance of developing the administrative infrastructure for the eventual transfer of health services from the federal government. Along with the hospitals in Yellowknife, Fort Smith, and Hay River, some programs were already being managed by the territorial Department of Health, such as services to the aged and disabled.

Building on these early activities, the Department of Health began a plan for further health promotion. In 1978, the Department formed a new section called Health Information and Promotion under the Community Health Programs and Standards Division. Influenced by the Lalonde Report, senior management at the time had a strong commitment to health promotion and the role it would play in the years to come as a cornerstone of health care. The newly formed Section modelled its approaches in keeping with the Lalonde Report's emphasis on lifestyle intervention and disease prevention. It aligned its activities with national/federal health promotion programs and developed initiatives in such areas as fitness, high blood pressure, and prevention of tobacco use.

In those days, departmental funding was considerably easier to obtain. Because of the small size of both the Department of Health and the territorial government, there was less political red tape when ideas and plans were put forth. Recommendations were readily accepted and decisions quickly implemented. As a result (and also due to the persuasive, enthusiastic, and committed efforts of the Department of Health senior management to health promotion), the new Section was accorded budgets that allowed it to engage in innovative activities. Continuous support and encouragement were also provided by Health and Welfare Canada in Ottawa, who included the territorial health promotion staff in the development of national strategies in health promotion. Health and Welfare was also instrumental in assisting and funding the Department of Health to conduct territorial health surveys on such practices as tobacco use. These contributions of the federal government were significant in providing the territorial Department of Health with an information base on which to create and develop health promotion programs.

Over the next several years, the Health Information and Promotion Section created a variety of health promotion programs and activities in the NWT. Early activities focussed on lifestyle intervention and disease prevention, such as fitness testing, blood pressure screening, lifestyle awareness, and the distribution of pamphlets and brochures on health topics. The Health Information and Promotion Section also developed and implemented activities for schools in nutrition and fitness. These school health efforts prepared the way for discussions with the Government of the NWT Department of Education on the need for a territorial-based school health program.

In the early 1980s, the Health Information and Promotion Section began to use mass media to communicate health messages to the public. This included radio announcements and, eventually, televised health information spots through the northern communications satellite Anik, which had recently been launched. This use of the media was a significant first effort in reaching the geographically isolated Aboriginal communities of the NWT.

The Health Information and Promotion Section became increasingly aware of the importance of developing culturally and linguistically appropriate materials for the Northern population. To this end, it collaborated with the Government of the NWT Department of Culture and Communications in the production of Northern-developed posters, pamphlets, and stickers. The Medical Services Branch, Health and Welfare Canada also supported this production.

Another thrust spearheaded by the Health Information and Promotion Section was to promote health careers for Northerners, particularly Aboriginals, in the management and delivery of health care. This included developing a slide-tape presentation and a pamphlet package on health careers for public dissemination. This initiative, with others, served as a foundation for more comprehensive programs in years to come.

The production of a newsletter, *HealthBeat,* was also started in the early days of the Health Information and Promotion Section. The newsletter was intended to convey health promotion philosophy and messages to health professionals working in the NWT and to create a profile for the newly formed Department of Health.

Transfer of Administrative Responsibility

The political scene in the NWT during the 1970s and '80s was one of great change. The Berger Inquiry of the mid-1970s on the effects of the Mackenzie Valley Pipeline on the health and culture of Aboriginal peoples gave strong recognition to Aboriginal issues and encouraged a Native political voice. The Inuit, Dene, and Métis were actively involved in land claims, the division of the NWT, and the devolution of federal government management to territorial government. Increasing numbers of Aboriginal people were elected to the territorial government and worked within the Cabinet.

The involvement of Aboriginal organizations in the devolution was particularly evident in the transfer of the administrative responsibility for health care from Health and Welfare Canada to the Government of the NWT. The federal government had specified that the transfer was conditional upon the involvement and support of Aboriginal groups. The Department of Health collaborated with the Inuit and Dene organizations and communities to form Regional Health and Hospital Boards that would work in partnership with the Department of Health in the management and delivery of health services and programs. The membership of the Regional Health Boards would comprise trustees appointed by the Minister of Health upon the recommendation by each municipal government in the respective regions. Thus, community participation in the management of health services would be assured. The concept of boards was recognized as timely for Northerners because of the size of the NWT and the tremendous diversity of its peoples.

This decentralized approach was important to the Department of Health's blueprint for health services in the NWT, as Native self-government and increased involvement by Aboriginal peoples in the management of all areas were increasingly critical issues among territorial Aboriginal groups.

It was foreseen that, as these Regional Health Boards matured, they would assume more responsibilities in the direct management and delivery of programs in many areas, including health promotion. The Department of Health anticipated that each Regional Health Board would eventually have its own Regional Health Promotion Officer and that the Department would take a consultative and supportive role.

The Department of Health also recognized the potential role CHRs could play in health promotion, particularly in community development.

CHRs were seen as an important cultural link between the communities and health professionals, who were usually non-Native. Consequently, the Department of Health negotiated that with the transfer of administrative responsibility, there would be an increase in the number of CHRs, revitalizing the CHR program.

The Baffin region was the first to experience transfer with the formation of the Baffin Regional Hospital Board in 1982. The management of the rest of the health services in the Baffin region transferred in 1986, resulting in all the Baffin health services being managed under the newly formed Baffin Regional Health Board. The final transfer of administrative responsibility for health care from the federal to the territorial government for the rest of the NWT took place in April 1988, with the formation of the Keewatin, Kitikmeot, and Inuvik Regional Health Boards and Mackenzie Regional Health Service.

Territorial Government Health Promotion

During the mid-1980s, the Health Information and Promotion Section confirmed its role as a significant force in health promotion in the NWT. The Department of Health was an active participant on the federal committee that produced the 1986 federal document on health promotion, *Achieving Health for All: A Framework for Health Promotion* (Epp, 1986), and encouraged the health promotion staff to subscribe to the principles and philosophy expounded in that position paper.

The Department's participation on the federal committee and its continuing close, co-operative relationship with the federal government ensured support from Ottawa for health promotion activities in the NWT as exemplified by the funding provided for development of the NWT School Health Program.

The School Health Program became a major activity of the Health Information and Promotion Section. The Health Promotion Directorate of Health and Welfare Canada not only supported the proposal for the NWT School Health Program but also provided core funding for its development. The territorial Department of Education entered into partnership with the Department of Health on this project. Over the next ten years, the two departments collaborated in developing a school health program that gained international attention for its comprehensive approach to health and sensitivity to the diversity of culture of the North. As a result of the program and the publicity it generated, the politicians made the progressive move to establish health as a mandatory subject in the NWT school curriculum, with the NWT School Health Program as its base.

Also as a result of its supportive relationship with the federal government, the Health Information and Promotion Section became responsible for overseeing the successful completion of Canada's first survey on the health of Canadians in the NWT, which included a valuable emphasis on Aboriginal peoples.

Territorial Health Library and Resource Centre

With the relocation of Medical Services Branch Northern Region head-quarters from Edmonton to Yellowknife in 1981, the Department of Health negotiated with Medical Services Branch the joint ownership and management of Northern Region's health resource library, which had also been transferred north. The Department of Health's portion of the deal was given to the Health Information and Promotion Section to administer, thus providing it an opportunity to expand its role significantly in health education and promotion.

Under Medical Service Branch Northern Region, the main purpose of the resource library had been to supply the nursing stations with health journals and health education materials such as films, video tapes, and pamphlets. Under the Health Information and Promotion Section, the service was also made available to schools and the general public. School and public use increased to the point where the Health Information and Promotion Section had to prepare posters and pamphlets to fill demands for culturally appropriate materials. The library/resource centre was named the Dr. Otto Schaefer Health Resource Centre and grew to become a unique and significant resource of health information for all sectors in the NWT.

Also during this time, the mandate of the Health Information and Promotion Section was redefined to focus specifically on health promotion, while the health information component was reassigned to other divisions within the Department. This reorientation increased staff efforts in health promotion.

The Family Life Program

The NWT School Health Program project was near completion by 1984-85, and the Health Promotion Section was expanding its sphere of activity. Health and Welfare Canada had redirected its financial support from NWT Planned Parenthood to the funding of a three-year term position with the Department of Health for a Family Life Co-ordinator. Although the position was not originally within the Health Promotion Section, it was moved there in the late 1980s.

The Department of Health succeeded in obtaining funding for the creation of a team of Family Life Education Consultants (FLECs). The FLECs were to support the Family Life unit of the NWT School Health Program and to act as an education resource to communities on such issues as sexually transmitted diseases, teenage sexuality, and birth control. Because of an increasing concern with family violence and child sexual abuse in the NWT, the FLEC project developed strategies to assist women in dealing with these issues based on the "popular education" approach to community development. The FLEC staff were eventually hired permanently and became an active force in community mobilization around family violence and child sexual abuse throughout the NWT.

The NWT AIDS Project

Because of concern over the growing incidence of HIV infection in Canada, the Health Promotion Section obtained federal funding in 1987 to develop and implement an AIDS prevention project of considerable magnitude in the NWT. Although the project was beset by administrative difficulties, it broke new ground in the development of innovative and culturally sensitive health promotion strategies aimed at increasing the awareness of Northerners to HIV/AIDS and the risks for infection. The project was completed in 1991 and was a fundamental and crucial step in preparing the way for the future development of a comprehensive NWT AIDS strategy, with the Health Promotion Section taking the role as leader and catalyst.

Revitalization of the CHR Program

With the transfer of administrative responsibility for health care in 1988, the Department of Health had negotiated an increase in the numbers of CHRs for the NWT with the intention of having a CHR in every community. In the initial years following the health transfer, the potential value of CHRs as front-line agents of health promotion was clearly recognized. Subsequently, the Department of Health developed, in co-operation with Arctic College and with the input of health professionals, a CHR training program that would more adequately provide CHRs with the knowledge and skills needed to promote health at the community level. To reflect this focus on health promotion, the Department of Health revised the job description for CHRs (with the input of CHRs) and assigned the role of overall support and development of CHRs to the Community Health Division, with the participation of the Health Promotion Section.

Enhancement of Nursing Skills

Nurses have been the cornerstone in delivering health services under both federal and territorial management of health care in the NWT. To promote the vital role that nurses play, not only through health education but also through collaborating with CHRs in community health promotion initiatives, the Nursing Services Division of the Department of Health developed a health promotion component as part of the Advanced Nursing Skills In-service Program.

This program is part of a plan to upgrade the skills and knowledge of community health nurses in the NWT. It will help address the need of community nurses to acquire a more comprehensive understanding of health promotion.

Community Health Committees

In 1986, in preparation for establishing the Regional Health Boards, the Department of Health charged the Health Promotion Section with responsibility for reactivating the community health committees. By that time, many of the health committees had been relatively inactive for years. In the Dene communities, the committees were virtually non-existent, while a few still struggled along in some of the Inuit communities.

The Health Promotion Section worked specifically on activating the community health committees in their advisory capacity to the Regional Health Boards and in their role as agents of health promotion in their communities. The original plan for the structure of the Regional Health Boards called for community representatives to be members of community health committees; this arrangement would help keep the Regional Health Boards informed of locally identified health issues and concerns.

However, the Aboriginal participants in the health transfer negotiations rejected this condition and demanded instead that communities be able to recommend whomever they wanted as their trustee, whether or not they were a member of the health committee. This flexible arrangement was ultimately agreed upon in the final transfer agreements. However, once the Regional Health and Hospital Boards were formed, the Department of Health continued to stress the importance of the role of community health committees to the new Board trustees. Community health committees were presented as a vital communication link between the trustees and their communities and as potentially strong advocates of community health promotion. If trustees were not members of health committees, they were strongly encouraged to become members.

In the years following the inception of the Regional Health Boards, community health committees did not flourish as hoped, for a number of reasons. One fundamental reason was that they were viewed and treated as advisory groups with little power of their own, much as they were in Medical Services Branch days. There appeared to be confusion among municipal and territorial governments as to the legal status of the committees: what was their association to the various levels of government? to the Health Boards? Because municipal governments and Band Councils were not obliged to choose Health Board trustees from community health committees, support for the committees was often lacking from local government.

The community health committees were further weakened by a lack of resources. The Department of Health was reluctant to provide core funding to the committees because they regarded them as the responsibility of municipal governments and because participation on the committees was strictly voluntary. But, as community health committees were not legislated components of the health system, the Boards were not obliged to support them financially, either. Consequently, while Boards may have provided project-based funding for health committees, no long-term coherent commitment to their development was made.

Still other factors contributed to the apparent weakness of the community health committees. Except for the larger regional centres, communities in the NWT are very small, ranging from 50 to 1000 people. There are often a great number of community committees on which one has the option to serve, and often the same people serve on many committees. Many of these committees have strong support from the municipal and territorial levels of government for either funding or resource allocation, or both. Health committees generally had neither funds nor resources other than what they might have raised themselves. This lack of resources and, ultimately, of power, made serving on community health committees frustrating for many participants.

Despite the difficulties and uncertainties that plagued many community health committees, some have carried on. A few have become well established and have been highly successful in their community-based health promotion initiatives. Both the Regional Health Boards and the Health Promotion Section of the Department of Health continue to support the community health committees. As well, the Health Promotion Section has recognized that there may be other community groups that have direct or indirect interests in health and that it is important to encourage and support these efforts. Further, as the Regional Health Boards mature, put their own regional health promotion teams in place, and develop strategies for health promotion, the barriers to community health committee development will likely be resolved.

Regional Health Promotion Officers

Supporting the rebirth of community health committees was an activity of the Health Promotion Section tied into the initial efforts to prepare the regions for the formation of Regional Health Boards. With the actual formation of the Boards in 1988, other issues began to take priority for the Health Promotion Section. The senior management of the Department of Health had also strategized that the Regional Health Boards would each have Regional Health Promotion Officers who would ultimately be responsible for facilitating community initiatives in health promotion.

With the gradual placement of the Regional Health Promotion Officers, the Health Promotion Section was able to move from direct delivery of service to the regions to a consultative role. This process took place over several years, beginning early in 1988, when the Department took the first steps in redefining the role of Health Promotion staff from specialists in certain areas such as school health, tobacco, and community health to that of generalists, each working as a consultant to one or more of the Regional Health Boards. This redefinition of the role of the Health Promotion Officers was refined over the ensuing three years. In addition to acting as consultants to the Regional Health Boards, the Health Promotion Officers were responsible for developing territorial health promotion policy and planning. In 1991, the Health Promotion Section was renamed Policy and Planning, Health Promotion.

By mid-1993, the Regional Health Boards had realized their full complement of regional health promotion staff and were well on their way to developing health promotion strategies tailored to the conditions and issues of their respective regions. The Health Promotion Section played a crucial role in this effort by decentralizing positions from within the Section to the Boards. It also assisted the Boards in preparing job descriptions and recruiting staff for the Regional Health Promotion Officer positions. The Department of Health had thus successfully devolved responsibilities for the direct delivery of health promotion to the regions and taken a consultative and supportive role in working with the Boards in developing their programs and activities.

Current Political Situation and Implications for Future Health Promotion

It is difficult to predict what forms health promotion will take or what priority it will be accorded by government and politicians in the NWT to the year 2000. Since 1991, the territorial government has been making efforts to streamline government administration and decentralize as many programs and services as possible to the communities and regions (e.g., territorial government Community Transfer Initiative). The government has also been making significant efforts to make government processes more meaningful for its residents, the majority of whom are Aboriginal. For example, substantial efforts have been made to translate government communications of all kinds into the eight official languages of the NWT.

Many of these changes have been made with respect to the territorial government report, *Reshaping Northern Government*. Another report, *Strength at Two Levels*, also recommended the merging of the Departments of Health and Social Services. However, this merger has not yet taken place, pending an additional internal review on the value of the proposal by non-Cabinet members of the NWT Legislature. Whether the mergers will be a complete one-time event or a program-by-program incremental process is unknown. A functional review of the Department, currently under way, may also change its internal structure and workings.

Whatever the process, administrative change within the Department of Health seems likely, including changes to the structure of the Health Promotion Section. Whether health promotion will continue to be defined independently or be recognized and encouraged as an inherent component of other health and social service areas is unknown at this time.

Healthy Public Policy

Now that the Regional Health Boards have had several years of experience, the Department of Health is engaging in efforts to refine the policies, legislation, and administrative structures upon which the system operates. A Memorandum of Understanding is currently being developed between the Department of Health and the Regional Health/Hospital Boards, clarifying the roles and responsibilities of each. The Department is also preparing a new NWT Public Health Act to replace the current one, which had been modelled on southern examples, to make it more meaningful to the unique conditions of the North. The new Act will clarify and strengthen the role of the Regional Health/Hospital Boards in all areas, including health promotion.

The territorial Departments of Justice and Health have played strong roles in raising the level of awareness of the territorial government as a whole to the importance of developing and implementing legislation that considers the health of its citizens. As a result, government departments are increasingly cognizant of the health effects of proposed legislation. The Department of Health itself has defined an approach to health and health services that is framed in terms of healthy public policy.

Division of the NWT and Settlement of Dene Land Claims

The Inuit negotiated a land claims settlement for the eastern arctic in 1992 and, a year later, secured federal government support for the formation of a new territory — to be called Nunavut — which would encompass most of the Inuit regions of the North. Scheduled for 1999, the formation of this territory will, in fact, divide the NWT into two. The future face of the management and delivery of health care in the North is indescribable at this time, as the administrative structures for the new government of Nunavut are unknown. Nunavut will include the Kitikmeot, Keewatin, and Baffin regions and will have a predominantly Inuit population. The Inuvialuit of the western arctic will remain connected with what will be left of the NWT.

New government relations will obviously be required between Nunavut and the remainder of the NWT. Whether the philosophy and structure of the health care system that has been set up by the Department of Health will remain intact is not known.

The settlement of Dene land claims and the realization of their desire for self-government may affect the structure of the new health system in the North. For example, a Regional Health Board has not yet been formed in the Mackenzie region because both the Dogrib and Slavey tribes want separate Boards and the territorial government has not been able to justify funding two Boards for such small, geographically proximate populations. (The Department of Health continues to manage the health services for that region.) Also, the five Dene tribes have been negotiating land claims separately with the federal government, considerably diminishing their support for the role of the Dene Nation to act as their governing body. What effect these moves toward regionalism will have on the eventual formation of one or more Regional Health Boards is unknown. It is conceivable that management of health might even be transferred to individual bands.

While the health and social problems of their peoples is of great concern for Aboriginal leaders, their political agenda is of top priority. The socio-economic and cultural factors at the root of many of the health and social problems of the Inuit, Dene, and Métis will not truly begin to be resolved until the issues of self-government and self-determination through political solutions are themselves resolved.

The impact of these political changes on the development of health promotion within and outside of territorial government is difficult to assess. The Department of Health is trying to build a health care system that meets the unique geographical and cultural needs of its citizens and which is sufficiently flexible to adapt to the significant political changes of the near future. The development of health promotion as a process for initiating and sustaining change in the conditions that affect the health of individuals will undoubtedly continue in the NWT. What shape it takes remains to be seen.

Sources

Personal Interviews

Helen Balanoff. Former Director, Student Support Division, Government of Northwest Territories, Department of Education, July 7, 1993.

Elaine Berthelet. Former Chief, Programs and Standards Community Health Division, Government of the Northwest Territories Department of Health; current Associate Deputy Minister, Government of the Northwest Territories Department of Health, July 7, 1993.

Jill Christensen. Founding member, Former President, Canadian Public Health Association NWT Branch, July 8, 1993.

Sandra Mackenzie. Director, Community Health Division, Government of Northwest Territories Department of Health, July 8-9, 1993.

Jo MacQuarrie. Founding member, Former Executive Director, Board member, Canadian Public Health Association NWT Division, July 6, 1993.

Maureen Morewood-Northrop. Former Nursing Officer, Medical Services Branch, Northern Region, Inuvik Zone; current Director of Nursing Services, Government of Northwest Territories, Department of Health, July 6, 1993.

Janice Stirling. Nurse-in-Charge, Yellowknife Public Health Unit, Mackenzie Regional Health Services, Government of Northwest Territories, Department of Health, July 8, 1993.

Rick Tremblay. Former Health Educator, Medical Services Branch, Northern Region, Mackenzie Zone, Current Policy and Planning Officer, Health Promotion, Government of Northwest Territories, Department of Health, July 5, 1993.

Telephone Interview

Margie Crown. Former Policy Officer, Government of Northwest Territories Department of Health; current Head, Policy and Planning Health Promotion, Government of Northwest Territories Department of Health, August 18, 1993.

Documentary Sources

Brett, H.B. (1969). A synopsis of northern medical history. *Canadian Medical Association Journal*, *100*(March 15), 521-525.

Butler, G. (1973). Delivery of health care in northern Canada. *Canadian Journal of Opthalmology, 8,* 188-195.

Epp, J. (1986). *Achieving health for all: A framework for health promotion.* Ottawa: Health & Welfare Canada.

Lalonde, M. (1974) *A new perspective on the health of Canadians.* Ottawa: Supply & Services Canada.

Health and Welfare Canada, Medical Services Branch, Northern Region. *Report on health conditions in the Northwest Territories 1963-1987.* Yellowknife: Author.

Government of Northwest Territories, Department of Health (1986). *Presentation to Dene Nation.* Paper presented to Dene Leadership Conference, Yellowknife, April 14, 1986.

Graham-Cumming, G. (1969). Northern health services. *Canadian Medical Association Journal, 100*(March 15), 526-531.

Lindquist, J., & McDermott, R. *Health care in remote areas.* Paper presented at the Canadian Hospital Association Convention, St. John's, Newfoundland, June 13, 1979.

Monpetit, Sister. *History of northern nursing in Indian communities.* Paper presented at Inukshuk Nursing Conference, Whitehorse, Yukon Territory, May 16, 1990.

Northwest Territories, Department of Health (1993). *A review of the Northwest Territories AIDS Project.* Yellowknife: Author.

Northwest Territories, Department of Health (forthcoming). *Working together towards health for all: The Northwest Territories way.* Yellowknife: Author.

O'Neil, J.D. (1987). Health care in the central Canadian arctic: Continuities and change. In D. Coburn et al. (eds.), *Health and Canadian society: A sociological perspective.* (2nd ed.) (pp. 141-158). Toronto: Fitzhenry & Whiteside.

O'Neil, J.D. (1991). Democratizing health services in the Northwest Territories: Is devolution having an impact? *Northern Review, 5,* 60-62.

Roberts, V. (1990). *History of nursing north of 60 in Canadian Inuit communities.* Paper presented at Inukshuk Nursing Conference, Whitehorse, Yukon Territory, May 16.

Uygur, Dr. A.O. (n.d.). *Mackenzie Area — Annual Report and Program Forecast, 1972-1973.* Yellowknife: Health & Welfare Canada, Medical Services Branch, Northern Region, Mackenzie Zone.

Weller, G.R. (1981). The delivery of health services in the Canadian north. *Journal of Canadian Studies, 16*(2), 69-80.

Yazdanmehr, S. (1993). *An overview of health promotion in the Northwest Territories.* Edmonton: Health Canada, Alberta/NWT Region, Health Promotion & Social Development Regional Office.

The Health Promotion Movement in Ontario: Mobilizing to Broaden the Definition of Health

Ann Pederson and Louise Signal

In April, 1989 the Ontario Premier's Council on Health Strategy outlined its vision of health:

> We see an Ontario in which people live longer in good health, and disease and disability are progressively reduced. We see people empowered to realize their full health potential through a safe, non-violent environment, adequate income, housing, food and education, and a valued role to play in family, work and the community. We see people having equitable access to affordable and appropriate health care regardless of geography, income, age, gender or cultural background. Finally, we see everyone working together to achieve better health for all (Premier's Council on Health Strategy, 1989a).

This vision, subsequently adopted by the government (Ontario Ministry of Health, 1992), reflects the incorporation of a broad, social view of health and its determinants — the core of the contemporary view of health promotion — into the discourse of health planning and policy making. Previously the rhetoric of health activists in the women's and community health movements (Grace, 1991; Hoffman, 1989), a social view of health is now articulated by government bureaucrats, politicians, academics, and public health workers in Ontario, in part as a result of the actions of professional social reformers.

In this chapter, we argue that it is the acceptance of a broad view of health and its determinants which has been the major accomplishment of the health promotion movement in Ontario to date. This is not to suggest that there have not been other achievements, but to stress that a fundamental change has taken place in the language of health policy makers, a change that may have far-reaching consequences for the organization and delivery of health services in Ontario.

This chapter describes and analyzes the evolution of support for health promotion in the province since the early 1970s. Our discussion is based on the findings of two studies, one focussing on the development of health promotion in Ontario (Pederson, 1989) and the other focussing on the political influences on the development of health promotion in the Premier's Council on Health Strategy (Signal, 1993).[1] Both projects employed a similar design and set of methods: in-depth, face-to-face interviews with key informants and the analysis of documents. A total of 60 people were interviewed in the course of the two projects and hundreds of documents reviewed, including the minutes of organizational meetings, ministerial briefing papers, official and unofficial organizational publications, newspaper accounts, news releases, and internal government memoranda.

Health promotion, as examined here, is conceived of as "a field of professional work within the health establishment" (Grace, 1991, p. 330), and its emergence can usefully be regarded as a professional social movement of health activists working within organizations (many of which are located within the apparatus of the state) (Pederson, 1989; Stevenson & Burke, 1992). Health promotion, thus conceived, does not constitute a popular social movement in the sense in which social movements are generally analyzed — a point argued elsewhere (see Grace, 1991; Labonté, earlier in this book; Stevenson & Burke, 1992) — but reflects a different phenomenon, the professionally sponsored social movement carried by professional social reformers and their organizational bases (McCarthy & Zald, 1987).

We examine initiatives within four organizations determined by observers as being key to the emergence of health promotion: the Ontario Ministry of Health, the City of Toronto Department of Public Health, the Ontario Public Health Association, and Paradigm Health. Each of these organizations had members or staff who were involved in the development of health promotion, many of whom were linked through an informal network of health activism and who influenced each other and their respective organizations. The description of events is strategic rather than exhaustive, and for simplicity, the activities of each organization are described in turn rather than combined into a single narrative.

We then consider the establishment and activities of the Premier's Council on Health Strategy, and its successor, the Premier's Council on Health, Well-being, and Social Justice, as they were important for bringing the health promotion approach further into policy making in the government of Ontario. Finally, we reflect on reasons for the development of health promotion in Ontario and explore possible implications for the future of health promotion.

Background

Ontario is the most populous province in Canada, having a population of 10 million, approximately 40% of the nation's total. The Regional Municipality of Metropolitan Toronto, consisting of six municipalities

[1] The research reported in this paper was supported in part by a fellowship to Ann Pederson from the National Health Research and Development Program and by a Canadian Commonwealth Scholarship to Louise Signal. We wish to thank Dr. Victor W. Marshall for his skillful and generous supervision of both the research projects upon which this paper is based and for his helpful comments on an earlier draft of this paper.

including the City of Toronto proper, has a population of some 3.5 million, making it the most densely populated urban area in the country.

From 1943 to 1985 the province was governed by the Progressive Conservative Party. During this period, one of increasing provincial prosperity, publicly funded health care was slowly introduced. In the 1950s, an extensive program of hospital construction was undertaken with the support of federal funds. The two prongs of medicare were subsequently established: hospital insurance in 1959, and a decade later, a universal publicly funded system of medical insurance (Ontario Ministry of Health, 1983a).

Since the mid-1980s, the province has experienced significant changes in government. In 1985, a minority Liberal (centrist) government was elected, ending 42 years of Conservative party leadership. The Liberals were subsequently re-elected with a large majority in the late summer of 1987. Then, in 1990, the New Democratic Party (social democratic) won a majority government. Each successive government was confronted by challenges in managing the province's health care system.

When the Liberals came to office in 1985, they inherited the requirement to bring Ontario into compliance with the terms of the Canada Health Act of 1984. This responsibility put health policy near the top of the Liberal government's agenda from its first days in office. The Canada Health Act had reinforced the five principles upon which medicare had been founded (universality, accessibility, comprehensiveness, portability, and public adminstration) and thus effectively outlawed the practice of "extra-billing," that is, charging fees higher than those payable by the public insurance scheme. Federal transfer funds were withheld from any province that failed to enforce the ban on extra-billing, and Ontario was among the worst offenders (Weller & Manga, 1983).

In Ontario, the government's intention to prohibit extra-billing led first to rotating strikes and then to a full-fledged, 25-day doctors' strike in June and July 1986, during which services were withdrawn to varying degrees across the province. Even emergency departments were closed on a rotating basis in some areas. Following the passage of legislation to ban extra-billing, the strike ended. The Ontario College of Physicians and Surgeons played a major role in ending the strike, arguing that medical withdrawal of service was illegitimate (Tuohy, 1988). Following the strike, the Premier promised a review of the health care system with physician input.

Since the introduction of medicare, cost control has been a dominant theme in Canadian health policy (Mhatre & Deber, 1992):

> Establishing a program of universal coverage, and making the federal and provincial governments responsible for its open-ended costs, guaranteed that the primary emphasis of the governmental agenda would shift from a concern with ensuring access to a concern with controlling costs (Tuohy, 1992, p. 288).

Successive Ontario governments have attempted to contain the costs of health care in Ontario, both directly through reducing the number of beds and attempting hospital closures, and indirectly through such strategies as de-institutionalization and decentralization (Deber & Vayda, 1985). However, their efforts have met with little success as health care costs have continued to increase well above inflation in Ontario every year and take up increasing amounts of the provincial budget. In 1977-78 health costs were 27% of the provincial budget (Ontario Ministry of Treasury & Economics, 1987). This had risen to 33% by 1990-91 (Ontario Ministry of Treasury & Economics, 1991). Thus, the climate in which health promotion came into prominence was an era of newly created access to health services but increasing concern over the costs of offering those services.

Health Promotion in the Ontario Ministry of Health

Health education has been used as a strategy for improving health in Ontario for over one hundred years. In 1882, the motto of the Ontario Provincial Board of Health was: "Ne pereat populus scientia absent" ("Let not the people perish for lack of knowledge") (Badgley, 1978, p. 21, reprinted earlier in this book), suggesting that the practice of health education stems from the earliest days of public health in the province. The term "health promotion," though, has a more recent history and in Ontario, as elsewhere, it is a descendant of health education. (Macdonald & Bunton [1992], for example, make a similar argument about health promotion in Britain.) Both health education and health promotion, however, have until recently been minor concerns of the Ministry of Health, which has long been preoccupied with the demands of establishing and maintaining the health care delivery system.

The federal working paper, *A New Perspective on the Health of Canadians* (Lalonde, 1974; hereafter, the Lalonde Report) may have introduced the term "health promotion" to most of the world, but it was already in use in Ontario: "health promotion" was part of the vocabulary of civil servants within the Ontario Ministry of Health by the early 1970s. Internal government memoranda show that the term was used to refer to a communication strategy to encourage the adoption of prescribed healthful behaviours. As well, health educators employed by the province from the mid-1960s on provided learning aids such as films and written materials to public health workers, particularly nurses, on such topics as smoking, fitness, nutrition, and illicit drug use.

Much has been written on the limited impact of the Lalonde Report within Canada (e.g., Evans, 1982; Hancock, 1986; McEwen, 1979). In Ontario, no formal action was taken in the immediate aftermath of the report's release; observers suggested that this might reflect traditional federal – provincial rivalries over jurisdiction for health.

Yet in 1975, the province's first Health Promotion Branch was established. Staff were charged with defining health promotion and devising a Ministry approach to its practice. A five-year review of existing health promotion programs conducted that year identified the following program

areas: venereal disease; dental health; smoking and health; cancer education; and a shared cost program for drug purchasing, Parcost.[2]

Throughout the 1970s, Ministry staff continued trying to define health
promotion. A one-page listing of definitions prepared in 1975 showed a
consistent thread: health promotion was viewed as an awareness-raising
activity aimed at increasing personal and community responsibility for
engaging in healthy behaviours. Health education was distinct from but
contributed to health promotion.

A Ministry reorganization in 1978 disbanded the Branch but established a five-person, short-term Health Education, Health Promotion Unit
which reported directly to the Deputy Minister. The Unit was to serve as a
"think tank" to define a direction for health promotion in the Ministry.
Staff formed liaisons within and outside the Ministry, provided advice to
Ministry staff, and investigated possible alcohol, nutrition, fitness, health
hazard appraisal, poison control, mental health, smoking, and holistic
health projects. The unit was disbanded in 1981 and the staff absorbed by
the Communications Branch.

The question of whether health promotion was principally a communications strategy or a broader approach was a persistent debate within the
Ministry; it was reflected in the shifting location of health promotion in the
organizational structure. Over the years, health promotion staff were shifted between the Communications Branch and various health promotion
units on several occasions.

Concerned about the rate of increase in health care costs, a growing
elderly population, new medical technology, the proposed Canada Health
Act, consumer demands for participation, and public interest in pursuing
healthy lifestyles (Ontario Ministry of Health, 1983b), the Minister of
Health initiated an extensive consultation process in 1982 to support long-
range planning. This Seeking Consensus process involved a series of consultative conferences during the spring and summer of 1983 to develop a
consensus on the characteristics of a desirable health care system (Ontario
Ministry of Health, 1983b). Participants were drawn from government,
academia, the health professions, District Health Councils (regional advisory councils made up of consumers, health care providers, and local government officials), and consumers. One of the items on which there was
significant agreement was that a desirable health care system "would focus
on disease prevention, health promotion and on individual responsibility
for health" (Ontario Ministry of Health, 1983b, p. 24).

In response to the Seeking Consensus process, the Ministry of Health,
in 1984, established an Office of Health Promotion reporting directly to
the Deputy Minister; its mandate was to implement and co-ordinate promotion and prevention programs across the Ministry. Staff were seconded
from various departments in the Ministry on the basis of their "entrepre-
neurial" spirit (B. Suttie, personal communication, November 1988), and

---

[2] It is interesting that Parcost, a program to provide free drugs to the elderly, that is, a financial
benefit to increase service access, was included in the list as this particular program was not consistent with the definition of health promotion espoused by the Ministry at the time.

one of the interests of the Office was corporate and workplace health promotion.

The Office of Health Promotion was replaced by a Health Promotion
Branch within the Ministry in the summer of 1987. The Branch has been
involved in several program directions, including cardiovascular health,
healthy lifestyles, community mobilization for health, and reducing
tobacco use. It has established a grants program to fund community-
based health promotion activities to increase individual control over
health, particularly through support for healthier lifestyles. The Branch
has also developed extensive resources to assist communities interested
in participating in health-related community mobilization, championed a
multidimensional tobacco strategy, and supported innovative health promotion program development, for example, on violence against women.

Public health has also been involved in health education and health promotion. Health educators were employed to support educational activities
in public health units as early as 1964 and health education — often, now,
health promotion — has become a regular part of health unit activity. In
1979, there was only one health educator working in a public health unit
(J. Murray, personal communication, September 1988); by 1992, there were
47 "health promotion specialists" employed in Ontario's 42 health units (A.
Stirling, personal communication, December 1992). The growth in the
number of such persons and pressures from other professionals interested
in accreditation in health promotion led to the emergence of the Ontario
Association of Health Promotion Specialists in Public Health in 1986.

On a statutory level, the Public Health Act of 1884 guided the activities
of public health units until it was replaced by the Health Protection and
Promotion Act in 1983. While the inclusion of health promotion in the
name of the Act suggests government support for health promotion, the
term was added only after the bill was drafted, in response to a proposal by
a member of the Opposition. The Act does not define health promotion and
contains only a single reference to public health education.

Overall, proponents of health promotion have regarded the Ontario
Ministry of Health as having responded to rather than led the health promotion field in the province. Critics argue that within the Ministry, initiatives
have been fragmented and unco-ordinated, and have tended to focus on a
lifestyle approach to health promotion. As well, the challenges of delivering
health care services consistently dominate the Ministry, limiting attention to
health promotion outside of the public health sector. Other organizations,
particularly the City of Toronto Department of Public Health, are seen as having been leaders in the development of health promotion. Nevertheless, one
of the ways in which health promotion advocates have been able to influence
government awareness of health promotion has been through consultation
processes, beginning with Seeking Consensus and continuing with three
direction-setting exercises conducted in the mid-1980s.

Three Reports

In 1987, three major Advisory Committees submitted their reports to the
government of Ontario. The report with the highest profile was that of the

Ontario Health Review Panel, established by the Premier in late 1986 following the physicians' strike. The Panel was chaired by John Evans, an influential physician with extensive academic administrative experience as well as involvements with the World Bank and the Rockefeller Foundation. The other reports were submitted by the Panel on Health Goals for Ontario, chaired by Robert Spasoff, a physician with epidemiological and policy interests from the University of Ottawa; and the Minister's Advisory Group on Health Promotion and Disease Prevention, chaired by Steve Podborski, a former world champion skier who had been appointed because of his public stance against accepting the sponsorship of the tobacco industry. The three reports, *Toward a Shared Direction for Health in Ontario* (Evans, 1987), *Health for All Ontario* (Spasoff, 1987), and *Health Promotion Matters in Ontario* (Podborski, 1987), while distinct and responding to different mandates, articulated a common vision of what would improve the quality of health for Ontarians and enhance the effectiveness and efficiency of the health care sector.

Each of the groups adopted the World Health Organization's (1984) definition of health as a resource for everyday life and identified similar core values on which to build their inquiry, such as equity and striving for quality of life. Three overriding themes were apparent in the reports: shift the emphasis from illness care to health promotion and disease prevention; provide a better balance within the service system between institutional care and co-ordinated, community-based services; and provide more opportunities for individuals to participate with service providers in making decisions on health choices. Each report acknowledged that this new approach requires different roles and responsibilities for the major actors in the health field. Each expressed frustration with the lack of progress on achieving new directions in health and called for immediate action (Corlett, 1988).

The Ontario Health Review Panel recommended establishing a vehicle for a governmentwide approach to health planning, a Premier's Council, while the Panel on Health Goals recommended the formation of a Health Goals Office. The Goals Office, like the Premier's Council, would be responsible for co-ordinating the processes associated with strategic planning for health. In December 1987, David Peterson, then Premier, announced the formation of a Premier's Council on Health Strategy (Peterson, 1987). With the establishment of the Council, a more social and ecological view of health and the various strategies to achieve it were brought into the mainstream of provincial government policy making. However, before elaborating on the Council and its activities, we review concurrent health promotion initiatives outside the provincial government.

City of Toronto Department of Public Health

The Department of Public Health of the City of Toronto has a long history of activism (MacDougall, 1990). Many of the key actors in health promotion in Ontario worked for the Department at one time or another. It was not only the workers of the Department who were influential in health promotion, however, but also successive Boards of Health and their chairs.

In the 1970s, for example, a subcommittee of the Board prepared a planning document on directions for public health, *Public Health in the 1980s* (Toronto Board of Health, 1978). The report took a broad view of health and the range of actions necessary to support it; in particular, it called for a decentralized structure, community health boards with lay representatives, and the establishment of "an issue-based, politically oriented advocacy capacity" (Toronto Board of Health, 1978, p. 22).

A Health Advocacy Unit was established in 1979 and in the three years of its existence, conducted investigations into the city's water quality, lead pollution in the soil, pesticide use in city parks, the health effects of video display terminals, and the relationship between poverty and health (City of Toronto, 1983; MacDougall, 1990). The Unit openly challenged the local and provincial governments for their inaction on health problems; informants reported that such openness contributed to the Unit's demise in 1982. Despite its formal dissolution, however, the staff of the Unit continued to be advocates for reform both inside City Hall and in their professional organizations.[3]

As described elsewhere (see Labonté, this volume), one of the most visible of the Department's contributions to health promotion was the Beyond Health Care Conference held to commemorate the city's sesquicentennial in 1984. Under the direction of Trevor Hancock, the conference brought together leading thinkers in health and health-related policy arenas from around the world (Beyond Health Care, 1985). Immediately following the conference, a one-day workshop on the Healthy City was conducted by Leonard Duhl; it subsequently inspired the international Healthy Cities Project and Canada's own Healthy Communities Project (see Manson-Singer, this volume). Toronto's own Healthy Cities office was established in 1989.

The Beyond Health Care conference established "healthy public policy" as part of the health promotion lexicon. Coined by Trevor Hancock to distinguish between public policy designed to foster health and public policy directed at the provision of public health services (see Hancock, 1982, 1985), healthy public policy became a key phrase in subsequent statements of the nature and practice of health promotion (e.g., Epp, 1986; *Ottawa Charter for Health Promotion*, 1986; Pederson, Edwards, Kelner, Marshall, & Allison, 1988).

Several staff members from the Department, notably those in the Advocacy Unit, decided that a unified vision of public health was needed for health policy reform in Ontario. Informants report that the group decided that rather than start a new group of their own, they would revitalize an existing organization — the Ontario Public Health Association — by running for office.

---

[3] While the Health Advocacy name still appears within the organizational chart of the Department of Public Health, respondents stressed that the current organization is a tamer version of the original.

Ontario Public Health Association

The Ontario Public Health Association (OPHA) was established in 1949 to represent the interests of those working in public health. The profile of the OPHA in health policy making waxed and waned with the fortunes of the public health field; traditionally, the OPHA has been a minor player in the health policy arena. Beginning in the early 1980s, however, the organization experienced a resurgence of membership and an increase in the perceived legitimacy of its self-declared role as the "voice of public health in Ontario."

As suggested, several individuals from the Toronto Department of Public Health sharing a vision of a revitalized public health movement in Ontario sought office in the OPHA in the 1980s. The new leaders successfully developed the Association into a group with continuing involvement in health policy making. Part of this process involved uniting diverse interests in the public health domain by negotiating with a number of public health organizations to become constituent members of the OPHA. These groups included the Registered Nurses Association of Ontario, the Ontario branch of the Canadian Institute of Public Health Inspectors, the Ontario Association of Health Promotion Specialists in Public Health, and the Ontario Chapter of the Canadian Health Education Society.

In 1987, the Association reconstituted itself and "for all intents and purposes became a new organization" (P. Elson, personal communication, 1992). At the time, it established a small secretariat with partial support from the Public Health Branch of the Ministry of Health. Additional monies were raised through individual and constituent society membership fees, fee-for-service contracts, and sponsored projects.

In 1987, the OPHA's mission was "to provide leadership in, and a unifying voice for, the health of the public in Ontario." In the fall of 1992, that mission statement was revised: "The mission of the OPHA is to strengthen the impact of people who are active in community and public health throughout Ontario" (P. Elson, personal communication, 1992).

The OPHA has approximately one thousand members, a third of those who work in public health in Ontario. Many other public health workers are represented indirectly, however, through their membership in the constituent societies.

The Association has been active in supporting the practice of health promotion in public health through sponsoring annual educational workshops, health promotion summer schools, a Literacy and Health project, conferences, and in public policy work. One measure of the success of the Association as a legitimate interest in health policy was the appointment of then President Peg Folsom to the Premier's Council on Health Strategy upon its establishment in 1987.

Paradigm Health

Paradigm Health was established in 1982 from among participants in the health and medicine track at the First Global Conference on the Future, held in Toronto in 1980. With approximately two dozen members, Paradigm Health provided an opportunity for its members to meet without the organizational constraints of either their employers or other voluntary associations. Members included health planners in the provincial government, community health professionals, students and professors in community health, and health administrators. Most of these individuals were also involved, whether as employees or volunteers, with key health and educational organizations within the province, including the Ontario Ministry of Health, the City of Toronto's Department of Public Health, and the University of Toronto's Division of Community Health.

Paradigm Health described itself as an independent "health futures group of Canadian professionals, based in Toronto" (Chenoy, 1985, p. 17), established "to address the perceived need for the creation of alternatives in public policy concerning health" (Jackson & Burman, 1985, p. 4). Concerned that there was too much "doom and gloom" about the future of health and health care in Ontario, the members set out to articulate a positive vision of health for the future.

Paradigm Health members conducted workshops, made presentations, published articles describing their positive vision of health, and developed a newsletter, *Paradigm Health Outreach*, which was circulated to some 600 subscribers on three continents. A series of articles on a positive vision of health and health care was published in a journal of health administration as a means of reaching professional health planners (see Chenoy, 1985; Chenoy & McQueen, 1985; Jackson & Burman, 1985; Paradigm Health, 1985). Through member contacts within the Ministry of Health, the group was invited to meet with then Minister of Health Larry Grossman in April of 1983. Mr. Grossman challenged Paradigm Health to translate its vision into practical measures and invited the members to prepare a speech for him; the speech was never given because there was a Cabinet shuffle, but the group continued to present the government with briefing papers (e.g., Paradigm Health, 1986).

Paradigm Health's vision of health and health care focussed on creating environments conducive to health, learning the art of well-being, and providing essential sick-care services to all. The group was explicit that it used health to talk about the nature of society, building its view of a desirable society on the base of what would be a society conducive to positive health (Chenoy & McQueen, 1985). Having articulated its positive vision of health, the group went into self-described "hibernation" in the late 1980s.

Summary

During the 1970s and '80s, reform-minded professionals and bureaucrats, working in various public health and health planning organizations both inside and outside the government of Ontario, articulated the view that health was distinct from the activities of the health care system. Initially a marginal or popular view, in time, and through the actions of commissions, consultations, organizational changes, reports to government, and conferences, this view came to be argued even by the highest level of health system review panels. It was within this context of health promotion development that the Premier's Council on Health Strategy emerged, late in 1987.

Premier's Council on Health Strategy

The Premier's Council on Health Strategy was an intersectoral institution that was created to recommend a strategy for health reform to the government of Ontario. The Council's work was framed by the health promotion approach: the institution itself represented a policy planning structures approach (Milio, 1987) to policy making, it adopted the World Health Organization's broad definition of health, and it used a number of health promotion strategies. The Council's mandate included the selection of health goals for Ontario, the development of healthy public policies, and the identification of policies to shift away from institutional care to an emphasis on health promotion and disease prevention (Peterson, 1987).

Although the first public mention of a Premier's Council on Health Strategy was made by the Ontario Health Review Panel, informants suggest that the original idea may have come from the Premier himself. There was already a precedent for such a Council in the form of a Premier's Council on the economy, which had been established in April, 1986.

Initially, 32 people were appointed to the Premier's Council on Health Strategy, including the Premier and seven other Cabinet ministers, seven academic physicians, representatives of the leading health interest groups in Ontario, and one representative from each of consumers, business, and labour. Senior bureaucrats from the ministries represented on Council attended Council meetings as observers. The role of the Council was advisory to government, but with eight members of the Cabinet at the table, the Premier in the chair, and the senior bureaucratic policy makers in the province sitting around the room, it had much more influence than is typical of advisory bodies to government, such as the now disbanded Ontario Council of Health.

Although initiated by the Liberal government of David Peterson, the Council was retained and transformed by the New Democratic Party government of Bob Rae, after its election in 1990. The council was renamed the Premier's Council on Health, Well-being, and Social Justice and its institutional structure altered. The new Council has a wider mandate, places more emphasis on the broad definition of health, and includes a number of social justice advocates.

Much of the detailed work of the Premier's Council on Health Strategy was carried out in four subcommittees consisting largely of Council members and the bureaucrats from particular ministries assigned to each committee, all of whom took an active role. The Health Goals Committee developed a vision of health (quoted at the beginning of this chapter), recommended five health goals for Ontario (Premier's Council on Health Strategy, 1989a), and subsequently developed objectives and targets for two of the goals (Premier's Council on Health Strategy, 1991d). The vision and goals have since been accepted as the overall health policy objectives of the New Democratic Party government of Ontario (Ontario Ministry of Health, 1992).

The Healthy Public Policy Committee developed an analytical framework on the broad determinants of health, *Nurturing Health* (Premier's Council on Health Strategy, 1991c), which was more comprehensive and nuanced than the Lalonde Report's "health field concept" (Lalonde, 1974). In particular, evidence was offered on the positive link between wealth and health, and the argument was made that population health improves when socio-economic differences are narrowed. *Nurturing Health* also argued that national prosperity is important for health and that "research suggests there may be an optimal ceiling for spending on the formal health care system — past a certain point such spending could be a drag on the nation's economy and hence its health" (Premier's Council on Health Strategy, 1991c, p. 17) (cf. Evans & Stoddart, 1990).

The main intention of the report was to provide a context within which to fit evidence, and develop policy, on the broad determinants of health. Progress has been made by the Premier's Council on Health, Well-being, and Social Justice on one of the three specific healthy public policies recommended in the report, healthy child development policy. Healthy public policy itself, defined as "public policy which encompasses all the determinants of health," was adopted as a goal of the Ontario government in January, 1992 (Ontario Ministry of Health, 1992, p. 1).

The Integration and Co-ordination Committee recommended the integration and co-ordination of health and social services at the local level (Premier's Council on Health Strategy, 1991b). This recommendation may have helped to legitimize the establishment under the Liberals, and subsequently the New Democratic Party, of community-based agencies for the delivery of long-term care, a joint policy of the Ministry of Health and the Ministry of Community and Social Services.

The Health Care Systems Committee's first report, *From Vision to Action* (Premier's Council on Health Strategy, 1989b), recommended changes in four areas of the health system: hospital funding, physician payment methods, community services, and co-ordination of the system. The focus was on more efficient use of existing resources. Progress has been made on meeting a number of these recommendations. The committee also recommended the establishment of a Health Human Resources Planning Agency, an intersectoral committee, outside the Ministry of Health, charged with strategic human resources planning and management (Premier's Council on Health Strategy, 1991a). This recommendation has met with little political support to date.

It is still early to be assessing the impact of the Premier's Council and difficult, in the complex world of policy making, to draw clear links between policy influences and policy outcomes. Nevertheless, some of the specific policy recommendations of the Premier's Council on Health Strategy have been implemented and many provide support and legitimization to policy decisions that have been inspired elsewhere. The Premier's Council on Health Strategy has also been important as a policy-making institution: it has been both an example of intersectoral policy making and a capacity-building vehicle for it (Milio, 1987).

More importantly, we would argue, the Premier's Council on Health Strategy brought the broad definition of health, promoted by health activists in a number of key health institutions over the previous 15 years, into policy making across the government of Ontario. It was the first time that a consensus had developed among key policy makers about an approach to health reform in the province based on the health promotion approach.

Reflections

The adoption by the Premier's Council and later, the provincial government, of a broad view of health as the basis for health policy in Ontario suggests that the health promotion movement has reached a significant level of institutionalization in Ontario. That is, a broad view of health, initiated in the 1970s with the Lalonde Report (Lalonde, 1974), has finally come to the centre of policy making for health, and health promotion has become accepted as an essential part of health policy making in the province. How has this been possible? We would suggest three major reasons: the dynamics of a professional social movement; the ambiguity of the concept of health promotion and the role that ambiguity plays in consensus building and social movements; and the role that health promotion plays in the cost containment debate, the priority issue in the health sector.

Social movements emerge and disappear. Not all are able to have their agenda enter the mainstream. But the health promotion movement, originating within the long-range health planning apparatus of the state (Laframboise, 1973) and appealing to progressive social reformers working within the public health field, has met with a fair degree of acceptance. Professional social movements such as this one benefit from their location within organizations that can carry the movement's agenda forward even as individual members of the movement leave it (McCarthy & Zald, 1987). Health promotion has been successful partly because careers have been built with it. Today, there are health promotion training programs, journals, grants programs, research institutes, and government bureaucracies. All this activity contributes to — but does not entirely account for — the degree of continuing interest in health promotion. We think that a larger factor in the success of health promotion, however, has been the concept's ambiguity.

Stone (1988, p. 125) suggests that "ambiguity facilitates negotiation and compromise because it allows opponents to claim victory from a single resolution." The view of health promotion articulated by the Ottawa Charter (1986), with its call for self-sufficiency and individual responsibility on the one hand and democracy and empowerment on the other, is sufficiently ambiguous to appeal to people across the political spectrum. Ambiguity allows constructive debate and policy making which might otherwise be impossible, although proponents of health promotion fear co-optation by a consensus that is more apparent than real. When discussions move beyond rhetoric to implementation and concrete policy making, will the consensus fall apart?

Health promotion suggests that health can be improved without spending more money on the health care system — the funding should be spent in other policy domains. This is an appealing argument at a time when the growth in health care costs has been the continuing concern of successive Ontario governments.

What of the future of the health promotion movement? Will it result in a significant reorientation of health policy making? Stone (1988, p. 124) warns that although ambiguity is beneficial in the early stages of a social movement, this ambiguity "usually masks internal conflicts that will become evident as the movement seeks concrete policies." Certainly, the broad definition of health has only recently come of age in Ontario. If Stone is correct, it is likely that significant conflicts, hidden by the consensus achieved at the Premier's Council, will emerge as policy makers across the government attempt to develop more substantive policies based on the broad definition of health.

We have argued that health promotion has been a professional social movement in Ontario. In order for it to be a truly liberating health strategy, health promotion needs to move beyond the professionals and become a more popular social movement. Initiatives such as the release of a popular version of *Nurturing Health* (Premier's Council on Health Strategy, 1991c), entitled *Nurturing Health: A New Understanding of What Makes People Healthy* (Premier's Council on Health, Well-being, and Social Justice, 1993) are important steps in this process. It remains to be seen whether these efforts to popularize health promotion are successful.

References

Badgley, Robin F. (1978). *Health promotion and social change in the health of Canadians*. Unpublished paper presented to the Seminar on Evaluation of Health Education and Behaviour Modification Programs, Toronto, December 1978.

Beyond health care: Proceedings of a conference on healthy public policy. (1985). *Canadian Journal of Public Health, 76*(Supp.1).

Board of Health, Health Planning Steering Committee (1978). *Public health in the 1980s.* Toronto: Department of Public Health.

Chenoy, N.C. (1985). An introduction to health futurism. *Health Management Forum, 6*(1), 17-25.

Chenoy, N.C., & McQueen, R.J.C. (1985). Beyond health care. *Health Management Forum, 6*(3), 52-58.

City of Toronto (1983). *The unequal society: A challenge to public health.* A joint report of the City of Toronto Department of Public Health and Department of Planning & Development. Toronto: Department of Public Health.

Corlett, S. (1988). *Synthesis of the major themes of three health strategy reports.* Unpublished paper prepared for the Premier's Council on Health Strategy, Toronto.

Deber, R.B., & Vayda, E. (1985). The environment of health policy implementation: The Ontario, Canada example. In W.W. Holland, R. Detels, & G. Knox (eds.), *Oxford textbook of public health* (pp. 441-461). Oxford: Oxford University Press.

Evans, J.R. (chair) (1987). *Toward a shared direction for health in Ontario: Report of the Ontario Health Review Panel.* Toronto: Ontario Ministry of Health, June.

Evans, R. (1982). A retrospective on the "New perspective". *Journal of Health Policy, Politics and Law, 7,* 325-344.

Evans, R.G., & Stoddart, G.L. (1990). Producing health, consuming health care. *Social Science and Medicine, 31,* 1347-1363.

Grace, V.M. (1991). The marketing of empowerment and the construction of the health consumer: A critique of health promotion. *International Journal of Health Services, 21,* 329-343.

Hancock, T. (1982). Beyond health care: Creating a healthy future. *The Futurist, 16*(4), 4-13.

Hancock, T. (1985). Health in transition. *Canadian Home Economics Journal, 35*(1), 11-13, 16.

Hancock, T. (1986). Lalonde and beyond: Looking back at "A New Perspective on the Health of Canadians". *Health Promotion (International), 1,* 93-100.

Hoffman, L.M. (1989). *The politics of knowledge: Activist movements in medicine and planning.* Albany, NY: State University of New York Press.

Jackson, S.F., & Burman, D. (1985). A positive vision of health. *Health Management Forum, 6*(2), 4-11.

Laframboise, H. (1973). Health policy: Breaking the problem down into more manageable segments. *Canadian Medical Association Journal, 108,* 388-391, 393.

Lalonde, M. (1974). *A new perspective on the health of Canadians.* Ottawa: Supply & Services Canada.

McCarthy, J.D., & Zald, M.N. (1987). The trend of social movements in America: Professionalization and resource mobilization. In Mayer, N. Zald & John D. McCarthy (eds.), *Social movements in an organizational society* (pp. 337-391). New Brunswick, NJ: Transaction.

Macdonald, G., & Bunton, R. (1992). Health promotion: Discipline or disciplines? In R. Bunton & G. Macdonald (eds.), *Health promotion: Disciplines and diversity* (pp. 6-19). London & New York: Routledge.

MacDougall, H. (1990). *Activists and advocates: Toronto's health department, 1883-1983.* Toronto & Oxford: Dundurn Press.

McEwen, E. (1979). Whatever happened to the Lalonde report? *Canadian Journal of Public Health, 70*(1), 13-16.

Mhatre, S.L., & Deber, R.B. (1992). From equal access to health care to equitable access to health: A review of Canadian provincial health commissions and reports. *International Journal of Health Services, 22,* 645-668.

Milio, N. (1987). Healthy public policy: Issues and scenarios. Unpublished paper prepared for *A Symposium on Healthy Public Policy,* Yale University, October 5-6, 1987.

Ontario Ministry of Health (1983a). *A century of caring.* Toronto: Author.

Ontario Ministry of Health (1983b). *Health care: The '80s and beyond.* Toronto: Author.

Ontario Ministry of Health (1992). *Goals and strategic priorities.* Toronto: Author.

Ontario Ministry of Treasury & Economics (1987). *1987 Ontario budget.* Toronto: Author.

Ontario Ministry of Treasury & Economics (1991). *1991 Ontario budget supplement: Managing health care funding.* Toronto: Author.

Paradigm Health (1986, July). *A vision for a healthy Ontario*. A report to the people of Ontario and their government from Paradigm Health. Toronto: Author.

Paradigm Health (1985). Vision of health in 2011. *Health Management Forum*, 6(4), 50-64.

Pederson, A.P. (1989). *The development of health promotion in Ontario*. Unpublished master's thesis, University of Toronto, Toronto, Canada.

Pederson, A.P., Edwards, R.K., Kelner, M., Marshall, V.M., & Allison, K. R. (1988). *Co-ordinating healthy public policy: An analytic literature review and bibliography*. Ottawa: Minister of Supply & Services.

Peterson, D. (1987). *Premier Peterson to chair Council on Health Strategy*. News release, 3 December, Office of the Premier.

Podborski, S. (chair) (1987). *Health promotion matters in Ontario*. A Report of the Minister's Advisory Group on Health Promotion. Toronto: Ontario Ministry of Health, September.

Premier's Council on Health Strategy (1989a). *A vision of health: Health goals for Ontario*. Toronto: Author.

Premier's Council on Health Strategy (1989b). *From vision to action: Report of the health care system committee*. Toronto: Author.

Premier's Council on Health Strategy (1991a). *Achieving the vision: Health human resources. Report of the health care system committee*. Toronto: Author.

Premier's Council on Health Strategy (1991b). *Local decision making for health and social services. Report of the integration and co-ordination committee*. Toronto: Author.

Premier's Council on Health Strategy (1991c). *Nurturing health: A framework on the determinants of health*. Toronto: Author.

Premier's Council on Health Strategy (1991d). *Towards health outcomes: Goals 2 and 4: Objectives and targets*. Toronto: Author.

Premier's Council on Health, Well-being, & Social Justice (1993). *Nurturing health: A new understanding of what makes people healthy*. Toronto: Author.

Signal, L.N. (1993). *The politics of the new public health: A case study of the Ontario Premier's Council on Health Strategy*. Unpublished doctoral thesis, University of Toronto, Toronto, Canada.

Spasoff, R.A. (chair) (1987). *Health for all Ontario*. Report of the Panel on Health Goals for Ontario. Toronto: Ontario Ministry of Health, September.

Stevenson, H.M. & Burke, M. (1992). Bureaucratic logic in social movement clothing: The limits of health promotion research. *Canadian Journal of Public Health, 83*(Supp. 1), S47-S53.

Stone, D. (1988). *Policy paradox and political reason*. Glenview, IL: Scott, Foresman & Company.

Tuohy, C.J. (1988). Medicine and the state in Canada: The extra-billing issue in perspective. *Canadian Journal of Political Science, XXI*, 267-296.

Tuohy, C.J. (1993). Social policy: Two worlds. In M. M. Atkinson (ed.), *Governing Canada: Institutions and public policy* (pp. 275-305). Toronto: Harcourt Brace Jovanovich.

Weller, G.R., & Manga, P. (1983). The development of health policy in Canada. In M. M. Atkinson & M. A. Chandler (eds.), *The politics of Canadian public policy* (pp. 223-246). Toronto: University of Toronto Press.

World Health Organization, Regional Office for Europe (1984). *Health promotion: A discussion document on the concept and principles*. Copenhagen: Author.

Health Promotion in Québec: Did It Ever Catch On?[1]

Michel O'Neill and Lise Cardinal

The [Québec] policy [on Health and Welfare] will rely on six strategies: (1) Foster the reinforcement of personal skills; (2) Support life settings and develop healthy and safe environments; (3) Improve living conditions; (4) Act for and with vulnerable populations; (5) Harmonize public policies and actions fostering health and welfare; (6) Orient the health and welfare services system toward more effective and less costly solutions (MSSS, 1992a, p. 134, free translation).

In order to sustain prevention and health promotion. . . the Minister will: (1) Devote to these activities a minimum of 20% of the new monies planned for the implementation of the reform; (2) Put in place as soon as possible the Centre of Expertise in Prevention and Promotion of Health and Welfare planned in the context of the reform (MSSS, 1992a, p. 176, free translation).

Québec is the second largest Canadian province, with just over seven million inhabitants, of whom about 80% are Francophone. Despite important differences from the rest of the country in culture, language, and the organization of major sectors of society (e.g., the school system, the civil code, and public health services), Québec underwent a questioning of its health and welfare system during the second half of the 1980s that reflected concerns similar to those of most of the other provinces. This examination was initiated by the Rochon Commission which worked from 1985 to 1988. The Commission's comprehensive report (CESSS, 1988) was followed by a first governmental proposal in April 1989, introduced by then Liberal Minister of Health and Social Services, Thérèse Lavoie-Roux (MSSS, 1989). Following an election in October of the same year, the Liberals of Robert Bourassa were returned to power and, Lavoie-Roux having retired from politics, a new Minister of Health and Social Services was appointed, Marc-Yvan Côté. Côté finalized the reform in several steps: with a white paper (MSSS, 1990), a major piece of legislation — Bill 120 — (Gouvernement du Québec, 1991), a position paper on the financing of the reformed system (MSSS, 1991) and a detailed health and social services policy outlining specific goals to be reached by the year 2002 (MSSS, 1992a).

---

[1] Preliminary versions of this paper have been presented in the Scientific Seminars Series of the Institute for Health Promotion Research, University of British Columbia, Vancouver, June 29, 1992, and at the États généraux de la promotion de la santé au Québec, Québec City, August 27, 1992.

Under the reforms, the central involvement of the provincial government in financing and managing the health and welfare system has been maintained (Pineault et al., 1993), but small and significant breaches in the universality of services have occurred and user fees have been imposed on previously free services. In this context, as illustrated by the quotes at the outset of this chapter, health promotion was identified as a key approach to deal with Québec's health problems. However, it is unclear how this commitment to health promotion will be operationalized, owing to the financial constraints that are threatening the implementation of the whole reform. Moreover, as this chapter will argue, in contrast with other provinces and with the federal government, health promotion has never been fashionable in Québec, at least in the system of health and welfare services.

In this chapter, we will first show that although the current status of health promotion is somewhat unclear, this province has a long and strong tradition in health education. Secondly, we will offer evidence of the paucity of interest in health promotion in Québec since 1986. In the third section, we will suggest some reasons why health promotion has never been popular. Finally, we will assess the consequences of this apparently weak interest.

1940–1986

From a Glorious Past in Health Education to an Uncertain Present in Health Promotion

The history of public health practice in Québec reveals a long tradition of health education activities (Desrosiers & Gaumer, 1987). In a study of health education in Québec from the 1920s to the end of the 1970s, one of us (O'Neill, 1977) identified four important periods in the history of the field. As the fourth period begins in the mid-1970s — when the time span covered by this book starts — we will discuss it in some detail. Let us, however, briefly consider the three earlier periods to provide a context for more recent developments.

Early Health Education Efforts

The early 1940s saw the formal birth of health education in Québec when Jules Gilbert, the medical officer of health for the Unité sanitaire (the County Health Unit) of Shefford, became intrigued by differences in the health-related practices in the Francophone and Anglophone villages of his territory. He persuaded the provincial Minister of Health of the day to send him for graduate studies in health education in the United States. On his return, in the mid-1940s, he created a Health Education division in the Ministry that he ran virtually single-handedly until 1960. By the end of the 1940s, the role of this low-budget division was to transmit materials prepared nationally in Ottawa, to develop other materials and campaigns, to negotiate (without much success) with the Ministry of Education to include health education in the school curriculum, and, most importantly, to provide guidance and assistance to the personnel of the County Health Units and the Municipal Health Services. The County and Municipal Health Units had been established in the 1930s to deliver public health services in Québec, and health education of various publics was a key responsibility.

The 1950s was the golden age of health education in Québec (O'Neill, 1977). Formal training in this field was then available through one additional year of specialization on top of the Diploma in Hygiene offered by the School of Hygiene at the University of Montréal, and also as a specialization for some elementary and high school teachers in some of the Écoles normales (Normal Schools) where teachers were trained. Specific jobs of "nurse educator" existed in most county health units. Meanwhile, Jules Gilbert was a whirlwind of activity, writing textbooks (Gilbert, 1959a, 1967) and papers (Gilbert, 1954, 1959b, 1967), editing a newsletter, teaching at the University of Montréal, providing support to "his" nurse educators, supervising the training in health education of people from foreign Francophone countries, and more.

This golden age came to an abrupt end during the early 1960s when the third (1960–1973) period in the history of health education in Québec began. Caught in the administrative nightmare of starting a hospital insurance scheme, of which Jules Gilbert became the first manager, the Québec Ministry of Health began to abandon its commitment to public health, and hence to health education (O'Neill, 1977). Under a major reorganization of the educational system which transferred the responsibility to train students in public health to various departments and professional schools in colleges and universities (medicine, nursing, dentistry, engineering, veterinary medicine), the Montréal School of Hygiene was closed (Gaucher, 1979). This situation lasted until the mid-1970s when, in the wake of the first major reform of Québec's health and welfare system (Lesemann, 1981; Renaud, 1981), public health services, renamed "community health," were reorganized.

1973–1986: Health Education and the Modern Era of Québec Public Health

In the reorganization following the Castonguay-Nepveu Commission, what was left of Public Health Services was removed from municipalities and County Health Units in 1973 and largely integrated into a new network of 32 Community Health Departments (DSCs). This marked the beginning of a new era, the fourth period of health education activities in Québec.

The health and welfare system reform of the early 1970s was based on clear ideological premises, including community participation and a broad concept of health in which social and medical aspects were considered two sides of the same coin. Services were to be multidisciplinary and were to integrate the preventive, curative, and readaptive dimensions of professional interventions — and hence the unusual decision was made to locate public health services in hospitals. Facilities were to be organized into a neat structure and a major reshuffling of organizational categories was done, including the creation of new organizational forms such as the DSCs. The DSCs have been abolished by the recent Côté reform, and the 20 years during which they were the major carriers of public health services are now being studied (Duplessis, 1981; O'Neill, 1983; Pineault et al., 1990), but there is still a lot to learn about them.

Since their inception, and particularly at the outset when they had to deliver the major part of preventive services that were subsequently transferred in the early 1980s to the network of Local Community Services Centres (CLSCs), health education and health promotion have been key tasks of the DSCs (O'Neill, 1983; MSSS, 1988). These programs were carried out with enormous good will and dedication, but usually on the basis of very little training, by dentists, nurses, dental hygienists, and physicians who had overly simplistic approaches to changing health-related behaviours.

However, before illustrating the lack of popularity of health promotion in Québec since 1986, it should be mentioned that in the late 1970s and early '80s, two other actors played a significant role in relation to health promotion. The first was the Conseil des affaires sociales et de la famille (Council on Social Affairs and the Family), a consultative board to the Minister of Health. Under the astute guidance of a former head of the Health Education Division of the Ministry, an epidemiologist-physician by the name of Madeleine Blanchet who has always been a firm believer in health promotion, this council undertook, through several studies, a major update of the epidemiological status of Québec's population health and welfare (e.g., Levasseur, 1983; Roy, 1983). This operation culminated in a famous document, *Objectif santé* (CASF, 1984), that was followed by several other important papers (e.g., CASF, 1989), all framed by health promotion rhetoric. However, despite widespread recognition both within and outside Québec of the quality and the relevance of these documents, the actual impact of this consultative body's recommendations on government policy and professional practice was very limited.

The second key player was the Association pour la santé publique du Québec (ASPQ), the Québec Public Health Association. Founded in 1943, the ASPQ is a dynamic body that has always been at the vanguard of public health thinking in the province. As early as 1984, it held a conference on the theme of health promotion. Moreover, it has been a major player in the launching of every major federal health promotion initiative in Québec (Healthy Communities, Strengthening Community Health, Knowledge Development in Health Promotion, etc.) and is currently very involved in consensus building over health promotion.

Lack of Popularity of Health Promotion in Québec Since 1986

If we take the period 1986–92, that is, the span when the public profile of health promotion has been very high nationally and internationally following the release of the *Ottawa Charter on Health Promotion* (Charter, 1986) and the Epp (1986) document, *Achieving Health for All: A Framework for Health Promotion*, what do we observe in Québec?

Health Promotion in the Québec Government

The quotes at the beginning of this chapter are somewhat misleading because they suggest that the Côté reform has confirmed the need for health promotion, whereas in actuality, in the years since the Ottawa Charter, there has been constant indecision within the Ministry of Health and Social Services (MSSS) about health promotion's definition, status, and organization.

Formally, a Health Promotion Service (the fifth and lowest level in the organizational structure of the Ministry) was created in the early 1980s. Since then, this unit has never been staffed by more than a handful of dedicated but not always specifically trained professionals, and it has experienced a high turnover of directors and personnel. As was true of earlier organizational incarnations, the Service made several plans and proposals for an overall health promotion strategy (MSSS, 1977, 1987a, 1987b). These documents integrated the most recent national and international visions of the field but never really received the attention, let alone approval, of the top administrative and political echelons of the Ministry. Thus, despite the rhetoric of healthy public policy and reducing health inequalities, the provincial Health Promotion Service has tended to work on lifestyle health problems (nutrition, accidents, cardiovascular diseases, tobacco, dental problems, etc.), the public media campaigns being designed and implemented by the Communications Division located in another Directorate of the Ministry. If we consider that during the same period provinces like Ontario and New Brunswick had Health Councils answering directly to the Premier, it is clear that Québec was not in the same ball game.

Another indication of the ambiguous status of health promotion in the Québec government is the way it was treated in the various operations that led to the Côté reform. Again, this was only a hesitant waltz, one step ahead, two steps back, despite documents prepared both internally (Duval & Paquet, 1991; Ferland, 1991; Martin, 1991) and externally (Godin, 1990; O'Neill et al., 1990) which made precise suggestions for a mandate, legislative program, and organizational structure for health promotion congruent with the most current Canadian and international developments in the field. Despite this input, the Côté reform integrates health promotion and disease prevention as a vaguely defined expertise to be developed by new Public Health authorities at the provincial and regional levels. In contrast, the health protection function has a well-defined legal mandate which is operationalized as interventions in infectious diseases, occupational health, and environmental health. This arrangement means that the development of expertise in prevention and promotion is very uneven in the 18 regions of Québec. Public health authorities thus begin to deal with their health protection functions and, depending on their interest, resources, and motivation, then move into prevention and promotion.

In the provincial bureaucracy, the Côté reform locates health promotion one level higher in the Ministry's hierarchy; it is now a Direction rather than a Service in a new General Direction of Public Health headed by an Associate

Deputy Minister. None of the suggestions made in the various working documents mentioned above to create intersectoral governmental structures answering to the Cabinet or the Premier in order to develop healthy public policies have been incorporated in the scheme. Although health promotion was identified in the final government documents (MSSS, 1990; MSSS, 1992a; MSSS, 1992b) as one of the six fields of public health where major research and development efforts would have to be made, at the moment of writing it is still unclear if a Centre of Expertise on this topic will be developed at all, although a centre will most likely be dedicated to the Québec version of Healthy Communities, Villes et Villages en santé (Poirier, 1993, personal communication). Overall then, health promotion in the provincial governmental structure following the Côté reform runs the risk of being more of the same: one-shot interventions, mostly on lifestyles issues, poorly co-ordinated with other relevant directions in the Ministry (let alone with other ministries) and conducted by a small but dedicated staff receiving little attention from the major legislative, administrative, or political decision makers within or outside the Ministry of Health and Social Services. Despite numerous interventions at the local or regional levels of public health agencies, the provincial government's commitment to health promotion has never translated into strong, clear structures or programs.

Health Promotion in Local Governments: Villes et Villages en Santé (VVS)

Municipal governments in Québec have legal jurisdiction over many of the determinants of health and well-being, including housing, safety, physical environments, and leisure. Born in 1987, Villes et Villages en santé is alive and well (Lacombe & Poirier, 1991) and has been formally identified by the Côté reform as a strategy (MSSS, 1992a) to reinforce the health promotion role of local governments. At the time of writing, this movement comprised over 80 municipalities, covering more than 25% of Québec's population. The project has been integrated since May 1990 in a non-profit organization, Le Réseau québécois de villes et villages en santé. This network is supported by a Centre of Information and Promotion located in Québec City. Since its inception, the network has already undergone an initial evaluation (Fortin et al., 1992), and a significant discussion of indicators and evaluation appropriate to VVS has been undertaken (Cardinal & O'Neill, 1992; O'Neill & Cardinal, 1992). The network is tied into the national and international Healthy Cities movement and has been identified by the World Health Organization (WHO) as a "model of good practice" (Giroult, 1990). In fact, the Québec network has been identified as one of the best-developed networks of Healthy Cities in the world (Tsouros, 1990). As noted elsewhere in this book, Healthy Cities (in Canada, Healthy Communities) is certainly the most visible embodiment of recent health promotion rhetoric.

However, if you asked the hundreds of people involved in the VVS movement in Québec to define health promotion, the vast majority would not know what you were talking about, especially the ones who are not

public health professionals. As a matter of fact, the leadership of the movement has even reframed the Healthy Cities concept to distance it from the
word "health," replacing it by "quality of life," which seems less threatening to non-health professionals (Fortin et al., 1991). Moreover, it has also
been found that to function, there is no need for the people implementing
Villes et Villages en santé in a municipality to have a common understanding of the ideology and the concepts inspiring the movement (Fortin
et al., 1991). Thus, but for the leadership of the movement, most people
trying to implement local policies, programs or projects favourable to
health in the context of VVS in Québec do not formally refer to health promotion and are not conscious that they are operating in such a framework.

Health Promotion in Community Health Agencies:
The DSCs and CLSCs

As already mentioned, the 1970s reform of the health and welfare system
totally reorganized preventive and public health services in Québec into
two networks. The first network consisted of the 32 Community Health
Departments (DCS) which were established in regional hospitals and given
a broader but somewhat more ambiguous mandate than the County Health
Units or Municipal Health Services they replaced (Desrosiers, 1976;
O'Neill, 1983). The second network comprises the 160 or so Local
Community Services Centres (CLSCs); these centres cover the whole
province and consist of facilities providing various unspecialized medical,
social, and community services. The story of these two networks is inter-
twined and fascinating but too complicated to be told here. Whereas the
DSCs have disappeared in the Côté reform, their functions and personnel
being assimilated by the new regional bodies created to decentralize the
management of the whole system, the CLSCs have been maintained and
their functions reinforced.

In Québec, it is clearly the professionals in the DSCs who have been the
most interested in health promotion since 1986, in part because these organizations were looking for an intervention niche that would be indis-
putably theirs, since some of their former roles had devolved to the CLSCs
or to other organizations. Individuals in DSCs all over the province have
become the most visible champions of health promotion rhetoric and practice, developing programs, writing numerous books and papers, and being
active nationally and internationally — especially in the Francophone
world, where some of them have won international awards. Some of these
individuals were even seconded to the Ministry in order to assist its own
Health Promotion Service.

However, these individuals were not always able to convince their organizations that health promotion practices were legitimate community
health endeavours. Whereas provincially the DSCs developed co-ordination committees on topics like infectious disease, environmental health,
trauma, and epidemiological monitoring, they were never able, despite
considerable effort (AHQ, 1988), to create a strong enough consensus
about health promotion to maintain a provincial committee on this topic.

Moreover, as testified by the members of one of the DSCs' most reputable teams in this domain (Perreault et al., 1992), the health promotion practices of these organizations have by and large maintained a focus on individual behavioural change and have been much less active in the more environmental dimensions of health promotion practice advocated by the Ottawa Charter and other similar documents.

As of 1993, 18 new structures (the Régies régionales) have to integrate the former network of 32 DSCs. The way in which they will organize the development of their prevention and health promotion expertise is still unclear; arrangements will likely vary according to region and be a delicate and controversial issue, as a first study has already shown (Déry, 1993).

On the other hand, because they were close to the population and operated under a mandate to be community driven and community oriented, the CLSCs have long conducted numerous interventions that would qualify as health promotion, even if people did not refer to them as such. Paradoxically, however, since the mid-1980s, there has been an important reorientation of the CLSCs away from community-directed practices and towards a curative orientation based on medical services, as suggested by a well-known government report (Brunet et al., 1987). This general orientation, moving away from the rhetoric and practices of health promotion that had been — under other names — the bread and butter of most CLSCs, has been reinforced by the Côté reform. It is still unclear how this shift in emphasis will be applied, because many CLSCs have a long history of community involvement and of professional practices linked to the community; many have been able to maintain this flavour in their services since 1987 despite the Brunet report. What is clear, though, is that in general, given the context, the CLSCs have been much less vocal about health promotion than the DSCs. Some CLSCs have gone as far as to say that health promotion was not part of their mandate! However, when compared to most DSCs, the practices of most CLSCs have been much closer to health promotion for a much longer period of time than have the activities of the DSCs.

Only the future will tell if and how these paradoxes in DSCs and CLSCs will be resolved, but it is clear that in the service networks in Québec most likely to adopt health promotion, it has not been popular.

Health Promotion in Grass-Roots Organizations and Among the General Public

Grass-roots organizations in the health and welfare sector have been extremely important in Québec, especially since the mid-1970s when, in the wake of the feminist movement, they began to provide services that the new health system was unable or unwilling to offer (Dumais & Lévesque, 1983; Fortin, 1993; O'Neill, 1989). As an example of grass-roots involvement in health promotion, let us consider the Strengthening Community Health initiative, a major federal health promotion project run by the Canadian Public Health Association (see the chapter by Hoffman earlier in this book). Since its launch in 1988, Strengthening Community Health has linked major institutional funders and provincial federations of grass-roots organizations in the province (O'Neill, 1989). This and other federal initiatives distributed approximately $800 000 annually of funds earmarked to grass-roots organizations and survived the demise of the national project in 1991. However, regular personal communication with the participants in these initiatives suggests that very few people in these organizations refer to the health promotion concept or to key health promotion documents to frame their activities. A close look at their work or their ideology would, however, undoubtedly show that many — if not the majority — of them do health promotion, but without knowing it!

As for the general population, even though to our knowledge no formal research has been undertaken on this point, there is no indication that the concept or rhetoric of health promotion has been sufficiently disseminated so as to become well known, let alone incorporated into everyday life.

Research and Training in Health Promotion

If someone looks at the programs of the three major provincial, peer-reviewed bodies funding health-related research in Québec — the Fonds de la recherche en santé du Québec (FRSQ), the Conseil Québécois de la recherche sociale (CQRS) and the Fonds pour la formation de chercheurs et l'avancement de la recherche (FCAR) — none has had a specific "health promotion" funding category during the period from 1986 to 1993. Indirectly, these bodies may have financed projects or even provided infrastructure monies to research teams whose work could be labelled health promotion but, as such, no earmarked money of this sort exists. It is the same situation with the research monies given each year by the Ministry of Health and Social Services for community health research: some of it might actually be devoted to projects that could be labelled health promotion, but no specific monies are devoted to this domain.

The Québec situation is thus very different from other provinces like British Columbia, for instance, where significant monies have been devoted to health promotion research through its Provincial Health Services Research Fund (see the chapter by Altman and Martin in this book) or the National Health Research and Development Program (NHRDP) of the federal government. NHRDP has had Health Promotion as a priority research area since the late 1980s. A specific health promotion competition was held in 1990 and a recent joint venture with the Social Sciences and Humanities Research Council will fund, from 1993 to 1998, six national research centres on health promotion (see the paper by Rootman and O'Neill in this book).

If we look at training in health promotion (O'Neill, 1992), given the fact that there is no specific professional occupation called health promoter or health educator in Québec (in contrast with Ontario or the United States), there has been almost no formal education in this domain. No undergraduate training is available, except the occasional course in the curriculum of certain types of health professionals (especially nursing). At the graduate level, both the University of Montréal and Laval University offer a specialization in health promotion as part of Master's degrees in community health. A few of the doctorates in Community Health at the University of Montréal or in the faculties of Education in Montréal, Sherbrooke, or Québec City have also been done in Health Promotion. Finally, on-the-job training in this domain, even though the Ministry of Health and Social Services has commissioned a series of documents to this end (MSSS, s.d., 1990a) and has significant budgets earmarked for training purposes, has only been occasional. Here again, health promotion has little legitimacy of its own, being usually considered an unclear subfield in the general domain of community health whereas in other provinces, specific programs exist at the undergraduate (e.g., Dalhousie University, University of Waterloo) or graduate (University of Toronto) levels.

Possible Explanations for the Lack of Interest

Beyond the usual cultural and political caution — if not resistance— of Québeckers to any attempt by the federal government to suggest directions in fields constitutionally belonging to the provinces, there are, in our view, a few additional explanations for the lukewarm reception in Québec to the health promotion approach that came as a tidal wave in the wake of the Ottawa Conference of November 1986.

No Need for a New Rhetoric of Health Promotion

A first explanatory factor for the lack of enthusiasm for health promotion is that what was promoted by the federal authorities as a "new" discourse to modify the way in which the health and welfare system was organized and professional practice was developed had been, in fact, the day-to-day situation in Québec for about 15 years. As mentioned previously, the early 1970s reform of Québec's health and welfare system was already couched in the same ideological terms as the ones proposed by the "new" health promotion vision. Moreover, the way the Québec system had been reorganized, with networks of public local community clinics (the CLSCs) and community health departments (the DSCs) covering the whole province, was exactly what some of the federal documents were arguing for, seemingly unaware that such networks had been in place for more than a decade in Québec. Hence, there was simply no need for the health promotion rhetoric!

Reluctance of Community Health Physicians to Accept a More Political Vision of Their Practice

The emphasis of the post-1986 "new" health promotion rhetoric is more on the political, policy, and environmental dimensions than on the more individual ones that had previously characterized health education for decades. This political emphasis contributed to the reluctance in adopting the new vision of health promotion in Québec.

As a matter of fact, the balance in the type of community health professionals employed in public health organizations has increasingly been tipped in the direction of physicians since the reform of 1973. For instance, in 1981, physicians accounted for 3.4% of DSCs' personnel (O'Neill, 1983), whereas they accounted for 29.2% in 1992 (AHQ, 1992). This situation has arisen primarily because of an economic arrangement favouring the hiring of physicians: when a medical specialty in community health was created in 1980, significant funds were earmarked to hire such physicians on a salaried basis by the Québec Health Insurance Board. Thus, from 1980 on, DSCs were able to hire almost any number of physicians at no direct cost to their budgets, whereas hiring any other type of personnel required a specific request to the Ministry — in a period of severe budget cuts. It is therefore not surprising that, especially in large urban areas, physicians have become the largest group of community health professionals in Québec DSCs. Moreover physicians, more or less consciously, were also able to monopolize the community health positions of authority in agencies, in the Ministry and in academia, and were then in a situation to define what was legitimate community health or health promotion practice.

This medicalization phenomenon has had mixed consequences that still need to be empirically studied. We think that for at least two reasons it has had, in relationship to the adoption of a more environmental vision of health promotion, a rather negative effect. First, given the economic barriers to hiring non-physician personnel in the DSCs, public health professionals who would have been more likely to be attracted to an environmental vision of health promotion (like the ones trained in social sciences, for instance) were not abundantly hired. Even when they were hired, such people were usually not in key positions of influence. Second, apart from a few notable exceptions, the way most Québec physicians have been trained and are practising community health reflects a classical scientific and technocratic approach to public health work. This approach is based more on the disciplines of epidemiology, biostatistics, and the organization of medical care than in the behavioural sciences, which are often perceived as less "scientific." This has had the effect of deterring most public health physicians from "buying in" to the community-oriented political approach advocated by the new health promotion rhetoric.

Thus, not only was there little need for a new health promotion rhetoric in the Québec of the mid-1980s, but the people who were in control of the definition of community health practice usually did not favour the approach promoted by this rhetoric. The fact that as a result of the Côté reform the concept of community health has been replaced by the more traditional one of public health — largely but not exclusively a result of the influence of community health physicians — is but one additional illustration of this phenomenon.

No Health Promotion Profession

As we have already pointed out, in contrast with Ontario or the United States, where there are professions of "health educator" or "health promoter," there has been no professional constituency in Québec who found its interests served when the concept came into fashion in 1986. We do not mean here that professionalizing health promotion is necessarily good: this is a tricky issue that deserves more detailed consideration. What is certain, though, is that part of the lukewarm interest in health promotion in Québec is probably explained by the fact that no professional constituency was there to fight vigorously for it, even if a small part of the public health profession, especially in the DSCs, were enthusiastic about it.

A Neo-Conservative Political Climate

Another phenomenon that may partly explain Québec's reluctance to adopt the health promotion discourse is the fact that, like almost everywhere else in the Western world, this province has moved in the direction of neo-conservatism since the beginning of the 1980s. This move has been less dramatic than in other parts of Canada or than in countries like Britain or the United States. The ideological mood, especially since the election in 1982 of Robert Bourassa's provincial Liberal government on a neo-conservative political platform, has nevertheless been concerned mostly with dismantling the welfare state, diminishing the size of the public deficit, decreasing government intervention, and privatizing certain areas of government service. In such a climate, from the viewpoint of people running state-funded community health agencies, becoming more political and community oriented is likely to be considered at high risk of political retaliation. Health promotion thus arrived at a moment when public organizations would rather maintain a low profile and survive than become more visible and risk ruin.

Low Political Visibility of Health Promotion

We think that another important reason why health promotion never became fashionable among provincial political decision makers is because of its low political payoff. The general population is highly sensitive to the availability of curative services which, given the current fiscal situation of governments, are constantly threatened for cost-containment reasons. Even if health determinants as important as jobs and income are very much valued by the general population, they are not associated with health. Politicians are thus precluded from going beyond the rhetoric by taking resources from the curative sector to transfer them to health promotion because it could severely jeopardize their very political survival.

Lack of Long-Term Financial Commitment to Health Promotion

Most innovative health promotion programs are suffering a crucial lack of continuity. They are usually funded on a demonstration project basis, burdened with unrealistic expectations, and threatened with the disappearance of funds. In contrast, most of the much more costly medical technology is not obliged to demonstrate its effectiveness before being financed. We see again how powerless the health promotion constituencies are as compared to those of biomedicine.

Chronic Conceptual Confusion

Finally, the last — but not the least — reason why we believe the health promotion discourse of the mid-1980s has never really caught on in Québec is because of what we have labelled, echoing the proposals for a Triple E Canadian Senate (Equal; Elected; Effective), the Triple C of Québec Health Promotion: Chronic Conceptual Confusion. Despite numerous efforts, health promotion proponents in academia, the Ministry of Health and Social Services, or in the network of DSCs have never succeeded in clarifying the concept of health promotion sufficiently to show how it differs from disease prevention or health protection. Thus, proponents have not been able to convince the decision makers of its specificity as a professional practice. This conceptual haziness is not exclusive to Québec, but it has surely contributed there in no small way to the paucity of interest and the implementation difficulties described earlier.

Consequences of the Lack of Interest

As must now be evident, except among a very limited group of civil servants, academics, and community health professionals, the discourse of health promotion as put forward nationally and internationally since 1986 has not been very popular in Québec. However — and this is the major paradox — many ideas and practices suggested by this discourse have been at the very core of the operation of the formal and informal (grass-roots) Québec health system since its reform in the early 1970s and have also been maintained in the Côté reform of the early 1990s.

So, what is the problem? How important is accepting the international or national health promotion rhetoric and movement if the concepts and practices suggested are implemented anyway, even if under other names? Would an additional push for health promotion just be a way for now marginal professionals to get access to legitimacy, jobs, or power at the expense of more mainstream professionals, as has been suggested about the 1970s rise of community health in Québec generally (O'Neill, 1982)? Even if the answers to these three questions are "none," "no," and "yes," we nevertheless think that the formal development of health promotion as a part of the current reform of the public health system is important. Without health promotion, some key elements that could have a significant impact on the health of the population are unlikely to be implemented. In order to push this argument further, we suggest a conceptual clarification of health promotion.

Figure 1   Health promotion: A philosophy and a set of practices.

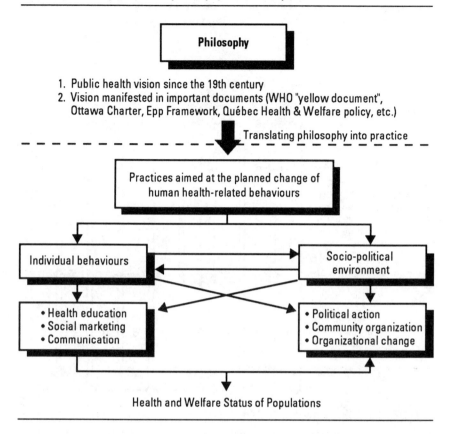

As shown in Figure 1, we think that an important part of the conceptual confusion surrounding health promotion is that the expression has been used simultaneously to identify an ideology or philosophy and a series of interventions to implement this ideology. A few authors have mentioned this distinction between the ideological and the practical dimensions of health promotion (e.g., Green & Kreuter, 1991; MSSS, s.d.) but, in our view, they have not realized the fact that keeping them under the same umbrella might produce the negative consequences seen in Québec.

Actually, we do not think that the ideology of health promotion as formulated in the World Health Organization's (1984) "yellow document," the Ottawa Charter (Charter, 1986), the Epp (1986) Framework, Québec's recent policy on health and welfare (MSSS, 1992a) or in other similar publications, is in any way original. As rightfully argued by Statchenko and Jenicek (1990), for instance, it is just a modern reformulation of the old public health approach to health issues that was born in the nineteenth century and has since taken various looks and names, such as "community health" (Conill & O'Neill, 1984).

Figure 2   Domains of application of health promotion and other public health approaches.

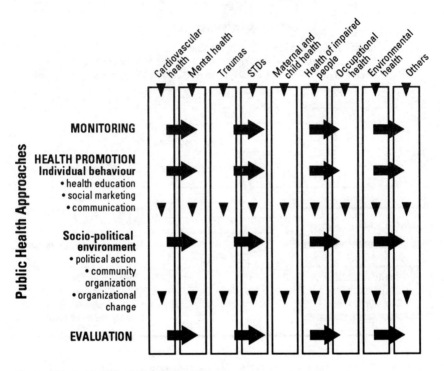

Source: Adapted from Cardinal & Lavoie, 1991.

The latest health promotion ideology includes a vision of health and its prerequisites, as well as the plurality of factors that foster or threaten it, and is based on a set of values that includes equity, democracy, political accountability, and social justice. In our view, using the word "health promotion" to label this specific ideology is misleading; we have argued elsewhere (O'Neill et al., 1990) that, in Québec at least, it has resulted in both the leadership and rank-and-file of public health professionals dismissing health promotion as just a relabelling enterprise. In doing that, many people have also dismissed what we think is the hard core of health promotion: the specific set of interventions presented in the bottom part of Figure 1 that can be developed, among others (see Figure 2), to foster the health and welfare of the population. We would thus argue that to label this ideological or philosophical dimension the proper concept is the "new public health" (Ashton et al., 1989; Frenk, 1993; Martin & McQueen, 1989) or the "ecological public health" (Kickbush, 1989) and that we should stop referring to it as "health promotion."

As indicated by the line between the two halves of Figure 1, which is dotted and not solid, separating the two dimensions of the health promotion concept does not mean that they are not intimately linked. However, we think (as shown by Figure 2) that health promotion designates more than anything else a set of specific intervention skills that, like epidemiological monitoring or evaluation, can be applied to any domain of health-related intervention, whether defined by disease categories, milieu, or target population. As suggested in the bottom of Figure 1, we would argue that what constitutes the specificity of health promotion interventions is the skills required for the planned change of health-related human behaviour, whether individual behaviour or the collective environmental dimension of this behaviour, the two being obviously related. This vision of health promotion is shared, among others, by Green and Kreuter (1991) in their authoritative book, *Health Promotion Planning*.

There are several strategies for intervening to shape human behaviour, most of which have been developed in the social, behavioural and educational sciences. In the health promotion literature (e.g., Martin, 1988; MSSS, 1990a; Matthias, in this book), we frequently find them organized in the six sets indicated in Figure 1, that is, on the one hand health education, social marketing, and persuasive communication usually targetted toward individual behaviour and, on the other hand, political action, community organization, and organizational development, usually more concerned with collective behaviour.

Our fear is that if the whole of health promotion is dismissed because the ideological part looks too much like the old public health philosophy, the development and use of the specific skills mentioned in the bottom of Figure 1 will never become part of the daily practice of public health professionals and others, decreasing significantly the capacity of the "new public health" to come about. This is, in our view, the major consequence of the lack of acceptance of the recent vision of health promotion in Québec. Our fear is confirmed by the way in which health promotion expertise has begun to be conceptualized and organized since the Côté reform (Cardinal & Lavoie, 1991; Déry, 1993), as discussed earlier in this chapter. For instance, in the framework of reference for public health practice published by the Ministry (MSSS, 1992b), political action has not been included among the series of legitimate health promotion interventions.

Conclusion

How can we answer the question posed in the title of this chapter: Did health promotion ever catch on in Québec? The answer, in our perspective, is no, but yes. No, because we have shown that the rhetoric of health promotion that arose in the mid-1980s has received much less attention in Québec than elsewhere in most of Canada. But yes, on the other hand, because most of the principles that inspire the health promotion ideology and several of the practices it suggests have been in place in Québec since the early 1970s Castonguay-Nepveu reform. Moreover, it is intriguing that despite an overall political economy of fiscal crisis at both the federal and provincial levels, and the strength of neo-conservatism since the early 1980s, the Côté reform is framed in ideological terms very like those of the Castonguay-Nepveu reform of 20 years earlier (Bergeron, 1990), ideological terms that are exactly the ones suggested by the "new" health promotion rhetoric of the mid-1980s.

However, history has taught us something about the period of 1970 to 1990, in Québec as well as in many other places in the world. The evolution of international macroeconomic conditions, whereby the major developments have clearly shifted from North America and Western Europe to the Asian side of the Pacific rim, can reframe or write off the social democratic commitments of governments, whether in health or other policy areas; the right-wing style measures undertaken by Ontario's New Democrat government under Bob Rae in 1993 or by the socialists in France before they were replaced are good recent cases in point. It is thus unclear at this time whether, even if not always formally labelled as such, the practices and policies of a health promotion of the type noted at the beginning of this chapter and advocated by the Québec government in the Côté reform documents will be allowed to take place. The general economic and political climate concerned with stopping the growth of government deficits in a weak economy and trying to solve the constitutional nightmare might absorb all available energies. Moreover, as the reform of public health services unfolds, it is far from obvious that health promotion's peculiar professional skills, as we have tried to specify them here, will be clearly enough defined and advocated to be allowed to contribute to improving the well-being of the population.

However, as history has also taught us, in part because of its unique status in Canada, Québec has frequently had to innovate. For instance, faithful to its tradition of being an important catalyst on major public health issues, the Québec Public Health Association was able to muster enough good will and energy to launch in 1991 a provincial consensus building on health promotion. To date, this has led to an experts' seminar in April 1992 and to a major provincial conference in August 1992 in the wake of which a Québec Declaration on Health Promotion (ASPQ, 1993) has been prepared. This declaration was officially launched in the fall of 1993, and a series of regional workshops on health promotion practices in the new reformed health and welfare system is due to take place in 1993-94. Moreover, in alliance with the ASPQ, leaders in the mental health field have released a policy proposal about prevention and health promotion in this domain (Blanchet et al., 1993). Perhaps these initiatives, which seem to be well received, as well as the rather grim political economic conditions awaiting us at the turn of the millennium, will force us to put the ideology and the practices of health promotion in place much faster than might be imagined — for survival's sake!

References

AHQ (Association des hôpitaux du Québec) (1988). *Promotion de la santé et prévention des problèmes de santé dans les DSC: Optimiser les actions.* Montréal, Comité promotion des DSC, AHQ.

AHQ (1992). *Qui fait quoi dans les DSC?* Montréal: Comité de co-ordination de la santé communautaire, AHQ.

Ashton, J., et al. (1989). *The new public health.* Buckingham: Open University Press.

ASPQ (Association pour la santé publique du Québec) (1993). *Déclaration québécoise pour la promotion de la santé.* Montréal: Auteur.

Bergeron, P. (1990). La commission Rochon reproduit les solutions de Castonguay-Nepveu. *Recherches sociographiques,* 31(3),359-81.

Blanchet, L., et al. (1993). *La Prévention et la promotion en santé mentale: préparer l'avenir.* Bondierville: Gaétan Drouin.

Brunet, J., et al. (1987). *Rapport du Comité de réflexion et d'analyse des services dispensés par les CLSC.* Québec: MSSS.

Cardinal, L., & O'Neill, M. (1992). Building information partnerships with communities: The necessity of strategic choices. In L. R. Scott (ed.), *Building partnerships in community health through applied technology* (pp. 245-248). Victoria, B.C.: University of Victoria.

Cardinal, L., & Lavoie, M. (1991). *Organisation régionale de la santé publique: La Place de la promotion de la santé.* Québec: Département de la santé communautaire de l'Hôpital de l'Enfant-Jésus.

CASF (Conseil des affaires sociales) (1984). *Objectif: santé. Rapport du Comité d'étude sur la promotion de la santé.* Québec: Conseil des affaires sociales et de la famille, Éditeur officiel du Québec.

CASF (1989). *Deux Québec dans un.* Boucherville: Gaétan Morin et CASF.

CESSS (Commission d'enquête sur la santé et les services sociaux) (1988). *Rapport de la Commission.* Québec: Gouvernement du Québec, Les Publications du Québec.

Charter (1986). *The Ottawa charter for health promotion.* Ottawa: WHO, Health & Welfare Canada, Canadian Public Health Association.

Conill, E., & O'Neill, M. (1984). La Notion de santé communautaire: Éléments de comparaison internationale. *Canadian Journal of Public Health,* 75, 166-175.

Déry, D. (1993). *L'Adoption d'un modèle organisationnel de l'expertise régionale en promotion de la santé*. Québec: Essai de maîtrise en santé communautaire, Université Laval.

Desrosiers, G. (1976). Les Départements de santé communautaire: Une Expérience québécoise. *Canadian Journal of Public Health, 67*, 109-113.

Desrosiers, G., & Gaumer, B. (1987). *Des réalisations de la santé publique aux perspectives de la santé communautaire*. Québec: Les Publications du Québec, synthèse critique no. 16 de la Commission d'enquête sur les services de santé et les services sociaux.

Dumais, A., & Lévesque, J. (1986). *L'auto-santé des individus et des groupes au Québec*. Québec: Institut Québécois de recherche sur la culture (IQRC).

Duplessis, P. (1981). Réflexions sur les Départements de santé communautaire dix ans après la réforme. *Administration hospitalière et sociale, 6*, 30-44.

Duval, L. & Paquet, G. (1991). *Réduire l'inégalité sociale devant la durée de la vie, la maladie et les problèmes sociaux entre les québécois bien nantis et les plus démunis*. Québec: Ministère de la santé et des services sociaux.

Epp, J. (1986). *La Santé pour tous: Plan d'ensemble pour la promotion de la santé*. Ottawa: Santé et bien-être social Canada.

Ferland, M. (1991). *Les Répercussions des conditions de vie et de l'environnement social sur la santé et le bien-être*. Essai de maîtrise en santé communautaire. Québec: Université Laval.

Fortin, J.P., et al. (1991). *Les Conditions de réussite du mouvement québécois de villes et villages en santé*. Québec: Université Laval, Centre de recherche du CHUL.

Fortin, J.P., et al. (1992). Villes et Villages en santé, les conditions de réussite. *Promotion de la santé, 31*(2), 6-10.

Fortin, A. (1993). *Les Organismes communautaires*. Texte inédit, Département de sociologie, Université Laval.

Frenk, J. (1993). The new public health. *Annual Review of Public Health, 14*, 469-490.

Gaucher, D. (1979). La Formation des hygiènistes à l'Université de Montréal 1910-1975. *Recherches sociographiques, 20*(1), 59-87.

Gilbert, J. (1954). The integration of research, service and teaching in public health work. *Canadian Journal of Public Health, 45*, 323-328.

Gilbert, J. (1959a). *L'Éducation sanitaire, théorie et pratique*. Paris: Masson.

Gilbert, J. (1959b). Vision et cauchemar d'un hygièniste. *Canadian Journal of Public Health, 50,* 360-367.

Gilbert, J. (1963). *L'Éducation sanitaire.* Montréal: Presses de l'Université de Montréal.

Gilbert, J. (1967). Grandeur and decadence of health education. *Canadian Journal of Public Health, 58,* 355-358.

Giroult, E. (1990). *Rapport sommaire, 2e Congrès interrégional Villes santé en langue française.* Copenhague: OMS Europe.

Godin, G. (1990). *Habitudes de vie et comportements.* Québec: Université Laval. Document préparé pour la Politique de santé et bien-être.

Gouvernement du Québec (1991). *Loi sur les services de santé et les services sociaux et modifiant diverses dispositions législatives.* Québec: Éditeur officiel du Québec, 176p. (Projet de loi 120, Ch. 42, législation 1991.)

Green, L.W., & Kreuter, M.W. (1991). *Health promotion planning, an educational and environmental approach* (2nd edition). Mountain View, CA: Mayfield.

Kickbush, I. (1989). *Good planets are hard to find.* Copenhague: FADL publishers, Série des "WHO Healthy Cities papers," No. 5.

Lacombe, R., & Poirier, L. (1991). Villes et Villages en santé. *Santé et société, 13*(3-4), 1-48.

Lavoie, M., & Cardinal, L. (1991). *Contribution de la promotion de la santé à la santé publique.* Québec: Département de santé communautaire de l'Hôpital de l'Enfant-Jésus.

Levasseur, M. (1983). *Des problèmes prioritaires.* Québec: Conseil des affaires sociales et de la famille. Collection: La Santé des québécois, Gouvernement du Québec.

Lesemann, F. (1981). *Du pain et des services.* Montréal: St-Martin.

Martin, C. (1988). La Vraie nature de la promotion de la santé. *Santé et société, 10*(1), 12-16.

Martin, C. (1991). *Politique de la santé et du bien-être. Stratégie: prévention et promotion de la santé.* Québec: Ministère de la santé et des services sociaux du Québec.

Martin, C., & McQueen, D. (eds.) (1989). *Readings for a new public health.* Edinburgh: Edinburgh University Press.

MSSS (Ministère de la santé et des services sociaux du Québec) (s.d.). La Promotion de la santé: Une Perspective, une pratique. *Santé et société*, Collection Promotion de la santé, Volume 1.

MSSS (s.d.). La Promotion de la santé: Concepts et stratégies d'action. *Santé et société*, Collection Promotion de la santé, Volume 2.

MSSS (s.d.). La Promotion de la santé: Les Actions en promotion de la santé; concertation et action intersectorielle. *Santé et société*, Collection Promotion de la santé, Volume 3.

MSSS (s.d.). L'Intervention éducative pour la promotion de la santé au travail. *Santé et société*, Collection Promotion de la santé, Volume 4.

MSSS (1977). *Une Politique de promotion de la santé de 1978-1981*. Québec: Auteur.

MSSS (1987a). *La Promotion de la santé au Québec: Une Stratégie de concertation pour la santé*. Québec: Auteur.

MSSS (1987b). *Le Choix de la santé: Plan d'action en promotion de la santé 1988-1991*. Québec: Auteur.

MSSS (1988). *Rapport du Groupe de travail sur l'analyse de l'action des DSC*. Québec: Auteur.

MSSS (1989). *Pour améliorer la santé et le bien-être au Québec: Orientations*. Québec: Auteur.

MSSS (1990). *Une Réforme axée sur le citoyen*. Québec: Auteur.

MSSS (1990a). La Promotion de la santé mentale. *Santé et société*, Collection Promotion de la santé, Volume 5.

MSSS (1991). *Un Financement équitable à la mesure de nos moyens*. Québec: Auteur.

MSSS (1992a). *La Politique de la santé et du bien-être*. Québec: Auteur.

MSSS(1992b). *Cadre de référence pour l'élaboration du programme de santé publique et pour l'organisation du réseau de santé publique*. Québec: Direction de la santé publique.

O'Neill, M. (1977). *Vers une problèmatique de l'éducation sanitaire au Québec*. Thèse de maîtrise en sociologie déposée à l'école des gradués de l'Université Laval.

O'Neill, M. (1982). L'Intervention sociologique en milieu public et parapublic: Application d'une problèmatique alternative au cas de la santé communautaire québécoise. In ACSALF (ed.), *L'Intervention sociale* (pp. 68-88). Montréal: Éditions Co-opératives Albert St-Martin.

O'Neill, M. (1983). Les Départements de santé communautaire. *Recherches sociographiques, 24*(2), 171-201.

O'Neill, M. (1989). Community health projects in Québec: Can they participate significantly to promote the health of the population in the years to come? *Health Promotion. International 4,* 189-198.

O'Neill, M. (1992). Former en promotion de la santé au Québec. In École nationale de santé publique (ENSP) (ed.), *Former en éducation pour la santé* (pp. 93-103). Rennes, France: ENSP & Comité français d'éducation pour la santé(CFES).

O'Neill, M., & Cardinal, L. (1992) (eds.). *Des indicateurs pour évaluer les projets québécois de villes et villages en santé: La Nécessité de faire des choix.* Québec: Université Laval.

O'Neill, M., et al. (1990). *L'Insertion de la promotion de la santé dans la législation et la structure gouvernementale québécoise.* Québec: Université Laval, équipe de recherche sur les aspects socio-politiques et environnementaux de la promotion de la santé.

Perreault, R., et al. (1992). Promotion de la santé: Un Exercice de mise en application de la charte d'Ottawa. *Canadian Journal of Public Health, 83,* 34-57.

Pineault, R., et al. (1990). Health promotion activities in Québec hospitals: Comparison of DSC and non-DSC hospitals. *Canadian Journal of Public Health, 81,* 199-204.

Pineault, R., et al. (1993). The reform of the Québec health care system: Potential for innovation? *Journal of Public Health Policy, Spring,* 198-219.

Renaud, M. (1981). Les Réformes québécoises de la santé ou les aventures d'un état "narcissique." In Bozzini, L., et al. (eds.), *Médecine et société: Les Années 1980* (pp. 513-549). Montréal: St-Martin.

Roy, L. (1983). *Des victoires sur la mort.* Collection la santé des québécois. Québec: Conseil des affaires sociales et de la famille, Gouvernement du Québec.

Statchenko, S., & Jenick, M. (1990). Conceptual differences between prevention and health promotion: Research implications for community health programs. *Canadian Journal of Public Health, 81,* 53-60.

Tsouros, A. (ed.) (1990). *World Health Organization Healthy Cities Project: A project becomes a movement.* Copenhagen: FADL Publishers.

World Health Organization (1984). *Health promotion. A discussion document on the concept and principles.* Copenhagen: World Health Organization, Regional Office for Europe.

Health Promotion in the Atlantic Provinces

Dale Poel and Frances Pym

This chapter reviews the extent to which health promotion concepts and practices have been adopted by the provincial governments, community organizations, professional groups, and the academic community in the four provinces of Atlantic Canada. We borrow from the diffusion of innovation literature (Green & McAlister, 1984; Rogers, 1983; Rogers & Kim, 1985) to place our descriptive findings into a conceptual framework.

The four Atlantic provinces are distinctive in several ways. Newfoundland, Prince Edward Island, Nova Scotia, and New Brunswick have the smallest population base of all Canadian provinces and this is dispersed across a wide geographic area. Prince Edward Island has just over 128 000 citizens, while Nova Scotia is approaching 900 000. Even Nova Scotia, then, has a population base only matching many of the regional health units in the larger provinces of Québec and Ontario.

In addition to their small population base, these four are also the poorest of the Canadian provinces. The economic environment has implications for health promotion. Many communities are one-industry towns dependent on a single pulp mill, mine, or fish plant for their very survival. The region pays for this economic structure with the stress of seasonal unemployment, fears of plant closures, and a willingness to tolerate working and living conditions that are not healthy. The dramatic closing down of the Atlantic cod fishery is only the most recent example of these economic and health impacts. Not surprisingly, the health status of Atlantic Canadians compares unfavourably with that in other provinces on a number of indicators (Nova Scotia, 1989).

As a consequence of population and poverty, the four provinces have the smallest overall provincial budgets, but the highest provincial expenditures per gross domestic product. Provincial expenditures on health, as well, are the highest relative to provincial fiscal capacity. Transfer payments from the federal government are a higher percentage of provincial revenue than in other provinces, potentially causing greater dependence on the federal government.

The Atlantic provinces, however, share some important characteristics with the other Canadian provinces. The context within which Atlantic provincial political and administrative leaders and health professionals respond to health promotion themes contains:

- The common presence of the Canadian federal government, especially the Department of Health;
- Common regional representatives of national-level community organizations such as the Canadian Mental Health Association, the Canadian Public Health Association, and other disease-related associations;

- Common professional associations of health care providers that influence roles and activities in health promotion and are affiliated with national professional bodies such as the Canadian Medical Association or the Canadian Nurses Association; and
- The health care hospital budgets and physician services costs that dominate provincial budgets in all Canadian provinces.

Several questions arise when we consider the adoption of health promotion concepts and practices in this context as the diffusion of innovation. The provincial characteristics (social inequities, dispersed populations, severe budgetary pressures on provincial governments) point to important questions concerning motivation and resources for and obstacles to the adoption of health promotion concepts, programs, and practices. Other questions focus on the organizational and professional climate for innovation. If health promotion initiatives are an added cost to a provincial health budget, then they will be competing for scarce resources in a professional field in which a clinical response to illness still dominates. The competition for funding will be more keenly felt within the budgetary framework of these four provinces.

Research Process

The editors of this book set the following broad questions in general and for the regional chapters in particular. They asked:
- Who has been promoting health promotion?
- How has the concept been used over time?
- What form have health promotion activities taken?
- What have been the consequences of these developments?

The task of describing and assessing the development of health promotion in Atlantic Canada is large and our experiential base is not sufficient to support an "armchair" approach. The fragmented environment of health promotion is another hurdle in the way of assessing health promotion developments in Atlantic Canada. Health promotion as a concept, program, or activity is not found in one tidy place. Where would you go to see health promotion in action? No single voice represents the field. Different professional communities represent multiple claims to ownership. Even the professional community competes with commercial ownership claimed in the advertisement of products that are "healthy" — from dietary fibre to passenger-side air bags. Who gets to say what it is?

There are two main sources of information concerning health promotion developments in Atlantic Canada: written documentation and professional experience. Written documentation exists in descriptions of federal and provincial programs that are fielded under the name of health promotion. References to health promotion are also found in the reports and recommendations of Royal Commissions (New Brunswick, 1989; Newfoundland, 1984; Nova Scotia, 1989) and Task Forces (New Brunswick 1991a, 1991b, Nova Scotia, 1972, 1990, 1992; PEI, 1992, 1993) created to review and make recommendations for the health system and in the written briefs prepared for these review bodies.

Experience in health promotion can be observed in the action of community groups or in televised spots urging a healthy, or at least safe, lifestyle. The experience is also recorded in the sessions of annual meetings of professional groups and in special workshops or seminars. The collective experience with health promotion in the Atlantic region has been episodic; focussed networks of professionals, practitioners, and community groups are just beginning to form.

A "knowledge development" health promotion workshop was funded by the national Health Promotion Directorate in each province in 1989-90. Following from that effort, an attempt has been made to form a regional health promotion group, the Atlantic Health Promotion Network. It hopes to link academic, professional, and community representatives and is still in the formative stages (e.g., a newsletter). Dalhousie University has recently received funding under the Social Science and Humanities Research Council/National Health Research and Development Program (SSHRC/NHRDP) competition for Centres for Health Promotion. In short, the experience is not collected in some easily accessed corporate memory bank.

We overcame some of these limitations by fielding a *Guide for Information Retrieval* on health promotion in Atlantic Canada. The covering letter to the *Guide* defined our intentions:

> We want the Atlantic chapter to be both accurate and interesting. Towards that end, we are asking your assistance (1) in documenting the bench marks of health promotion in the four Atlantic provinces since the early 1970s and (2) in suggesting the broad themes and issues which characterize this field in our provinces.

The *Guide* (available from the authors) included both closed and open-ended questions. It was sent to every Atlantic Canadian listed in the Health Promotion Directory produced through the Knowledge Development Initiative, to members of the Atlantic Health Promotion Network, to provincial civil servants whose job description suggested a connection to the field, and to individuals in related agencies or councils. A total of 77 *Guides* were mailed to people in government, in professional organizations, community groups, and the region's universities.[1] Thirty-four percent (n=26) were returned. About half the responses came from Nova Scotians, but responses came from all four provinces and, within each province, from the major categories of informants. We are most grateful to all those who shared their experience and expertise with us.

It is important to think of these responses not as a sample of a population, but as an extension of the authors' knowledge base. The information

---

[1] Provincial government included representatives from the Departments of Health and Community Services, Health Councils, and Task Forces. Professional organizations were represented by the provincial medical and nursing associations and associations of social workers, nutritionists, physiotherapists, and public health professionals. Community groups included Association for Community Living, Canadian Mental Health Association provincial divisions, The Self-Help Connection, Health Action Coalition, St. John Health Action Council, and Alzheimer Societies.

provided was important to our analysis. In addition, we supplemented the *Guide* responses with several personal interviews with key informants in each province.

The Adoption of Health Promotion

A Diffusion Framework

The diffusion of innovation literature, having started in a mythical Iowa cornfield with the adoption of hybrid corn seed, has been described as a "mile wide and one inch deep" (Rogers, 1983). A mile wide refers to its applications to many different contexts of innovation. One inch deep refers to its theoretical development. We are willing to risk perpetuating the characterization by borrowing just a few concepts from that literature within which to place the diffusion of health promotion in the Atlantic provinces.

Our interest is in the context and process of the adoption of new ideas, concepts, and programs in health promotion. Although much of the literature deals with individuals as adopters, we are primarily interested in governmental, professional, and community organizations as adopters of health promotion concepts and practices within their work. This choice both recognizes the importance of organizational context and also is a useful limit to our scope of research.

The process of adoption is defined in several phases (Green & McAlister, 1984) such as awareness, interest, trial, and adoption. We are working from an organizational frame of reference within which we think of three phases of adoption. The first is comprehension and includes awareness and interest. The second is use in language, e.g., in organizational documents, public reports, or announcements. The third is use in action through the development of or participation in health promotion programs. We are not focussing on the adoption of one specific health promotion program, nor on individual adopters of such an initiative, but rather trying to describe regional patterns and trends. Two areas from the diffusion literature are especially interesting to us here: the timing or phases of adoption and the characteristics of early versus later adopters.

Green and McAllister (1984) have distinguished between innovators, early adopters, the early majority, the late majority, and late adopters, and locate these groups along a logistic (S-shaped) curve which can characterize a particular pattern of adoption within a population. On the individual level there are interesting socio-economic and behavioral differences between adopters at the several stages. The earlier adopters, for example, are described as more affluent, more attuned to national media, more "cosmopolitan," and with greater knowledge about health. The later adopters tend to be more socially or economically disadvantaged, socially isolated, and suspicious of government.

The insights from this individual-level analysis can be integrated with other research on innovators from both the individual and the organizational

Table 1   Contrasting characteristics of early and later adopting organizations.

EARLY ADOPTERS	LATER ADOPTERS
Abstract thinking, capacity for planning	Micro-management, fewer resources for and less interest in planning
Positive orientation towards change	
External professional linkages	Resistance to change, tendency to favour status quo
Large size, availability of "slack" resources	Relative professional isolation
Communication openness at all organizational levels	Smaller size, limited organizational resources
	Centralization, formalism as an organizational style

perspectives (Chapman, 1986; Mohr, 1969; Rogers, 1983; Rogers & Kim, 1985). Table 1 borrows from this literature to contrast characteristics of early and later adopters, considered in an organizational context.

How do provincial governments, professional organizations, community groups, and the academic community in the four Atlantic provinces compare in their relative capacity for planning, orientation towards change, extent of external professional linkages, size and resources, and communication styles? Are the greater differences between provinces or between groups within the provinces? We will attempt to reach some conclusions about the capacity for the adoption in language and action in the Atlantic provinces, using these attributes to structure our findings. But first, we will turn to the actual experience with health promotion in these provinces.

Experience in Health Promotion in the Atlantic Provinces

What is health promotion in the four provinces of Atlantic Canada — its definition, its historical development, its current directions? The first question of our *Guide* asked people from the four provinces to note "major events, developments, or programs in health promotion." These responses of the informants are summarized within five time periods in Appendix A at the end of this chapter.

Major Events, Developments, and Programs

The responses to our survey did not create an exhaustive enumeration of health promotion events and developments in the region, but are useful for illustrating patterns of experience. People were asked only to note developments in their own areas of work or interest. The events and programs volunteered, combined with written documentation and the authors' own experiences, provide a representative profile of provincial developments and responses to federal initiatives. The responses also point out how diverse the perceptions of health promotion can be.

1972–1975

In our first period, 1972-75, we found a focus on health *education* in all four provinces. Lifestyle themes were also found in anti-smoking campaigns and some programming around sexually transmitted diseases. New Brunswick can claim a leadership role in developing a Council on Smoking and Health. The most diverse references were found for Nova Scotia, where respondents mentioned community-based initiatives such as MOVE (a citizen-based action group), the Ecology Action Centre, and the opening of the North End Community Medical Centre. These initiatives were, of course, volunteered with the benefit of hindsight and may reflect present-day rather than contemporary organizing frameworks. That is, during the 1970s, many health professionals might not have located MOVE or the Ecology Action Centre within a health promotion framework.

There was provincial recognition of national developments, as noted by references to discussions of *A New Perspective on the Health of Canadians* (Lalonde, 1974; hereafter, the Lalonde Report). The difficulty of maintaining health promotion on the political agenda can be noted in a reference to the 1972 Nova Scotia Council of Health. This Council's review of the Nova Scotia health care system and its report, *Health Care in Nova Scotia: A New Direction for the '70s*, was the first systematic opportunity for professional and community groups to voice health promotion themes. In the end, however, the government of the day let both the Council and its policy and program themes die on the vine.

1975–1980

References given for the 1975-80 period began to identify health promotion programming for women with a broader focus than clinical concerns for pregnancy and fetal development or community concerns for pregnancy avoidance. The Women's Health Education Network (WHEN) was an especially important community-based initiative in Nova Scotia and later in Newfoundland. New Brunswick also piloted a Well Women's Clinic during this period.

The health promotion continuum was defined broadly in the region to include work related to disease prevention and epidemiological studies. The medical approach to health promotion reflected the dominant medical values of the region's largest tertiary care, teaching, and research hospital complex associated with Dalhousie University's Faculties of Health Professions, Medicine, and Dentistry.

Nutrition programming was a key focus within the region's general emphasis on health education. Special emphasis to this area and school-based nutrition education was found in Newfoundland. The mid-1970s was also a period when a variety of community-based organizations began to be formed, especially in Nova Scotia and New Brunswick. The influence of nationally organized non-governmental organizations (NGOs), such as the Victorian Order of Nursing and the Canadian Public Health Association, was noted as having contributed to the awareness of health promotion issues. The 1977 International Public Health Association meeting in Halifax was a significant event in the continuing development of health promotion themes in the Atlantic region.

1981–1985

Lifestyle and health education programming continued to be important in each of the provinces. The references to health education as an emphasis were strongest on a provincewide basis in New Brunswick and Newfoundland, especially for school-based programs. A major school-based project was funded by the National Health Research and Development Program (NHRDP) in Dartmouth, Nova Scotia.

This period began to show the pattern of provincial responses to specific federal initiatives through targetted funding of health promotion programming. Nova Scotia led with the creation of its Heart Health program. Provinces also responded to federal initiatives around parenting and child development (Nobody's Perfect) and federal government targetted funding for Seniors, AIDS, and Aboriginal AIDS programming.

Nova Scotia's second review of health services was carried out by its Legislative Select Committee on the Health Care System. This legislative committee repeated the provincewide public consultation process first implemented by the defunct (1981-85) Nova Scotia Health Council. Community and professional groups again dutifully prepared their briefs and called for more community-based health care and stronger programming in health promotion. The Public Health Association of Nova Scotia's 1985 annual meeting focussed on health promotion and coincided with the release of the Select Committee's first (and only) report. We also found additional references to the development of health advocacy groups in Nova Scotia.

Another national but non-governmental association, the Canadian Council for Social Development (CCSD), contributed to the discussion of community-based health services at the end of this period. The agency's discussion of health emphasized the more complex determinants of a health model that is important to health promotion and represents participation in the discussion by an agency outside the narrower clinical focus of health/illness. Although the CCSD was mentioned within the region, its presence as a policy and program reference point was likely unevenly felt among the various health promotion actors. We argue in our conclusion that national linkages of this sort are more common and important for NGOs and are more tenuous for the respective provincial Health and Social Service Departments in the area of health promotion.

Newfoundland led the 1980s round of Royal Commissions and Task Forces dealing with the health care system. Its Royal Commission on

Hospital and Nursing Home Costs reported in 1984. Its mandate was somewhat narrowly defined around issues of costs, but its public hearings, with their focus on a continuum of care, allowed broader themes to be heard as well. PEI created a new department that brought health and social services under the same Minister, recognizing organizationally the relationship between the two.

1986–1990

The latter half of the 1980s reflected the "coming of age" for health promotion in Atlantic Canada, although the process was not linear. Nova Scotia and New Brunswick had major Royal Commissions and developed health strategies that included strong references to community-based health and health promotion. The other three provinces joined Nova Scotia in participating in the Heart Health program. Dartmouth became the only city east of Québec to participate in the national Healthy Communities Project. A major self-help project, The Self-Help Connection, was funded by the Health Promotion Directorate in co-operation with the Canadian Mental Health Association/Nova Scotia Branch. The Knowledge Development initiative of the federal Health Promotion Directorate brought a diverse group of community representatives, health professionals, and academics together in each province to share views on health promotion and led to the formation of the Atlantic Health Promotion Network. At the end of this period, Nova Scotia committed its first uniquely provincial funding to community health promotion with the establishment of CHIPS, the Community Health Initiatives Program.

The language of the Ottawa Charter and a national conference (1989, Vancouver) began to influence the work and language of the provincial governments as well as NGOs during this period. The Nova Scotia Department, however, distinguished itself at the conference by presenting material on lifestyle education while others were "shifting their paradigm" to community development and healthy public policy. While the occasion may reflect on Nova Scotia's (lack of) progress in health promotion programming to that date, the event is important generically in documenting the responsive nature of the four provincial governments to developments in health promotion at the national and international levels.

The Canadian Public Health Association and the Public Health Association of Nova Scotia, along with community groups and registered nurses, continued to contribute to the dialogue around issues in health promotion. Both professional groups and community organizations were fully represented in the briefs to provincial Royal Commissions and provided the community support underlying the recommendations for increased emphasis on well-being and health promotion in Nova Scotia and New Brunswick.

1991 to Today

Nova Scotia has recently re-established a Provincial Health Council as a result of recommendations by its Royal Commission on Health Care and the response to those recommendations by its Department of Health. The Council is gradually gaining visibility through its work and reports, especially with the development of health goals for Nova Scotians and community consultations. Its permanency, compared to the 1970s Health Council, will depend on the Council's establishing a working relationship with the new Liberal provincial government, as well as the Department of Health. The potential for this should be good since the new Premier (the Honourable John Savage) was first the mayor of Dartmouth and the driving force behind his city's participation in the national Healthy Communities Project.

The integration of national developments in health promotion with provincial concerns has broadened and "updated" the content of health promotion in each province. This can be seen in attention to family violence prevention in Prince Edward Island, recent attention to primary health care initiatives in Nova Scotia and New Brunswick, and the recognition of the health impact of the fishery closures in Newfoundland.

Some themes persist, however. New Brunswick continues to show leadership in smoking prevention initiatives, and one respondent suggests Newfoundland will continue with "more of the same," including a strong emphasis on school-based health education programs. Recent years also witnessed continuation of the pattern of setting national priorities with monies attached leading to provincial responses. This can be seen in the focus on breast cancer screening and fetal alcohol syndrome that have become themes of federally supported programs.

Developments of health promotion in the 1990s may be gleaned from hints offered in the final category of "1991+." The financial pressures on the institutional health care system may finally force an integration of planning around the full continuum of well-being/health care. The document, *A Health and Community Services Plan for New Brunswick* (New Brunswick, 1992), is a good example of these pressures at work, at least in language, if not practice. The impact of such planning on practice and the health of populations remains to be seen. New Brunswick, for example, is into the second year of a major restructuring of its health care system, but the full impact of these changes will not be felt for some time. Prince Edward Island, with little fanfare, is in the process of adopting major reforms to its health care system with strong themes of health promotion and community participation (PEI, 1992, 1993). The Transition Team of the PEI Cabinet Committee on Government Reform is recommending the establishment of regional structures and a Health Policy Council along the lines of Nova Scotia's Health Council.

The comments for this final period include references to a more comprehensive setting of health goals and actions for reform, combined with the findings of Task Forces considering alternatives for primary health care, pilot projects, and community-based planning. The course is set.

The Concept of Health Promotion

Development and Diffusion

Our *Guide* asked, in an open-ended format, for people to describe "health promotion" from the standpoint of their own work and experience. The question asked was not a test to see whether Atlantic Canadians could give the "correct" definition of health promotion. Our intention was to collect definitions *in use*. The definitions that were provided certainly varied across the professional community. Throughout Canada, professionals and communities have yet to agree upon a definition of health promotion. We suspect our responses are similar to those that would be forthcoming in other regions. The definitions offered represent a continuum of beliefs and orientations, ranging from the traditional disease prevention/public health model to the newer ideas embodied in the Ottawa Charter:

> "As a family physician, health promotion means primarily patient education to me — lifestyle changes, healthy eating, exercise, stopping smoking, etc."

> "Health promotion is active living — developing and maintaining a physically active lifestyle, designed to enhance cardiovascular fitness, muscular strength and flexibility."

> "Community development. Citizen participation."

> "Enabling people to take control of their own health, especially by addressing the power differential."

> "The process of community development — knowledge, skills, and resources to improve control or take control of their health and the environment that affects their health."

Some discussions of health promotion seem to suggest that new concepts of health promotion articulated at different stages (the Lalonde Report; the Epp Framework; the Ottawa Charter) replace earlier versions or, ideologically, should do so! That view would see the adoption of health promotion language and practice as linear or sequential like this:

■ hp1   ■ hp2   ■ hp3   ■ hp4

While there has clearly been a progression in the field from a focus on disease prevention to lifestyle/health education, to broader concerns about community development, healthy public policy, and social action as cornerstones of health promotion, our information shows that many of these earlier themes remain under the conceptual umbrellas of our informants. Many people and organizations seem to add new health promotion ideas to their conceptual framework without discarding older ones. Thus, hp2 is added to hp1, rather than replacing it.

The diversity of responses suggests that evolving ideas of health promotion have diffused into the professional and organizational cultures within the region, but have done so differently in different places. Among our informants, the community groups seemed most ready to adopt the newer additions to the health promotion lexicon, perhaps because these ideas are readily compatible with the beliefs and values articulated by those working in community-oriented contexts. For others (members of the university community, civil servants, even some health professionals), the ideas embodied in the Ottawa Charter may be less congruent with their professional socialization and organizational culture. Many within the university come to health promotion from a clinical health science, or a health education perspective grounded in an individual, treatment-oriented approach, rather than a community development or public policy focus. People within the government sector work in a context where power, planning, and control have traditionally been centralized.

Multiple concepts of health promotion are currently operative in Atlantic Canada and ownership of the concept, unless by ideological fiat, is not narrowly controlled by accredited "health promoters." Reading through the responses and in talking with other informants, we had a sense of inclusion — that people working in the health promotion field in Atlantic Canada did not feel the need to exclude individuals whose orientation to the field differed from their own.

One clear message we received is that there is more than enough work to go around and conceptual correctness, or expending effort negotiating it, are luxuries the region cannot afford. An alternative explanation could be that professional and community groups have not had sufficient opportunity to talk to each other or work together and, as a result, have not fully appreciated the different nuances they attach to the notion of health promotion.

Leadership in Health Promotion

The Role of Governments

A recent synopsis of a health promotion knowledge development workshop described health promotion ". . . as a concept and practice. . . devolving from senior government through provincial and local government to more 'grassroots' community and social movement groups" (Labonté, 1993). Borrowing from Labonté (1993), our *Guide* invited people to tell us whether health promotion leadership in their province came from government, community-based groups, professional associations, or the university community. The more critical informants volunteered that none of the options were leaders in the field; the more optimistic or enthusiastic checked each option.

The responses to this question and others in the *Guide*, however, suggest that until very recently the diffusion of new health promotion concepts and programming in Atlantic Canada went *around* rather than through provincial and local governments. The federal government, community groups, and professional associations were more frequently characterized as leading in the field than were provincial or municipal governments. Some informants gave examples of provincial agencies or individuals within provincial departments actually blocking participation in specific health promotion initiatives.

Role of the Federal Government

The federal government has contributed to the development of health promotion through the resources and programming of the Health Services and Promotion Division of Health Canada, especially its Health Promotion Directorate. Federal contributions in community health, health promotion, and mental health were generally viewed as positive. The acknowledged contributions include conceptual development, program funding, and the dissemination of information through the journal *Health Promotion* (formerly *Health Education*). The beginnings represented in the Knowledge Development conferences were acknowledged, but a lack of follow-through was noted. The regional staff of Health Canada were seen as extremely supportive, and developments around Strengthening Healthy Communities and the Atlantic Health Promotion Network were given as examples.

The relationship between the federal government and provinces was most often characterized as co-operative. Some noted it as a forced co-operation, driven by the incentives of cost-shared programs and the heavy reliance on federal monies for programming in this area. Until recently, the absence of federal initiatives in health promotion would have meant the absence of health promotion in the four provinces. Later provincial initiatives were fairly narrowly defined in areas of health education or health promotion through lifestyle advertisements.

The role and impact of federal government can also be seen in areas of shared cost funding such as the Heart Health or Strengthening Healthy Communities programs, Health Promotion Contribution Funding, or the AIDS Community Action Fund. When the federal government declares a certain direction or initiative a major priority and gives that area significant financial support, all the provinces usually respond. Program diffusion takes place in a relatively short period of time and within criteria that are largely defined by the federal government. Some provincial informants were critical of this federal dominance of the field.

Provincial participants in the AIDS Community Action Fund show interesting patterns of response to a federal intiative, for instance. PEI is distinctive within the region and nation for not having participated in this program by 1991. Newfoundland also stands out for not having participated in the first round (1985-87) of program funding. With these exceptions, the timing and level of participation is remarkably similar. By 1991, all provinces except PEI had participated in the program at levels that roughly matched their population and provincial budgets as a percentage of national totals.

A federal civil servant administering the program will not be surprised at this proportionate distribution of federal monies across the provinces. What this means, however, is that the development of new initiatives is an external pressure to which provinces respond. In poorer provinces, the federally sponsored initiative is likely to be the only initiative. The adoption and participation pattern also reinforces a federal role that is crucial to poorer provinces, namely, the support for national and minimum standards of program delivery and access, even in the field of health promotion.

The Provinces in Atlantic Canada

In all four provinces, most informants described their provincial government as "reactors." The provinces have reacted to the federal conceptual development of health promotion, its publications in the field, to shared-cost programs, to federal cost containment efforts (e.g., the cap on Established Program Funding). When asked for examples of provincial initiatives, some informants gave examples that, in fact, were federal in origin (e.g., the Heart Health Program). The provinces have also gradually reacted to public interest in and pressures for health promotion initiatives. These pressures have been articulated primarily by organized community groups and some professional organizations.

As reactors, the provinces have gradually added positions or departmental divisions with specific mandates to address health promotion issues and develop programs. Some provinces have hired "health educators" but our informants seemed unsure whether this represents the most appropriate use of scarce resources — or is in fact a conceptually appropriate way to work on health promotion.

Yet, in the last few years there have been distinctly provincial initiatives. Examples that were volunteered include the New Brunswick Premier's Council and VISION 2000, seat-belt and anti-tobacco legislation, the New Brunswick Council on Smoking and Health, the Nova Scotia Provincial Health Council and, in Newfoundland, an interagency committee on smoking and health. The Community Health Initiative Program in Nova Scotia was noted, as well as the recent Task Force on Primary Health Care. Newfoundland's health education in schools and the province's Breast Feeding Council also were cited.

Most informants did not identify any significant differences between the Atlantic provinces in terms of their health promotion activities. Any provincial differences are small. The four provinces are responding to the financial pressures caused by reduced transfer payments while, at the same time, introducing "health care reform" packages that include greater emphasis on health promotion.

All four provinces have had to date a fairly centralized approach to planning and resource allocation — despite increasing rhetoric to the contrary. This limits their ability to foster newer versions of health promotion because devolution through the provinces means giving community groups both resources and power to define needs and program directions. Even newly developed regional structures for the provincial health care system in New Brunswick and Nova Scotia do not necessarily bring decentralization. In fact, in New Brunswick, new regional structures have been criticized for restricting community-based participation in decision making.

Task Forces, Study Committees, Royal Commissions, and Health Councils

Each provincial government in Atlantic Canada conducted some review of its health care system during the 1980s. The review took the form of a Royal Commission in Newfoundland (1984), Nova Scotia (1989), and

New Brunswick (1989), while a Task Force on Health worked for a Cabinet Committee on Governmental Reform in Prince Edward Island (PEI, 1992, 1993). In Nova Scotia and New Brunswick, the Royal Commissions were preceded by earlier reviews and, most importantly, were followed by other formal activities that led to adoption by governments of themes and positions from the health promotion field.

In Nova Scotia, for example, the 1989 Royal Commission was preceded by a 1972 Council of Health study and a report from a 1984 Select Committee on Health from the Nova Scotia legislature. Both used provincewide public consultations as part of their information base and both heard calls for shifts towards prevention and health promotion. The groups who complained in 1988-89 that they had already presented their views earlier were ignoring the fact that the continuity had been lost. The politicians and administrators needed to "hear it again," and they did.

Following the Royal Commission's report, a Departmental Task Force reviewed the Commission's recommendations and produced its own report (Nova Scotia, 1990). That Departmental report recommended the legislation that created the Nova Scotia Health Council, the first legislated health council of its kind in Canada. After a quiet beginning, the Council has been actively establishing health goals for the province, engaging citizens and organized groups in further discussion of health care reform. The Council's statement of goals has health promotion and healthy public policy front and centre (Nova Scotia, 1992, 1993).

There is continuity in and potential for continuing public participation through the Nova Scotia Council that does not exist in New Brunswick, given the Council's statutory basis of existence. In New Brunswick, a merger of health and community services into one Department was related to attempts to broaden the perspectives on health policy. The structural merger, however, has not become functional at the service level. The New Brunswick Royal Commission was more narrowly defined around health care costs than Nova Scotia's and its sixty-four recommendations had a strong cost containment flavour, while acknowledging the need for public participation and nodding to health promotion as an ultimate solution.

The main outcome of the New Brunswick Commission's work was the creation of a Premier's Council on Health Strategies. The Council's mandate included advising the government on policy options, recommending innovations in health services, and emphasizing health promotion and disease prevention. Before its demise, the Council produced a creditable discussion paper on "health promotion and prevention issues" (New Brunswick, 1991b). A subsequent policy paper (New Brunswick, 1991a) called for health promotion as a central policy thrust in shifting resources from the curative, institution-based system towards community-based prevention and health promotion.

In the meantime, however, the Premier's Council has been terminated, health system planning is completely within the provincial Department, and cost-saving measures are being taken on the institutional care side.

New Brunswick informants, though, have yet to see plans or policy instruments to support the development of community-based health promotion alternatives. The most recent Departmental planning document (New Brunswick, 1993) has all the right language and the advantage of linking health and social services within one department, but action to date primarily has taken the form of bed closures.

Our more cynical informants saw the Royal Commissions and Task Forces as ploys to divert attention from the real political issues of power, money, and control. We are more inclined to see the Royal Commissions in all three provinces as important vehicles for the dissemination of health promotion ideas to the public, the media, and government and for the sharing of concepts among professionals. They represented important opportunities for community groups, professional organizations, and interested citizens to express views in a forum not previously available. Especially in New Brunswick and Nova Scotia, the Royal Commissions were precursors to policy and structural changes important to the further development of health promotion initiatives, i.e., use in language and in action. They have increased the legitimacy of health promotion concepts and programs within the larger discussion of the health care system (and cost control of the same).

Health promotion's legitimacy may be stronger within the professional associations and organized community groups. Individual citizens still tend to identify health and health care with beds, specialists, and technology. Surveys in both New Brunswick and Nova Scotia are consistent in this finding. One New Brunswick respondent said:

> While participation in this process might have done something for the "consciousness " of politicians, administrators, and health care providers, the public, the consumers of health care services, do not seem to have been influenced. In a sense, it was preaching to the converted. New Brunswick "users" still see heath care as beds, hospitals, doctors — health promotion has a very low public profile.

The various commissions and councils have brought the adoption of health promotion to the Atlantic provinces through the stages of comprehension and use in language by transferring knowledge and policy positions from national and international forums to the provinces and by providing a forum for regionally based groups to reinforce these external themes.

A Prince Edward Island informant said it most succinctly: "Words are there. It remains to be seen if this will translate into action." PEI's most recent recommendations for reform very clearly represent a health promotion approach to health planning and services. The recommendations speak explicitly about "the development of a new organizational culture" (emphasis added) that will "foster people and communities working together and developing creative strategies to address health issues." The Health Transition Team document is probably the clearest expression of health promotion concepts applied to an Atlantic province health care system (PEI, 1993) and the strongest statement supporting implementation of those concepts.

Capacity for Adoption of Health Promotion

The capacity to move to the third stage of adoption, use in practice, will continue to be influenced by the five characteristics we have extracted from the innovation literature (See Table 1, p. 288). Early adopters will have a greater capacity for abstract thinking and planning, a positive orientation towards change, and stronger external professional linkages. Early adopters will also be larger, have more slack resources available, and will build communication patterns that are open at all organizational levels.

To what extent do the four provincial governments, professional organizations, community groups, and the academic communities in the Atlantic provinces share these attributes of early adopters? The authors' own experiences and the comments received from our *Guide* suggest an assessment on at least some of these dimensions for the four categories of actors.

Provincial Governments and Their Agencies

Until very recently, the Nova Scotia government and its Department of Health (and Fitness) could be described by all the characteristics associated with later adopters. It specialized in micro-management instead of planning. It resisted change and was relatively isolated professionally. It had limited resources and was extremely centralized with a very closed communication system.[2]

Anyone familiar with the Nova Scotia government and its Department through the 1970s and '80s has at least one good example that fits this description. For instance, in 1988 a Department report was prepared on the health status information of Nova Scotians and included some regional comparisons. A senior Departmental official withdrew the preliminary draft of the report from its limited circulation just before a provincial election. The equivalent study for the 1989 Royal Commission did not include regional information. The first report has not yet been released.

The Nova Scotia Provincial Health Council has had a similar experience with government control of information. Like the Nova Scotia Royal Commission, the Health Council has had difficulty gaining access to reports. A recent newspaper article makes the point:

> The Provincial Health Council's request for specific pieces of information from the government, particularly the Department of Health. . . has been frustrating.
> The council. . . says over half the information requests it made to the Health Department in 1992 were not filled or only partially filled.
> The provincial auditor general's report has specifically criticized the government for not releasing reports about the province's co-ordinated home care program to the Provincial Health Department (Mellor, 1993, p. A5).

---

[2] Lest we seem to be picking on Nova Scotia, it represents to some extent only the most convenient and familiar example. Informants provided similar characterizations of agencies/civil servants in the other provinces. In professional circles, however, Nova Scotia is commonly said to have the weakest civil service in the nation, an accusation presently being confronted by a new Liberal government through the use of external administrative audits of key departments.

Until very recently, Nova Scotia's capacity for planning, generally and in the field of health, has been limited by scarce resources and handicapped by political inclination. One respondent called a former premier of Nova Scotia, the Honourable John Buchanan, the "milli-second contingency analyst." In very centralized decision systems, the emphasis can be more on control than planning in its normally understood professional sense.

Nova Scotia, New Brunswick, and PEI are moving toward a more regionally defined health care system and intend to include the planning function in this regionalization. Newfoundland already has a regionalized structure. A stated reason for regionalization is to take planning "closer to the people." Regionalization to date has not been accompanied by decentralization, i.e., the loosening of centralized control. In addition, regional concerns have focussed on the institutional health system more than health promotion. Ironically, in centralized regionalization, local communities actually can have a sense of loss of control (e.g., "they" closed our hospital).

Both New Brunswick and PEI have a structural advantage for health- and health promotion-directed planning because their departments bring together health and community services. We noted earlier the clear language of integration in New Brunswick's recent planning documents. In both provinces, however, the two fields have tended to co-exist within a single department up to the level of the Deputy Minister. Of the four provinces, New Brunswick probably has had the strongest formal capacity to plan since that function was integrated within one unit in the Department. PEI's impending changes remain untested.

Centralized micro-management tends to focus on incremental change in and control of the line item budget, rather than new directions. The four provinces, generally, have not been open to change, broadly defined across the field of health promotion during this twenty-year review period. Each province has had some special interest or initiative, but change has come very slowly. The increased pace in recent years (even months) has been produced by the extreme financial crisis facing the provincial governments. It is not clear yet whether the change induced by these pressures will strengthen health promotion programming or simply close beds and introduce user fees. We must comment that within each provincial department there are individuals with a clear understanding of health promotion issues and a strong interest in its development. The numbers are not large, though.

The external professional linkages of the Atlantic provincial governments and their departments have been primarily in the areas of health care management and federal – provincial financing in the health care system (hospitals, doctors, pharmacare) and much less in the areas of health promotion. These linkages have often consisted of federal – provincial committees organized around national areas of concern defined by the Canada Health Act.

Outside of government-to-government relationships, linkages often have been contractual in nature, rather than part of a continuing network. External relationships to the regional academic community have been shaped by the limited presence of health profession education in PEI and

New Brunswick and by the dominance of the medical sciences in Nova Scotia and Newfoundland. There has not been a large academic or professional health promotion community in the Atlantic region with which government departments could interact, even if they wished. These disadvantages combine with relatively small Departments and, within the Departments, scant human resources committed to the field of health promotion. Except for in Newfoundland, the Premiers, recognizing this problem in scale, are currently discussing merging or integrating their three Departments of Health.

If we look only at the past it would be easy to become discouraged about the ability or willingness of provincial governments to move beyond the rhetoric and adopt health promotion initiatives in practice. Recent developments suggest that unfreezing has occurred and change may finally be underway. Health Councils, already established in Nova Scotia and built into new legislation in PEI, provide a structure for new, more equitable relationships among politicians, professionals, and communities. As well, the current financial crisis obliges even the most resistant to reflect upon the very limited ability of high-cost institutional sickness care to improve health status.

Professional Organizations

Regional views on professional organizations may be similar to those held elsewhere in Canada. There are different orientations toward health promotion across the professional groups. The values and directions of health promotion are more congruent with some professional values and interests than with others. There are few provincial differences in the professional organizations, since the national organizational cultures dominate, rather than the political culture. The traditional patterns in professional education, which emphasize central authority and professional knowledge over shared authority and community-based experience, can incapacitate professional organizations from adopting health promotion as a practice paradigm.

Professions like nursing, physiotherapy, and occupational therapy can more easily incorporate health promotion concepts into their goals, since these are also congruent with their organizational interests in decreasing the gatekeeping role of physicians and in expanding the scope of their professional practice. The nursing profession, at least at the national and regional association level, has been an "early adopter" of health promotion concepts and has enthroned health promotion as a central plank of its *raison d'être*. But, just because a professional association endorses health promotion as policy, it has not necessarily diffused into the culture of more grass-roots working professionals. Most nurses, for example, still work in the institutional health care system where sickness care still dominates the organizational culture. However, concept diffusion — including changes in pre-service education to incorporate health promotion — and the increasing pace of health care reform are contributing to changing perceptions among many groups of professionals. Physicians, long attached to the disease prevention view of health promotion, have begun to incorporate lifestyle counselling as a central element of their practice. In New Brunswick, the Medical and Nursing Associations recently collaborated in the development of a blueprint for a new style of community-based health centre and worked hard to incorporate current health promotion concepts into the design.

Professional organizations in the region also have links to other, more community-based organizations. On a less formal level, the small size of communities in Atlantic Canada means that individuals often wear more than one hat. People whose "day job" may be nutritionist or nurse are often involved with local groups and projects or with the disease societies.

Community-Based Organizations

As with the professional organizations, many of the larger community-based organizations engaged in health promotion in Atlantic Canada have "external linkages" to national bodies, which give them additional resources for developing health promotion initiatives. The Canadian Mental Health Association, the Cancer Society, and the Lung Association are examples of community groups that have active structures of local volunteer groups delivering programs throughout the region. The local chapters use nationally designed materials to get their message across to the public. The planning skills and resources of the national body make it easier for community volunteers to work, for example, with school children on smoking issues or in fostering the development of self-help groups. Working with these organizations is a "way in" to health promotion for many Atlantic Canadians.

These community organizations gain resources for early adoption of health promotion in language and action. They have a capacity for planning beyond their regional size. Particularly, those not narrowly defined around a specific disease have a stronger orientation towards change because of the interdisciplinary or cross-professional nature of their own membership and their external professional linkages.

Other community organizations do not have the same resources for change and adoption of health promotion, but may be organized around a single issue that represents the group's driving force or source of momentum. SODA, the Sprayers of Dioxin Association in New Brunswick, is a good example of a clearly local group with limited, formal linkages to external resources. These groups often lack the resources available to the groups with national offices, and can find it more difficult to plan and evaluate programs. The Community Action Pack, a kit of materials produced by Health Canada to assist community groups, has been enthusiastically received by some groups and may help bridge this gap. In addition, resources produced at the federal level for Active Living and other programs are available and being used by people trying to meet the needs of their communities.

For both types of community groups, the most important link to resources for health promotion initiatives has not been provincial and local governments but from outside the region — most often Health Canada — as well as their national bodies. The provincial government may have endorsed a federal grant, but the financial and conceptual resources came from out of the region. The support given to self-help and mutual aid by the Self-Help Connection is a good example of the combination of federal and community organization interests and resources — in this instance, the Health Promotion Directorate (nationally and through its regional office) and the Canadian Mental Health Association/Nova Scotia Division.

One difficulty with this dependency on federal support has been that the support often comes in the form of "demonstration project" funding. Health Canada is not in the business of sustained funding. When the demonstration is successfully completed, an extension may be negotiated, but in the end something that may have become an integral part of community-based services either passes out of existence or has to be adopted by someone with local resources. The Self-Help Connection has finally attracted some support from the province of Nova Scotia. A successful community centre for the mentally ill, however, closed its doors for lack of local support and because it refused to think of a new way it could "demonstrate" the basic service it was providing.

The Academic Community

We have come this far generalizing about diverse groups over four provinces, but at our "home base" we start by noting some reluctance to do so. Some members of the academic community in Atlantic Canada work in areas with a full range of graduate and undergraduate programs in the health sciences. Others are in smaller centres with fewer resources. Memorial University, Saint Francis Xavier and, more recently, Henson College at Dalhousie University have supported community development outreach that has included health promotion programming. All three have or are facing severe financial cutbacks. The University College of Cape Breton, though, has recently introduced an undergraduate degree in Community Development. The Dalhousie University Health Promotion Research Centre for Productive Living is the first organizational structure in the Atlantic region dedicated solely to the field of health promotion.

The capacity of the academic community in the Atlantic region to adopt health promotion concepts and practice is influenced by some factors unique to the region and others common to the Canadian academic community. The factors held in common with other Canadian academics are probably the most significant.

The main factor unique to the region is geographic: the distances over which academics need to travel to communicate face-to-face or to work with community groups and the distances from national-level events that often are located in the centre of the country, if not British Columbia. The increasing costs of travel and declining conference travel budgets limit many from having significant contacts out of the region. Conference calls, teleconferencing, and electronic mail are substitutes only in part.

Academics in Atlantic Canada share with the rest of the country their academic disciplines and the sources of funding for academic research. The disciplines and funding structures within which academics traditionally work and within which career progress is defined are barriers to acquiring the interdisciplinary networks called for by the health promotion framework and to thinking beyond the discipline. As well, direct work with community groups is time consuming. The production of community-based, participatory, or action research does not have the same status as traditional, peer-reviewed publications and does not always translate readily into the more acceptable form (see, for example, Canadian Mental Health Association/Nova Scotia, 1989). The academic community has many of the capacities for adoption of health promotion as an orientation to their academic work; the incentives to do so have not been strong over the twenty-year period of this review.

Talking/Doing Health Promotion

The provincial governments of Atlantic Canada seem to be on the verge of doing health promotion. For adoption in action to take place, the doing will have to be supported by a fundamental change in organizational culture. The language and direction of the most recent document (June 1993) from Prince Edward Island suggests such changes are possible. The change must include a stronger capacity for planning, an openness to change, and a communication style that is open and a two-way process. Nova Scotia's Health Council, and PEI's announced version of the same, is a critical organization to link politicians and civil servants to their communities.

While the governments seem open to change at present, this is a recent phenomenon. We attribute this new and more substantial interest in health promotion to the present financial crisis of the institutional health care system and of the governments in general. At a recent presentation of research findings concerning partnerships between health professionals and self-help group members (Stewart et al., 1993), a Nova Scotia Department of Health representative came, invited but somewhat unexpectedly given his areas of work. At the conclusion of the workshop, his "bottom line" question was: "Have you identified which self-help groups are cost-effective alternatives to traditional physician and hospital services?"

We might think he missed the point. That was not one of the research questions. Yet, that may be the point around which the next stage of development in health promotion takes place. The proponents of health promotion currently have the attention of provincial decision makers in Atlantic Canada. The sustainability of that attention and the strengthening of the larger network of health promotion professionals and community groups will hinge, we anticipate, on establishing the linkage between health promotion and the health status of Atlantic Canadians and showing how this link can foster health for lower costs than the still dominant hospital-based medical service.

References

Canadian Mental Health Association/Nova Scotia (1989). *Speaking out about mental health: A needs assessment.* Halifax: CMHA/Nova Scotia, The Self-Help Connection.

Chapman, E.A. (1986). Diffusion theory: A review and a test of a conceptual model in information diffusion. *Journal of the American Society of Information Science, 37*, 377-386.

Green, L.W., & McAlister, A.L. (1984). Macro-intervention to support health behavior: Some theoretical and practical reflections. *Health Education Quarterly, 11*, 322-339.

Labonté, R. (1993). *Health promotion knowledge development: Report of a meeting.* (Toronto, January 27 & 28, sponsored by the Health Promotion Directorate, Health & Welfare Canada).

Mellor, C. (1993, July 30). Health council reveals secret of government. *The Chronicle Herald*, p. A5.

Mohr, L.R. (1969). Determinants of innovation in organizations. *American Political Science Review, 63*, 111-126.

New Brunswick (1989). *Report of the Commission on Selected Health Care Programs* (McKelvey-Lévesque Commission). Fredericton: Author.

New Brunswick (1991a). *Health 2000: Vision, principles and goals.* Fredericton: Department of Health & Community Services.

New Brunswick (1991b). *Health promotion and prevention issues: Draft report.* Fredericton: Premier's Council on Health Strategy.

New Brunswick (1993). *A health and community services plan for New Brunswick.* Fredericton: Department of Health & Community Services.

New Brunswick Hospital Association (1991). *Health promotion and prevention issues: Response to the draft report.* Fredericton: Author (unpublished report).

Newfoundland (1984). *Report to the Government of Newfoundland and Labrador.* St. John's: Royal Commission on Hospital & Nursing Home Costs.

Nova Scotia (1972). *Health care in Nova Scotia: A new direction for the seventies.* Halifax: Nova Scotia Council of Health.

Nova Scotia (1984). *Report.* Halifax: Nova Scotia Legislative Select Committee on Health.

Nova Scotia (1989). *The report of the Nova Scotia Royal Commission on Health Care: Towards a new strategy.* Halifax: Royal Commission on Health Care.

Nova Scotia (1990). *Health strategy for the nineties: Managing better health.* Halifax: Department of Health.

Nova Scotia (1992). *Toward achieving Nova Scotia's health goals: An initial plan of action for health care reform.* Halifax: Provincial Health Council.

Nova Scotia (1993). *Working together to renew Nova Scotia's health care system: Discussion guide and workbook.* Halifax: Provincial Health Council.

Prince Edward Island (1992). *Health reform: A vision for change* (Report of the PEI Task Force on Health). Charlottetown: Cabinet Committee on Governmental Reform

Prince Edward Island (1993). *Partnership for better health.* Charlottetown: The Health Transition Team.

Rogers, E.M. (1983). *Diffusion of innovations* (3rd ed.). New York: Free Press.

Rogers, E.M., & Kim, J-I. (1985). Diffusion of innovations in public organizations. In R. Merritt & A.J. Merritt (eds.), *Innovation in the public sector* (pp. 85-105). Beverly Hills: Sage.

Stewart, M., Crossman, D., Poel, D., & Banks, S. (1993). *Partnerships between health professionals and self-help groups.* Halifax: Project report to NHRDP, Health & Welfare Canada (Grant # 6613-1477-61).

Appendix A

Major Events, Developments, or Programs in Health Promotion Volunteered by Informants to the *Health Promotion Information Guide*

Nova Scotia	New Brunswick	PEI	Newfoundland	Atlantic Region/National Events
1972-75 • Lalonde Report • Cardiovascular epidemiology unit funded by NIH • Dalhousie's Bachelor of Health Education program • MOVE formed (Movement for Citizens Voice in Action). Focus on empowerment, self help, inequities • 1972 NS Council of Health report, Health Care in NS: A new direction for the 70s. • North End Clinic opens • Ecology Action Centre established • Some co-op & non-profit housing set up	1972-75 • "Didn't hear much then" • Limited HP activity. Health educator hired for brief time; left. Written materials came from federal government • NB Council on Smoking & Health was "prototype for all other provincial councils and Canada"	1972-75 • Lalonde Report, "discussion, little action" • Children's Dental Care Program, health education for school children • Diabetes Education Centre opens	1972-75 • Public awareness programming, focus on STDs • Family planning • Poison prevention • Establishment of inter-agency committee on smoking and health	1972-75 • Lalonde Report • 1st Nat'l Conference on Community Health Centres (held in Ontario)

Nova Scotia	New Brunswick	PEI	Newfoundland	Atlantic Region/ National Events
1976-80 • Epidemiology studies on hypertension in NS • Women & Alcohol conference • Women's Health Education Network • Development of multisectoral approach to service delivery, e.g., Cobequid Multi-Service Centre • Founding of Prepared Childbirth Association of NS	**1976-80** • Well Womens' Clinic in Fredericton, Moncton (2 years) • New initiatives in School Health (e.g., sexuality education) • Fredericton High School piloted a School Nurse position • Provincewide prenatal education program (VON leading plus PHN, Fredericton Childbirth Assoc.) • Beginning of mass education campaigns (e.g., seatbelts) • Public Health develops own HP materials; health fairs; some HP programs institutionalized; Nutrition Month.	**1976-80** • Major revision of Canada's Food Guide • Establishment of Mental Health Day Centre programs • Discussion paper on health issues (1977) calls for increased public participation in developing future health policy	**1976-80** • Nutritionists hired for all regions; increase in nutrition focus of HP • Prenatal nutrition program • School-based nutrition programming	**1976-80** • 1977 International Public Health Association meeting in Halifax — a catalyst prior to Alma-Ata • New federal-provincial fiscal arrangement — Established Program Funding (EPF) for health and higher education • 1980 Vancouver conference on health promotion, Shifting the Paradigm: From Disease Prevention to Health Promotion

Nova Scotia	New Brunswick	PEI	Newfoundland	Atlantic Region/ National Events
1981-85 • Heart Health Program • Atlantic working group on hypertension funded by Pharmaceuticals Ltd. • Dartmouth Health Promotion study (NHRDP) • "Concept not well defined; working from disease prevention framework" • Health Coalition of NS sponsors public forums on new directions in health care • Seatbelt legislation • PHANS conference on HP (1985) • NS Nutrition Council formed as advocacy group (1985) • NS Legislature's Select Committee on Health Report (Vol. 1; 1985)	**1981-85** • Mass media directed at smoking, seat belts, etc. • Reproductive Health Centres set up in communities around the province (with some federal funds) • National Strategy to reduce tobacco use • Further institutionalization of some HP programs in DPH work: nutrition, dental health, school health days, supported by provincially (centrally) developed a/v, pamphlets, etc.	**1981-85** • "The talk began" (Epp Framework) • Teen Health Information Service (personal health & community resources) • Cardiac education programs • Baby Help Guide to Infant Nutrition • Creation of Dept. Health & Social Services • Born Free (to assist pregnant women to quit smoking)	**1981-85** • School-based health education • Preschool screening for 3-year-olds • Promotion of B/F/Lifestyle media campaigns • Policy focus on tobacco education • Public Health decentralized in theory; still much central control • Royal Commission on Hospital & Nursing Home Costs	**1981-85** • Nobody's Perfect program (HPD/H & W) • Small increases in federal monies for HP Contributions Programs (Seniors, AIDS, Aboriginal AIDS funding) • Canada Health Act (1984) • Beyond Health Care Conference (1984) • National Conference on Improving Community-based Health & Social Services (CCSD; 1985)

Nova Scotia	New Brunswick	PEI	Newfoundland	Atlantic Region/National Events
1986-90 • Self-Help Connection Project • Challenges in Participation • Healthy Communities; Dartmouth only community east of Québec to participate • CPHA annual conference: Strengthening Community Health • PHANS conference features Epp Framework (1986) • National HP conference: "NS talks lifestyle education while others talk new health promotion," but "gradual recognition that HP is distinct from disease prevention" • NS Occupational Health & Safety Act • Change Dept. to Health & Fitness • Royal Commission on Health Care emphasizes shift to HP (1989) • SCHR partnership with Health Action Coalition (1990) • 1989-92 study of rural seniors & medication • NS Heart Health Program (1989) & Survey report (1987) • Community Health Promotion fund set up by Dept. (1990) • Health Strategy for '90s by Dept. of Health • Appointment of NS Provincial Health Council (1990)	1986-90 • AIDS comes to NB: community-based response, some gov't programs • Heart Health Program & Report of NB Heart Health Survey • Legislation on seatbelts • Health Promotion & Disease Prevention Unit set up within Dept. Health & Community Services • Report of Commission on Selected Health Care Programs (McKelvie/Lévesque; 1989) • Premier's Council on Health Strategy • Health 2000 (corporate plan for DHCS) • Playing for Keeps (improving children's quality of life) • Enhancing Seniors' Independence ("offices" set up to oversee programs for children, seniors, with Cabinet-level oversight) • Mental Health Commission established, responsible for in-hospital community care and HP: focus so far on bed closures at mental hospitals	1986-90 • HP knowledge development workshop gained interest of professionals & community groups but no followup or leadership • Initiative of Reproductive Care Program (Medical Society & PEI Dept of H&SS) • Heart Health Program (1990)	1986-90 • Heart Health survey completed, leading to risk reduction programs by PHNs • Pilot PHC project by ARNN, others • Public education programs: AIDS, drinking/driving, teen pregnancy • School-based programs of teen mums • Janeway Hospital starts HP outreach • Streetproofing for kids • Women's Health Centre(s) set up • Preschool 3- & 5-year screening switched to one at 3 years • Federal-provincial AIDS programming; PHNs follow up via Train the Trainer approach with PTAs, community groups • Other federal-provincial: Nobody's Perfect, Break Free • Interagency B/F Council set up • School health: nutrition, dental stressed	1986-90 • Epp Framework • Ottawa Charter • Federals have limited relationship with "disease" societies, more applications for funding from community-based groups • 1989-90 Knowledge Development workshops held in each region and bring academics, practitioners, community groups together

Nova Scotia	New Brunswick	PEI	Newfoundland	Atlantic Region/ National Events
1991+ • Workshops on community development in HP • Slow transition in provincial Dept. to Ottawa Charter concept of HP • Pilot geriatric assessment of rural seniors, then mobile assessment team for frail elderly. More on medication; seniors in nursing homes • Dept makes HP part of Policy & Planning Division; to affect all planning • Provincial Health Council & associated Task Forces, incl. working group on Primary Health Care • Cheticamp Primary Health Care project 3-year pilot • NS Coalition on Rights of Children & Youth (1992) • Provincial Health Council: 1992 Health Goals & Action Plan for Health Care Reform	1991+ • Proposal from Dept. H&CS for provincewide breast cancer screening program • Excellence in Education Commission (new push on screening/early intervention for at-risk children) • Monies for HP through Health Care Reform (i.e., bed closures) • Alcohol & Drug Dependency Commission shut down, responsibilities transferred to Dept. • More "targeting" of programs, e.g., high-risk pregnancies, feeding poor children in schools, but continuing with other basic HP programs • Healthy Public Policy on Tobacco Initiative with new legislation on tobacco • Formation of NB Heart Health Program & co-ordinating committee (war with Positive Heart Living) • McAdam project: Primary Health Care	1991+ • Brighter Futures • Continuation of Heart Health Program • Completion of Health Care Task Force Report • Learning Today for a Better Tomorrow (project that increased public awareness, understanding re:elder abuse) • Appointment of family violence prevention co-ordinator and development of partnerships between gov't and community to reduce and prevent family violence	1991+ • "More of same" • Some Task Forces to examine impact of fishery closure	1991+ • Strengthening Community Health Leadership • Atlantic Health Promotion Network • CPHA document on roles, functions of public health nurses "very helpful" • New initiatives: breast cancer screening and fetal alcohol syndrome become themes for regionally funded programs • H&W asked to identify "partners," e.g., well womens' clinics, support groups • Beginning of H&W Brighter Futures program • Publication of Health Promotion journal cancelled

INTERNATIONAL

PERSPECTIVES

Canadian Health Promotion: An Outsider's View From the Inside

Lawrence W. Green

Canadian health promotion is probably a topic best avoided by a landed immigrant until his citizenship is secure. Canadians are rightly proud of their health care system, and those working in the field of health promotion sometimes blush when reminded how much the rest of the world has looked to Canada for inspiration and leadership. If I were a newcomer to the United States who had the *hubris* to criticize a cherished U.S. institution — especially if I had benefitted from it — I would be greeted with mutterings of "Love it or leave it" in some quarters, dismissed as naive in others. But I promised to do this chapter a year ago, when I was still enjoying the honeymoon of my New Canadian status and the deadline seemed a long time away.

Now, with trepidation and humility, I must offer a perspective on health promotion in Canada. My background includes just eighteen months of living in this country. As well, I had the dubious advantage of viewing the Canadian system with admiration for five years as an American responsible for national programs in the United States; for seventeen years as a professor in the United States; and for four years as a student in a U.S. school of public health during the 1960s, with one eye on the Vietnam War and the other on Canada.

I would like to approach this topic by citing another New Canadian, an Englishman who has lived and worked in Canada much longer than I, who identified the major differences between Canadian and European health promotion on the one hand, and U.S. health promotion on the other (Table 1). This approach will allow me to discuss the contrasts, rather than criticize the policies of my new home country. It will also enable me to stay closer to the subject I can presume to know best — U.S. health promotion policy and programs. I also hope to offer some counterpoint to the distinctions that many Canadians (and Europeans) might draw between their own style of health promotion and that of the Americans.

Canadian vs. U.S. Health Promotion

A Canadian Perspective

Trevor Hancock, at a meeting of American Academic Health Center deans and vice-presidents (Hancock, 1993), bravely presented a chart contrasting the Canadian and European view of health promotion vis-à-vis the American view (Table 1).

Table 1   How Canadian/European health promotion contrasts with U.S. health promotion.

Canada/Europe	USA
Social focus	Individual focus
Collective responsibility	Personal responsibility
Risk conditions	Risk factors
Blame society	Blame the victim
Excuse the victim	Excuse society

The audience accepted this characterization politely, without protest or defensiveness. This acceptance of an apparently embarrassing portrayal of U.S. health promotion perhaps reflected the fact that these Academic Health Center executives came mostly from the field of medicine. They may have considered this view of the U.S. model to be flattering, or at least credible and comfortably close to the medical model. Or perhaps they, as I, saw it as damning but accepted it as truth, because they knew so little of the scope of U.S. or Canadian health promotion that they had no basis for challenge. Dr. Hancock did add a caveat that these distinctions reflected the "extremes," which he explained in terms of historical and cultural differences. This qualification may have defused the reaction.

Whatever the explanation for that audience's acceptance, Hancock's view seems to fit a widely held stereotype, as articulated by de Leeuw (1989). This study contains such politically loaded phrases as "blame the victim" and "personal responsibility" versus "collective responsibility." The ironies in de Leeuw's critique are multilayered — and irresistible as an outline for my task of commenting obliquely on Canadian health promotion.

Recasting the Contrasts

Blaming the Victim

The first irony is that the phrase "blaming the victim" comes from an American author commenting on U.S. social policies (Ryan, 1971). Specifically, it referred to the fault ascribed by liberals to the poor for having their problems in the first place (the usual meaning intended by critics of

U.S. health promotion). Later in the 1970s, it often included blaming the poor for failing to use the services provided by the liberal policies of the 1960s under legislation arising from the New Frontier initiatives and the War on Poverty (Andersen et al., 1975).

The irony here is that critics of U.S. health promotion, especially in the 1980s, used an American phrase that was formulated as a criticism of American liberal professionals and of policies that were, in retrospect, communitarian compared with the prevailing individualism of most U.S. (and Canadian and British) social policies of the 1980s. Americans must, nevertheless, accept the criticism that the deterioration of social policies in the 1980s does not mean that equity was ever achieved (although the socio-economic gaps in access were largely closed in the years immediately following the passage of Medicare and Medicaid legislation in 1966), or that the underlying social problems were successfully addressed.

Canada's remarkable contributions to the "new public health" and the health promotion initiatives of the WHO European Regional Office were based in part on the publication of *A New Perspective on the Health of Canadians* (Lalonde, 1974; hereafter, the Lalonde Report), which repositioned health policy in relation to (a) lifestyle and environmental determinants of health and (b) subsequent concerns with issues of social justice, economic determinants, and equity. These were the same concerns reflected in U.S. legislation arising from the War on Poverty in the 1960s (Sardell, 1983).

A distinctive mark of the Kennedy – Johnson War on Poverty legislation of the 1960s was the appearance in virtually every Congressional Act of the phrase, "maximum feasible participation." By the definition of this clause, the federal government required of local community grantees that they have policy and planning boards consisting of at least 51% lay consumer (non-professional, non-provider) membership (Green, 1986). The intent of the federal policy was thus to provide not only the resources but also the political clout and positions for the have-nots to participate in the reform of local policies. Unfortunately, the Vietnam War siphoned off many of the resources that were intended to go to the community health centres, the economic opportunity agencies, and other local organizations created by the legislation and the federal grants. As a result, these programs were understaffed, and many of the consumer volunteers on their boards thus had to do double duty as volunteer or underpaid staff as well. This tended to sap participants' energy and compromise their independence and credibility as policy makers on the boards. Daniel Patrick Moynihan referred retrospectively to this perversion of the legislative intent as "maximum feasible misunderstanding" (Moynihan, 1969).

My point here is not to detract from the Canadian contributions to global concepts of health promotion and a new order of public health, nor to reassign credit for those contributions to the U.S. policies of the 1960s. My purpose is only to suggest that the contrasts between Canadian concepts and policies vis-à-vis U.S. public health policy — at least in the previous decade — were not so great as the more recent stereotyping of American health promotion would have us believe.

Canadian health promotion has been conceptualized as more than public health, as has public health policy for disease prevention and health promotion in the United States. The characterization of American health promotion as limited to changing the behaviour of individuals is perpetuated by the fact that health promotion is but one leg of the three-legged stool of public health policy: health promotion, preventive health services, and health protection. Health protection's emphasis on the environmental determinants of health precludes health promotion from laying exclusive claim to this focus. Getting at the more basic socio-economic determinants of health remains a problem for the health sector in the United States, as it does in Canada.

It would be more precise, and more accurate, to contrast Canadian federal policy (e.g., Epp, 1986) and some provincial health promotion policy papers of the 1980s with the highly visible private-sector and medically oriented health promotion in the United States, as reflected in workplace wellness programs and risk-factor reduction programs, as well as research sponsored by the U.S. National Institutes of Health. However, the deeper roots of American health promotion lie in the traditions of the public health infrastructure at the federal, state, and local levels. These are reflected in the research and training that is based in schools of public health. Such American traditions square much more closely with what the WHO European Office of Health Promotion dubbed the "new public health," possibly because Europe has not had a tradition of schools of public health. However, the traditional public health concern with social, economic, and environmental determinants of lifestyle and health finds its roots in nineteenth-century European public health, especially in England (Chadwick, 1865). The emergence of vaccines and antibiotics to fight communicable diseases during the first half of this century diverted attention from social concerns to biomedical approaches to public health, both in Europe and in North America. The 1960s were a turning point back to social, economic, and political concerns in both the United States and Canada.

The real shift in American and Canadian policy since the 1960s has been from strong federal leadership and initiative in addressing problems of social justice, economic determinants, and equity as health issues to increasingly decentralized policies and, especially in the United States, privatization of the problems and the solutions. The emphasis in the United States on "states rights" under Ronald Reagan's New Federalism has been mirrored in Canadian revenue sharing and the devolving of federal powers to the provinces. The effect on health promotion in both countries has been that states and provinces now pass on to communities the encouragement, and to a lesser extent some resources, for communities to take primary responsibility for setting health promotion priorities and for developing their own programs. Community "empowerment," in most instances, looks a lot like the War on Poverty programs of the 1960s. As in the U.S. social experiment of the 1960s, Canadian resource support has been curtailed, this time by recession rather than war.

Individual vs. Social Focus

A second irony in the stereotyped contrast between American and Canadian/European health promotion is the issue of individual focus versus social focus. What makes this irony poignant is that the 1966 inclusion of Medicare and Medicaid in U.S. legislation as part of the War on Poverty overwhelmed many public health agencies at the federal, state, and local levels with the task of administering these new programs — which focussed on individual medical needs rather than community social and health needs. Failure to enact a universal system of health insurance left the patchwork of entitlements and welfare benefits to public health agencies to administer.

As a result, the American Public Health Association (APHA) created a Medical Care Section that quickly became the largest and most influential in the Association, driving much of the advocacy agenda of APHA toward issues of medical care rather than community-oriented public health as we knew it before 1966. That agenda attracted disaffected physicians from the American Medical Association who joined APHA and further forced the legislative agenda toward issues of personal coverage, financing, and access to medical care. This was a worthy agenda. Had it succeeded, the United States today might have a system more like Canada's. But the cost of this single-minded focus of public health advocacy was that it failed to respond to the crumbling federal, state, and community public health and welfare infrastructure, which was being systematically dismantled by the Nixon administration. The public health advocacy establishment became so preoccupied with medical care issues that it lost sight, in my opinion, of the population health issues which were the heart of its science and philosophy.

Even the U.S. Health Information and Health Promotion Act of 1976, which created the Office of Health Information and Health Promotion (now the Office of Disease Prevention and Health Promotion) in the Department of Health, Education and Welfare (now the Department of Health and Human Services) had as a lead clause in its mandate:

(1) coordinate all activities within the Department which relate to health information. . . and education in the appropriate use of health care;

(2) coordinate its activities with similar activities of organizations in the private sector; and

(3) establish a national information clearinghouse to facilitate the exchange of information concerning matters relating to health information. . . and education in the appropriate use of health care, to facilitate access to such information, and to assist in the analysis of issues and problems relating to such matters. (Public Law 94-317, 1976)

The Congressional preoccupation with medical cost containment resulted in a mandate for the new health promotion policy office that focussed on issues of public use of medical care services and on self-care issues (Viseltear, 1976).

The lesson in this experience, from a Canadian perspective, is that Canada might well lose the gains of its health care system in the face of recessionary forces, which could erode the social focus of Canadian health promotion just as the siphoning of resources by the Vietnam War did in the United States. It is an insidious, if not subtle, process. The parallel scenario in Canada might go something like this:

- First, the support and priority given to health promotion at the federal level declines as pressures for decentralization and revenue sharing take precedence.
- Second, the attention of provincial Ministers of Health to health promotion initiatives becomes increasingly distracted by the erosion of medical care resources and the public's tendency to give greater political support to addressing these matters than to health promotion.
- Third, the local coalitions and agencies trying to launch Healthy Communities (and less ambitious projects) find their lifelines to provincial resources drying up or strained by mixed signals.

Much of this scenario may already be recognizable in some provinces. The abandonment of the Healthy Communities initiative at the federal level was a first volley.

The irony is that a social-equity focus on health can become a social-equity focus on providing for medical care, which then converts to a focus on the individual's personal medical needs, access to care, and provision of services. Health promotion then becomes an agent of the driving forces of medical imperatives or curative priorities over preventive niceties. Health promotion is called upon through research funding, cost/benefit analyses, community and hospital grants, demonstration projects, and government service positions to serve the interests of cost containment in medical care. This purpose is expected to be accomplished through public education on appropriate use of health services, patient education on self-care and management of chronic diseases, and community organization to mobilize local resources in support of medical care needs.

Risk Factors vs. Risk Conditions

Canadian contributions to theory on "the broader determinants of health" have given credence to the new public health, which is actually a renaissance of nineteenth-century European ideas of public health and 1960s North American attempts to redistribute resources. The irony here is that it was a Canadian document — the Lalonde Report — that turned policy attention to risk factors and perhaps away from the broader risk conditions determining health. Other Canadians called the Lalonde Report into question (Labonté & Penfold, 1981). During the same period, research in the United States from the Alameda County study was building the case simultaneously for behavioural risk factors (Belloc & Breslow, 1972) and for risk conditions such as social support, income, and education (Berkman & Breslow, 1972). Then, the megaprojects on cardiovascular risk reduction at Stanford (Farquhar et al., 1990), Minnesota (Carlaw et al., 1984), and Pawtucket (Lasater et al., 1984), building on the experience of the North Karelia project in Finland (McAlister et al., 1982), combined the risk-factor approach of preventive medicine with a community public health approach.

The encouraging results of these projects have spurred a similar approach to cancer prevention and greater policy attention to health promotion.

The recognition that these projects were narrowly conceived around cardiovascular or cancer risk factors and were driven by a scientific agenda controlled by the investigators (rather than a social or health agenda controlled by the communities) led to a community health promotion grant program from the Kaiser Family Foundation. The intention here was to put the same state-of-the-art behavioural science and public health methods into community projects conceived and directed by the communities themselves (Tarlov et al., 1987). Drawing on Canadian concepts of healthy public policy and healthy communities (Hancock, 1985), and the experience of the U.S. Centers for Disease Control with the Planned Approach to Community Health (PATCH) (Nelson et al., 1986), the Kaiser program expanded to the Southern region of the United States with a reconnaissance approach to building state – local partnerships and supportive policies for community development (Green & Kreuter, 1991). This approach has been adapted, in turn, by the Ontario Ministry of Health in some of its provincial – local partnering for health promotion, and in part by the federal – provincial Heart Health Initiative (Federal – Provincial Heart Health Initiative, 1991).

These programs attest to the compatibility of approaches that address specific risk factors while attempting to bring about more comprehensive changes in the social, organizational, and economic environments. The give-and-take of ideas between the United States and Canada, with both countries drawing on research and experiences from Europe, Australia, and developing nations, attests to the universality of some of the principles emerging from various mixes of risk-factor and risk-condition approaches. In retrospect, I find the distinction difficult to maintain in practice.

Personal Responsibility vs. Collective Responsibility

The cultural and historical distinctions between Canada and the United States are probably greater on this point than on any of the others. Whether this translates into real differences in the implementation of health promotion in the two countries needs more systematic study than I am presently able to offer. Nor have I seen a systematic study of this question in the professional or scientific literature. One study that would be a model is a recent comparison of U.S. and British health promotion policies (Leichter, 1991). My hypothesis, based on unsystematic observations, is that Canada's higher taxes on alcohol and tobacco provide the clearest example of the public's willingness to allow government a larger role in lifestyle matters than one finds in the United States. A more extensive ban on the advertising of tobacco products is another example. A Canadian court declared this act unconstitutional, but that decision was reversed in January 1993. In other areas related to lifestyle, the United States has been just as aggressive as Canada, if not more so, in letting government regulate (i.e., collective responsibility) rather than leaving such matters to individual responsibility. For example, in occupational health, federal legislation in the United States has provided for much more aggressive regulatory authority by two federal agencies, the Occupational Safety and Health Agency and the National Institute of Occupational Safety and Health, to regulate worksite hazards and unsafe conditions of work.

The greater emphasis on individual responsibility in U.S. health promotion policy, compared with that of Canada and Europe, is fostered in part by the separation of health promotion from health protection in those U.S. documents that set the stage for the 1980s, namely, *Healthy People: The Surgeon-General's Report on Health Promotion and Disease Prevention* (U.S. Department of Health, 1979; hereafter, the Surgeon-General's Report), and *Promoting Health, Preventing Disease: 1990 Objectives for the Nation* (U.S. Department of Health, 1980; hereafter, the Objectives). Thus, health promotion was more narrowly defined within U.S. federal policy, but not without providing for the environmental determinants of health under the official rubric of health protection. Health promotion was to remain focussed on the lifestyle determinants of health. At the same time, these policy documents were driven by an analysis that gave priority to those determinants that could most directly be linked with the leading causes of death. This approach ranked behavioural determinants over the more pervasive and powerful (but less direct) social and economic factors.

These U.S. policies had barely reached publication when President Jimmy Carter was replaced by Ronald Reagan. The disease prevention and health promotion initiative that we had nurtured so lovingly was now at risk of being flushed with one pull of the White House chain. To our surprise, the new administration embraced it. The new Assistant Secretary for Health instructed the agencies of the Public Health Service to prepare their 1982 fiscal year budgets with the Objectives as their justification. This unexpected endorsement of disease prevention and health promotion policies by the Reagan administration was partly a recognition of the broad consensus that had gone into the Objectives; they could hardly be seen as a Democratic policy platform (Green, 1991). However, the endorsement was a smokescreen of support for relatively inexpensive activities, while the new administration cut deeply into the budgets and authority of the health services and health protection agencies (Allegrante & Green, 1981). By the mid-1980s, the contrasts presented by Hancock between the U.S. programs and the Canadian/European philosophy of health promotion probably approached their extremes, at least as reflected in the rhetoric of individual responsibility and risk-factor reduction on the one side versus that of collective responsibility, equity, and environmental determinants on the other.

Canada, too, has federal agencies devoted to health services and health protection. Its Health Promotion Directorate has had responsibility for numerous behaviour-specific programs, for example, in drug abuse and smoking prevention. Yet the image persists of a much more socially progressive, comprehensive, multisectoral health promotion in Canada. Is this image living on borrowed time in the afterglow of the Lalonde Report, the Ottawa Charter (WHO, 1986), and *Achieving Health for All: A Framework for Health Promotion* (Epp, 1986)? Is it being kept alive by a few notable provincial initiatives and the high-profile WHO initiatives built on

Canadian models? Is it nurtured by *Health Promotion*, the widely circulated magazine of the Health Promotion Directorate, and the disproportionately frequent appearance of Canadian authors in the journal *Health Promotion International*, inaugurated around the time of the Ottawa conference in 1986? Or, is it truly etched into the hearts and minds of Canadians, new and old?

There is reason to believe that the socially progressive view goes deeper than mere puffery, rhetoric, and bureaucratic posturing. Canadian history and cultural traditions lend themselves to an ethic of social support and social responsibility. "Peace, order, and good government" is the motto cited in Canada in the same situations in which Americans might be moved to recite, "Life, liberty, and the pursuit of happiness." In the matter of immigration policy, the Canadian rejection of the American-style melting pot in favour of a multicultural mosaic symbolizes a tolerance of diversity. Canadians, as a people, never fought a war of independence with Britain; many loyalists to the Crown in the United States moved across the Canadian border during what Americans call the Revolutionary War. America's suspicion of government as a result of the "taxation without representation" issue led to a federalist structure blatantly designed to minimize the powers of central government; the Civil War further strained the relationship between the federal government and the states. Only recently has Canada felt the strain of provincial separatism to the point of posing a constitutional crisis. This could mitigate against Canadian historical and cultural traditions.

Whatever differences might be attributed to history and culture, with regard to the individual-versus-social-responsibility continuum, the ethos of Canadian health promotion discourages intolerance of any one community's preferences. Indeed, condemning the American emphasis on individual responsibility in some of its health promotion programs seems inconsistent with the Canadian tradition of multicultural tolerance.

Conclusion

At the end of the conference in Florida at which Trevor Hancock courageously presented his table of contrasts to the assembly of American Academic Health Center directors, I asked him where that chart had originated. I had seen it elsewhere, sometimes attributed to him, sometimes not. He said he recalled first coming up with the contrasts by comparing the first issue of the new journal *Health Promotion International*, which appeared about the time of the Ottawa Charter in 1986, with the first issue of the *American Journal of Health Promotion*, which came out at about the same time. This information made everything suddenly clear to me as to how apparently vast differences between two neighbouring countries had been created and perpetuated.

I recounted to Dr. Hancock how Michael O'Donnell, the young editor and publisher who started the *American Journal of Health Promotion*, had come from a business background and had written a best-selling book on worksite health promotion (O'Donnell & Ainsworth, 1984). At the time he started the *Journal*, O'Donnell's perspective on the field was heavily influenced by one arm of the pluralistic (not to say multicultural) American health promotion community. He subsequently took up doctoral studies at the University of Michigan School of Public Health, where his perspective broadened apace with his editorial and publishing responsibilities. Evidence of this metamorphosis can be seen in the contrast between his definition of health promotion in the first issue (O'Donnell, 1986) compared with his redefinitions over the next three years (O'Donnell, 1989).

My conclusion of this insider-outsider reflection is that Canadian health promotion has, indeed, been innovative in its conceptualization of a social rather than an individual focus, of collective responsibility rather than personal responsibility, and of risk conditions rather than risk factors. But these ideas have had some life in the United States. Some of them have suffered setbacks with the flow of international events such as the Vietnam War in the 1960s; political trends such as the conservative government's emphasis on decentralization, privatization, and deregulation during the 1970s and 1980s; and economic trends such as the recession of the 1990s. Canada will not be immune to such setbacks in its own health promotion policies and programs, as recent events have demonstrated.

The brief window of opportunity during the Carter years to break out of the conservative mould in U.S. national health promotion policy resulted in the Surgeon-General's Report in 1979 and the Objectives in 1980, inspired in part by the Canadian Lalonde Report. The U.S. documents had many of the social concepts and focuses that later appeared in the Ottawa Charter (1986) and the Framework (1986). They also contained objectives particular to those factors that would be measurable at the individual level, those for which individuals could take some degree of personal responsibility, and those for which risks could be pinpointed as proximal if not ultimate causes.

These became the objectives widely quoted by those who sought to characterize the U.S. brand of health promotion as individualistic, risk-factor oriented, and victim-blaming. Add to that the emergence of an *American Journal of Health Promotion* out of the private-sector oriented, workplace health promotion and fitness tradition (which is one of many species of health promotion in the United States), and the impression was sealed that American health promotion was hopelessly mired in individualistic, personal risk-factor thinking.

As I review manuscripts for Canadian journals, grant applications for Canadian funding agencies, and attend site visits to Canadian health promotion projects, I am proud of the extent to which American science and theory has served Canadian investigators, and proud as a New Canadian to see how creatively and forcefully Canadian investigators and health practitioners have adapted, complemented, and applied these and other ideas out of the richness of this multicultural society.

References

Allegrante, J.P., & Green, L.W. (1981). When health policy becomes victim blaming. *New England Journal of Medicine, 305,* 1528-1529.

Andersen, R., Kravitz, J., & Anderson, O.W. (1975). *Equity in health services: Empirical analysis in social policy.* Cambridge, MA: Ballinger.

Belloc, N.B., & Breslow, L. (1972). Relationship of physical health status and health practices. *Preventive Medicine, 1,* 409-421.

Berkman, L.F., & Breslow, L. (1983). *Health and ways of living: The Alameda County study.* New York: Oxford University Press.

Carlaw, R.W., Mittlemark, M.B., Bracht, N., & Luepker, R. (1984). Organization for a community cardiovascular health program: Experiences from the Minnesota Heart Health Program. *Health Education Quarterly, 11,* 243-252.

Chadwick, E. (1865). *The sanitary condition of the labouring population of Great Britain,* Edinburgh, Scotland. Edinburgh: Edinburgh University Press.

de Leeuw, E.J.J. (1989). *The sane revolution: Health promotion: Backgrounds, scope, prospects.* Assen/Maastricht, The Netherlands: Van Gorcum.

Epp, J. (1986). *Achieving health for all: A framework for health promotion.* Ottawa: Health & Welfare Canada.

Farquhar, J.W., Fortmann, S.P., Flora, J.A., Barr Taylor, C., Haskell, W.L., Williams, P.T., Maccoby, N., & Wood, P.D. (1990). Effects of community-wide education on cardiovascular disease risk factors — The Stanford Five-City Project. *Journal of the American Medical Association, 264,* 359-365.

Federal – Provincial Heart Health Initiative (1991). *Evaluation guidelines for heart health.* Ottawa: Health Services & Promotion Branch, Health & Welfare Canada.

Green, L.W. (1991). "Foreword." In *Healthy people 2000: National health promotion and disease prevention objectives.* Boston: Bartlett Publishers.

Green, L.W. (1986). "The theory of participation: A qualitative analysis of its expression in national and international health policies." In W. Ward (ed.), *Advances in health education and promotion* (Vol. 1, part A, pp. 211-236). Greenwich, CT: JAI Press.

Green, L.W., & Kreuter, M.W. (1991). *Health promotion planning: An educational and environmental approach.* Mountain View, CA: Mayfield.

Hancock, T. (1993, in press). Healthy communities: The role of the academic health centre. Presented at the annual meeting of the Association of Academic Health Centers, Amelia Island, Florida, September 30, 1992; forthcoming in M. Osterweis et al. (eds.), *Promoting community health: The role of the academic health center.* Washington, DC: Association of Academic Health Centers.

Hancock, T. (1985). Beyond health care: From public health policy to healthy public policy. *Canadian Journal of Public Health, 76,* 9-11.

Labonté, R., & Penfold, S. (1981). Canadian perspectives in health promotion: A critique. *Health Education, 19*(3/4), 4-9.

Lalonde, M. (1974). *A new perspective on the health of Canadians.* Ottawa: Information Canada.

Lasater, T., Abrams, D., Artz, L, Beaudin, P., Cabrera, L., Elder, J., Ferrerra, A., Kniskey, P., Peterson, G., Rodrigues, A., Rosenberg, P., Snow, R., & Carleton, R. (1984). Lay volunteer delivery of a community-based cardiovascular risk factor change program: The Pawtucket experiment. In J.D. Wiley et al. (eds.), *Behavioral health: A handbook of health enhancement and disease prevention.* New York: Wiley.

Leichter, H.M. (1991). *Free to be foolish: Politics and health promotion in the United States and Britain.* Princeton, NJ: Princeton University Press.

McAlister, A., Puska, P., Salonene, J.T., Tuomilehto, J., & Koskela, K. (1982). Theory and action for health promotion — Illustrations from the North Karelia Project. *American Journal of Public Health, 72,* 43-52.

Moynihan, D.P. (1969). *Maximum feasible misunderstanding: Community action in the war on poverty.* New York: Free Press.

Nelson, C.F., Kreuter, M.W., Watkins, N.B., & Stoddard, R.R. (1986). A partnership between the community, state, and federal government: Rhetoric or reality. *Hygiene, 5*(3), 27-31.

O'Donnell, M.P. (1989). Definition of health promotion: Part III: Expanding the definition. *American Journal of Health Promotion, 3,* 5.

O'Donnell, M.P. (1986). Definition of health promotion. *American Journal of Health Promotion, 1,* 4-5.

O'Donnell, M.P., & Ainsworth, T. (eds.) (1984). *Health promotion in the workplace.* New York: Wiley.

Public Law 94-317, 94th Congress, S. 1466, June 23, 1976, Sec. 1706, 90 Stat., p. 700.

Ryan, W. (1971). *Blaming the victim.* New York: Vintage Books.

Sardell, A. (1983). Neighborhood health centers and community-based care: Federal policy from 1965-1982. *Journal of Public Health Policy, 4,* 484.

Tarlov, A.R., Keher, B.H., Hall, D.P., Samuels, S.E., Brown, G.S., Felix, M.R.J., & Ross, J.A. (1987). Foundation work: The health promotion program of the Henry J. Kaiser Family Foundation. *American Journal of Health Promotion, 2,* 74-80.

U.S. Department of Health, Education & Welfare (1979). *Healthy people: The Surgeon-General's Report on health promotion and disease prevention.* Washington, DC: Public Health Service, DHEW-PHS-79-55071.

U.S. Department of Health & Human Services (1980). *Promoting health, preventing disease: 1990 Objectives for the nation.* Washington, DC: Public Health Service.

Viseltear, A. (1976). "A short history of P.L. 94-317." In *Preventive medicine USA.* New York: Prodist.

World Health Organization (1986). *Ottawa charter for health promotion.* Ottawa: Canadian Public Health Association.

The View from Down Under: The Impact of Canadian Health Promotion on Developments in New Zealand

John M. Raeburn

Early Influences

Ron Draper

New Zealanders who go to Canada, and Canadians who go to New Zealand, immediately recognize that there is a kind of spiritual bond between the two places. We share the British parliamentary tradition and the Queen. Each of our countries has a dominant neighbour, for whose citizens we are frequently mistaken because of the way we speak. We both love the outdoors and beautiful landscapes. And each of our countries is fundamentally bicultural. (In New Zealand, our two cultures are Maori and European, and the relationship between the two often parallels the French-English situation in Canada.)

However, compared with Canada, the term health promotion is a relatively recent arrival in New Zealand. It was only at the beginning of the 1980s that we started to hear about it here, stimulated by three significant events. Two of these were visits to New Zealand by Lawrence Green (whose chapter precedes mine in this book), and the third was a visit by Ron Draper, then Director of the Health Promotion Directorate in Ottawa.

The first visit by Green had relatively little impact, mainly because he was brought to New Zealand by the national Dental Association and spoke primarily to dentists. Then came Draper in 1980. He visited as an advisor to the New Zealand Department of Health, and as far as I know, he gave no public talks. However, his presence had far-reaching repercussions. During his time in New Zealand, he made a visit to Northland, a mainly rural area at the top of the North Island, and I was among a number of people there who met him. Northland was the location for a comprehensive pilot experiment in the reorganization of New Zealand's health services. The people co-ordinating that project were on the lookout for good ideas, and were impressed by Draper and what was happening in Canada. What followed was the establishment in Northland of the first "official" health promotion unit in New Zealand (Snelgar & Jackson, 1987). This unit combined several influences: the Canadian orientation to lifestyle and social marketing, the New Zealand proclivity for grass-roots community development, and a planning approach based on goals, needs assessment, and evaluation.

Ron Draper had a strong contribution to make in each of these areas. In 1980, the lifestyle and social marketing approach to health promotion was in its heyday in Canada. Ron gave us the Lalonde Report, and I still have on my bookshelves several of the copies he sent us. (Generations of New Zealand medical and other students have since received photocopied chapters out of the Lalonde Report.) In terms of community activity, the Canadian Health Promotion Contributions Program served as an inspiration, especially the idea that community groups should receive public funds to generate and run their own health promotion programs. Subsequently, some of the best community-based health promotion programs in New Zealand — especially one involving Maori people called Ringa Atawhai (The Helping Hand) — originated in Northland, more or less based on the Contributions model (Cooney & Jackson, 1988). Finally, Draper's public administration background came through in his goals-oriented approach to organization. Some of us continue to work in this idiom, which we find especially useful for the planning and evaluation of health promotion interventions (Raeburn, 1987b).

So the early Draper visit had an important impact on health promotion initiatives in the experimental Northland scheme, and it was this scheme that subsequently served as a model for the reorganization of the entire New Zealand health system. In 1983, the Area Health Boards Act was passed, setting up fourteen Boards throughout the country. The first objective of the Boards, as stated in the legislation, was "to promote, protect and conserve the public health, and to provide health services," and the first of each Board's functions, duties, and powers was "generally to promote and protect the health of the residents of its district, and, towards that end, to consult and co-operate with individuals and organizations. . . concerned with the promotion and maintenance of health."

Some of the Northland people were influential in helping to draft this legislation, and although one cannot be certain, I believe this forthright emphasis on health promotion had much to do with Ron Draper's visit in 1980.

Draper's visit had another important influence on the national scene. Not long after he came, the New Zealand Department of Health set up a program called the Community Health Initiatives Funding Scheme (CHIFS). It was only some years later, when I visited Ottawa and worked with the Contributions Program, that I discovered that CHIFS had been modelled directly on Contributions as a result of Draper's visit. The CHIFS program survived for many years, and gave out money to community groups undertaking their own health-related activities. However, there were some important differences between CHIFS and the Contributions Program, some good, some not so good. On the good side, CHIFS funding decisions were made by local community committees set up for that purpose, and these decisions did not have to be ratified by the Minister (which was the case, I was astonished to find, with the Contributions Program in Canada). On the not-so-good side, the supportive infrastructure found in Canada (i.e., advisors on hand in offices across the country to assist community groups with applications and their work) was never set up in New Zealand. This, I believe, marks one of the strengths of the Canadian program.

Health Promotion Emerges

Lawrence Green and the Health Promotion Forum

Around 1984, Lawrence Green returned, this time at the invitation of the New Zealand Medical Research Council. He gave a series of well-attended workshops throughout the country, aimed at looking at the future of health promotion activity in New Zealand. Larry Green is, of course, American by birth (even though he now lives in Vancouver). But it is worth discussing his visit here, since it had important consequences for health promotion in New Zealand.

The climax of Green's visit was a meeting in Wellington that brought together a variety of national agencies to discuss health promotion. As a consequence, the Medical Research Council co-ordinated the establishment of an independent body called the Health Promotion Forum of New Zealand, funded in part by the Council, and in part by a consortium of such bodies as the Heart Foundation, the Alcoholic Liquor Advisory Council, the Cancer Society, and others. The Forum was intended to co-ordinate voluntary sector and community activity in health promotion. By chance, its first director was a Canadian, Dr. Larry Peters, who had been teaching community psychology at the University of Waikato in Hamilton.

Peters held the Health Promotion Forum position for a couple of years, during which time he became conversant with what was happening back in his homeland, and this was evident in the way he worked. In particular, he was interested in doing a New Zealand version of the 1985 Canadian Health Promotion Survey (Epp, 1987). Indeed, Peters became so conversant with what was going on in Canada that he returned there in 1988 to take up a job in the Health Promotion Directorate in Ottawa to work on analyzing the survey. Since that time, the Forum has not had a particularly Canadian flavour. It does, however, subscribe strongly to the *Ottawa Charter for Health Promotion* (WHO, 1986; hereafter, the Charter).

The Ottawa Charter

Until now, we have mainly discussed the period up to 1986. Just as the Western world dates its calendar B.C. and A.D., it is likely that the health promotion world will date its calendar BOC and AOC, referring, of course, to the Ottawa Charter as a turning point in the history of health promotion.

Although the Ottawa Charter is not a strictly Canadian document, Canada played an active role in formulating and initiating its principles even before it was published. I would like briefly to elaborate on this.

Nineteen eighty-six was a special year for me personally. I had been granted sabbatical leave from the university. As has been the case for several New Zealanders, I decided I would go to the Health Promotion Directorate in Ottawa, which for a health promoter was like going to Mecca. Ottawa was where health promotion had been born and nurtured.

When I arrived, the Directorate was in the throes of discussing policy as a lead-in to the 1986 Ottawa Health Promotion Conference, and was evidently strongly committed to the social model enshrined in the Charter. There was clearly a tension developing between the old lifestyle approach and the new social-model approach. Nobody quite knew how it would all work out, but everyone was very stirred up about it.

There had obviously been much discussion between the World Health Organization and Ottawa, and it was hard to tell who had come up with which strands of the social model. In any case, it seemed that Canada was to be the guinea pig for the new way. Just as Canada had led the world with the Health Promotion Directorate based on the Lalonde Report, so the same Directorate would lead the way with a national policy based on the social model. This was to be embodied in a "new" Lalonde Report, which subsequently appeared as *Achieving Health for All: A Framework for Health Promotion* (Epp, 1986).

To make a long story short, I was privileged to be a participant in some of the policy development work in the Directorate in 1986, and all the time I was taking notes about how we could use the same tactics in New Zealand. I also managed to attend the Conference as one of the two New Zealand delegates (the aforementioned Canadian, Larry Peters, was the other).

Health Reforms, Phase One

Area Health Boards

When one attends such an event as the Ottawa Conference at public expense, there is general expectation that, when one returns home, the event will be reported to as many people as possible. Over the following year (1987), both Larry Peters and I spoke about the Charter in many settings around the country. We also wrote a couple of articles for a now-defunct public health journal, *New Zealand Health Review* (Raeburn,

1987a; Raeburn & Peters, 1987), one of which was titled, "Options for Health Promotion: What Can We Learn from the Canadians?" These events occurred at a critical moment historically speaking, when the entire health system was starting to undergo a major reform, namely, the establishment nationally of Area Health Boards.

As mentioned, these Boards were required by law to have a strong orientation to health promotion, yet it was not clear what this meant. Although there were important health promotion events and developments around New Zealand at that time — such as the Great New Zealand Smoke-Free Week (Laugeson, 1987), the research coming from the public health oriented Alcohol Research Unit at the School of Medicine (Casswell & Stewart, 1986), and the setting up of the Department of Health's Health Promotion Programme in Head Office in Wellington (Kill, 1987) — there was no overall view or guiding philosophy for health promotion suitable for Area Health Boards. The Ottawa Charter seemed to provide this.

In conjunction with the health reforms, in 1987 the Minister of Health in the Labour government set up a Board of Health to advise him. This, in turn, was made up of several topic-oriented committees, one of which was for health promotion. Subsequently, this committee published a widely distributed document, *Promoting Health in New Zealand* (New Zealand Board of Health, 1988), which included a full transcript of the Ottawa Charter. (Interestingly, this document had little influence, probably because it was caught precariously between the old lifestyle approach and the new social model).

Meanwhile, Area Health Boards were starting to hold public meetings on community involvement and health promotion, and some had set up their own planning groups. Virtually every Area Health Board in New Zealand chose the Ottawa Charter as its basic philosophical statement regarding health promotion, with particular emphasis on community action and policy. (In practice, little was accomplished by the Area Health Boards in health promotion, with most efforts focussed on prevention strategies in such areas as smoking and cervical screening).

However, in 1991, one of the Area Health Boards (Waikato) did start to plan a comprehensive community-based health promotion approach. This was thanks to the efforts of Canadian Ron Labonté, another contributor to this book. Labonté had been invited to spend several months at the University of Waikato in Hamilton, to teach graduate courses there in health promotion. The Waikato Area Health Board took advantage of Labonté's presence in their region. They asked him to design, on a consultancy basis, a health promotion system that they could use. So New Zealand stood at the threshold of adopting a Toronto-style approach to health promotion in the heart of its dairy farm country! Sadly, this plan never materialized. Not only did the bureaucracy succeed in burying it, but the whole Area Health Board system suddenly came under threat of disestablishment, thanks to new government policies. Nevertheless, Ron Labonté managed to reawaken an interest in Canadian-style health promotion, both through the students he inspired, and the various workshops he held around the country at the invitation of the Health Promotion Forum.

Health Reforms, Phase Two

The New Right

As readers may know, New Zealand is currently undergoing a comprehensive political restructuring of the New Right variety. This is the latest example of a well-established tradition in which New Zealand politicians treat their country as a social laboratory. Such things are possible because of New Zealand's small, cohesive population (three million), its insularity, and its single-tiered, centralized government. In the past, most of these experiments have been generally positive in respect to health and social well-being. For example, New Zealand was the first country in the world to have universal suffrage. (Nineteen ninety-three marks the centenary of women's gaining the vote.) It also has a unique treaty, for a colonized country, between the Crown and the indigenous people (the Treaty of Waitangi). And in the 1930s, New Zealand began the world's first welfare state, which included a "free" comprehensive public health service equally available to all. As a result, New Zealand's population is one of the healthiest in the world.

The current political experiments are as revolutionary as anything that has gone before, but there are few who regard them as positive from the standpoint of health and social services. Starting with the "Rogernomics" of the supposedly left-wing Labour Party elected to power in 1984 (named after the monetarist dogma of then finance minister Roger Douglas), and pursued with even greater vigour by the subsequent conservative National government, New Zealand has instituted what is possibly the most radical New Right state in the world. The welfare state is being systematically dismantled, with education, social services, and health being especially targetted. Education and social services have already been radically restructured. By 1992, it was the turn of health services. The Minister of Health, Simon Upton, is a New Right enthusiast, and has set in train a process of disestablishing the Area Health Boards, replacing them with four Regional Health Authorities which will contract out all services, with a view to cost saving and generating a profit. For the first time, New Zealanders must pay to go to hospital. Health is now to be run as a business like any other. Public health is to have separate funding (which may turn out to be a plus), and health promotion will come under this umbrella. But the shape this will ultimately take is yet unknown.

In case readers think I may be exaggerating the New Right revolution in New Zealand, along with its present and future impact on health, they may be interested and amused to read the following passage by Denis Welch, a well-known and respected political columnist, published at the same time this chapter was being written:

> It's also vital to remember that for many on the New Right this country has barely scratched the surface of what's politically possible. . . . If they had their way, what remains of the state would be ideologically nuked, leaving only a few diplomats and a couple of armed guards standing. . . . As for health reform, why shilly-shally? Chile is already privatising state-owned hospitals, says Business Roundtabler Roger Kerr [leading New Right lobbyist], adding:

"We have left undone those things which we ought to have done, and we have done those things which we ought not to have done." Even the prayer-book has been co-opted to the New Right cause. (Welch, 1992, p. 25)

Conclusion

We understand that Canada is currently in a phase of recession, with unemployment rising. We also understand that Canada has consulted New Zealand about some of its monetarist reforms. As can be seen from what has been written here, New Zealand has benefitted greatly from health promotion influences coming from Canada. Indeed, if we include the Ottawa Charter, one could assert that the Canadian influence has been the dominant one. However, perhaps the tables are about to be turned. What happens now to health promotion in New Zealand under the latest reforms may have considerable relevance to Canada. What an irony it would be if, in the years to come, Canada starts to look to New Zealand to see how to do (or more likely, how not to do) health promotion in a post-welfare-state environment!

In the meantime, O Canada, we thank you for your role in our health promotion. It couldn't have come from a nicer place.

References

Casswell, S., & Stewart, L. (1986). *From a public health perspective: Availability of alcohol in New Zealand.* Auckland: Alcohol Research Unit.

Cooney, C., & Jackson, S. (1988). The community link. *New Zealand Nursing Journal, 81,* 12-16.

Epp, J. (1986). *Achieving health for all: A framework for health promotion.* Ottawa: Health & Welfare Canada.

Epp, J. (1987). *The active health report: Perspectives on Canada's health promotion survey 1985.* Ottawa: Health & Welfare Canada.

Kill, B. (1987). Guest editorial. *New Zealand Health Review, 6,* 13.

Laugeson, M. (1987). The 1986 Great New Zealand Smoke-Free Week. *New Zealand Health Review, 6,* 19-20.

New Zealand Board of Health (1988). *Promoting health in New Zealand.* Wellington: Author.

Raeburn, J.M. (1987a). Options for health promotion: What can we learn from the Canadians? *New Zealand Health Review, 6,* 24-27.

Raeburn, J.M. (1987b). People projects: Planning and evaluation in a new era. *Health Promotion (Canada), 25,* 2-13.

Raeburn, J.M., & Peters, L. (1987). The First International Conference on Health Promotion: A New Zealand perspective. *New Zealand Health Review, 6,* 24-27.

Snelgar, D., & Jackson, S. (1987). Health promotion and the Northland Area Health Board. *New Zealand Health Review, 6,* 27-28.

Welch, D. (1992). Welch's week. *New Zealand Listener,* May 18, p. 25.

World Health Organization (1986). *The Ottawa charter for health promotion.* Ottawa: Canadian Public Health Association.

Health Promotion Research in Canada: A European/British Perspective

David McQueen

This paper has two themes. The first is that health promotion as a broad concept, stemming from a public health perspective that is societally rather than individually focussed, has developed largely from a European and Canadian base. The second is to suggest that health promotion as a concept must now move beyond the rhetoric of its developmental years if it is to continue as a viable force in public health.

Biography and Definitions

A Personal View

This is an age of reflexivity, where our biography is as important as our thoughts and the two may not be separable. My public health background began in the late 1960s, following a period of study and interest in the history and philosophy of science. Through rather tortuous paths of study I developed an interest in the sociology of science, followed by medical sociology. Then came a doctorate at the American citadel of public health, Johns Hopkins University, followed by ten years as a faculty member in the Department of Behavioral Sciences at Hopkins.

Early in the 1980s, the opportunity to establish, and become the first director of, a research institution in Edinburgh could not be resisted and I moved to Scotland. During my years there, my links with the rest of Europe increased, notably through the World Health Organization European Regional Office (WHO-Euro), while my North American connections diminished — except for Canada, that is, where a number of personal and professional ties developed, ties that were established from my European base.

Now I have many ties with Canada — personal, intellectual, and institutional — and almost regard Canada as European rather than North American, with regard to health promotion. I was one of the lucky ones to be there when the *Ottawa Charter on Health Promotion* (WHO, 1986; hereafter, the Ottawa Charter) was drafted. Since then, I have followed Canada's fortunes in health promotion with considerable interest. Thus, I am not an unbiassed observer of health promotion in Canada.

Three Decades of Health Promotion in Canada and Europe

The term health promotion dates from the 1970s and stems from several sources. Most notable is the influence of *A New Perspective on the Health of Canadians* (Lalonde, 1974; hereafter, the Lalonde Report). (Cf. Laframboise, 1973.) The health field concept presented in the Lalonde Report made health the locus of four factors: human biology, lifestyles, organization of medical care, and environment. What was critical was the placing of medical care in a broader and equal context with biological, social, and environmental factors. Over the next two decades the idea of health promotion, particularly in Canada and Europe, would emphasize in different measures each of these factors or dimensions of health promotion.

Clearly, the Lalonde Report and other events of the 1970s initiated a groundswell of support for health promotion, but many followers of this concept had only vague notions about what it was. Some ten years later, a key World Health Organization paper, *Health Promotion: A Discussion Document on the Concept and Principles* (WHO,1984), would attempt to clarify what was rapidly becoming a very loosely defined field of research and practice.

Two decades is a more than adequate gestation period for a field that should encompass theory, research, and practice. The 1990s represent the watershed for health promotion. Now health promotion must show its utility to the sceptics, as well as to those who have had their consciousness raised by its rhetoric. The challenge is one of proof: Can health promotion deliver what it professes? While any emerging field is distinguished by its theory and practice, one looks to research for the empirical evidence. In Canada, the research setting appears relatively well developed.

Issues in Health Promotion Research

Background

Health promotion research is difficult to define. It encompasses much of the research in health policy, lifestyle, and socio-epidemiology. Studies of policy development, community participation, and the anthropology of health are pertinent. It is also possible to define health promotion research by priority areas (though the areas would vary greatly from culture to culture), such as exercise, youth, or AIDS. However one defines health promotion research, there seems to be some consensus on its parameters. Health promotion research should:

- Be concerned with the conditions for change and the obstacles to change;
- Identify patterns of life and health chances, patterns of behaviours, and patterns for policy making in health;
- Look at "natural experiments" taking place in the real world, e.g., Healthy Cities;
- Emphasize the study of diverse methods, multidisciplinary approaches, and the collaboration of different sectors with different traditions; and finally,
- Involve the community of interest in the research.

Some of those who are concerned with health promotion research might disagree on the relative importance of its critical areas, but most would agree that those critical issues include:

- Theories and concepts in the field;
- Methodology and the style of research that is appropriate; and
- Application of research findings, ranging from dissemination to utilization of research.

With regard to theories and concepts, the criteria for any new theory should include: (1) contextualism (i.e., the theory should incorporate the wider context of health and health behaviour); (2) dynamism (the theory must be capable of explaining states of behaviour and health at different points in time); and (3) an interdisciplinary approach (the theory should arise from multiple sources and represent research from diverse theoretical traditions).

The application of research is perhaps the thorniest problem in the list. Most would argue that application should be seen as central to health promotion research, and would make some of the following points:

- A redistribution of power should be effected in setting the research agenda. This recommendation holds at many levels; for example, it is argued that community perceptions and priorities for action should initiate research projects, the results of which should then be returned to the community. Community and lay perceptions of knowledge and expertise should be recognized and deployed.
- The application of research must be seen in the context of action.
- To ensure an increased uptake and utilization of research findings, an assessment needs to be made of ways of presenting these findings to non-professional and lay groups in the community as well as to policy makers.

The Behavioural Risk-Factor Tradition

During the past three decades, the socio-epidemiologically based risk-factor survey has been the approach of choice for gaining baseline data on population parameters related to social factors in health and illness. These parameters include public attitudes, opinions, beliefs, and behaviours. The premise of such surveys is straightforward: if public health efforts are to be successful on a broad scale, then public health practitioners and health promoters must have an informed basis upon which to practise. Furthermore, opinions, beliefs, and attitudes are seen as an essential component of necessary behavioural change (although it is widely recognized in health behaviour research that there is only a weak association between individual beliefs and actual behaviours). Thus, most lifestyle-oriented surveys and questionnaires stemming from the risk-factor model reflect this premise.

There is worldwide interest in lifestyle surveys. Lifestyle and health-type surveys have ranged from rather small, simply designed surveys to serve local needs (e.g., surveys by local health boards or small communities) to large-scale, methodologically complicated endeavours to assess broad population trends (e.g., national surveys by computer-assisted telephone interviews). In almost every case, such surveys produce large amounts of data that provide public health researchers with seemingly infinite points for analysis.

The idea of a European-wide health promotion survey has been discussed at length in a number of European meetings. Many European researchers, including some associated with the lifestyles and health movement in WHO-Euro, pushed for a comprehensive health promotion survey for Europe. Nevertheless, despite considerable interest and good intentions, such a survey has not yet been undertaken. Of course, there were a number of surveys that flew the banner of "lifestyle and health," but many of these were essentially studies of epidemiologically based risk factors for disease. This is not a criticism of behavioural risk-factor surveys; they serve a critical role in the research agenda of public health. Nevertheless, the rhetoric of health promotion has argued for a broader perspective of health and demands the collection of data that are relevant to inform that broader perspective.

Despite the vast amount of health-related statistical data that are available in most modern industrialized countries, it is remarkable that Canada may be the only country that has managed a nationwide health promotion survey. The fact that such a survey has now taken place twice in the past five years is a tribute to the importance that Canada places on health promotion.

Methodological and Theoretical Issues

In general, much health promotion research has been driven by a need to satisfy fairly rigid research criteria established by statisticians, for example, rigid adherence to the established statistical sacred cows of randomness, normality, and significance, often at the expense of any sensitivity to the research problem being addressed. In fact, alternative statistical and methodological procedures and their underlying rationales are rarely taught at the elementary levels, despite the likelihood that actual research conducted in health promotion will largely be in violation of the statistical assumptions underpinning classical parametric procedures. Thus, a central issue for health promotion research is how to break free legitimately from a rigid orthodoxy that is increasingly inadequate for the special areas of study needed.

Much is known about the distribution of some health-related individual behaviours in populations. Drinking patterns and smoking behaviours are two highly researched areas; slightly less well understood are eating habits and physical exercise. These four behaviours have been measured extensively over the years in Britain and most European countries. Probably most behavioural research currently carried out continues to assess these, and accepts the necessity for doing so. Some individual behaviours, regarded by many public health practitioners as important, are assessed in a myriad of studies, e.g., drug use, sexual behaviour, care seeking, and suicide, to name a few.

Other individual behaviours that take up much time in daily routine (such as driving, shopping, and watching television) are rarely measured or included in studies, even though a case could be made that they may have profound effects on people's health. Thus, researchers have emphasized a limited selection of possibly relevant behaviours for health promotion. Furthermore, despite the extraordinary documentation of some health-related behaviours, there is less information about how these behaviours relate to one another within populations and within population subgroups. This relative dearth of data is not simply a measurement problem; it influences the manner in which much behavioural research is funded and carried out. The Canadian approach to lifestyle and health research, notably through the Health Promotion Survey, has tried to engage some of these broader perspectives.

The Role of Epidemiology

How much the role of epidemiology has figured in the arguments for health promotion research remains an open question. It may well be that epidemiology as a base for health promotion is one key to understanding the distinctions between the British, European, American, and Canadian views of health promotion. Many Canadian arguments for health promotion research (e.g., Maclean, 1988; O'Neill, 1988; Raeburn & Rootman, 1988) are notable for either an absence or a diminution of an epidemiological perspective.

On the epidemiological side, it has been argued that behavioural epidemiology is the science of health promotion and therefore has a very central place in health promotion research (Raymond, 1989). The argument is that epidemiology has gone well beyond a narrow concern with infectious diseases to a concern with the prevalence and incidence of problems. Raymond states:

> Behavioral epidemiology as the science of health promotion and disease prevention seems to be the next major breakthrough area in public health science. Health promotion is necessarily transactional, developmental, dynamic and ecological. My hope is that our behavioural epidemiology will acknowledge these four attributes of health promotion by pushing beyond the conventional borders of behavioural risk factors research to the excitement of discovering the antecedents of health in the social contexts of behaviour (p. 286).

Kok and Green (1990) put forward six propositions to assist in the development of co-operation between research and health promotion practice. Their argument, based on practice, is that "health promotion activities that are not strongly grounded in previous epidemiological and psycho-social research are more likely to be ineffective and sometimes even counter-effective" (p. 303).

This statement shows not only how key is the discussion about epidemiology in health promotion, but also illustrates the increasing global network of activity in this field, because one author, Kok, is European and the other, Green, is American, now living in Canada. Future historians trying to puzzle out the influence of the various countries and nationalities in the development of health promotion must contend with these interrelationships. Nonetheless, one point is certain: a Canadian perspective always plays an important role.

It is highly likely that over the next few years the debate will continue on how, or if, epidemiology should enter into the emerging repertoire of health promotion research, and what form it should take. Whatever the conclusion (if indeed there can be one), it is clear that this question is central in determining the contribution of health promotion research to public health. While there is little doubt that epidemiology *was* for years the science of public health, the question remains as to whether it will or can be the science of the *new* public health and health promotion.

The Institution of Research

What may be termed the institution of research (McQueen, 1990) consists of a complicated mix of three components: (1) individual researchers, (2) research organizations, and (3) research funding bodies. Depending on the particular field, there is some agreement among the three components about what constitutes appropriate research. In the case of well-established areas of medical research — for example, epidemiology — there is undoubtedly a high degree of consensus within all three components about what constitutes the subject matter and methodology of epidemiological research. Put in a Kuhnian perspective, there is agreement on which puzzles to solve and the appropriate paradigms for research among researchers, research organizations, and the funders of research. It is reasonable to assert that those who carry out research in epidemiology are supported by research organizations and funding bodies that share many ideas about research approaches. This situation is the direct result of a well-established research paradigm for epidemiology and years of people's being trained in a generally agreed-upon methodology.

By contrast, there is much less consensus about what health promotion research is, and there is no established paradigm for such research. The consequence of this lack of a clear research agenda for health promotion is that there is little agreement among the components of the institution of research about what constitutes health promotion research.

As a result, there is a lack of clarity about what sorts of research projects should be supported. Consequently, projects are sometimes proposed that promise to fulfill multiple goals, or have multiple aims. This is an old problem in public health research. For example, it has been commonplace to carry out a survey with the twin goals of measuring the prevalence of some phenomenon in the population and simultaneously developing and validating the measure of that phenomenon. From a methodological perspective, these goals are essentially incompatible; nevertheless, many studies have proceeded with this approach. While some might question this practice, it could be argued that it has been legitimized over years of research in public health. Health promotion research, on the contrary, has no bank of established practice to counteract this problem of multiple goals in research, and has a long task ahead to establish accepted practice. No doubt this is also a consequence of a field that is not discipline-based and states catholic goals for its research. One argument (McQueen, 1990) is that a comprehensive approach to health promotion research should be built around broad themes that are understood by all sectors of the institution of research.

The Development of Health Promotion Research

Debate Manifested as *Ethos*

In late 1990, a national conference on health promotion research was held in Toronto (Maclean & Eakin, 1992). This conference, Health Promotion Research Methods: Expanding the Repertoire, was notable for several reasons. There were numerous papers and keynote talks that addressed fundamental problems in research theory and methods for health promotion research. The meeting well illustrated the emerging character of health promotion research, both in Canada and in Europe. While it is notable that the meeting occurred in Canada, much of the evidence presented was international in scope. Furthermore, this meeting illustrated the consensus that was building about research in health promotion, as seen from a Canadian/European perspective.

What emerged at this meeting was evidence that there is considerable consensus in health promotion research and practice regarding what I would term an *ethos* of health promotion, that is, a widely shared set of expectations about health promotion with respect to the subject matter and approach to research (McQueen, 1991).

This *ethos* is the culmination of decades of initiation and development, and has research consequences. For example, it emphasizes less sophistication in analysis, particularly in quantitative approaches. Sophistication in data analysis may have the effect of providing detail too elaborate or inscrutable for the general needs and use of public health workers and policy makers. The paradox, of course, is that such notions as dynamism and context in multidisciplinary research often result in the need for innovative and complex data collection procedures and analyses, whether they are quantitative or qualitative. Thus, in health promotion research, the criterion of usefulness is often at loggerheads with analytic prerequisites.

One can appreciate the difficulties by examining some of the basic concerns of health promotion. Consider, for example, the implications for research and analysis that would be driven by the priorities and policies implied in the five major areas of activity of the Ottawa Charter (build healthy public policy; create supportive environments; strengthen community action; develop personal skills; reorient health services). The research agenda deriving from these areas of action implies a need for discourse between researchers and research users. This co-operative process will determine the types of data collected and pose problems for analysis of different types of data sets; in addition, it has implications for what one does with already existing sources of data, notably vital statistics. Thus, data analysis that is a part of the essence of any health promotion research is often compromised by the imperatives of usefulness.

The importance of the *ethos* is how health promotion ideas fit into one important, continuing debate in health promotion research. The debate is over research methods, notably the continued allegiance to and use of conventional public health methods versus a shift to other, perhaps unconventional, methods. The debate centres around the idea of to what extent those who use conventional methods can be considered health promotion researchers. There are many elements to this debate. One issue is the qualitative versus the quantitative approaches to research; another is the subjective versus the objective. What is implied by many is that the emerging paradigm for research in health promotion will require a subjectivistic epistemology. This subjectivistic epistemology means that the world (reality) is what we say it is. This notion, lying partly in hermeneutic understanding (Palmer, 1969), and relating clearly to the idea of reflexivity, fits well with that part of the *ethos* of health promotion which asserts that people (e.g., community) know what they want. The methodological problem for the researcher is an old one, that is, how to measure what is wanted. Measurement is thus saddled with the problem of understanding through method; the method or methods that seem immediately appropriate involve dialogue and discussion among all parties.

Searching for Legitimacy

Health promotion research is searching for legitimacy. In its current emerging state, it is difficult to sort theory from ideology, and this has implications for research methodology. One dilemma recurs: is health promotion research (particularly the variety called action research) a conduit for the expression of the ideology of health promoters, or is it a conduit for the public expression of health-related needs? In the past, health professionals were often accused of not listening to their patients; in the present, the health promoter runs the risk of arrogance in not listening to the community. This problem is further compounded by the emerging view that health promotion research is seen as a mechanism or conduit between the community and the policy maker. Put another way, research is a tool that helps the community communicate to the policy maker, and vice versa. All of this relates to the combined problems of dissemination and use of research, which in turn challenge current methodological approaches.

In actuality, the problem of dissemination and use is a great challenge to health promotion research and, by implication, to public health in general. The challenge is particularly acute for methods, both data collection and data analysis. Health promotion researchers often talk about extending the research repertoire, broadening the base for public health research, and the dawn of a "new" public health. However, the situation is complex. Consider the implications of the *ethos* that health promotion research is focussed on research that has a particular set of end users, namely, policy makers, decision makers, communities, and individuals in the general population. What do researchers know about the appropriate strategy and methodology for reaching these diverse groups? Probably very little, partly because few researchers are trained to be end users. Academic training exists to produce research on models and methods that are understandable to promotion committees, peer group committees, and journals; in other words, "people like academics." Hence, one is confronted with the established institution of research, its acceptable methodologies, and its views on appropriate dissemination.

The Canadian Contribution

Canada as the Fulcrum

There are slight variations between the European and the American views of health promotion research. In referring to the definitions of health promotion that came out of WHO-Euro (1984) and the Ottawa Charter, Green and Raeburn wrote that "these definitions have evolved in an essentially industrialized and European setting, and take little account of the history of health promotion in other parts of the world, notably the United States, the Western Pacific, Asia and the third world in general" (1988, p. 151). This is a valid point, although one might argue that Canada has been a fulcrum for American and European views. Certainly the Canadian perspective emphasizes empowerment as a key concept, and the community remains the centre for health promotion action.

Even though the U.S. style of health promotion would appear to take a more individualistic approach than the more socially oriented European/Canadian style (a point discussed at length elsewhere in this book), the net result is that often both emphasize similar elements of health promotion. Most importantly, Green and Raeburn note that:

> . . . health promotion is one of the first and few (along with public health) truly interdisciplinary enterprises (not to say professions) in health that seems genuinely emancipated from the domination of medicine. While medicine has its part to play in health promotion, health promotion does not take its primary impetus from medicine or the medical model (p. 152).

One would probably find wide concurrence in this statement among health promotion practitioners and researchers on both sides of the Atlantic, whether American, Canadian, British, or European. But these are statements about the *ethos* of health promotion as a field in general. The question remains as to whether health promotion research is pursued in a similar fashion in all places. Judging by the consensus-building efforts on health promotion research carried out in the *American Journal of Health Promotion*, one could make the case that a particular piece of research has been judged "better" to the extent that it follows classical biomedical, epidemiological guidelines. Indeed, health promotion research projects are regularly reviewed in the *Journal* and given asterisks in relation to how much the reported study has adhered to classical, quasi-experimental designs and other canons of traditional sociomedical research. There is little to be seen of broad-based ethnographic approaches, community development, or other less quantitative approaches to health promotion research. Furthermore, there is considerable emphasis on health promotion programs that feature single diseases or single behaviours as the "outcome" of the health promotion intervention.

Canadian Influence on the European Perspective

First, Canada, like much of Europe, has acted upon a broad perspective of health promotion that moves away from strategies based on individuals to those in which context becomes paramount. To appreciate this perspective fully would require an elaborate exegesis of hundreds of documents produced in Europe, Canada, and the United States over the past two decades. As this would be a long and tedious process, let it suffice to argue that when public health is under discussion, the Canadian emphasis has been on such words as "community" in contrast to "individual"; "promotion" in contrast to "education"; "social environment" in contrast to "individual risk"; "health" in contrast to "disease"; and "public policy" in contrast to "individual strategy."

Second, Canada and Canadians have actively participated in health promotion activities that clearly identify with a European base. This activity is seen both in practice and in research. In practice, the Healthy Cities movement stimulated by WHO-Euro owes much to past and continuing links with Canada and Canadians. Since its beginning, the Healthy Cities Project has flourished, with much of that growth fostered and stimulated by many Canadians, notably Trevor Hancock, Ron Draper, and Michel O'Neill (Curtice & McQueen, 1991). Of course, it is impossible to know to what extent the Healthy Cities Project would have taken a different direction had it not had the stimulus of the Toronto meeting and the underpinning of the Ottawa Charter. But the concern with the ecological context of the city and its relationship with public health fits well with the emergent Canadian perspective on public health. It is for future historians to document links in the history of ideas, but in the meantime, the ties seem obvious.

Health Promotion Research in Canada

The overall perception from the European side of the Atlantic is that the institution of health promotion research in Canada is in relatively good order. That is, there appears to be a well-developed mixture of public and governmental support for health promotion research and practice. This is manifest not only in the resourcing and support for major research initiatives such as the Health Promotion Survey, but also in the continuous financial backing for six Centres of Excellence in health promotion research and practice. One cannot help but admire the growth and development of the governmental policies leading to health promotion strength, e.g., the Epp initiatives at the federal level in Canada, and the very strong health promotion initiatives that have occurred at the provincial level as well. In turn, these programs are further enhanced by initiatives at the local level. In short, across a very broad spectrum of research and practice, Canadian developments in health promotion must be acclaimed. Given the small population of Canada, it appears that a proportionally large effort is going into health promotion; the impression is certainly one of high activity in contrast to Britain.

Yet one must not simply compare financial resources going into health promotion in one place relative to another. Simple financial comparisons often miss the point and get mired in quibbles over whether one or another budget is being channelled into health promotion efforts. The point here is that from a European/British perspective, Canada appears to be putting health promotion high on the health agenda.

While it is always difficult to assess impact, historically (that is, with the advantage of hindsight), it is clear that Italy was a dominant force in the Renaissance; that Britain was the engine of the Industrial Revolution; that Germany was at the forefront of the chemical and physical sciences in the nineteenth century; and that the United States was the powerhouse of Western capitalism in the twentieth. But these are large and powerful movements. In this century, medicine has assumed a large and powerful role within Western industrialized countries. What place has health promotion had in this enormous activity?

I would hazard a guess that its place remains relatively small, both in terms of resources and of workers in the field. At best, one can only try to assess the relative proportion of the power of the total medical/health establishment that might be attributed to health promotion. What is clear is that Canada would appear to have a relatively larger proportion of its resources and power going to health promotion than any of the European countries.

It could be argued that health promotion, particularly as conceptualized in the Canadian/European perspective, goes well beyond medicine for its strength. This may well be true; initiatives such as Healthy Cities/Communities clearly draw on a wider perspective than medicine alone. A future task for those interested in assessing the impact of health promotion will be to uncover the extent to which funding and support for health promotion has come from agencies, either governmental or private,

outside the medical sector; to uncover the extent to which individuals
enter careers of health promotion from disciplines remote from medicine
and public health; and to reveal the extent to which research methods and
approaches from other disciplines dictate the standard for health promotion research.

References

Curtice, L., & McQueen, D.V. (1990). *The WHO Healthy Cities Project —
An analysis of progress.* Edinburgh: Research Unit in Health &
Behavioural Change, University of Edinburgh.

Green, L.W., & Raeburn, J.M. (1988). Health promotion. What is it? What
will it become? *Health Promotion International,* 3(2), 151-159.

Kok, G., & Green, L.W. (1990). Research to support health promotion in
practice: A plea for increased co-operation. *Health Promotion
International,* 5(4), 303-308.

Laframboise, H. (1973). Health policy: Breaking the problem down into
more manageable segments. *Canadian Medical Association Journal, 108,*
388-391, 393.

Lalonde, M. (1974). *A new perspective on the health of Canadians.* Ottawa:
Information Canada.

Maclean, H.M. (1988). Implications of a health promotion framework for
research on breastfeeding. *Health Promotion International,* 3(4), 355-360.

Maclean, H.M., & Eakin, J.M. (eds.) (1992). Health promotion research:
Expanding the repertoire. *Canadian Journal of Public Health, 83,* Supp. 1,
88 pages.

McQueen, D.V. (1990). Comprehensive approaches to health research. In
de Leeuw, E., Breemer ter Stege, C., de Jong, G.A. (eds.), *Research for
Healthy Cities* (pp. 52-58). Proceedings of the International Conference
on Research for Healthy Cities, Supplement TSG 11/90, The Hague.

O'Neill, M. (1988). What kind of research for what kind of health promotion? *Health Promotion International,* 3(4), 337-340.

Palmer, R.E. (1969). *Northwestern University studies in phenomenology and
existential philosophy.* Evanston: Northwestern University Press.

Raeburn, J.M., & Rootman, I. (1988). Towards an expanded health field
concept: Conceptual and research issues in a new era of health promotion. *Health Promotion International,* 3(4), 383-392.

Raymond, J.S. (1989). Behavioural epidemiology: The science of health promotion. *Health Promotion International,* 4(4), 281-286.

World Health Organization (1988). *Five-year planning framework.* Copenhagen: WHO Regional Office for Europe. Healthy Cities Papers, No. 2.

World Health Organization (1986). *The Ottawa charter on health promotion.* Ottawa: Canadian Public Health Asociation.

World Health Organization (1984). *Health promotion: A discussion document on the concept and principles.* Copenhagen: WHO Regional Office for Europe.

CONCLUDING

THOUGHTS

Health Promotion in Canada: Did We Win the Battle But Lose the War?

Trevor Hancock

Readers will forgive me, I hope, for my militaristic metaphor; however, they would doubtless like an explanation. What battle am I referring to — what war are we in the health promotion field fighting? And for that matter, is this even an appropriate metaphor for a movement that puts peace at the top of its list of prerequisites for health and that believes very strongly in processes of peaceful and negotiated change?

Let me hasten to reassure readers that I am not espousing violence, nor am I suggesting we resort to force to achieve our ends. But at the same time I think we have to recognize that, like it or not, we are engaged in a power struggle — a battle, if you will — with the forces that run counter to the process of enabling people to increase control over and improve their health. The "war" is the war against poverty, hunger, disease, environmental degradation; against militarism and war itself. Let me begin, then, by discussing what this power struggle is, why power comes into health promotion at all, with whom we are struggling, and for what end.

Health Promotion: A Struggle for Power

In 1848, the Prussian health reformer Rudolph Virchow had recently returned from an examination of health conditions in the coal fields of Upper Silesia. Virchow was a leader in the health reform movement of that time (which was part of the wider reform movement) and was the editor and publisher of a magazine called *Medical Reform*, published in 1848-49. His trip to Upper Silesia, undertaken on behalf of the Prussian government, had resulted in a report that we today would call a health promotion report based upon social epidemiology. What Virchow concluded was that the health problems of the coal miners of Upper Silesia would not be alleviated by better medical facilities but by "education, freedom and prosperity," or — a dangerous notion in those times — "full and unlimited democracy." That same year, the pressure for reform led to a revolution and Virchow was there, on the barricades, pistol in hand (Ackernecht, 1981, pp. 14-18)!

Virchow's report was not all that well received, and certainly his recommendations were not put into place. In the midst of all that activity, Virchow was moved to write: "Medicine is a social science, and politics nothing else but medicine on a large scale" (Ackernecht, 1981, p. 46) and that "The medical reform that we meant was a reform of science and society" (p. 44).

Virchow was not alone, nor was he the first, in recognizing the relationship between health, medicine, politics, and power. Edwin Chadwick, the "father" of the English public health movement, had noted in his famous 1842 report that the appalling health conditions in the industrial slums of England were threatening political stability by weeding out older workers and replacing them with "a population that is young, inexperienced, ignorant, credulous, irritably passionate and dangerous." Thus, it has been argued that Chadwick believed in the importance of a stable state that maintained the status quo and that he recognized that ensuring the health of the population was an important means of ensuring the stability of the state (Ringen, 1979).

In this he was preceded by Johann Peter Frank, Director of Public Health for the Austrian province of Lombardy in northern Italy in the late eighteenth century. In his massive six-volume work, *A Complete System of Medical Police* (perhaps best translated in our modern times as health administration, since the "science of police" in those times really meant public administration), he proposed that the state should protect and enhance the health of its citizens both because their health is the nation's wealth and because he well understood the links between health and power and the need for the state, for its own sake, to maintain stability (Frank, 1976).

The point here is not that public health is a means of maintaining order — though to some extent it is — but that the links between health, politics, and power have long been understood. And politics is about power: who has it and who does not have it, who uses it and to what ends. Health promotion is thus part of a rich public health tradition that recognizes the relationship between health, politics, and power. One need only look at the definition of health promotion to understand that. According to the World Health Organization (WHO) (1986) and Health and Welfare Canada (Epp, 1986), health promotion is "the process of enabling people to increase control over and improve their health."

Health promotion can be said to be about power at two levels: first, the extent to which individuals and groups are able to take more control over their lives and their health at a personal and community level, and second, the extent to which health becomes established as a vital part of the political agenda. It is no coincidence that the first health promotion strategy in the Ottawa Charter is healthy public policy; public policy, as an expression of political intent and power, is the framework within which the other strategies of health promotion can operate; without health-promoting public policy, the rest fails. But the definition of healthy public policy is that it is ". . . characterised by an explicit concern for health and equity in all areas of policy and by an accountability for health impact" (World Health

Organization, 1988), and that accountability implies democracy; or, as Draper and Harrison (1991) put it, "healthy public policy is impossible without healthy democracy," another clear expression of the link between health promotion, politics, and power. To the extent that we are able to achieve the two aims of empowering people and communities and establishing health as a vital part of the political agenda, we can be said to be winning some battles, if not the war. To the extent that we fail in those regards, we cannot be said even to be winning the battles.

But before turning to a discussion of our successes and failures in these battles, I want to examine the issue of politics and power in health promotion, an examination prompted by a recent critique of health promotion. I also wish to discuss the links between health promotion and the approach to politics and power that lies at the heart of Green political philosophy.

Politics, Power, and Naiveté: Critique and Response

Enabling people to increase control over their health, and over the events and conditions that determine their health, is a process of political empowerment. Health promotion says that people should have more power — "people power" — and if that is not a political statement, I don't know what is! So at its heart, at its very roots, health promotion is about politics and power, and about the sort of social reform that motivated Virchow and his colleagues 150 years ago. The need for health promotion — the "new" public health — to retain those links to social reform (and his fear that the links had been forgotten) was addressed by Halfdan Mahler, then Director-General of WHO, at the Second International Conference on Health Promotion in Adelaide:

> Many of the early public health pioneers were also social reformers, pioneers in the organisation of labour, education, housing and sanitation. Much of this link has been lost in public health development. Social medicine and social policy have taken separate roads. Recent textbooks on public health or epidemiology frighten me by showing how much public health has lost its original link to social justice, social change and social reform. . . (Mahler, 1988).

But although I may assert — and I do — that health promotion is ultimately concerned with politics and power, there are critics who suggest, not without some reason, that we in the health promotion field are naive and that we do not even understand the issues of politics and power. In their critique of health promotion research (and more broadly of health promotion), Stevenson and Burke (1991), for example, argue that health promotion is restricted in its potential owing to its origins in the bureaucracy, its relationship with "new social movements like the peace movement, the environmental movement and the women's movement" and its inadequate understanding of politics and power. As they see it: "To state the matter baldly, the movement for health promotion is not a social movement but a bureaucratic tendency; not a movement against the state but one within it. . . ."

Thus they argue that even compared to other new social movements, health promotion is depoliticized. Even worse, "[T]his depoliticisation. . . compounds a deficiency in the conceptualisation of politics that is common to the discourse of all new social movements. . . including. . . a superficial understanding of the social meaning of power."

Stevenson and Burke criticize health promotion's emphasis on community empowerment, which they see as too "soft and vague":

> Gaining power in any meaningful sense of the term "power" will involve the "community" in economic, political, and ideological struggle with the state, capital, the medical profession, and alternatively defined communities. The health promotion literature lacks a clear conception of these obstacles to empowerment and largely ignores the politics of competition and struggle.

Once one overcomes one's irritation with the patronizing tone of this article and the apparent assumption that no one in the health promotion field had given these matters any serious consideration, one is left with the uncomfortable feeling that the criticism, while perhaps unduly harsh, is not without foundation. Indeed, authors from within the health promotion field have made similar points (see, for example, Baum, 1990; Farrant & Taft, 1988; Labonté, 1989; Watt & Rodmell, 1987) and, with others, raise important challenges to health promotion and concerns about our ability to deliver on what is, after all, a very ambitious agenda.

But in the final analysis, I believe that contrary to the views of Stevenson and Burke, we have indeed been undertaking some important economic, political, and ideological struggles, not least within the professional and bureaucratic systems, as I describe later. And while I take seriously the charge that we have not yet become a truly popular social movement, but remain mainly within the state (even the Healthy Communities movement, arguably the closest we have come to crafting a truly popular social movement, is still heavily based in the bureaucracy and the professions), I am mindful of the fact that among the fourteen transformational roles identified by James Robertson (1978) is not only the role of "liberators," who work outside the system to take power away from the system, but also the role of "decolonizers," who work from within the system to give power away. So while the current position of health promotion within the system makes it difficult to raise the political nature of our work (precisely, I hear our critics cry) it does not prevent us from seeking to give power away or to catalyze a true social movement for health which is sadly lacking, but which should take its rightful place alongside the other great social movements of our age. Finally, let us not forget that advocating for empowerment and democracy, for community involvement and greater social equity, can still get you into a great deal of trouble, even killed, in some parts of the world.

Health Promotion, Green Politics, and Power

I have argued elsewhere that health promotion is perhaps best understood as an expression of Green political philosophy in the health field, just as in the nineteenth century public health was an expression of the reform agenda of Socialist political philosophy (Hancock, 1989a). It is no coincidence that Stevenson and Burke see health promotion as allied with the peace, environmental, and women's movements, for these are the pillars of the

Green movement and its political expression, the Green parties, that have emerged everywhere in the past twenty years (Capra & Spretnak, 1984; Porritt, 1984). Yet as I have also argued, to tie health promotion to a particular political philosophy may be to reduce its potential effectiveness by politicizing it. Thus I believe that ultimately Stevenson and Burke's critique, while valuable, is mistaken because it is based in an "old paradigm" view of politics and power: they miss the main point of these new social movements, which is that they are about a different sort of politics and a different sort of power. As Kickbusch (1992) has noted, ". . . the new risks and the new social perceptions of risk have led to new ways of perceiving and *doing* politics and policy."

Green politics is not simply about the environment, although its proponents seek to portray it as such. Rather, it is about a new way of ordering our relationship with the earth, with other species, and with each other. The fundamental values of Green politics are based on respect: respect for the earth and for the finite limits of local, regional, and global ecosystems; respect for all the plants and animals that make up the web of life of which we are but one small part; and respect for human beings in our own communities and elsewhere in the world. Green politics embraces the political concerns of the environmental, peace, and women's movements and takes from them a new approach to power, one that seeks consensus, that emphasizes true participatory democracy and a sharing of power, much as was summarized in the mid-term review of the European Healthy Cities Project (Tsouros, 1990, p. 19):

> In this new approach, power has to be wielded by influence more than authori-
> ty and health advocates have to learn to share power with people rather than
> wield power over people; this means giving fewer directives and participating
> more in negotiations. It also means that, although a structure to facilitate the
> process is important, the process needs more attention and the structure less.
> The structures that are implemented should be more collegial and less hierar-
> chical. . . should enhance collaboration rather than competition, analyse issues
> holistically rather than sectorally and use both/and rather than either/or
> approaches. . . . As much as anything, the Healthy Cities project intends to
> change the organisational culture of cities and some basic social values.

And what is true of the Healthy Cities project (itself an application of the Green maxim of thinking globally and acting locally) is true of health promotion as a whole. It is, or should be, a fundamental challenge to the established order, the established way of doing things. It is a new way of "doing" politics and policy, a new way of sharing power more equitably — an approach wholly consistent with the social movements that lie at the heart of the Green political philosophy.

The Battle to Establish Health Promotion

For health promotion to become a reality, we need first to establish it as an idea, as an ideology with its own set of values and principles. Next, we need to establish a health promotion agenda and finally to establish health promotion programs. In the sections that follow, I will discuss the extent to which I believe we are winning the battle, which I take to be the battle to establish a health promotion ideology, agenda, and program; I will then discuss the extent to which I think we are succeeding in winning the war, which I take to be the extent to which we are making progress in achieving health for all — because ultimately health promotion is a means of improving the health and well-being of the population as a whole, both nationally and, in the final analysis, globally.

A Health Promotion Ideology

In terms of an ideology, health promotion has had to establish itself as distinct from health education, disease prevention, and health care; this, to a fair extent, it has achieved.

As distinct from health education. The Lalonde Report (Lalonde, 1974) led at first to a focus upon lifestyle rather than environment, and to health education programs intended to create behavioural change. But already by 1981, at the First Canadian Conference on Health Promotion, Labonté and Penfold (1981) were making the case that health promotion, if it was to be effective, had to focus on the socio-environmental conditions that established the context for poor health, using socio-political rather than educational strategies. By 1986, with the Ottawa Charter and *Achieving Health for All: A Framework for Health Promotion* (Epp, 1986; hereafter, the Framework), it was clear that health promotion was much more than health education; indeed, health education barely figures in those documents. Rather, health education is seen as but one of many strategies, relating in particular to the strategy of developing personal skills, for achieving change within a health promotion framework.

At the international level, this differentiation of health promotion from health education has been slower, perhaps in part because of the influence of the American health education establishment, acting through the International Union for Health Education, in equating health promotion, American style, with health education. Until recently in the United States, health promotion has focussed primarily upon lifestyle approaches intended to bring about behavioural change in individuals, with little or no attention paid to the socio-environmental context (but see Green, in this book, for a response to this view). However, at the international level, the World Health Organization recognized in 1990 the relevance of the health promotion approach to achieving health for all globally, and this strategy was cemented at the 1991 Sundsvall Conference, which was described as the first global conference on health promotion (World Health Organization, 1991a, 1991b).

As distinct from disease prevention. The second ideological differentiation has been to distinguish health promotion from disease prevention. These two concepts are often lumped together (as in the U.S. Office of Health Promotion and Disease Prevention) and in fact are sometimes confused with each other, occasionally leading people to talk about "health prevention," which is, of course, the business of the tobacco industry! The differentiation of health promotion from disease prevention is important because many in the medical system who are involved in disease prevention (particularly family physicians and to some extent specialists and hospitals) see little or no distinction between their disease prevention activities and health promotion, and thus think they have been doing health promotion for a long time. There are, however, vitally important differences between health promotion and disease prevention, and there are arguments to be made that the role of physicians — and in particular the role of hospitals — in health promotion should be limited and confined primarily to disease prevention (Hancock, 1989b).

Perhaps the most important difference is to be found in the distinction between disease and health. Disease prevention is based on the medical model, and focusses upon disease: it is "anti-pathogenic." As such, its success can be measured in terms of reductions in disease, disability, and death. Health promotion, on the other hand, is based on a health model: it is "salutogenic" (Antonovsky, 1978). Its success is to be seen in terms of enhanced health, well-being, quality of life, sense of self-esteem and self-worth, control over resources for health, etc. These are not the same; it is entirely possible to prevent death and yet increase poor health (adding years to life without adding health to years); conversely, it is entirely possible to be healthy while dying, in as much as there are healthy ways of dying — in a warm, loving, home-like environment and free of pain — just as there are unhealthy ways of dying — in pain and in an isolated and alienating hospital setting.

Health promotion differs from disease prevention in a number of other important respects: it focusses upon the health of populations rather than individuals, it looks for a pattern of interaction rather than causal links, and it develops interventions aimed at the common life situations of certain groups rather than interventions aimed at specific diseases (Kickbusch, 1986).

In these terms, health promotion is ideologically fairly well differentiated from disease prevention. However, it is not necessarily more attractive. That is because the outcome measures of health promotion are more difficult to measure and also because disease prevention fits more securely within the still-dominant medical paradigm than does health promotion. There is thus a tendency to fall back upon disease prevention measures rather than health promotion measures, a tendency that also strengthens the health education ideology.

As distinct from health care. The third ideological differentiation is between health promotion and health care. On the face of it, this is a comparatively simple differentiation, easily established by being more explicit and referring to our "health" care system more exactly as a sick-care system — a system that cares for sick people. That is what the system of health (more correctly, medical care) insurance was established for. The problem that arises, however, is that it has been difficult to establish in the public mind — and even more difficult to establish in the political mind and on the political agenda — that more medical care does not equal better health. Intuitively, people understand that, but when it comes to discussing the reallocation of funds from medical care to health or to defining the responsibilities of the Ministry of "Health" as the management of the sick-care system, it has not been easy. In fact, as Proctor (1991) puts it, there has been a "bitter debate over health policy."[1]

If we suggest, for example, that we should take money away from hospitals and doctors and put it into better housing, improved public transportation, environmental protection, or social assistance, then we have a fight on our hands. The medical model and the medical and hospital establishments are very powerful and it is not easy to shift priorities or reallocate resources, as Proctor points out:

> In the health debate, those seeking to defend and expand the dominant paradigm are well organised and established in the professions, education, research and the institutions of the health care system. They have access to the media and the government. Those attempting to develop a new paradigm have not organised themselves into a force with similar access. Nor have they the same numbers and influence. . . . there is a struggle for power and control, to define the meaningful questions, interventions, methods and theory which will dominate our understanding of health and illness.

This is not to suggest that we have failed in our attempt to establish the health promotion ideology as distinct from the health/sick-care ideology. Politically, the ideology has been accepted for some years, both nationally — where the Deputy Ministers of Health convened a national symposium on health promotion and disease prevention as one of three priority areas in 1989 — and provincially, as seen throughout this book. In Ontario, for example, the Spasoff report on health goals (Spasoff, 1987) and the Evans report that led to the establishment of the Premier's Council on Health Strategy (Evans, 1987) opened the door to a health promotion policy. The result has been the adoption by the Ontario government and by the Ministry of Health of a vision of health, a set of health goals and a health policy framework all of which clearly distinguish between health promotion and health care (Premier's Council on Health Strategy, 1989; Ministry of Health, 1991). At least at the policy level, there is thus a recognition of a distinction between health promotion, which is seen as a government-wide issue, and health care, which is seen as the responsibility of the Ministry of Health.

Recently, Québec has gone even further down this road in its health and welfare policies, declaring that reducing health inequalities and poverty are priority policy objectives (MSSS, 1992). The policy goes "beyond the simple question of health and social services" in describing strategies to improve public health and welfare that "apply not only to the service system, but to all of society." Québec continues to be concerned with "the persistence of sharp inequalities in the area of health and welfare between the

---

[1] Given her position as a senior policy advisor in the Ontario government's Cabinet Office, dealing with the Social Policy Committee of Cabinet, Proctor's views are of particular importance.

sexes, social and occupational classes and communities." As in Ontario and elsewhere, greater recognition is paid to the importance of socio-economic factors and the social environment in influencing health.

From a focus on ideology then, where we have been generally successful, let us turn now to an examination of the extent to which we have been able to implement a health promotion agenda and programs.

A Health Promotion Agenda and Programs

A convenient framework for examining health promotion programs is the *Ottawa Charter for Health Promotion,* with its five strategies for health promotion, namely, building healthy public policy, creating supportive environments for health, strengthening community action, developing personal skills, and reorienting health services. To this can be added as subcomponents three elements from the Epp Framework (reducing inequity, developing mutual support and enhancing coping skills) and two elements of the presentation I gave at the National Symposium on Health Promotion and Disease Prevention in Victoria (Hancock, 1989b), namely, support for health promotion research and the creation of structures for health promotion. This gives us a ten-point agenda for health promotion (see Table 1), and for each point on the agenda we can determine whether a program or series of programs and related activities exists.

In the sections that follow, I will briefly — and from a purely personal point of view — review the extent to which we have achieved success in developing programs and activities in several of these agenda items at the national, provincial, and local levels. However, space does not permit a comprehensive review of all ten agenda items (which have in any case been the topic of this book), and my view is of necessity biassed toward my Toronto and Ontario-based experience, although it incorporates knowledge I have acquired at various occasions in the last few years across the country. Specifically, I shall address the topics of building healthy public policy, reducing inequities, creating supportive environments, strengthening communities, reorienting health services, supporting research, and establishing new structures.

Table 1	An agenda for health promotion.
• Build healthy public policy	• Develop personal skills
• Reduce inequity	• Enhance coping skills
• Create supportive environments	• Reorient health services
• Strengthen community action	• Support research
• Develop mutual support	• Establish new structures

Build Healthy Public Policy

In terms of developing healthy public policy, there has been no progress whatsoever at the national level, nor has there been any indication of any particular interest or willingness to take action. No real work has been done to follow up on the review of healthy public policy commissioned by Health and Welfare Canada (Pederson et al., 1988), nor was any follow-up action taken as a result of the report of the Canadian participants at the Second International Conference on Health Promotion in Adelaide in 1988, which suggested a number of specific measures including research, coalition building, and dissemination of information. This is clearly the result of an indifferent or hostile Conservative government, making the point that while rhetoric can be useful, it requires political will and action to make change.

Provincially, perhaps the most significant development in healthy public policy has been the establishment of the Premier's Council on Health Strategy in Ontario in 1987 and its identification of three strategic policy areas for development of healthy public policy: healthy child development policy, environmental policy, and adult adjustment and labour market policy — whatever the latter may mean. However, the process slowed to a crawl with the change of government in 1990 and although the Council was retained (with the new title of the Premier's Council on Health, Wellbeing and Social Justice and with an expanded membership), there is as yet no evidence that a mechanism or process for the establishment of healthy public policy has been put in place. What is needed is a government commitment — mandated through the Cabinet Office and its policy committees — with an interministerial working group (preferably at the Deputy Minister level, with technical support from the relevant ministries) actually to develop and implement healthy public policy (Hancock, 1992a).

The Manitoba Healthy Public Policy Committee, which is organized at the Deputy Minister level, appears to hold out more promise, though again, the commitment beyond rhetoric is uncertain. Thus, the recent strategic direction outlined in the document *Quality Health for Manitobans* (Manitoba Health, 1992a) states that the first foundation for restructuring the system is "developing a broad government focus on healthy public policy" that "focusses on the underlying causes of good or bad health": "In simple terms, this commitment means that *every major action and policy of government will be evaluated in terms of its implications for the health of Manitobans*" (emphasis in original).

In the Manitoba scheme, the Human Services Committee of Cabinet is responsible for healthy public policy, while the Deputy Minister's Steering Committee of Healthy Public Policy, chaired by the Deputy Minister of Health, is the vehicle for implementation (Manitoba Health, 1992b). Only time will tell how effective this approach will be, but at least healthy public policy appears to have a supportive structure within the Manitoba government.

The recent change in government in British Columbia may also prove to be one that is supportive of healthy public policy. The report of the Royal Commission on Health Care and Costs (1991) recommended the establishment of a Provincial Health Council that would be completely independent of government, the Ministry of Health, and the health care industry, and would report to the Legislative Assembly. The Commission also recommended establishing a set of measurable indicators with which to plan and evaluate public policies for health; evaluating the possible health effects of all proposed provincial programs or legislation; including studies of potential health effects in all environmental impact assessments; and increasing support for the Healthy Communities movement.

In addition, the B.C. government is establishing a Policy Co-ordination Office as part of the Cabinet Office, the intent being to link policy across ministries; this could obviously be important for the development of healthy public policy. As a recent Ministry of Health report on examples and outcomes of healthy public policy notes, ". . . thinking about policy in terms of health is a natural and obvious way to improve our lives. Very often, 'healthy public policy' is simply a matter of common sense" (British Columbia Ministry of Health/SPARC, 1991b; see also British Columbia Ministry of Health/SPARC, 1991a).

In Québec, a new provincial policy for health and welfare sets objectives for 19 policies in five areas (social adaptation, physical health, public health, mental health, social integration) and defines six strategies: promote a reinforcement of human potential; support the individual's surroundings and develop healthy, safe environments; improve living conditions; act for and with vulnerable groups; co-ordinate public policies and action to promote health and welfare; and orient the health and social services system toward finding the most effective and least expensive solutions (MSSS, 1992). The co-ordination of public policies is focussed on five priorities: reinforcing the home; strengthening the school environment; developing and reinforcing social networks; providing access to jobs; and reducing poverty. It is acknowledged that "these priorities cannot be dealt with on a sectoral basis" and that the government must "co-ordinate public policies for implementing intersectoral action plans [and]. . . rely on local and regional dynamics by supporting the development of initiatives to promote health and welfare at the municipal level. . . . "

At the local level, there has been considerable interest in healthy public policy in many parts of Canada. Healthy Communities projects across the country — and especially in Québec and B.C., where there has been provincial government support — have encouraged the development and implementation of healthy public policy by local governments, and we are beginning to see evidence of practical, hands-on experience.

For example, a report on the Québec project (Lacombe & Poirier, 1992) notes that the Québec network — Villes et Villages en santé — which was created in November, 1987, has grown "to more than 600 members. . . from more than 300 different organizations, including over 150 municipalities, 78 CLSCs and 32 DSCs." A formal association was established in May, 1990. The association is controlled by those municipalities which have officially adopted a Healthy Communities project; by the end of 1991, 70 municipalities comprising some 40 percent of Québec's population were members.

While local projects often begin by undertaking small-scale community activities, the report notes that "after experiencing such small co-operative projects, municipal officials start questioning their own decision making and practices"; thus municipal governments "become not only important partners but most legitimate facilitators of local intersectoral co-operation for health as well as potentially powerful advocates for the development of healthy public policies by higher governments." An addendum to the report gives examples of activities underway in communities ranging in size from 700 to one million people. These municipalities are addressing a variety of issues, including: the use and disposal of toxic home products; youth drug abuse, vandalism, and crime; home or motor vehicle accidents; urban green areas or other city planning issues; well-being of the elderly; family policies; physical activities and environmental programs.

The experience in British Columbia has been similar, though the approach is somewhat different. Unlike the Québec model, which emphasizes a network, an association, and a central information and resource centre, the B.C. Healthy Communities initiative provided grants to communities at a level of funding between $2000 and $30 000. A review of the project in the form of a *Yearbook* (British Columbia Ministry of Health, 1992) reveals that there are 91 communities in the B.C. project and that 38 communities received grants and implemented initiatives during 1991. All the participating local governments passed resolutions endorsing the adoption of Healthy Communities principles and the majority of the projects were able to establish a multisectoral approach to health, involving more than three sectors on their Steering Committees. The principles they integrated included developing new partnerships for health, using community skills for problem solving, resident participation (over 45 000 people were involved in the Healthy Communities process in 1991), developing new leaders, involving local government, stimulating community planning, developing healthy public policy and fostering community pride. The report also notes that

> Communities will become more adept at identifying government policies and actions that act as barriers. Government ministries need to reflect 'healthy community' principles and philosophies and, in fact, this is already happening with ministries linking to forge consistent and responsive approaches to communities.

In short, healthy public policy is non-existent at the federal level, developing slowly at the provincial level, and seemingly developing swiftly at the local level. This has obvious implications for our strategy for health promotion and serves to reinforce the importance of the slogan "think globally, act locally."

Reduce Inequity

Here lies the rub. If health promotion is to succeed, current inequalities in health — and inequities in access to basic prerequisites to health — must be reduced. But there has been little or no action at any level. Federal government policies have increased economic inequities in the last decade, and no significant policy initiatives have been developed to address inequalities in health. Similarly, there has been little or no action at the provincial level. Indeed in Ontario, where the Spasoff Committee proposed as a first health goal the reduction in inequities in health opportunities in Ontario (Spasoff,

1987), this goal was deliberately excluded from the health goals adopted by the Liberal Government in 1989, and was not reinstated by the NDP Government when they came to power in 1990, in spite of the fact that the Premier's Council on Health Strategy was renamed the Premier's Council on Health, Well-being and Social Justice!

Given the lack of federal and provincial initiatives, it has been difficult for local communities to address the reduction of inequities in health opportunities or to reduce inequalities in health, though some health departments, notably the City of Toronto's, have drawn attention to the issue for years and have tried in a number of small ways to address the issue. But significant reductions in inequalities in health depend on a change in such societal determinants of health as economic and social welfare policies, which in turn depend on a significant shift in our values, in what we believe society is all about and what our strategic priorities are as a society. A recent report from the (Ontario) Premier's Council on Economic Renewal (1993) proposes a new approach to the determination of strategic societal priorities that involves an integration of economic, social/health and environmental policy making through a process of "co-determination" involving government, business, labour, and other key social sectors. Until we make the sort of changes in our structures and processes that this report calls for, until we "reinvent government" (Osborne & Gaebler, 1991), we will make little progress in developing healthy public policy and reducing inequalities in health.

Create Supportive Environments

In discussing this topic, which is vast, I will confine myself to the physical environment, and in particular to two related aspects of the links between the physical environment and health, namely, ecosystem health and land use planning.

In terms of creating supportive physical environments for health, progress at the national level has again been disappointing. The Health Promotion Directorate of Health and Welfare Canada organized a 1989 conference on the links between health, environment, and economy (Hancock, 1989c) and has been interested in exploring the links between health for all and sustainable development. However, apart from commissioning a review of the literature (Small, 1988) and preparing the briefing book on supportive educational environments for the Third International Conference on Health Promotion in Sundsvall (Wilson et al., 1991), the Directorate seems to have done little else to pursue the issue of supportive environments for health. Instead, the Health Protection Branch has been responsible for preparing the report and action plan on Health and Environment as part of Canada's Green Plan (Health & Welfare Canada, 1992), in the process conspicuously ignoring issues of environmental inequity, despite linking issues of health and environment to the Canadian Healthy Communities Project.[2]

One relatively bright light has been the Health Protection Branch's Great Lakes Health Effects Program, which is a serious effort to address the issues of ecosystem health and ecotoxicity in the Great Lakes basin and to recognize the psychological and social dimensions of the health threats posed by ecosystem contamination, an approach that is more consistent with the health promotion approach to environmental health than the traditional health protection approach. (For a critique of this approach and a description of a health promotion approach to health and the environment, see Hancock, 1992b).

At the provincial level, there is also little evidence of a willingness to support the creation of physical environments supportive of health. For example, environmental health continues to be an area of disputed jurisdiction between the Ministries of Environment, Labour, and Health, and is in any case under-resourced in all those areas, at least in Ontario. Alberta, on the other hand, has been making some serious efforts to strengthen environmental health, while there is a strong network of DSCs (Département de Santé Communautaire) involved in this topic in Québec. However, there is no evidence that any serious, comprehensive effort is underway to address such issues as the creation of healthy homes and housing, healthy schools, healthy workplaces, healthy hospitals[3], or even, at the provincial level, to support healthy communities through modifying provincial planning acts and the municipal planning process to take greater account of health, although to be fair it may still be too early in the process for that to happen.

One promising development is the recent report from the Ontario Premier's Council on Health, Well-being and Social Justice (1993) on "Our Environment, Our Health," which lays out a set of health goals under the headings of healthy ecosystems, healthy communities, and healthy workplaces. The goals are laudably broad and ambitious, addressing such issues as energy production, agricultural practices, urban planning and design, and workplace organization. In the area of urban planning, the report supports many of the characteristics of a healthy community that have emerged from the Healthy Cities/Communities movement's calls for a greater integration of social and land use planning. This latter point has also been taken up and expanded upon by reports from the (Crombie) Royal Commission on the Future of the Toronto Waterfront (1992) and the province's Office for the Greater Toronto Area (1992), both of which urge an integration of environmental, social,

---

[2] In fairness, it must be pointed out that the Health Promotion Branch, through its support of the Canadian Healthy Communities Project and in particular, through its linkage via that project to the Canadian Institute of Planners, has helped with respect to some aspects of creating supportive physical environments for health, at least in the sense of urban planning; however, that support was severely curtailed for short-sighted political reasons when support for the project was not renewed in 1991.

[3] If any facility in the community should be environmentally friendly, one would think it would be the hospital. But it seems that hospitals seldom are. Instead, the environmentally unfriendly design and operation of hospitals (they are often sealed buildings, use a lot of energy, water, toxic materials, and disposables, and some are even exempt from air pollution control regulations!) is a major scandal, and one that Ministries of Health and hospital boards have shown little concern over. Recently, in a more positive development, a group of mainly middle-level managers in and around Toronto has established the Health Care Environment Network.

economic, and land use planning and support the Healthy Communities concept. Also in Ontario, a provincial commission headed by John Sewell, a former Mayor of Toronto, is currently reviewing the Planning Act and does appear to tend to include a broader range of social and health concerns in the planning process.

But again, it is at the local level where the links between health and supportive environments, particularly physical environments, have been most clearly established and where the most active efforts are underway. In communities across the country, people are creating strong links between healthy community and sustainable community concepts, and often these are seen as simply two sides of the same coin, one concerned with human well-being, the other with environmental well-being. In British Columbia, for example, the University of British Columbia has established a Task Force on Healthy and Sustainable Communities (housed, interestingly enough, in the Department of Family Medicine) which, in addition to developing a series of background papers, is supporting a pilot project in the City of Richmond to apply the ideas. In Alberta, the Alberta Environment Council was an early supporter of the Healthy Communities approach. In Manitoba, Ontario, and Québec, many of the Healthy Communities projects are addressing the relationship between health and the environment. For example, Sudbury has now held three "Healthy People/Healthy Places" conferences to address the links between health, environment, and economy, while Rouyn-Noranda — the first community in Canada to formally declare itself a Healthy Community — has from the start seen the environmental problems it faces (due, like Sudbury, to metal mining and smelting) to be central to its Healthy Communities project.

In Ontario, municipal Round Tables on Environment and Economy and Healthy Communities projects are working closely together in a number of communities. The idea is even spreading to the development industry, with at least one developer — the Daniels Group — proposing to build a "Healthy Village" in Brampton which will incorporate many of the design characteristics of a Healthy Community. And at least one municipality — the Regional Municipality of Halton to the west of Toronto — has two main sections in its draft revised Official Plan, one devoted to land stewardship and one devoted to Healthy Communities, complete with proposed goals and policies covering environmental quality (air, water, land, waste management), human services (basic material support, public safety, learning services, social support services, involvement in decision making, cultural and recreational services, heritage services, health services), economic development, transportation and energy (Regional Municipality of Halton, 1993) — the shape of things to come?

Clearly, we are succeeding at the local level — and to some extent, at the provincial level — in our efforts to put health on the agenda of land use planners and local governments and to change the way in which we plan, design, and build the physical and social infrastructure of our communities.

Strengthen Community Action

In the area of strengthening community action, the national perspective has been quite encouraging. From its early days, the Health Promotion Directorate has believed strongly in providing resources and support to community groups through its Health Promotion Contributions Program, and has been a strong supporter of the strengthening of community resources, capacity and action. The Directorate also funded both the Healthy Communities Project and the Strengthening Community Health Project, both of which emphasized the strengthening of community action. Similarly, as noted in many chapters in this book, most provinces have been strong supporters of the strengthening of community action, with community development approaches to health promotion being an important facet of provincial programs. Not surprisingly, given such supportive national and provincial environments, community action at the local level has generally been strengthened.

There are, however, a couple of caveats. The first is that often these projects are just that — time-limited projects — and when they've run out, the community capacity that has been created may wither. There is a danger that these projects will create dependence on national and provincial governments and build up expectations that are later crushed when funding is withdrawn. At the same time, these community activities often cannot get off the ground and cannot be sustained without an infusion of outside support, especially since these projects are often in communities that lack resources and capacity in the first place. More attention must be given to ensuring that good projects continue to receive support, which might mean reallocating resources from other programs that are not as effective.

The second caveat is that the relative lack of action at the national and provincial levels in terms of healthy public policy and the creation of supportive environments might lead a cynic to believe that national and provincial governments are only too keen to encourage communities to take responsibility and action for health promotion, but are not too keen when it comes to their own areas of jurisdiction and authority!

Reorient Health Services

When it comes to reorienting health services, there has been little or no action at the national level. Admittedly, the federal government does not have jurisdiction over health care services, but it missed a golden opportunity in the early 1980s, with the passage by the Liberal government of the Canada Health Act, to address the medical monopoly and the over-emphasis on hospitalization. Since then, the (Conservative) federal government has shown little or no interest in reorienting health services, other than a wish to duck out of its financial responsibilities for medicare as quickly as possible.

At the provincial level, there were numerous Royal Commissions on the reorientation of health services during the 1980s and early 1990s (e.g., the Royal Commission on Health Care and Costs [B.C.], 1991; Premier's Commission on Future Health Care for Albertans, 1989; Saskatchewan

Commission on Directions in Health Care, 1990; Ontario Health Review Panel, 1987; Commission d'enquête sur les services de santé et les services sociaux, 1987; Nova Scotia Royal Commission on Health Care, 1989), and all of them came to essentially the same conclusions:

- Shift the priority to health promotion and disease prevention;
- Shift resources from institutions to communities;
- Develop a more managed, co-ordinated, or even integrated system;
- Decentralize and regionalize the system;
- Encourage alternative payment systems and the use of non-physician practitioners;
- Increase public accountability and involvement; and
- Do efficiently what is known to work.

In practice, however, there has been little progress towards achieving these goals. Most Ministries of Health (sic) have preferred to continue business as usual, ignoring the crisis until it overwhelms them. There have been some important pilot projects, such as the Victoria Health Project (Iles, 1991), but until very recently no province has made any serious, comprehensive effort to reorganize the health care system. However, there are now promising developments in a number of provinces, most notably British Columbia, Saskatchewan, Québec, New Brunswick, and Newfoundland, all of which have recently begun to decentralize and regionalize their health care systems.

At the local level, there is little role for local governments in health care services, but a number of local health planning bodies and local groupings of health care service deliverers have taken interesting and exciting initiatives, and some hospitals in particular are showing greater interest in a "bottom-down" approach to health planning (Hancock, 1993a) — as is the Canadian Hospital Association itself (Canadian Hospital Association, 1993) — and in their role in creating healthier communities (Hancock, 1993b, 1993c).

Support Research

In terms of research, the federal Health Promotion Directorate, in conjunction with the National Health Research and Development Program (NHRDP), has supported the development of a health promotion research and knowledge development program and with both NHRDP and the Social Science and Humanities Research Council (SSHRC) has supported the establishment of Centres for Health Promotion Research. However, there has been little success in shifting the NHRDP granting criteria to take more account of health promotion approaches such as participatory and qualitative research, and little evidence that there has been any significant shift from the bloated biomedical research funding of the Medical Research Council to the sparsely funded public health and health promotion research budget of NHRDP.

Provincially, there has been little or no support for health promotion research, though the Ontario Premier's Council's Innovations Fund did support some semi-innovative programs; however, much of what was supported was not innovative, and true innovation proved to be beyond the capacity of the innovations program to support! At the local level, there has been a growing interest in community-based research involving participatory techniques, subjective information, and qualitative methodologies, and the community seems to be leading academic researchers in this respect. Indeed, it appears that there is a growing gulf between many of the academic researchers and their community-based colleagues and the communities they serve, if some of the anecdotal feedback from the Second National Conference on Health Promotion Research is anything to go by. One answer, it seems to me, is to adopt the strategy of a recent Kellogg Foundation program: give the research funds to the communities and let them hire researchers from competing universities based on their abilities to meet the communities' self-defined research needs.

Develop New Structures

Finally, in terms of structures for health promotion, at the federal level there has been no structure or mechanism established to support healthy public policy, while the recent reorganization of Health and Welfare Canada appears to have significantly weakened the Health Promotion Directorate. At the provincial level, there are Premiers' Councils or their equivalents in several provinces now, and most provinces have a health promotion branch within the Ministry of Health or its equivalent. However, health promotion continues to be a small part within a large ministry devoted primarily to sick-care services; the elevation of health promotion to higher prominence and status within the Ministry and/or the creation of an entirely separate ministry for health, environment, and well-being (or some such combination) has yet to be seriously addressed in most provinces. At the local level, the Healthy Communities movement in particular has led to the establishment of a variety of formal and informal structures that support health promotion both within local government and across communities as a whole.

Summing Up

One would have to conclude that while the initial leadership and support of the federal government was very important in establishing health promotion as a concept and in supporting health promotion programs at the community level, the federal commitment to health promotion is now drastically diminishing. There is and has been no commitment from the Conservative government to health promotion since Jake Epp was Minister of Health and Welfare, and no evidence that they are willing to develop the policies, mechanisms, or structures that will ensure that healthy public policy is developed, that supportive environments for health are created, that the health care system in Canada is reoriented, that inequities in health opportunities and inequalities in health are reduced, or that adequate research support is provided to health promotion. In short, the federal government, having shown great leadership from the mid-1970s to the mid-1980s, is now fading from the health promotion scene.

At the provincial level, the picture is somewhat happier. The development of Premiers' Councils and other mechanisms to explore healthy public policy, together with the establishment of health promotion branches, indicates that the shift from federal to provincial responsibility for health promotion is underway. The extent to which this shift will be real rather than rhetorical is yet to be determined, but so far there has been little evidence that the provinces are seriously prepared actually to develop and implement healthy public policy, place more emphasis on the creation of supportive environments for health, comprehensively and effectively reorient their health care services, address inequities in health opportunities, and reduce inequalities in health or provide adequate research funding for health promotion. However, several provinces, notably Québec and B.C. (and soon, it is to be hoped, Ontario), have made important contributions by establishing provincial Healthy Communities initiatives.

It is at the local level where we see perhaps the best hopes for health promotion, and in fact the best implementation of health promotion. Through the Healthy Communities projects (supported, it must be acknowledged, by the federal and some provincial governments) there have been numerous exciting initiatives in the development of healthy public policy, the creation of supportive environments for health, the strengthening of community action, and mutual support and the development of personal skills, including coping skills. However, the development of Healthy Communities projects is still to be found only in a minority of municipalities, and in some of those the true understanding of, and commitment to, the concepts and principles of health promotion and of healthy communities is rather minimal. Moreover, local municipalities and communities may lack the jurisdiction and power to address some of the fundamental determinants of health that will reduce health inequalities; they are dependant upon national and provincial leadership in the development of healthy public policy and of policies for the creation of supportive environments for health (Hancock, 1990). But nonetheless, local action holds out the greatest promise for the further development of health promotion in Canada, and hopefully this can lead to pressure on provincial governments to be more supportive of health promotion; it seems unlikely that there will be any progress at the federal level while the present (Conservative) government remains in power.

Losing the War?

As must be apparent from the previous sections, while we have been reasonably successful in establishing a health promotion ideology and agenda, and somewhat successful in establishing health promotion programs, particularly at the local level, the prospects of developing healthy public policy at the federal and provincial levels, and thus establishing a framework for the other elements of health promotion, appear somewhat bleak. If we look at the global scene, moreover, the situation appears even more bleak. Globally, while there was much talk at the 1992 Earth Summit in Rio de Janeiro, significant progress toward sustainable development was stalled by the power of American multinational corporations in particular, expressed through their puppet president (George Bush), while European and Japanese commitments were less than adequate. As a result, it seems that globally, economic and political inequalities will persist and indeed are likely to grow, while the depletion of resources and the damage to ecosystems will continue. Moreover, as recent events in Europe, the Persian Gulf, Africa, and to a lesser extent, Asia and Latin America have shown, war continues to be a means for settling disputes that is too frequently resorted to, and the global community is only likely to be allowed to intervene when the industrialized world's oil or other vital resources are threatened.

The recent growth in respect for human rights and democracy and thus citizen empowerment, especially in Central and Eastern Europe or in some parts of Latin America and Africa, appears to be a step in the right direction, but democracy and human rights are far from being achieved in many other parts of the world. And even where human rights and democracy are reasonably well respected, here in the Western democracies, there is little evidence of a truly empowered citizenry and indeed, little evidence that the political and business élites have any interest in seeing an empowered citizenry that would threaten their own power.

Recently, J.K. Galbraith (1992) mused on whether, having now defeated communism, our next (and more important and more difficult) task is to defeat capitalism? Certainly the greatest threat to health now comes from a consumption-oriented, growth-oriented ideology — industrialized capitalism — that accepts the necessity of inequality and that seeks control over the earth's resources, including its human resources. We are a very long way from winning that war!

To win this war against industrialized capitalism, we in the health promotion field will need to become part of the worldwide movements for peace, social justice, and environment that are the essence of the philosophy and politics of the Greens. This means that health promotion itself must become a popular movement, not just a professional movement, and must ally itself politically with the Green movement. To some extent, we have started that process through the Healthy Communities projects and the community development approach, but we still have a long way to go. Certainly our strategy, an application of the environmental maxim of thinking globally and acting locally, is the right one. But the value shift, and the power shift, that will lead us to a healthier future for all takes time, perhaps a generation or two, maybe more. As the crisis of unsustainability and inequity worsens globally and in our communities, the pressure for change may lead to more rapid change. But the key question is whether there is enough time left to win this war.

References

Ackernecht, E. (1981). *Rudolf Virchow*. New York: Arno Press.

Antonovsky, A. (1978). *Health, stress and coping*. New York: Jossey Bass.

Baum, F. (1990). The new public health: Force for change or reaction? *Health Promotion International, 5*, 145-150.

British Columbia Ministry of Health/SPARC (1991a). *A guide for communities to enact health-promoting policies*. Victoria, B.C.: Office of Health Promotion.

British Columbia Ministry of Health/SPARC (1991b). *Examples and outcomes of healthy public policy*. Victoria, B.C.: Office of Health Promotion.

British Columbia Ministry of Health (1992). *Healthy Communities 1991 Yearbook*. Victoria, B.C.: Author.

Canadian Hospital Association (1993). *An open future: A shared vision*. Ottawa: Author.

Capra, F., & Spretnak, C. (1984). *Green politics*. New York: E. P. Dutton.

Commission d'enquete sur les services de santé et les services sociaux (Rochon Commission) (1987). *Summary of the Report*. Québec: Gouvernement du Québec.

Draper, P., & Harrison, S. (1990). Prospects for healthy public policy. In P. Draper (ed.), *Health through public policy* (pp. 144-158). London: Greenpoint.

Epp, J. (1986). *Achieving health for all: A framework for health promotion*. Ottawa: Health & Welfare Canada.

Evans, J. (1987). *Toward a shared direction for health in Ontario*. Toronto: Government of Ontario.

Farrant, W. (1991). *Building healthy public policy: The healthy community movement as an entry point*. Vancouver: Social Planning & Research Council.

Farrant, W., & Taft, A. (1988). Building healthy public policy in an unhealthy political climate: A case study from Paddington and North Kensington. *Health Promotion (International), 3*, 287-292.

Frank, J.P. (1976). *A system of complete medical police: Selections from Johann Peter Frank* (ed. with an introduction by E. Lesky; trans. from 3rd rev. ed. of Vienna, 1786 by E. Vilim). Baltimore: Johns Hopkins University Press.

Galbraith, J.K. (1992). *The culture of contentment*. Boston: Houghton Mifflin.

Hancock, T. (1989a). Greening health: Health promotion, the living economy and ecological politics. In *Proceedings, Conference on Community Empowerment and Social Movements in Health Promotion.* ZiF (Centre for Interdisciplinary Studies), University of Bielefeld, Federal Republic of Germany.

Hancock, T. (1989b). Where the rubber meets the road. In *Proceedings, First National Symposium on Health Promotion.* Victoria, B.C.: Office of Health Promotion, British Columbia Ministry of Health.

Hancock, T. (1989c). *Sustaining health: Achieving health for all in a secure environment.* (Mimeo.) North York, Ontario: Faculty of Environmental Studies, York University.

Hancock, T. (1990). Developing healthy public policy at the local level. In A. Evers et al. (eds.), *Developing local healthy public policy.* Frankfurt/Boulder: Campus/Westview.

Hancock, T. (1992a). *Making public policy healthy.* Report to the Health Promotion Branch, Ontario Ministry of Health.

Hancock, T. (1992b). Promoting health environmentally. In *Supportive Environmnents for Health.* Copenhagen: WHO Europe.

Hancock, T. (1993a). *Bottom-down health planning.* Unpublished paper.

Hancock, T. (1993b). Healthy communities: The role of the Academic Health Center. In *Promoting community health.* Washington, DC: Association of Academic Health Centers.

Hancock, T. (1993c). Seeing the vision, defining your role. *Healthcare Forum Journal, 36*(3), 30-37.

Health & Welfare Canada (1992). *A vital link: Health and the environment in Canada.* Ottawa: Author.

Iles, S. (1991). *Victoria health project.* Unpublished paper prepared for Canadian health care management. Victoria, B.C.: Victoria Health Project (841 Fairfield Road, Victoria, B.C. V8V 3B6).

Kickbusch, I. (1986). Health promotion: A global perspective. *Canadian Journal of Public Health, 77,* 321-326.

Labonté, R., & Penfold, S. (1981). Canadian perspectives in health promotion: A critique. *Health Education, 19*(3), 4-9.

Labonté, R. (1989). Community empowerment: The need for political analysis. *Canadian Journal of Public Health, 80,* 87-88.

Lacombe, R., & Poirier, L. (1992). *The Québec network of Villes et Villages en santé.* Québec: Villes et Villages en santé.

Lalonde, M. (1974). *A new perspective on the health of Canadians.* Ottawa: Health & Welfare Canada.

Mahler, H. (1988). Keynote address (Second International Conference on Health Promotion). *Health Promotion (International),* 3, 133-138.

Manitoba Health (1992a). *Quality health for Manitobans: The action plan.* Winnipeg: Author.

Manitoba Health (1992b). *Terms of reference, Deputy Ministers' Steering Committee of Healthy Public Policy.* (Mimeo.) Winnipeg: Author.

Ministère de la santé et services sociaux. (1992). *Health and welfare policy: A summary.* Québec: Author.

Ministry of Health, Ontario (1992). *Strategic plan.* Toronto: Author.

Nova Scotia Royal Commission on Health Care (1989). *Towards a new strategy* (summary). Halifax: Author.

Office for the Greater Toronto Area (1991). *GTA 2021: The challenge of our future.* Toronto: Author.

Osborne, R., & Gaebler, T. (1991). *Reinventing government.* Reading, MA: Addison-Wesley.

Pederson, A.P., Edwards, R.K., Kelner, M., Marshall, V.M., & Allison, K. R. (1988). *Co-ordinating healthy public policy: An analytic literature review and bibliography.* Ottawa: Minister of Supply & Services.

Porritt, J. (1984). *Seeing green.* Oxford: Blackwell.

Premier's Commission on Future Health Care for Albertans (1989). *The rainbow report: Our vision for health* (Volume 1). Edmonton: Author.

Premier's Council on Economic Renewal (1992). *Ontario 2002* (draft report). Toronto: Author.

Premier's Council on Health Strategy (1989). *A vision of health: Health goals for Ontario.* Toronto: Author.

Premier's Council on Health Strategy (1991). *Nurturing health: A framework on the determinants of health.* Toronto: Author.

Premier's Council on Health, Well-being and Social Justice (1993). *Our environment, our health.* Toronto: Author.

Proctor, R. (1991). The bitter debate over health policy. *Policy Options,* 12(8), 3-7.

Regional Municipality of Halton (1993). *Draft revised official plan.* Oakville: Regional Planning Department.

Ringen, K. (1979). Edwin Chadwick, the market ideology and sanitary reform. *International Journal of Health Services, 9,* 107-120.

Robertson, J. (1978). *The sane alternative.* London: James Robertson.

Royal Commission on the Future of the Toronto Waterfront (1992). *Regeneration* (final report). Toronto: Author.

Royal Commission on Health Care and Costs (1991). *Closer to home.* Victoria, B.C.: Author.

Saskatchewan Commission on Directions in Health Care (1990). *Future directions for health care in Saskatchewan* (summary). Regina: Author.

Small, B. (1987). *Healthy environments for Canadians.* Ottawa: Health Promotion Directorate/NHRDP.

Spasoff, R. (1987). *Health for all Ontario.* Toronto: Ministry of Health.

Stevenson, H. M., & Burke, M. (1991). Bureaucratic logic in new social movement clothing. *Health Promotion International, 6,* 281-289.

Tsouros, A. (ed.) (1990). *The WHO Healthy Cities Project: A project becomes a movement.* Copenhagen: World Health Organization Regional Office for Europe.

Watt, A. & Rodmell, S. (1988). Community involvement in health promotion: Progress or panacea? *Health Promotion (International), 2,* 359-368.

World Health Organization (1984). *A discussion document on the concepts and principles of health promotion.* Copenhagen: Author.

World Health Organization (1986). Ottawa charter for health promotion. *Health Promotion (International), 1*(4), iii-v.

World Health Organization (1988). *The Adelaide recommendations: Healthy public policy.* Copenhagen: Author.

World Health Organization (1991a). *Health promotion in developing countries* (briefing book for Sundsvall Conference on Supportive Environments). Geneva: Author.

World Health Organization (1991b). *Report of the Sundsvall Conference on Supportive Environments.* Geneva: Author.

Wilson, D., et al. (1991). *Creating educational environments supportive of health* (briefing book to the Sundsvall Conference on Supportive Environments). Ottawa: Supply & Services Canada.

Beyond Lalonde: Two Decades of Canadian Health Promotion

Michel O'Neill, Irving Rootman, and Ann Pederson

In her Introduction to this book, Ilona Kickbusch personified health promotion on the international scene as a child who would have to be astute and tough to survive in the years to come. Having gathered the observations and thoughts of nearly two dozen contributors, the editors would have to concur. And, to extend Ilona's image, we would argue that this child will also need to be flexible, responsive, and opportunistic if she is to come to be considered a mature member of the health enterprise.

When we began this venture about three years ago, we had ideas about the prospects for health promotion in Canada and we expected to learn more through compiling this manuscript. In this final chapter, we offer some concluding remarks based on the international and the Canadian scenes. In both cases, we will first try to draw some lessons from the past and then offer some predictions about the future.

Looking back, we must accept that while this book breaks new ground, it nevertheless has limitations. Specifically, while our contributors represent a very diversified group of academics, health professionals, and policy makers, we are conscious that several significant people who could have shed additional light on the developments of Canadian health promotion, both here and abroad, have not been included. For instance, the international impact in the Francophone world has not been touched upon, and several important Canadian scholars and practitioners did not have the opportunity to express their views here. Moreover, little space has been devoted to the perspective of communities. Despite these gaps, however, we think that this book offers a broad picture of what has happened in Canada regarding health promotion over the past two decades.

Reading the chapters as a whole, we are struck that, despite numerous comments about the lack of clarity of health promotion, the writers share a "health promotion culture" of key common values and concepts. There is even what we could call a "health promotion tone" in the papers — a mix of rigorous scholarship blended with personal concern.[1] The book thus offers a dialectic between stories and analyses, both of which we think are useful and necessary to understanding and furthering health promotion. Even

---

[1] This shared culture and approach to health promotion may also have been partly responsible for the remarkably smooth process involved in preparing this manuscript. We are grateful to the contributors for their co-operative spirit and hope that they are as pleased with the final product as we are.

allowing for some bias in our selection of contributors, we believe that there is now a clear consensus on what health promotion is and on how to go about implementing it, both within Canada and abroad.

International Impact of
Canadian Health Promotion

Lessons from the Past

Geopolitically, Canada is not a significant international power, yet Canada compensates somewhat for this by promoting ideals and ideas that occasionally reach international importance. We are thinking here of such Canadian ideas as the United Nations' blue caps, put forward by former Prime Minister Lester Pearson, or the firm anti-apartheid position of former Prime Minister Brian Mulroney. In the world of international co-operation between "developed" and "developing" countries, in part because of its bilingual capacity and its lack of a colonial past beyond its own frontiers, Canada's governmental and non-governmental agencies are highly respected.

Moreover, we think that Canada has been at the core of the processes that are leading to global change in the visions of health and environmental issues, as well as in the understanding of the connections between health, economics, and ecology. Canada strongly supported the process that led to *Our Common Future* (World Commission on Environment & Development, 1987), the now famous report produced by a special U.N. commission chaired by the former Norwegian Prime Minister, Gro Harlem Bruntland. In the same manner, through the Lalonde Report, Canada was a catalyst in the international shift in thinking about health and in the ways in which health issues should be addressed.

We contend that the recent shift of the field of health education toward health promotion is largely due to an alliance between the European Regional Office of the World Health Organization (WHO), under the leadership of Ilona Kickbusch, and some key Canadian players. This alliance has been so successful that the whole field has repositioned itself. Even the mainstream International Union for Health Education has altered (in 1993) its name to the International Union for Health Promotion and Education — a change due, among other reasons, to the proposals introduced to its board by a Canadian.

Important institutions and individuals have put Canada in this leadership position. Among the institutions, the federal government, and especially the Health Promotion Directorate of Health and Welfare Canada, has clearly been central. While politicians like Marc Lalonde and Jake Epp were highly prominent, other politicians (and, more importantly, civil servants) maintained the orientation and commitment over time. The Department of Public Health of the City of Toronto has also been a hotbed of innovations that have had international impact. Moreover, the Canadian

Public Health Association has always been an important ally in the development and the international marketing of the "new" health promotion. Among individuals, such key people as Ron Draper and Lavada Pinder in the federal structure and Trevor Hancock and Ron Labonté in Toronto are well known; many others have played less spectacular but often crucial roles. The fact that Canada has recently attracted such a driving force in the field as Larry Green is but another indication that the country is still a spearhead in the international developments of health promotion.

The chapters from our international contributors force us, however, to ask questions. First, Larry Green convincingly challenges the stereotype that the Canadian/European vision of health promotion, as David McQueen labels it, has always been more structural than its American counterpart. Larry contends that, given the neo-conservative political context of the early 1980s, all the energy of the numerous structurally oriented Americans has been diverted to fighting for basic health services and thus been distracted from other battles. Moreover, John Raeburn describes how a radical move to the right in New Zealand seriously shook a health promotion orientation that was inspired by the Canadian one. Both authors alert us to the fact that the current international political economy (which in Canada is manifest through the North American Free Trade Agreement with the United States and Mexico, monstrous public deficits, and constitutional nightmares) can be fertile ground for an evolution of health promotion in a direction very different from the one it has had over the last twenty years.

In reading this book we note the extent to which health promotion has entered the mainstream of health discourse and activity. This process is evident in changes in the names of journals and associations, in the use of the words "health promotion" in the reconstruction of health services in Eastern and Central Europe, in countless government documents worldwide, in professional meetings, and in position papers of more conservative bodies like Hospital or Medical Associations. If we use diffusion of innovations terms (Rogers, 1983), Canada was one of the key promoters of an innovative idea that took some time to get off the ground but which is now well diffused and adopted. One issue that remains, however, is that the words "health promotion" continue to encompass a wide range of visions and practices sometimes quite remote from the original concept.

For some Canadians who were instrumental in the promotion of the original vision of health promotion, its widespread acceptance can be unexpectedly problematic. The fear is that the original innovative aspects of health promotion are lost when it is appropriated by mainstream organizations and institutions. By becoming everybody's business, health promotion may become distorted. Many of the original promoters (including several Canadians) question their role because they are losing the leadership and control they once had over the field. Nevertheless, one could argue that health promotion's becoming mainstream is still a positive development because many more people are likely to have access to it through mainstream channels than when it was the vision of a few innovators. We are not in a position to assess whether becoming mainstream is good or bad; but it is interesting to observe that, as with other successful processes of change, health promotion is becoming co-opted by the dominant order it first set out to challenge, creating significant dilemmas for the promoters and the early adopters of its credo.

A Few Predictions

Predicting the future is a hazardous enterprise at the best of times, and especially so in this era of rapid social change. Nevertheless, we think it is desirable to try to do so, if for no other reason than to be able to look back later and find out how wrong we were. A better reason, however, is that predictions can sometimes help to shape the future through challenging people and institutions to confront themselves and change. Accordingly, we offer our predictions of the future of health promotion based on the material contained in this book and our own perceptions of where things are going in this domain. Here, we will make predictions about health promotion on the international stage and, in the final section, in Canada. With regard to the former, we feel confident in offering three major suggestions.

The first is that health promotion will continue to be primarily a phenomenon of developed countries. This does not mean that it will not spread to developing countries; indeed, this is already happening. It is simply to say that given the enormous and growing health and economic problems of the developing world, health promotion is unlikely to move to centre stage. Developing nations are more likely to continue to emphasize primary health care and prevention, strongly shaped by the economic constraints of structural adjustment programs put forward by the World Bank and the International Monetary Fund. In this context, health promotion is likely to seem a luxury that few developing countries can afford. Whether this perception continues will depend in part on the role that the central office of the World Health Organization in Geneva plays in supporting health promotion in developing countries. This is a role which it has not yet pursued vigorously, despite important internal efforts for the definition and implementation of a health promotion and protection framework. Some of this reticence arises from continuing debates over whether health education is the same as health promotion. The change in the name of the International Union for Health Promotion and Education augurs well for the resolution of this debate.

Related to the first prediction is our belief that the European Office of the WHO in Copenhagen will continue to show global leadership in health promotion. This office has built an important track record in the field through the leadership of the former health promotion project officer, Ilona Kickbusch, who has moved to a more powerful position in the organization. She and her successor, Erio Ziglio, should help to maintain the leadership role of WHO-Euro. Moreover, the projects that are currently being supported by this office through its "settings approach" (e.g., Healthy Cities, Healthy Workplaces, Health-Promoting Schools, etc.) are demonstrating to the rest of the world how health promotion can work in practice.

Finally, we would predict that Canada will continue to play an important role in health promotion on the international stage. At this time, for reasons that will be discussed, it is not clear what role the federal government will play in this regard, but it is clear that individual Canadians and institutions will continue to make a contribution to health promotion internationally. Not only are people such as Trevor Hancock and Ron Labonté likely to continue to be called on to share their ideas and experience, and others, like Jean Rochon, to be appointed to positions like the Health Promotion and Protection Direction of WHO in Geneva, but, increasingly, new organizations such the university-based health promotion centres are being called upon as well. For example, the Centre for Health Promotion at the University of Toronto, which is a little more than three years old, is involved in projects in the Caribbean, Costa Rica, and Eastern Europe; the Institute for Health Promotion Research at the University of British Columbia is involved in initiatives in the Western Pacific; and the GRIPSUL at Laval University has undertaken projects in African French-speaking countries as well as in Latin America. These involvements are likely to grow with the maturing of these groups. As well, the Canadian Public Health Association and the Canadian Society for International Health are likely to continue to stimulate Canadian contributions to health promotion internationally.

Thus, by and large, it appears that health promotion will continue to thrive in developed countries at least, and that Canada will continue to play a significant role in ensuring that it does.

Twenty Years of Health Promotion in Canada

The National Scene: The Decline of Federal Leadership

Turning to developments within Canada, we note that in Robin Badgley's chapter in this book (a paper originally published in 1978), he remarks that despite a very strong and visible health promotion discourse over the last 20 years, especially since the mid-1980s, perhaps not as much has been accomplished as one might have expected. In addition, perhaps the leadership of the federal government in health promotion, as was the case for the Lalonde Report, has been felt more outside Canada than within it. As Lavada Pinder argues in her chapter, several key opportunities have been missed and successive Canadian governments, under different parties, have never fully realized the potential of the discourses on health promotion that they were espousing and disseminating.

Yet, the accounts in this book clearly show that, especially after 1986, many of the activities that went on under the name of health promotion in the provinces and territories were stimulated or directly supported by federal initiatives. Moreover, in almost every part of the country, the regional offices of Health and Welfare Canada's Health Promotion Directorate played a key role. Through the vigorous marketing of the Epp (1986) Framework, as well as extensive consultation following its release, and initiatives like the

Knowledge Development process, it has been next to impossible for health-related constituencies in Canada not to have been exposed to the new gospel (and to position themselves in relation to it). What is intriguing, though, is that little hard money has been invested; most of the innovative national developments (like the three discussed in this book: Healthy Communities, Strengthening Community Health, and Knowledge Development) were funded for short periods of time at modest levels and yet generated very significant activities and results.

However, it is also clear that after the peak commitment leading to and immediately following the First International Conference on Health Promotion in Ottawa in November 1986, federal leadership has steadily declined. This has occurred for a variety of reasons, including important structural changes in the Ministry and in key personnel. The major reason is probably a series of fiscal and political crises that have resulted in a loss of confidence by Canadians in national political institutions and in the necessity of cutting expenses at any price, leaving little room in the 1990s for ventures such as health promotion.

It should be pointed out that since the 1970s, the Canadian Public Health Association, often in collaboration with the federal government, has also been a central player on the national scene. This was perhaps best exemplified in the co-sponsorship of the First International Conference on Health Promotion by WHO, Health and Welfare Canada, and the Canadian Public Health Association. Thus, while all the sectors of Canadian society could have been mobilized by health promotion, certain voluntary associations and professionals from the public health domain have clearly been at the forefront along with the federal government.

The Provincial and Territorial Scenes: Similarities and Differences

From the nine case studies in the Provincial Perspectives section of this book, we see that the ways in which health promotion has taken shape in the various parts of the country are much more diverse than the uniform discourses of the Lalonde Report, the Epp Framework, or the Ottawa Charter might lead one to suspect. There is no such thing as a Canadian way to do health promotion that applies, as the Canadian motto goes, from sea to sea (a mari usque ad marem). Hence, while there are some interesting similarities among the provinces and territories, there are also some striking differences.

Among the similarities, the most important is probably that the arrival of health promotion in the mid-1980s occurred when all the provinces and territories were questioning the organization of their medical care systems. These systems, constitutionally under provincial and territorial authority, were established during the 1950s and 1960s under strong federal incentives. By the end of the 1980s, all the provinces were confronting mounting deficits and escalating costs for health care, both as a result of their own financial problems and because of a steady decline since the mid-1970s in health-related transfer payments from the federal government.

The case studies show that in virtually every province or territory the rhetoric of health promotion permeated the official health planning discourse: numerous commissions of inquiry analyzed the various health care systems and employed health promotion as a key approach in their reports. Differences will undoubtedly appear, however, in the degree to which this rhetoric is employed in health system reform. It will be interesting to see if health promotion is used to reposition health in the general policy-making system in the direction of healthy public policies or if it is used only as a rationale for cutting services without fundamentally altering their nature. It is still too soon to have a clear sense of how this will work out, as most of the provinces are only now implementing their system reforms.

A second important similarity among the case studies is the fact that despite the presence in many provinces of visions that were close to health promotion before it was fashionable, the bulk of what was done in the name of health promotion was, and still is, lifestyle-oriented. Initiatives such as the Premier's Council on Health Strategy in Ontario or the healthy public policy vision developed in the Yukon are still uncommon and too new to have manifested their full potential.

A third important similarity pertains to the actors that have been influential in the development of health promotion. In most provinces/territories, we see activity by institutions like the provincial government, the regional office of the Health Promotion Directorate of Health and Welfare Canada, the Public Health Association, and local universities. Ann Pederson's conclusion that health promotion in Ontario was championed by a group of progressive public health professionals, policy makers, and academics (the community being virtually absent) captures well what is described for most provinces and territories, with the possible exception of B.C., where the community was centrally involved, and of Alberta, where the public health sector lagged behind a strong network of community development agencies.

If we look for differences in the ways in which health promotion evolved in the various provinces or territories, we first see variation in the speed at which the health promotion discourse was adopted in these jurisdictions. In many places, the term "health promotion" was in use not only before the Epp Framework but, in the case of Saskatchewan, even before the Lalonde Report. Yet, in contrast, O'Neill and Cardinal argue that Québec was very reluctant to adopt the health promotion rhetoric at all and did so after almost everyone else — although similar concepts had been employed in Québec since the beginning of the 1970s.

We also see variation in the level of new activities created by the "new" health promotion discourse, especially since the mid-1980s. In some cases, as in B.C., this discourse was used to stimulate new practices and programs, whereas in other areas it was used to legitimize existing practices or not used at all, as in Québec, where a large number of professional and grass-roots practices compatible with health promotion operated for years without being known as health promotion.

A fuller analysis of the variations in the use of health promotion rhetoric and its application in the various provinces and territories is beyond the scope of this chapter. Mining the case studies further will no doubt result in additional insights and questions. For now, we would like to address a key issue that arises throughout this book, including the nine provincial/territorial case studies: health promotion's status as a social movement.

Is Health Promotion a Social Movement?

The question of whether health promotion is a social movement is important because if it has the strength and pervasiveness of a social movement, health promotion is more likely to have significant impact on the health of Canadians than if it has not. Several chapters of this book, including those by O'Neill and Pederson, Labonté, Manson-Singer, and Kickbusch, query whether health promotion is a social movement. Overall, our conclusion is that health promotion as it has existed over the last 20 years, and more specifically since the mid-1980s, is not a social movement solidly rooted in practices and actions of large groups of people. Rather, we think that it is a professional movement that has successfully advanced a discourse about health and the production of health which has gained significant acceptance. As suggested by people such as Ron Labonté in this book or Stevenson and Burke (1992) elsewhere, this discourse is a professional and bureaucratic response to the challenges put forward by other social movements, including feminism and environmentalism.

In many ways, this discourse is not new; as O'Neill and Cardinal argue in their chapter, the health promotion discourse is the old public health discourse (which has been around for well over a century) revamped to take into account the different nature of health problems at the end of the twentieth century; hence their argument for relabelling it as the "new" or the "ecological" public health. What is intriguing, though, is why this discourse has gained such popularity now, both in Canada and elsewhere.

We think there are several reasons. The first is the ambiguity of the discourse, which as Pederson has shown can be legitimately used by the left and the right or by the collectivist and the individualist, thus serving a whole range of political agendas (Pederson, 1989).

Another reason for the current popularity of health promotion is its conjunction with other intellectual enterprises of this time. Regardless of their starting point, it seems as if analysts from various social arenas share a similar analysis of the problems confronting Spaceship Earth, whether in economic, social justice, environmental, or health terms. If this proposition is true, health promotion can be usefully regarded as the realization by the health constituencies of developed countries that there is no way to solve health problems if they are not put in the context of global environmental, social, and economic developments. We must think globally but act locally, as the adage goes. If there is currently more receptivity to the health promotion discourse, it may well be because it is the health version of a global discourse that has gained increased legitimacy in Canadian society as well as in many other developed and developing societies. This global discourse, as in the Ottawa Charter, the Bruntland Report, and countless other documents of a similar nature, maintains that the health of human beings, individually and collectively, is linked to the health of other species and of the planet as a whole, to sustainable economic development, and to the dissipation of major social inequities. It is thus not surprising to see Trevor Hancock's chapter in this book, which — like the visionary public health physicians before him — calls for political action in the name of health.

To use an argument put forth by Kelly, Davies, and Charlton (1993) in a recent discussion of the Healthy Cities phenomenon, health promotion is, first and foremost, one among many knowledge challenges of a post-modern type being made to a declining modern society. As sociologists have observed for several decades now, and as Toffler (1980) formulated in his unique way, we are currently experiencing the "third wave" of global change in human kind. After a "first wave" of change which produced traditional agricultural civilizations out of societies of fishers, hunters, and gatherers, the "second wave" produced the modern world of industrial societies. We are currently living the turbulent transition toward post-modern, post-industrial societies generated by the "third wave" of global planetary change. In that sense, if we agree with Eyerman and Jamison (1991) that knowledge challenges can be considered important elements of social movements, we could consider health promotion a social movement, but in that sense alone because it is a knowledge challenge that has until now been disconnected from actual social movements like feminism or environmentalism. It is these movements, and not the health promotion discourse promoted by bureaucrats and professionals, that have created meaning in the daily lives of people, and through which important political struggles have been expressed, based on the same values and aimed in the same direction as health promotion.

Health promotion can thus be considered the formulation in the health domain of a more general post-modern discourse that inspires and is promoted by the multiform, anti-technocratic social movement that, according to Touraine (1978), will slowly but surely bring about the post-industrial society. What does this imply about the future of health promotion in Canada?

The Future of Health Promotion in Canada

We draw on the material in this book and our own perceptions to hazard some predictions. The first prediction is that new players will continue to become involved in health promotion. Increasingly, we are seeing individuals and organizations from a wide range of sectors becoming interested in health promotion. Most obvious in this regard perhaps is the medical care sector. Some of this interest is undoubtedly self-serving, intended to try to preserve medicine's shrinking power, but some of it is a genuine desire to find out what health promotion can contribute. Our challenge is to welcome medicine and to help it and other disciplines develop initiatives that reflect the basic principles of health promotion, without permitting the powerful constituencies of biomedicine to redefine the field to fit their own vision of the world.

Other sectors that are showing increasing interest in health promotion are the educational sector (which has become involved in the Canadian Association for School Health and its provincial affiliates), the social service sector (which is adopting concepts such as quality of life that are related to health promotion), and the private sector (which is increasingly looking at health promotion as a way of enhancing the productivity of the workforce). Still other sectors are bound to follow as a result of the efforts of bodies that are consciously seeking to involve a broad range of players in health issues such as the Ontario Premier's Council on Health, Well-being and Social Justice. Moreover, as the population becomes more enlightened about the determinants of health through such efforts as the establishment of a health television channel, support for and involvement in health promotion is bound to increase.

Partly as a result of the entry of new players, we believe that leadership in health promotion will become increasingly diffused in Canada. As noted, until recently the federal government has been acknowledged as a key, if not the key, leader in health promotion in this country. However, its leadership role has diminished, partly through actions on its part (e.g., withdrawing funds from the national Healthy Communities Project) but also through other parties' assuming a more active role (e.g., some provinces and voluntary organizations). Whether the federal government will try to reclaim this role is unclear, especially given the splitting of Health and Welfare Canada. Health promotion was not mentioned as one of the areas of concentration for Health Canada in the press release announcing its creation and it is unclear what the commitment of the new Liberal government, elected in the fall of 1993, will be to health promotion. Moreover, as it increasingly reduces its transfer payments to provinces, the federal government is losing most of its power to maintain national leadership in the health arena. In any case, it is clear that others, including provincial health promotion branches, councils, voluntary organizations, and universities, want to be perceived as leaders. Under these circumstances, it is unlikely that the federal government can ever be the leader in health promotion in Canada again, either in reality or perception. This is not necessarily undesirable, as it could mean that health promotion will become increasingly accepted as a legitimate endeavour throughout society.

Another related prediction we would make is that local communities will become more important in health promotion. One reason for making this prediction is the growing diffusion of Healthy Communities initiatives in Canada. In spite of the withdrawal of federal funds from the national project, the number of Healthy Communities projects across the country grows and is likely to continue to do so as such efforts demonstrate their worth. Another interesting local development is the increase in the number of positions for people with training in health promotion in public health units, community health centres, district health councils, and other locality-based organizations.

A fourth prediction is that beyond the ideological arguments about structural versus individual interventions, there will be more integrated or comprehensive approaches to health promotion. Increasingly, it is being recognized and scientifically documented that social issues are connected to one another and that it is impossible to deal with one without dealing with others. In addition, the sheer cost of dealing with matters on an issue-by-issue basis will force us to look towards comprehensive approaches. Already, this approach is gaining momentum in Healthy Communities projects, or in school systems that are being urged by organizations such as the Canadian Association for School Health to adopt Comprehensive School Health as a way of responding to competing issues. Similarly, it is increasingly being argued that hospitals and other health care institutions that want to get into health promotion should adopt comprehensive approaches that deal with patients, staff, and the community within the same framework. Attempts are also being made in some provinces to integrate the various provincially funded health promotion initiatives.

We predict that there will be increasing sharing of experience in health promotion. Certainly, the development of communication technology enhances the chances of this happening, but it is also increasingly recognized that experience is as valid a basis for knowledge as research: as already mentioned, both stories and data are necessary and legitimate means to understand and change the world. It is thus expected that the university-based health promotion centres will play a significant role in encouraging and supporting such sharing of experience.

Finally, we predict that there will be increasing research and evaluation of health promotion efforts. As Larry Green pointed out at the Second National Conference on Health Promotion Research in Vancouver, we have a brief window of opportunity in which to provide scientifically sound evidence that health promotion works. It is one of the main responsibilities of the new university-based centres to provide this evidence.

Conclusion

We think that Canadian health promotion is clearly at a crossroads and that it can go in at least two directions. On the one hand, we might see the dawning of a golden era of health promotion in Canada — one tempered less by ideology and more by reality than was the case in the past. In this direction lies the seemingly inescapable scientific proof of health promotion's efficacy in order to compete successfully with other approaches for the health dollar. But it is a direction, as Badgley foresaw in 1978, in which there might not be much future. In fact, even if within the realm of health promotion there is strong consensus on what the field is all about, it is likely to remain marginal and lack legitimacy in the cost containment games that lie ahead of us. As a cautious observer of the Canadian public health scene for several decades has mentioned, while he is personally very sympathetic to the vision of health promotion, when money gets tight, "the walls of biomedicine get higher and thicker." Thus, potentially fruitful ventures like health promotion, if they have not been able to prove themselves in the terms defined by the biomedical world, are at risk of disappearing. And there is no question that health sector funding will continue to decline with the pressure on the federal and provincial governments to decrease their deficits.

Looking at current signs, the window of opportunity for health promotion to prove itself scientifically may not even be five years. One of these signs is the possibility, currently being explored, that the Medical Research Council (a wealthy and biomedically oriented federal granting agency) will become involved in behavioural and social research pertaining to health. This proposal raises questions about the survival of the National Health Research and Development Program (the less wealthy agency currently funding health promotion and public health research and which, over the years, has become significantly more responsive to the social aspects of health) that would eventually come under the supervision of the MRC. Another sign is the "biologization of society" that, according to leading futurists cited by Renaud (1993), is back in force after a few decades in which social explanations were well received, leaving enterprises like health promotion very vulnerable.

However, there is another direction. Perhaps the solution lies apart from realism and in ideology. As discussed previously, health promotion has, from a very marginal social position, challenged the conceptualization of health. If, until now, it has been difficult for health promotion to clarify its vision and to have it accepted by others, it might well be, as hypothesized by Kelly, Davies, and Charlton (1993), that we have not yet fully appreciated the fact that it really represents a paradigm shift in our understanding of and interventions in health. This shift, according to Kelly and his colleagues, is one from the modern to the post-modern mode of understanding the world.

The current tensions about the future of health promotion can thus be interpreted as the tensions between a still dominant modern, rational vision of the world and the emerging post-modern vision of a chaotic, random, and individually meaningful universe. Whereas, given the current power structure, health promotion has to play a modern game of showing its usefulness, maybe its real potential lies in the more fundamental changes toward post-modernism, of which it is but one driving force. There are also signs that some of these fundamental changes are currently occurring, as evidenced by the Royal Society of Canada's embarking on assessing the potential of participatory research in health promotion. Perhaps the dramatic social and economic changes that have already begun and that lie ahead of us at the end of the millennium will make the relevance of a post-modern vision of the world even more apparent.

As history has taught us, the real direction is likely to lie somewhere in the dialectical tension between these two future visions. We probably have no choice but to try to play the game of showing the effectiveness and usefulness of health promotion but, at the same time, we need to ally ourselves with and participate in the creation of the various social movements that are transforming our modern societies into post-modern ones. Once more, the power of words and ideas may pave the way to more material changes, as has been the case several times in the past (such as prior to the French Revolution). We hope all of you will join us as participants in this exciting process so that we can achieve our common goal of "health for all," which might not be reached by the year 2000 but towards which many groups, individuals, and organizations will continue to work for many years to come.

References

Epp, J. (1986). *Achieving health of all: A framework for health promotion.* Ottawa: Ministry of Supply & Services.

Eyerman, R., & Jamison, A. (1991). *Social movements: A cognitive approach.* University Park: Pennsylvania State University Press.

Kelly, M.P., Davies, J.K., & Charlton, B.G. (1993). Healthy Cities: A modern problem or a post-modern solution? In J.K. Davies & M.P. Kelly (eds.), *Healthy cities: Research and practice* (pp. 159-168). London: Routledge.

Lalonde, M. (1974). *A new perspective on the health of Canadians.* Ottawa: Ministry of Supply & Services.

Pederson, A.P. (1989). *The development of health promotion in Ontario.* Unpublished master's thesis, University of Toronto.

Renaud, M. (1993). Social science and medicine: Hygeia versus panakeia. *Health and Canadian Society, 1,* 229-247.

Rogers, E.M. (1983). *Diffusion of innovations* (3rd ed.). New York: Free Press.

Stevenson, H.M., & Burke, M. (1992). Bureaucratic logic in social movement clothing: The limits of health promotion research. *Canadian Journal of Public Health, 83*(Supp. 1), S47-S53.

Toffler, A. (1980). *The third wave.* New York: Macmillan & Morrow.

Touraine, A. (1978). *La voix et le regard.* Paris: Seuil.

World Commission on Environment & Development (1987). *Our common future.* Oxford & New York: Oxford University Press.

Contributors

Jack L. Altman is Director of the West-Main Unit, Vancouver Health Department. This health unit has integrated health promotion as a major component of both its internal activities at the worksite and its programs in the community. He is also current President of the B.C. Public Health Association and one of the original members of the B.C. Healthy Communities Network Steering Committee.

Robin F. Badgley is Chair of the Graduate Department of Community Health at the University of Toronto. He has chaired two national inquiries for the government of Canada, on the operation of the abortion law (1975-77) and on sexual offences against children (1980-84). Between 1977 and 1984, he was a member of the Pan American Health Organization's Advisory Committee on Medical Research, and has also served as a consultant (1985-87) on foreign aid for health to the Commonwealth Secretariat (London). In 1993, he was appointed Chair of the Ontario Minister of Health's Community Health Framework Committee. With co-author Samuel Wolfe, he has written two books: *Doctor's Strike: Medical Care and Conflict in Saskatchewan* (1967) and *The Family Doctor* (1973).

Lise Cardinal received her M.D. degree from Laval University in Québec City and practised as a general practitioner in a local centre for community care (CLSC) in a rural community from 1983 to 1985. She is a specialist in community medicine. Currently, she is a health consultant in the health department of the Hôpital de l'Enfant-Jésus and is involved in health promotion and health monitoring. She has also been involved in research on the Québec Healthy Communities Network through contributing to the evaluation of the network and to the development of indicators for a healthy city.

John C.B. English is an Associate Professor in the Department of Nursing and Health Studies at Brandon University, Brandon, Manitoba. He has helped spearhead the formation of VisionQuest, Brandon's Healthy Communities project, and founded the Westman Association for Terminal Care in Hospice. He has published *The Systems in Transition: Paradigm for Healthy Communities*, which is a model for understanding a community system as a vital organism. Currently, John chairs the Prairie Region Health Promotion Knowledge Development Network.

Joan Feather is a research scientist in the Department of Community Health and Epidemiology at the University of Saskatchewan in Saskatoon. She began her research career with the Canadian Centre for Community Studies. With a master's degree in sociology and additional studies in history, she has been active in social research in a wide variety of subject areas including health survey methodology, health insurance history, health care utilization, community health organization, program planning and evaluation, and indicators of health status and social risk conditions. Some of this research stemmed from unique research and development partnerships with community agencies and Northern and First Nations communities. She has served on several National Advisory Committees. She was appointed co-ordinator of the Prairie Regional Health Promotion Research Centre in 1993.

Ann Goldblatt is the Community Participation Program Co-ordinator within the Health Promotion Division of the Edmonton Board of Health. She is a graduate of social work (McMaster) and community health (Toronto). She has been a facilitator, educator, and policy advocate on inequities in health. She has held leadership roles in building a network for health promotion in Alberta, including on the board of the Alberta Public Health Association.

Lawrence W. Green is Director of the Institute of Health Promotion Research and Professor of Health Care and Epidemiology at the University of British Columbia. He received his degrees in public health at the University of California at Berkeley. He worked as a health educator in local, state, and federal health agencies in California and for the Ford Foundation in Dhaka, Bangladesh, and served as the first Director of the U.S. Office of Health Information and Health Promotion. He has been on faculty at Berkeley, Johns Hopkins, Harvard, and the University of Texas, and was most recently the Kaiser Foundation's Vice-President and Director of the Health Promotion Program. He is the author of some 200 chapters, monographs, and articles. Several of his books have been widely adopted as college texts.

Trevor Hancock is a Toronto-based public health consultant working in health promotion, Healthy Cities/Communities, healthy public policy, and health futurism. He is also an Associate Professor in the Faculty of Environmental Studies at York University. From 1980 to 1986 he worked for the City of Toronto Department of Public Health, initially in the Health Advocacy Unit and later as an Associate Medical Officer of Health. In 1984, Trevor organized the ground-breaking Beyond Health Care conference on healthy public policy, from which grew the Healthy Cities movement. He served as President of the Ontario Public Health Association from 1986-87 and Vice-President (Canada) of the American Public Health Association in 1991-92.

Ken Hoffman is currently Director of Community Development at the Sandy Hill Community Health Centre in Ottawa, Ontario. His main interest is in applying a community development and Healthy Communities approach to health promotion and in community health organizations. He has worked in a number of capacities with local, provincial, national, and international organizations. From 1989 to 1991, Ken was Assistant Program Director of the Strengthening Community Health Program conducted by the Canadian Public Health Association.

Ilona S. Kickbusch is Director of the Lifestyles and Health Department at the WHO Regional Office for Europe. Her areas of responsibility include health promotion, Healthy Cities, mental health, the tobacco and alcohol action plans, abuse of psychoactive drugs, nutrition, and AIDS. She has been the key instigator of WHO's approach to health promotion and was responsible for the *Ottawa Charter for Health Promotion*. She also developed the

WHO Healthy Cities project. Ilona has published widely on health promotion issues, is on faculty at Yale University's School of Public Health, and teaches regularly at universities in Europe and elsewhere. She holds a Ph.D. in political science.

Nancy Kotani is Director of the Health Promotion Division of the Edmonton Board of Health. She holds a master's degree in social work from the University of Toronto. She has been an advisor to a number of provincial and federal initiatives, including the National Advisory Committee on AIDS, and is President-Elect for the Canadian Public Health Association.

Ronald Labonté has worked in health promotion for 20 years, locally, nationally, and internationally. He works with health professionals, community health centres, labour unions, social service organizations, social action-oriented heath groups, the WHO, and UNICEF. This breadth of learning opportunities enriches his thinking about the capacity of health professionals to engage in emancipatory forms of practice. Ron has taught in Australia and New Zealand as well as Canada. He currently teaches part-time at the University of Toronto, where he is also a member of the Centre for Health Promotion. He is the author of many articles on health promotion, community development, and social policy.

Sharon Manson-Singer is an Assistant Professor in the School of Social Work and a Faculty Research Associate at the Centre for Human Settlements at the University of British Columbia. She serves on the Executive Committee of the Institute for Health Promotion Research at UBC, which she helped to found. From 1989 to 1991, she was a member of the Steering Committee for the Canadian Healthy Communities Project. Sharon is involved in health promotion research development and models for healthy and sustainable development.

Sharon M. Martin is Executive Regional Director, Vancouver Region, for the B.C. Ministry of Health. Despite her many professional positions in public health, she is best known for her extensive work in the community. She is currently on the executive of the board of the Canadian Public Health Association, is past president of the B.C. Public Health Association, and is also one of the original members of the B.C. Healthy Communities Network Steering Committee.

Sharon J. Matthias operates her own management and policy services consulting firm, building on her more than 20 years of government experience, most recently as Assistant Deputy Minister of Health and Regional Social Services in Yukon Health and Social Services. She holds a B.S.P., M.Sc. (pharmaceutical chemistry) and an M.B.A. Her interest and focus on health promotion strategies began with the development of the policy framework for community and occupational health and with her reflection on the influences and determinants of her own health and well-being.

David V. McQueen holds a doctorate in behavioural sciences from Johns Hopkins University. From 1973 to 1983 he was Assistant and then Associate Professor in Behavioral Sciences at Johns Hopkins University School of Hygiene and Public Health. In 1983 he was named founding Director of the Research Unit in Health and Behavioural Change at the University of Edinburgh, Scotland. As a Professor at the University of

Edinburgh he oversaw many health research projects, but was principally involved with a large five-year lifestyle and health survey. In October 1992, Professor McQueen joined the Centers for Disease Control in Atlanta as Chief of the Behavioral Surveillance Branch.

Michel O'Neill is a Professor in the School of Nursing at Laval University in Québec City. He obtained his doctorate in sociology from Boston University and has been involved in community health for 20 years as a community health worker, professor, researcher, consultant, and activist. His long-standing teaching and research interests pertain to the political and policy dimensions of health promotion. He is co-editor of two books, has authored and co-authored several dozen chapters and articles, and has presented over one hundred papers in various scientific and professional meetings.

Ann Pederson is a doctoral candidate in the Department of Behavioural Science in the Division of Community Health and an Associate of the Centre for Health Promotion at the University of Toronto. Prior to graduate school, she worked as a traffic safety educator in British Columbia. She has co-authored several papers on healthy public policy and community interventions to prevent substance abuse. Her doctoral thesis examines the experience of mothering small children.

Lavada Pinder was with the Health Promotion Directorate of Health and Welfare Canada for fifteen years, first as a Division Director (1977-87) and then as Director-General (1987-92). She was one of a number of people who had a hand in the development of *Achieving Health for All* and then went on to try to promote and implement the ideas. Prior to joining the federal government, she spent ten years with the Addiction Research Foundation of Ontario and also worked for several years in child welfare in Ontario and Saskatchewan. She is presently retired and working as a volunteer with the International Union for Health Promotion and Education and the Canadian Public Health Association.

Dale H. Poel is an Associate Dean in Dalhousie University's Faculty of Management and Director of the School of Public Administration. He is a specialist in applied research and teaches program evaluation in the M.P.A. program. He has conducted evaluation research for a number of federal and provincial agencies and served as a Senior Research Associate with the Nova Scotia Royal Commission on Health Care.

Frances Pym is an Associate Professor and Assistant Dean in the Faculty of Nursing at the University of New Brunswick. She is currently completing doctoral studies at Dalhousie University. Once a public health nurse in rural Nova Scotia, she teaches courses in community health nursing and health promotion. She has been actively involved with the Strengthening Community Health Project and is a founding member of the Atlantic Health Promotion Network.

John Raeburn is Associate Professor and Head of Behavioural Science at the University of Auckland Medical School, New Zealand. His main research and practice interests are in the area of community-based health promotion using an empowerment model. He has spent considerable time in Canada, including a year in the Health Promotion Directorate, Ottawa, in 1986 and was one of the two New Zealand representatives at the First International Conference on Health Promotion that year. He is currently an Associate of the Centre for Health Promotion at the University of Toronto and is married to a Canadian.

Irving Rootman obtained his Ph.D. in sociology from Yale University in 1970. He joined Health and Welfare Canada in 1973 as Chief of the Epidemiology and Social Research Unit of the Non-Medical Use of Drugs Directorate until 1978, when he became Chief of the Health Promotion Studies Unit in the new Health Promotion Directorate. He was appointed Acting Director of the Program Resources Division of the Health Promotion Directorate in 1986 and Director in 1988. From 1986 to 1990, he led a project to develop knowledge for health promotion in Canada. In September 1990, he became Director of the Centre for Health Promotion and Professor in the Department of Preventive Medicine and Biostatistics at the University of Toronto. Since July 1991, he has been a Co-Director of the North York Community Health Promotion Research Unit.

Louise Signal has worked in New Zealand as a policy analyst in the Health Promotion Program of the Department of Health, and prior to that as a community worker for local government. She completed a doctorate in community health at the University of Toronto while on a Commonwealth scholarship. Her dissertation was a study of the Ontario Premier's Council on Health Strategy. She continues health promotion research in her current position as a behavioural scientist with the New Zealand Public Health Commission.

Susan Yazdanmehr has a bachelor's degree in health education from Dalhousie University. Her interest in health promotion began in the late 1970s with volunteer work in community-based organizations in the Northwest Territories. She has worked for the territorial government as a research writer and as a community health promotion officer. Susan is currently working with Health Canada on the development and implementation of children's health initiatives in the NWT.

Index

To the Owner of This Book

We are interested in your reaction to *Health Promotion in Canada*. With your comments, we can improve this book in future editions. Please help us by completing this questionnaire.

1. If you are a student, please identify your school and the course in which you used this book.

_____

SCHOOL _____

PROGRAM _____

2. In what way did this book assist you in your course?

_____

_____

_____

3. What did you like best and least about the book?

_____

_____

_____

4. Please add any comments or suggestions.

_____

_____

_____

☐ May we contact you for further information?

☐ Do you wish to receive information on Saunders Reference Books?

NAME _____

_____

ADDRESS _____

_____

POSTAL CODE _____   PHONE _____

(fold here and tape shut)

MAIL POSTE

Canada Post Corporation
Société canadienne des postes

Postage paid   Port payé
if mailed in Canada   si posté au Canada
Business Reply   Réponse d'affaires

0116873899   01

0116873899-M8Z4X6-BR01

WB SAUNDERS CANADA
c/o Gerry Mungham
Manager, Marketing and Acquisition
PO BOX 35211 STN BRM B
TORONTO ON M7Y 6E1

Notes

Notes

Notes

Notes